Efficient and Flexible Reading

Efficient and Flexible Reading

Kathleen T. McWhorter

Niagara County Community College

Little, Brown and Company
Boston   Toronto

Library of Congress Cataloging in Publication Data

McWhorter, Kathleen T.
  Efficient and flexible reading.

  Includes index.
  1. Developmental reading — Handbooks, manuals, etc.
I. Title.
LB1050.53.M38 1983   428.4′3   82-25880
ISBN 0-316-56408-7

Library of Congress Catalog Card No. 82-25880

ISBN 0-316-56408-7

9 8 7 6 5 4 3 2 1

HAL

Published simultaneously in Canada by Little, Brown & Company (Canada) Limited

Printed in the United States of America

Acknowledgments

The author wishes to thank the following authors and publishers for permission to reprint their material in this text.

Reading Selections

1. Paul G. Hewitt, *Conceptual Physics: A New Introduction to Your Environment*, 4th ed. Copyright © 1981 by Paul G. Hewitt. Reprinted by permission of the publisher, Little, Brown and Company.
2. Robert A. Fleck and C. Brian Honess, *Data Processing and Computers: An Introduction.* Copyright © 1978 Charles E. Merrill Publishing Company. Reprinted with permission.
3. Thomas Ford Hoult, Lura F. Henze, and John W. Hudson, *Courtship and Marriage in America.* Copyright © 1978 by Little, Brown and Company (Inc.). Reprinted with permission.
4. From *Well-Being: An Introduction to Health,* by John Dorfman, Sheila Kitzinger, and Herman Schuchman. Copyright © 1980 Scott, Foresman and Company. Reprinted by permission.
5. Reprinted with permission of Macmillan Publishing Co., Inc., from *The Non-Runner's Book,* by Vic Ziegal and Lewis Grossberger. Copyright © 1978 by Vic Ziegal and Lewis Grossberger.
6., 15., and 23. Mary Gander and Harry W. Gardiner, *Child and Adolescent Development.* Copyright © 1981 by Mary J. Gander and Harry W. Gardiner. Reprinted by permission of the publisher, Little, Brown and Company (Inc.).
7. From *Overcoming Math Anxiety* by Sheila Tobias. Reprinted by permission of W. W. Norton and Company, Inc. Copyright © 1978 by Sheila Tobias.
8. From *The Story of Rock,* Second Edition, by Carl Belz. Copyright © 1972 Oxford University Press, Inc. Reprinted by permission.
9. From Molly S. Wantz and John E. Gay, *The Aging Process: A Health Perspective.* Copyright © 1981 by Little, Brown and Company (Inc.). Reprinted by permission.
10. Denis T. Raihall, *Family Finance: Money Management for the Consumer.* Copyright © 1969 Time, Inc.; copyright 1975 by Little, Brown and Company (Inc.). Reprinted by permission.
11. A. B. C. Whipple, "An Ugly New Footprint in the

In-Text Readings

Roger Penske, *Reader's Digest,* April 1981. Reprinted by permission of the author.

p. 176: Excerpt from "Is It Worth the Risk?" by David Roberts, *Reader's Digest,* April 1981. Reprinted by permission from *Outside* Magazine. Copyright © 1981 Mariah Publications Corporation.

p. 177: Excerpt from "Strategic Minerals," by Fred Warshofsky, *Reader's Digest,* February 1981. Reprinted by permission of the author.

p. 180: *Psychology and Life,* 10th ed. by Philip G. Zimbardo. Copyright © 1979 Scott, Foresman and Company. Reprinted by permission

p. 207: "Campus Values in Mate Selection," from Hoult, Henze, Hudson, 1978. By permission.

p. 277: Excerpt from p. 330 *Roget's International Thesaurus,* 4th ed. Revised by Robert L. Chapman (Thomas Y. Crowell Company). Copyright © 1977 by Harper & Row Publishers, Inc. Reprinted by permission of Harper & Row Publishers, Inc.

p. 305: "I Want a Wife," originally appeared in *Ms.* Magazine, Spring 1972. Reprinted by permission of the author, Judy Syfers.

p. 345: Lillian Borgeson, "Used Cars," from *Vogue,* February 1982. Copyright © 1982 by The Condé Nast Publications, Inc.

p. 349: "Money and Myth in Disney," by David Nyhan. Reprinted courtesy of the *Boston Globe.*

p. 352: Barbara Stern, "Calm Down in Six Seconds," from *Vogue,* October 1981. Copyright © 1981 by The Condé Nast Publications, Inc.

p. 356: "Macomber Animal Farm with a Mission," by Emilie Tavel Livezey. Reprinted by permission from the *Christian Science Monitor.* Copyright © 1981 The Christian Science Publishing Society. All rights reserved.

p. 359: "Jobs for New College Grads," reprinted with permission from *Changing Times* Magazine. Copyright © 1982 Kiplinger Washington Editors, Inc., March 1982. This reprint is not to be altered in any way except with permission from *Changing Times.*

p. 385: "Road Test Review," reprinted from *Car & Driver* Magazine, November 1981. Copyright © 1981 Ziff-Davis Publishing Company.

Selected Excerpts

Joseph B. Aceves and H. Gill King. *Introduction to Anthropology.* Copyright © 1979 by Random House, Inc.

Louis Berman and J. C. Evans. *Exploring the Cosmos,* 3rd ed. Copyright © 1980 by Louis Berman and J. C. Evans. Reprinted by permission of the publisher, Little, Brown and Copmany.

Leonard Broom and Philip Selznick. Selected excerpts from pp. 574, 455, and 65–66 in *Sociology,* Third Edition. Copyright © 1955, 1958, 1963 by Harper & Row Publishers. Inc. Reprinted by permission of the publisher.

Richard H. Buskirk. *Principles of Marketing: The Management View,* Third Edition. Copyright © 1961, 1966, 1970 by Holt, Rinehart and Winston, Inc. Reprinted by permission of Holt, Rinehart and Winston, CBS College Publishing.

Joseph S. DeBrum, Peter G. Haines, and Dean R. Malsbary. *General Business,* 10th ed. Copyright © 1971 by South-Western Publishing Company of Cincinnati, Ohio. Reprinted by permission.

Edward J. Fox and Edward W. Wheatley. *Modern Marketing.* Copyright © 1978 Scott, Foresman and Company. Reprinted by permission.

Martin J. Gannon. *Management: An Organizational Perspective.* Copyright © 1977 by Little, Brown and Company (Inc.). Reprinted by permission.

Morris K. Holland and Gerald Tarlow. *Using Psychology: Principles of Behavior and Your Life.* Copyright © 1980 by Morris K. Holland and Gerald Tarlow; copyright © 1975 by Little, Brown and Company (Inc.). Reprinted by permission.

David H. Knox. *Exploring Marriage and the Family.* Copyright © 1979 by Random House, Inc.

Alan H. Monroe and Douglas Ehninger. *Principles and Types of Speech,* 6th ed. Copyright © 1967 Scott, Foresman and Company. Reprinted by permission.

Kenneth J. Neubeck. *Social Problems: A Critical Approach.* Copyright © 1979 by Random House, Inc. Reprinted by permission of the author.

Marilu Hunt McCarty. *Dollars and Sense,* 2nd ed. Copyright © 1979, 1976 Scott, Foresman and Company. Reprinted by permission.

David Ogilvy. Excerpt from house advertisement, Wall Street Journal, June 14, 1972. Reprinted by permission of Ogilvy & Mather, Advertising, New York.

John Perry and Erna Perry. *Face to Face: The Individual and Social Problems.* Copyright © 1976 by Little, Brown and Company (Inc.). Reprinted by permission.

Irwin Unger. *These United States: The Questions of Our Past,* Vol. II, 2nd ed. Coyright © 1982 by Irwin Unger. Copyright © 1978 by Little, Brown and Company (Inc.). Reprinted by permission.

S. L. Washburn and Ruth Moore. *Ape into Human: A Study of Human Evolution,* 2nd ed. Copyright © 1980 by S. L. Washburn and Ruth Moore; copyright © 1974 by Little, Brown and Company (Inc.). Reprinted by permission.

Gary Wasserman. *The Basics of American Politics,* 3rd ed. Copyright © 1982, 1979 by Gary Wasserman; copyright © 1976 by Little, Brown and Company (Inc.). Reprinted by permission.

Burton Wright and John Weiss. *Social Problems.* Copyright © 1980 by Burton Wright and John Weiss. Reprinted by permission of the publisher, Little, Brown and Company.

For Ruth and Harry Thompson

Preface

The rapid expansion of knowledge and the exponential increase of information over the past decade make efficient and flexible reading essential. No longer does the student, businessman or -woman, lawyer, secretary, or technician have the time or energy to read everything leisurely, thoroughly, and completely. Instead, in order to keep abreast, each is forced to read selectively, paying more attention to and spending more time on what is important and devoting less time to that which is less important. Each must learn to adjust his or her rate, expected level of comprehension, and method of reading to suit the needs of particular situations. The purpose of this text, then, is to present techniques and guided practice that will enable the reader to develop skills for reading efficiently and flexibly. It presents techniques that allow the reader to accomplish reading tasks with the most realistic expenditure of time and effort, adjusting both reading rate and level of comprehension to suit the purpose, type of material, and familiarity with the material.

This text provides a balanced, integrated approach to the development of reading rate and comprehension. Each is treated as an interactive part of reading efficiency and flexibility. Reading rate, then, is approached as a variable that, in conjunction with others, must be controlled and adjusted to achieve the reader's goals.

The book offers a blend of reading comprehension, retention, vocabulary development, critical reading, and rate building techniques that have proven essential for college students and all other serious readers. Unit One presents the organization and framework for the text, establishes expectations for rate improvement, and dispels unrealistic expectations about speed reading, while emphasizing the relationship between rate and comprehension. Pretests are included to allow the student to assess his or her entry level skills and to establish realistic expectations. The second section presents specific techniques for efficient reading, including reading with a purpose, using textual aids, improving eye-movement patterns, phrase reading, and prereading. Unit Three presents techniques for increasing basic comprehension skills necessary for efficient reading. It deals with the organization and structure of ideas in sentences, paragraphs, and articles, and emphasizes methods for reading each in the most efficient manner. The fourth unit focuses on retention techniques that have a direct bearing on both rate and comprehension improvement. Concentration and review strategies, as well as underlining and notetaking skills, are discussed. Because of its importance in the development of mature reading behaviors, vocabulary improvement is the focus of Unit Five. Topics presented include multiple word meaning, technical vocabulary, word parts, and contextual aids. The abilities to interpret, evaluate, and apply what one reads are discussed in Unit Six. Such skills as making inferences, asking critical questions, and considering the source and authority of information are included. Unit Seven provides an extensive treatment of two selective reading techniques: skimming and scanning. The final section is intended to consolidate skills and techniques taught throughout the text and includes posttests that will enable students to assess their improvement.

Each chapter, except the initial and final chapters, includes two reading selections. These selections serve as a means by which students can measure and observe their progress and as suitable material with which to practice techniques taught in the respective chapters. Two difficulty levels are provided; Level B selections are more difficult than those designated Level A. The multiple choice questions that follow each selection are intended to test literal and interpretive comprehension and to assess the ability to determine word meaning in context.

A Reading Efficiency Score is utilized throughout the text as a single number that combines achievement in both rate and comprehension. It is used as a relative standard for pretest and posttest achievement and for measuring progress on each of the reading selections.

A worktext format was chosen for the text to provide ample instruction as well as necessary practice and application. Each explanation of a new technique is followed by exercises that illustrate the use of that technique and allow the student to test its effectiveness. With this method, students are given the opportunity first to understand the ideas and then to try out each new skill.

An answer key is included to make the text adaptable to self-instruction and to provide immediate feedback for students as they complete practice exercises. A words-per-minute conversion chart and a reading progress graph are also provided to enable students to compute their reading rates and to record and visualize their improvement. An Instructor's Manual presents the instructor with a detailed description of the text and offers specific suggestions for classroom use.

I wish to recognize my colleagues for their many useful suggestions on the development of this text, and my typist, Joyce Pawelczyk, for providing excellent manuscript preparation services. My editor, Molly Faulkner, deserves special thanks for her warm support, encouragement, and guidance throughout the writing of this text. I wish to thank Kathryn Daniel, my production editor, for her enthusiastic assistance and careful attention to the complexities of bringing this text into print.

Contents

Contents

optional
op

optional

Contents

Unit One:
Getting Started

The purpose of this unit is to help you get started reading better and faster. Before you learn specific techniques for increasing your reading rate and comprehension, it is important that you learn a little about reading efficiency and flexibility. You will need to know what is involved in each and how you can improve your skill levels. Also, before you begin working on improving your rate and comprehension, you must assess your present level of skill. For unless you obtain some estimate of your skill levels before you begin, you will be unable to measure the improvement you make.

Chapter 1 explains reading efficiency and flexibility and presents the basic principles that govern reading rate improvement. It also describes the factors that affect how well and how fast you read and discusses the issue of "speed reading." Chapter 2 contains four pretests designed to measure your present level of reading efficiency and flexibility. When you finish the text, you can compare these results with the results of four posttests included in the last chapter.

Chapter 1:
Some Facts About Efficient and Flexible Reading

We have all heard about cars that are "fuel efficient." They are cars that use fuel "efficiently" and conserve energy. Another phrase, "efficiency apartment," is commonly used to describe a small apartment that is relatively inexpensive and easily kept in order. Further, an "efficient" secretary is one who calmly and easily does his or her job well and on time. Efficiency, then, suggests the ability to achieve or perform with the minimum amount of effort, expense, or waste. In the case of the fuel-efficient car, you get distance, mileage, and speed for the least possible amount of fuel. In an efficiency apartment, necessary living space is available for the least possible amount of upkeep and cost. In the case of an efficient secretary, the job is accomplished with minimum stress, delay, or wasted time.

You can see, then, that "efficiency" means the effective utilization of time or resources in a specific task. As you begin to think more about the concept of efficiency, you may begin to realize that it is a major objective in our work-oriented society. For example, a secretary who takes an hour to type a letter, a short-order cook who takes twenty-five minutes to prepare a cheeseburger, or a sales clerk who takes five minutes to package a purchase is not regarded as efficient. Although each of these tasks may eventually be accomplished correctly, it will not have been accomplished within a realistic time frame.

DEVELOPING READING EFFICIENCY

When applied to reading, then, efficiency means the accomplishment of reading-related tasks within an appropriate time frame. As a college student, you are concerned with reading or studying a piece of material in the least possible time while still understanding and remembering what you read. Tasks such as reading and studying a textbook chapter, reviewing notes for a weekly quiz, or organizing class discussion questions based on a reading assignment, then, are all included in the concept of reading efficiency.

Many people assume that reading rate is the primary determinant of reading efficiency. They believe that slow reading is poor reading. Generally, it is assumed that in order to become more efficient one must simply read faster. This is *not* the case. The techniques you use to accomplish the task are at least as important to reading efficiency as your reading rate. For example, in reading a textbook chapter, the techniques you use may be more important than your reading rate. Similarly, *how* you review the material is more important than how fast you read in preparing for a weekly quiz. Also, how much you were able to remember what you read is more important than how fast you read an assigned article.

You can see, then, that reading efficiency implies the effective use of techniques as well as of time. For instance, if you take ten hours to read a twenty-page textbook chapter, you are not reading efficiently. Under most circumstances, you should be able to read more than two pages per hour. On the other hand, if you read a twelve-page assignment in one hour, but remember only 30 percent of what you read, you are not reading efficiently either. You can see, then, that efficient reading involves adequate comprehension and recall within a reasonable time frame. To increase your reading efficiency, you need to develop techniques that will help you read with comprehension and retention, and also enable you to use your time most economically.

One major focus of this book is the development of reading efficiency techniques that will enable you to get the most out of what you read within a reasonable time frame. In each unit and chapter you will learn specific techniques for improving efficiency in various reading tasks.

In Unit 2 you will discover some techniques to use before beginning to read and while reading. They can make reading much easier and enable you to remember more of what you read.

In Unit 3 you will learn how to recognize important ideas rapidly and to follow the author's development and progression of thought. After you have developed skills to increase your comprehension, you will learn in Unit 4 how to organize, record, and review information so that you can retain it easily.

Next, since vocabulary is crucial to understanding whatever you read, Unit 5 will present ways to develop vocabulary and will discuss how an awareness of vocabulary can contribute to increased comprehension. Then, Unit 6 will demonstrate the importance of an ability to interpret and evaluate what you read.

In Unit 7, you will learn two selective reading techniques — skimming and scanning — to be used when thorough reading is neither necessary nor efficient. Finally, in Unit 8, we will present specific techniques for increasing your rate, enabling you to become a more flexible, versatile reader.

DEVELOPING READING FLEXIBILITY

Do you read the newspaper in the same way and at the same speed that you read a chemistry textbook? Do you read poetry in the same way and at the same speed that you read an article in *Time* magazine? Surprisingly, for most adults the answer to these questions is yes. Most adults, and this includes college graduates, read everything in nearly the same way at the same rate.

A good reader, on the other hand, reads the newspaper both *faster* than and *differently* from the way he or she reads a chemistry book because the newspaper is usually easier to read and because he or she has a different purpose for reading each. A flexible reader reads poetry more slowly and in a different way than a magazine article. The reader's purpose is different for each, and poetry is usually more difficult and the meaning is often very compact. Generally, this ability to adjust your reading rate and methods to suit the type of material you are reading and your purpose for reading is called *reading flexibility*.

There are three factors or variables that are involved in reading flexibility:

1. the characteristics of the material to be read
2. the attitudes and purposes with which you approach the material
3. the level of reading skills that you bring to the reading situation

To develop reading flexibility, you need to be aware of each of these variables and make them work together in a way that will enable you to read in the most efficient manner possible.

Textual Features

Many features of the reading material itself influence how and how fast you read it. Here are a few important characteristics to consider:

1. *The format.* The physical arrangement of a page, often called the format, or layout, can influence how easily material can be read. For example, it is often more difficult to read a page that is a solid block of print than it is to read a page on which the ideas are broken up by headings, spacing, listing, and so forth.
2. *Graphic and visual material.* The inclusion of maps, pictures, graphs, and charts also may influence your reading. Maps, graphs, and charts present detailed information and require close, careful study, whereas pictures provide an impression or overview and require less careful study.

3. *Typographical aids.* Features of print such as boldface headings, italics, colored type, and headings often make a page easier to read and to understand. Headings usually announce the topic about to be discussed and together form an outline of ideas covered in the material. Italics and words in boldface or colored type make certain words and phrases stand out and emphasize their importance.

4. *The difficulty of the material.* Factors such as sentence length, paragraph length, and vocabulary level largely determine how difficult a piece of material is to read. Generally, the longer the sentences and paragraphs in a selection are, the more difficult they are to read. Of course, more difficult words also make a selection harder to understand.

5. *The subject matter.* The manner in which you approach a piece of reading matter is partially determined by the type and number of ideas and concepts that an author presents. For instance, a passage that explains a complicated scientific theory or procedure would require close reading, whereas material discussing everyday newsworthy topics would normally require less careful attention. Also, a passage that explains one new idea is often easier to read than a passage that presents three or four new, separate ideas in the same amount of space.

Although you can do nothing to change these features of writing, you can alter your approach to the material. You can deliberately slow down if you encounter a passage with long, complicated sentences or an article that presents complex ideas or uses technical vocabulary. Or you can deliberately speed up when you come across material that presents simple, straightforward ideas and uses everyday vocabulary. In other words, you should adjust your rate to suit the characteristics of the material you are reading. Also, you should adjust the manner in which you read the material, using different techniques to suit different types of material. A major portion of this book is devoted to techniques that will enable you to use features of the text to increase your efficiency and to approach difficult or complicated material.

Adjusting your rate and method to the style and content of what you are reading is what is meant by reading flexibility. The development of reading flexibility is one of the primary concerns of this text. Throughout the text, you will see that the type and nature of the material to be read are used as reference points for determining appropriate reading rate.

Reader Characteristics

Although various features of the material to be read directly affect the ease with which it can be understood, the characteristics of the reader are equally important. Many features about you also directly affect your understanding of a particular passage. Here is only a partial list of the characteristics that can affect your reading rate and level of comprehension.

Your Purpose in Reading. Your purpose or reason for reading a particular piece of material can greatly influence how you read it. Different situations require different levels of comprehension and recall. For example, you do not need to recall every fact when reading an article in the newspaper, but you do need a high level of comprehension when reading a contract that you plan to sign.

You can see, then, that purpose and comprehension are closely related. Throughout this text, you will see that a close relationship also exists between rate and comprehension and that both are controlled by purpose for reading. You will find that as your desired level of comprehension (as determined by your purpose in reading) decreases, reading rate increases. Table 1-1 illustrates this relationship.

Your Interest Level. Although not as important as purpose, your interest level also affects how you read. Most people have little difficulty understanding and remembering material if the subject is highly interesting. For example, a sports fisherman could read an article in *Fishing*

Table 1-1. THE RELATIONSHIP AMONG PURPOSE, RATE, AND COMPREHENSION

TYPE OF MATERIAL	PURPOSE IN READING	DESIRED LEVEL OF COMPRE-HENSION	APPROXI-MATE RANGE OF SPEED
poetry, legal documents, argumentative writing	analyze, criticize, evaluate	100%	under 150 wpm
textbooks, manuals, research documents	high comprehension recall for exams, writing research reports, following directions	95–100%	150–250 wpm
novels, paperbacks, newspapers, magazines	entertainment, enjoyment, general information	60–80%	250–400 wpm
reference materials, catalogs, magazines, nonfiction	overview of material, rapid location of specific facts, review of previously read material	below 50%	600+ wpm

World on landlocked salmon quickly and with high comprehension, and a gourmet cook would have no difficulty reading articles on pastry making. Interest, then, can facilitate comprehension and rate; also, a lack of interest or motivation can have an adverse effect. Many people admit that when they are not interested in what they are reading, they have trouble concentrating and often cannot remember what they have read.

Your Background Knowledge. The amount of knowledge you have about a topic influences how easily and how fast you will be able to read about it. Suppose you were asked to read an excerpt from an organic chemistry text. If you have completed several chemistry courses, the excerpt would be fairly easy to understand. On the other hand, if you had never taken a chemistry course, even in high school, the excerpt would be extremely difficult to read, and you would probably understand very little.

Your Physical State. How you feel, how much sleep you have had, whether you are trying to recover from a cold, and whether you are happy or relaxed after enjoying a dinner, all can affect your ability to read and concentrate. Ideally, you would complete analytical or careful reading assignments when you are at your physical peak and can maintain an optimum level of concentration.

Although there is little you can do to alter any of these characteristics, it is important to be aware of them and to take them into account as you read. Of those discussed, purpose is perhaps the most important to consider before you begin reading. You will see throughout the text that adjustment of your rate and technique to suit your purpose for reading is a key factor in reading flexibility. Also, you will learn techniques that can help you accommodate any of these characteristics that may seem to affect your rate or comprehension adversely.

Level of Reading Skill

A third set of factors that most directly control how well and how fast you are able to read is your level of reading skill. Your ability to understand the meaning of words, sentences, paragraphs, and longer selections directly influences how well and how fast you are able to read a given page. If your vocabulary is limited, for example, then you will encounter numerous unfamiliar words that will impair your comprehension and slow you down. On the other hand, an extensive, well-developed vocabulary will enable you to grasp meanings accurately and rapidly. Or, using another skill as an example, if you are not able to remember what you read, then you must waste time rereading or be forced to settle for a low level of comprehension.

Unlike textual features and reader characteristics such as interest and background, reading skill can be controlled and improved. Of course, all students possess a base of reading skills, but everyone can improve his or her skill to become a more efficient and effective reader. Significant portions of this book will concentrate on ways you can improve your reading and retention skills. The book has been organized into sections that focus on particular types of reading skills. Units 3, 4, and 6 are concerned with understanding, remembering, and interpreting and evaluating what you read, whereas Unit 5 presents techniques for vocabulary development.

PRINCIPLES OF READING EFFICIENCY AND FLEXIBILITY

Are you surprised by any of the following statements? Do you disagree with any of them? Do any of the statements seem to contradict what you have been taught previously?

1. You do not always have to read everything.
2. Not everything on a page is of equal importance.
3. There are shortcuts that can save valuable time and make reading or studying easier.
4. It is possible to increase your reading rate without losing comprehension.
5. Reading is a thinking process.
6. Not everything that appears in print is true.

Each of those statements expresses one of the major principles on which the techniques presented in this book are built. You must understand and accept each of these principles in order to profit by the skills and practices contained in this text. Because each is a vital principle, a brief rationale for each follows.

1. *You do not always have to read everything.* Throughout your educational experience, you may have been taught the contrary; you may even recall certain teachers who insisted that you read everything on a page or in a chapter and that you skip nothing. In this text you will see that, depending on your purpose for reading, there are situations in which it is perfectly acceptable and even advisable to skip portions of sentences, paragraphs, and articles.
2. *Not everything on a page is of equal importance.* Sentences, paragraphs, and longer selections each contain a mixture of important and less important information. In each, some parts are essential to the meaning whereas others only explain and provide additional

information about these key parts. A necessary skill in reading efficiently and flexibly is the ability to identify what is important and to be able to see how the remaining parts of the sentence, paragraph, or article relate to it.

3. *There are shortcuts that can save valuable time and make reading or studying easier.* Reading is not simply a matter of opening a book, reading the assigned material from beginning to end, and then closing the book. There are specific techniques you can use before you begin reading, while you are reading, and after you have finished reading that will greatly increase your efficiency.

4. *It is possible to increase your reading rate without losing comprehension.* It is an established fact that most people do not read as fast as they are capable of reading. Most students can increase their rate by applying techniques for improving their comprehension and retention. Of course, you cannot expect to double or triple your rate while maintaining a high level of comprehension, but a significant increase is usually noted.

5. *Reading is a thinking process.* Reading is thought of by many people as a visual, physical process in which the eyes move back and forth across lines of print. Although this eye movement is a part of reading, it is only the means by which information is taken from the page and transferred to the brain. It is the brain's function to attach meaning to the symbols that the eyes see. Because the meaningful activity in reading occurs in the mind, reading can then be regarded as a mental activity. However, there is another sense in which reading can also be considered as a mental, or thinking process. To read efficiently, a reader must interpret, react to, and evaluate what he or she reads.

6. *Not everything that appears in print is true.* A common assumption made by many people is that if a statement or idea appears in print, it must be true. Actually, printed materials contain many assumptions, generalizations, opinions, and judgments that often cannot be proved to be either true or false. As part of the thinking process, an active reader must question and evaluate the source, authority, and evidence offered in support of statements that are not verifiable.

Now that you more fully understand the concepts of efficiency and flexibility and are familiar with the basic principles of reading efficiency and flexibility, you are nearly ready to begin work. Before you actually begin, however, two last steps are necessary. First, you must establish reasonable, realistic expectations for the type of improvement you will make. The next section of this chapter will address this concern. Second, before beginning a program of improvement, you will want to know your present level of skill so that, at its end, you will be able to assess your progress. Chapter 2 is intended to provide you and your instructor with a quick estimate of your incoming level of skill. Chapter 19 is designed to indicate the level of skill you have achieved as a result of your instructional program.

IS IT POSSIBLE TO SPEED READ?

Have you heard some people say they can read thousands of words a minute? Have you read or heard advertisements for commercial speed reading courses that claim you can double, triple, or quadruple your reading rate? Do you wonder whether it is really possible to read at these high rates? Do you feel you have been missing something all along because you don't read this fast? The purpose of this section is to present information about reading rate improvement that will enable you to develop realistic expectations about reading efficiency or "speed reading" courses.

The most important fact about reading rate is that the physical limit for reading every word is around 800 words per minute. Numerous research projects have established this fact through eye movement photographs of very good and very fast readers. The best readers studied were unable to read every word if their rate exceeded 800 words per minute. And, when their speeds did exceed that rate, the photographs showed that they were skipping words, phrases, or even whole sentences. So, if you meet or hear of someone who claims to read 1000 words per minute, you know that he or she is not reading every word. Instead, the person probably reads selectively, reading some words or lines and skipping others. More than likely, the person is using one or more of the selective reading techniques that are suggested in this text.

We are still faced with this question: Can someone read 2000 words a minute or not? You are probably beginning to see that the answer depends on your definition of "reading." If we mean understanding and remembering everything on a printed page, the answer to the question is no. It is not possible, for instance, to read a college textbook selectively and retain enough to perform well on an exam. You must read everything. However, if by reading we mean reading selectively, skipping material, and, at times, settling for less than complete comprehension and recall of the material, then it is possible to read at those higher rates. In this case, it would be appropriate to read selectively at a rate above 800 words per minute. You should have begun to realize that different rates may be appropriate for different situations and for different types of reading. This awareness should make the concept "reading flexibility" meaningful.

Chapter 2:
Where Are You Now?
Pretests

Whenever you work hard or spend a great deal of time on a task, it is satisfying to be able to see your end result — clear evidence that you have accomplished something. For example, if you spend several hours repairing a car engine, your end result is clear: You have a car that runs. Similarly, if you work hard writing and revising a paper for your English class, you end up with a paper that expresses your ideas clearly and earns a good grade. At this point, you have realized that you will be devoting considerable time and effort to becoming a more efficient flexible reader and probably wonder whether you will actually improve. As you work through the chapters in this text, you may be able to "see the difference" in how well and how fast you are able to read day-to-day materials such as newspapers or textbooks. However, since this improvement will be gradual, it is easy to lose sight of the improvements you have made and to begin to feel as if you are not getting anywhere.

This book contains two features that enable you to measure your short-term and overall progress. The first is a pretest-posttest comparison. A pretest is provided in this chapter to let you measure your current level of reading efficiency. When you have finished the text, you can take a posttest that will tell you your level of skill at that time. By comparing your pretest scores with your posttest scores, you can then compute how much you improved. The posttest is provided in Chapter 19.

A second feature of the text that measures your improvement is built into each chapter. Two reading selections appear at the end of each chapter, accompanied by comprehension questions and a word count to enable you to compute your rate. By completing and scoring the questions and plotting your comprehension and rate on the progress graph included in the Appendix, you can keep track of your improvement.

The next section contains four pretests. The first test, the Reading Efficiency Pretest, measures both your rate and comprehension on a general interest article. The remaining three tests measure your reading flexibility. Complete each pretest following the directions given. After you complete the tests, you will see how to interpret your results.

MEASURING YOUR READING EFFICIENCY

To assess your present level of reading efficiency, complete the following pretest. Be sure to time yourself accurately and to read the passage according to the following directions:

1. Assume that the following article appeared in a magazine you are reading. Assume further that you are interested in skiing and have been considering trying cross-country skiing. Read the selection to find out as much as you can about cross-country skiing.
2. Before you begin reading, record the time in minutes and seconds in the space marked Starting Time. Then begin reading the selection. Read it only once. When you finish, record the time in the space marked Finishing Time. Compute your Reading Time by subtracting your Starting Time from your Finishing Time.
3. Complete the comprehension questions that follow the selection. Do not look up the answer to each question. You may refer back to the selection to answer questions that refer to a particular word, phrase, sentence, or paragraph.
4. Score your answers using the Answer Key at the back of the book. Give yourself 10 points for each correct answer. Since a perfect score would be 100, your score is really a percentage based on the number of questions you answered correctly. Record your score in the space marked Comprehension Score.
5. Use the words-per-minute conversion chart included at the back of the book to find the average number of words that you read per minute and record it in the space marked WPM.

READING EFFICIENCY PRETEST
CROSS-COUNTRY INNS ARE IN

In summer, the Home Ranch, north of Steamboat Springs, Colo., is a modestly successful dude ranch, luring urban cowboys and cowgirls with live horseflesh and barbecued beef. When the snows come, the ranch, like scores of summer inns and resorts from the California Sierra to Massachusetts, becomes a cross-country skiing resort. The demand for cross-country accommodations — and the carefully prepared trails through snowy woods, mountains and meadows they offer — has risen dramatically.

According to estimates by the U.S. Ski Association, in 1970 a mere 1,000 skiers were attracted to cross-country, while this year the number has leaped to more than 4 million. New techniques, products and uncharted areas are developing to serve regiments of "skinny-ski" addicts. Yellowstone, Crater Lake, Sequoia and other national parks are offering winter ski touring. In 1973 the 34-

13

mile Birkebeiner race and an accompanying 17-mile contest drew only 75 contestants. This year's outing will be the sport's Boston Marathon, attracting more than 7,000 participants.

Racing, however, is not the main attraction for the kick-and-glide set, many of whom have never skied before. The allurement is the sport's unhurried solitude. At big downhill resorts there are often agonizing waits for ski lifts, and eateries are jammed. Mobs of hot-doggers and snow bunnies have turned Stowe and Vail into adrenalized assembly lines of sport. At the Home Ranch the pace slows. Its 580 aspen-studded acres offer cross-country skiers 20 miles of trails glistening in 2 ft. of new powder. Twenty guests — the inn's capacity — enjoy wine-and-cheese parties in the meadows, photograph elk, ermine and eagles, soak in private hot tubs and feed resident tame llamas. No sounds of sports cars, chain saws, chairlifts or rock music from *après*-ski lounges pollute the mountain air. At $75 a day, including instruction, equipment and dinners of prime rib and smoked turkey, the ranch is half the price of similar downhill digs. But half price is only half the reason for the appeal. Ranch Operator Ken Jones says: "Most of our clientele are ex-downhillers. They're here to relax, unwind and get away from the throngs. Gliding through the trees without seeing or hearing anything is what's turning people on."

The Jackson Ski Touring Foundation in New Hampshire, one of the premier facilities in the country, provides more varied but equally successful enticements. Some 25,000 skiers enjoy everything from saunas to home-cooked meals offered by the ten inns that dot more than 100 miles of trails. "There is a madness in cross-country skiing," says Thomas Perkins, executive director of the Jackson group. "You take the absolute minimum in equipment and do extremes with it."

Some cross-country fanatics, in fact, refuse to accept the comforts of touring centers. For purists, there are challenges like the 35-mile, six-day trek across the ridge line of the Sierra in Sequoia and Kings Canyon national parks. It is an experience in mountaineering as well as skiing. The route rises 6,000 ft., almost straight up from the roadhead, to peaks of 13,000 ft. and more. One requirement: a small radio transmitter for avalanche protection. Other arcana may include polypropylene underwear, vapor-barrier booties and avalanche-probe ski poles. The reward of the trek is skier's cocaine: unmarred 1,500-ft. alpine slopes. Experts claim the trail is the equal of Europe's Haute Route from Chamonix, France, to Zermatt, Switzerland.

The search for pristine slopes has led thousands of escapists into the back country. There, distinctions are blurred: touring fans discover the speedy pleasure of schussing, and downhillers get an aerobic workout on cross-country skis. The two passions meet in a 120-year-old technique called telemarking — a turn of great difficulty — which offers balance to the free-heeled skier. One ski is extended beyond the other until the skier is crouching. The rear ski rudders the front one into the turns necessary for steep downhill flights. One aficionado calls it "genuflecting on the run." A new generation of skis, slightly wider than the usual touring model and metal-edged for downhill curve cutting, is doing a brisk business in sports shops. Telemarking classes have become standard fare at the larger touring centers. There are even the first North American Telemark Championships in the offing. They will be held this March in Aspen. Says Suzanne Hogan, 32, a self-described ski bum and waitress at the Home Ranch: "Telemarking has all the excitement of white water and hang gliding. You're in the snow and part of it."

But for most participants, the pleasures of cross-country are not concocted from thrills and chills. Many tourers are family groups that simply strike out from the back door after a snowfall. Unplowed roads, golf courses and frozen lakes provide paths for the basis of the sport: rhythmic, exhilarating exercise in the country air. Observes Buck Elliott, operator of Colorado's Crooked Creek Ski Touring ranch: "We're back to a simpler life. Out here, you become more aware of what breathing and eating are all about."

COMPREHENSION TEST

Directions: *Circle the letter of the correct answer.*

1. The author feels that cross-country skiing is
   a) growing in popularity
   b) declining in popularity
   c) increasing in costs
   d) decreasing in costs

2. For some fanatics, cross-country skiing has become a (an)
   a) opportunity to demonstrate their skill
   b) challenge to do the most with the least equipment
   c) opportunity to demonstrate the superiority of cross-country over downhill skiing
   d) challenge to cover more miles per day than downhill

3. The primary appeal of cross-country skiing is its
   a) competitiveness
   b) speed
   c) peace and quiet
   d) companionship

4. Cross-country skiing is
   a) costly for most individuals
   b) a sport for the over-thirty crowd
   c) more beneficial than downhill skiing
   d) an opportunity to escape to the back country

5. Telemarking is a technique
   a) for teaching downhill skiers to cross-country ski
   b) that provides more physical exercise than cross-country skiing
   c) that is most effective in deep snow
   d) for turning on steep slopes

6. *Ermine* is a
   a) type of animal
   b) a gnat or bug
   c) type of food
   d) skiing technique

7. If you were a person who enjoyed being alone yet liked the excitement of downhill speed, telemarking would be
   a) fun
   b) too repetitious
   c) boring
   d) difficult to adapt to

8. Telemarking is a technique that is
   a) easily mastered
   b) difficult to perfect
   c) used in both downhill and cross-country skiing
   d) very dangerous

9. Which of the following might be a possible substitute title for this selection?
   a) "The Thrill of Victory"
   b) "It Takes Money to Make Money"
   c) "All Talk and No Action"
   d) "Back to Basics"

10. The purpose of the last paragraph of the selection is to show the
    a) expense of skiing
    b) simplicity of the sport
    c) sights and sounds of the countryside
    d) speed of cross-country skiing

Efficiency Pretest:			839 words
Finishing Time:	_____ HR.	_____ MIN.	_____ SEC.
Starting Time:	_____ HR.	_____ MIN.	_____ SEC.
Reading Time:		_____ MIN.	_____ SEC.
WPM Score:	_____		
Comprehension Score:	_____		%

Computing Your Efficiency Score

From your calculations, you now have two scores: a words-per-minute (WPM) score and a comprehension score. When working with two scores, it is often difficult to know just how efficiently you read. Your comprehension score may be high, and your rate low, or vice versa. One indicates how rapidly you read; the second indicates how well you understand the article while reading at that rate. The next step, then, is to use these two numbers to compute a single Reading Efficiency Score (RES). This score combines your reading rate with your level of comprehension to produce a number that you can use to measure your overall level of efficiency.

To compute this score, first convert your comprehension score (percentage correct) to a decimal. You could divide by 100, but it is easier just to place a decimal point in front of your score if it is less than 100. For instance, if your comprehension score is 70%, then it would be .7 as a decimal, and a score of 90% would be converted to .90. If you had a perfect score of 100%, then convert it to 1.00.

Then multiply this decimal by your words per minute (WPM) score to obtain your reading efficiency score (RES). Round off your answer to the nearest whole number. Here is an example:

WPM Score: 216
Comprehension Score: 80%
RES = Comprehension Score (in decimal form) × WPM Score
RES = .80   × 216
RES = 172.80
RES = 173

This number may not seem meaningful at this point. However, as you complete reading selections at the end of each chapter, you will also compute reading efficiency scores, and you will begin to notice a gradual increase in this score. Now, record your RES for Pretest 1 on the Pretest Summary at the end of this chapter (p. 33).

MEASURING YOUR READING FLEXIBILITY

The following pretests are designed to measure your current level of reading flexibility. They consist of a number of different reading selections with very specific directions for completing each. As you work through these pretests, be sure to read and follow the directions carefully.

Reading Flexibility Pretest 1

To assess your present level of reading flexibility, complete the following pretest. Be sure to time yourself accurately and to read the passage according to the following directions:

1. Assume that the following selection was assigned by your psychology instructor. You are expected to read the material carefully so that you are able to take an exam based on its content. Read this selection in a manner to ensure that you will be able to recall most of what you read.

2. Before you begin reading, record the time in minutes and seconds in the space marked Starting Time. Then begin reading the selection. Read it only once. When you finish, record the time in the space marked Finishing Time. Compute your Reading Time by subtracting your Starting Time from your Finishing Time.

3. Complete the comprehension questions that follow the selection. Do not look back at the selection to answer the questions.

4. Score your answers using the Answer Key at the back of the book. Record your score in the space marked Comprehension Score.

5. Use the words-per-minute conversion chart included at the back of the book to find the average number of words that you read per minute and record it in the space marked WPM Score.

READING FLEXIBILITY PRETEST 1
NONVERBAL COMMUNICATION

James Geiwitz

Verbal language — that is, the written or spoken word — is the main way we humans communicate with each other, but it is not the only way. Intentionally or unintentionally, we deliver messages by the tone of our voice, the tilt of our eyebrows, the position of our body, the fire in our eyes. Some of these signals are deliberate and understood by most members of a particular culture. Certain gestures by a traffic officer are well known to mean "Stop," "Go," or "Get that clunker moving!" We nod our heads when we want to answer yes and shake them to say no.

When I was a teenager, I was amazed how many thoughts one could communicate simply by sticking up a finger or two — and I wondered why all these thoughts were obscene. A friend of mine, whom I will call Steve, and I decided to invent a new hand gesture and assign it a benevolent meaning: "I love you." An upraised ring finger on the right hand was, at the time, the only unused configuration, so it was chosen. Steve thought so highly of our new gesture of love that he flashed it to a female classmate, who slapped his face, and the high school principal, who told him he was now on probation. Steve's excuses that the gesture meant "I love you" fell on deaf ears, just as his gesture had fallen on eyes unable to perceive, at a distance, the difference between the ring finger and the middle finger.

HOW YOU SAY IT

It's not always *what* you say that counts, but *how* you say it. A high-pitched, squeaky voice communicates excitement or stress. It may betray the intense feelings of embarrassed teenagers on an important date, the fear of a soldier in battle, the nervousness of a job applicant. Several studies have shown that the pitch of someone's voice tends to rise when she or he is lying, one of the bases for checking "voice stress" in lie detection. Similarly, loudness may be used to emphasize a statement, or it may indicate anger. Pauses and hesitations often communicate uncertainty about what is being said. Thus, "Out of my way, you bully! Or I'll beat you to a pulp!" said in a soft, squeaky, hesitant voice will probably fail in its intended purpose; the verbal communication is in jarring contrast to the nonverbal message.

Changes in the pitch, loudness, or rhythm of part of a sentence — different inflections, they are sometimes called — also carry meaning. An actor's exercise is to repeat a simple sentence, giving the emphasis to each word in turn and thus conveying quite different messages. Try it on something like, "You want to become mellow?" Emphasizing "you" turns it into "Why *you*, of all people?" Emphasizing "become" suggests you are too laid back already.

THE FACE AND EMOTIONS

It is generally to your advantage for others to know how you are feeling. Expressing anger, for example, indicates to someone that what she or he is doing is meeting with your displeasure. In addition, it communicates the possibility of attack if the behavior in question is not discontinued. It is clearly preferable to express anger *before* attacking than simply to attack, because the anger itself might do the trick and save both people a lot of grief. In a similar vein, it is to your advantage, usually, to indicate to others what causes you pleasure. If you love jokes but never laugh, no one will tell you jokes.

On the other hand, it is sometimes to your advantage to disguise your emotion. You do not care to broadcast your loathing of your boss or your astonishment at the ugliness of her or his children. The ability to put on a "poker face" is highly valued. With its origins in the ability to conceal joy over an outstanding hand of cards, or fear while pushing a weak hand to its limits, the expression "poker face" has taken on a more general meaning, that in any situation the person has the ability to keep her emotions from being "written all over her face."

Naming Emotions from Faces

When psychology became an empirical science, one of the first topics it investigated was people's ability to judge emotions from the faces of other people. Pictures, either drawings or photographs, were presented, and the subject was requested to identify the emotion they showed, either from a list prepared by the experimenter or by giving her or his own label. In an early experiment, 11 subjects were shown photographs and tried to guess the emotions an actor was trying to convey. The best subject was correct 58 percent of the time; the worst was graded as being in close agreement only 17 percent of the time. These data were hardly encouraging to those who claimed the face is the major communicator of emotions.

It is possible that the facial expressions of an *actor* are not as communicative as a person's real expressions. Another psychologist photographed people subjected to an incredible set of situations, each situation designed to elicit a particular emotion. One of the 16 situations had the subjects witnessing the beheading of a white rat. Many subjects responded to this sight with a sickly smile, the same sickly smile that appeared in many other situations. The psychologist concluded that in ordinary people there was no significant relationship between emotions and facial expressions.

Other psychologists, puzzled at the negative results for what appeared to be a quite reasonable hypothesis, looked for flaws in the design of prior experiments. One psychologist concerned himself with the problem of *naming* an emotion. It was clear that in many experiments judging the facial expression of actors, subjects were penalized for using odd words; if the actor intended anger, for example, and the subject guessed rage, is this a hit or a miss? By carefully examining the judgments of 100 subjects judging 86 poses, Woodworth devised a crude scale, as follows:

1. Love, Happiness, Mirth
2. Surprise
3. Fear, Suffering
4. Anger, Determination
5. Disgust
6. Contempt

This is a scale; it is not simply six categories. If every judgment is placed in one of these six categories — both rage and anger go into category 4 — subjects agree with each other extremely well. And, if they disagree, the disagreements almost invariably fall into neighboring categories. If most subjects call a particular expression *fear* (category 3), the few who don't are most likely to call it *surprise* (2) or *anger* (4).

Once the scale was devised, it was used in a typical face-judging experiment. This time both the emotion intended by the actor and the emotion guessed by the subject were listed by one of the broad categories, not by the specific emotion. For example, if the actor intended to show anger — category 4 — and the subject guessed rage — also category 4 — the subject was given credit for a correct judgment. Using this method, subjects were nearly perfect in their judgments.

COMPREHENSION TEST

Directions: *Circle the letter of the correct answer.*

1. The article is primarily concerned with
   a) the various types of communication humans employ
   b) the importance of unspoken messages
   c) how voice changes carry messages
   d) how facial expressions reveal feelings

2. Early experiments in judging emotions from facial expressions
   a) proved that emoting cannot be read from faces
   b) were inconclusive in their results
   c) proved that emotions can be read from faces
   d) showed that actors could "read" faces better than ordinary people

3. A loud voice
   a) always communicates fear
   b) always communicates truth
   c) may express distrust
   d) may express anger

4. A high-pitched voice may suggest any of the following emotions *except*
   a) fear
   b) embarrassment
   c) anger
   d) excitement

5. According to psychologist Woodworth, love and happiness are
   a) similar emotions
   b) different
   c) revealed by different facial expressions
   d) primarily revealed through verbal expression

6. The word "benevolent" means
   a) kind
   b) insulting
   c) confused
   d) evil

7. The verbal message and the nonverbal message that a person communicates
   a) always agree
   b) never agree
   c) may conflict
   d) never conflict

8. Woodworth's scale was devised to
   a) avoid confusion in describing emotion
   b) explain various types of emotion
   c) help actors display emotions more clearly
   d) show that there are only six categories of emotion

9. The author and his friend may have developed their new hand gesture that meant "I love you" to
   a) avoid having to repeat the words to someone either one cared for
   b) anger the female classmate
   c) anger his high school principal
   d) test out how gestures can convey meaning

10. The author explains nonverbal communication primarily through the use of
    a) personal experience
    b) research studies
    c) statistics
    d) historical records

```
┌─────────────────────────────────────────────────────────┐
│                                                           │
│   Flexibility Pretest 1:                   1083 words     │
│                                                           │
│   Finishing Time:     _____  _____  _____        │
│                          HR.       MIN.       SEC.        │
│   Starting Time:      _____  _____  _____        │
│                          HR.       MIN.       SEC.        │
│   Reading Time:                 _____  _____        │
│                                    MIN.       SEC.        │
│   WPM Score:                    _____        │
│                                                       %   │
│   Comprehension Score:          _____        │
│                                                           │
│   Reading Efficiency Score:     _____        │
│                                                           │
└─────────────────────────────────────────────────────────┘
```

Reading Flexibility Pretest 2

Complete the second reading flexibility pretest following these directions:

1. Assume that you have found this article in a magazine that you are paging through. The title suggests that the article is about new TVs. You hope to purchase a new set, so you decide to read the article *only* for the purpose of finding out what is available on the market. You are not ready, at this point, to select a set, but you do want to know what is available and generally what costs are involved. Read the selection, then locate *only* these most important ideas.

2. Before you begin reading, record the time in minutes and seconds in the space marked Starting Time after the Comprehension Test. Then begin reading the selection. Read it only once. When you finish, record the time in the space marked Finishing Time.

3. Complete the comprehension questions that follow the selection. *Do not look back at the selection to answer the questions.*

4. Score your answers using the Answer Key. Record your score in the space marked Comprehension Score. Because there are five not ten questions, your score will be the number correct multiplied by 20.

5. Use the words-per-minute conversion chart included at the back of the book to find the average number of words that you read per minute and record it in the space marked WPM Score.

6. Compute your Reading Efficiency Score.

READING FLEXIBILITY PRETEST 2
THE NEW TVS: GETTING BIGGER, GETTING SMALLER

The newest model television sets mark the dawn of the era of component TV, in which various pieces of equipment can be purchased separately and tied together much like the pieces of a stereo sound system.

Most state-of-the-art TV sets now have the built-in capacity for plugging into video cassette recorders (VCRs), videodisc players, cable channels, game and computer keyboards, even stereo sound components. At least one manufacturer offers a projection system without a TV receiver for use with a VCR or a standard TV set.

Projection television is the newest item in the growing catalog of home TV options. More than a dozen manufacturers are making sets that project the picture onto a screen as big as or bigger than those used to show home movies and slides. Up to now seen mainly in bars, clubs and other gathering places, projection TV is expected to find its way into more than 100,000 American homes by the end of this year.

Henry Kloss, pioneer of projection TV for the home and head of Kloss Video Corp., believes a new age is dawning for TV sets. "For nearly 30 years technology kept television restricted to a small size of 19 to 25 inches," he says. "A whole generation has grown up thinking that the conventional 19-inch TV set is the best way to watch television."

But those screen dimensions are "incongruous and unnatural to watch," Kloss says. "Even 35mm slides are viewed on a screen at least four feet high, and movie theater screens are enormous."

Kloss Video makes TV systems with screens measuring six and a half feet diagonally. Other manufacturers, including such industry giants as RCA, Sony and Zenith, are also selling home projection TV. Prices, starting close to $3,000, match the scale of the screens.

At the opposite end of the size spectrum are the increasingly popular mini sets, with screens not much bigger than a credit card. Manufacturers call them "personal size" TVs.

These little sets may be natural complements to giant-screen models. A big screen can accommodate the whole family or guests watching special events, but mini sets, because they are easily portable, allow you to catch your favorite program wherever you are. Prices start under $200.

WHAT TO LOOK FOR

There is more to know about the mini TV sets and the projection systems before you buy.

Mini TV.   If you want a set that is truly portable, both around the house and outdoors, look for one that operates on household current (AC) and on car and other types of batteries (DC). Some of the new mini sets are so compact that they fit easily into a briefcase or beach bag. Those listed in the table on the next page

23

operate on AC and DC. Most will work on a car battery or a rechargeable battery pack (an optional accessory). In some cases the sets will even operate on flashlight batteries, although D-cells won't power a set for long before running down.

The mini sets have mechanical tuners, meaning you turn a knob to change channels. Some models are strictly TV sets; others include such features as AM-FM radio, cassette recorder/player and digital clock/timer. Generally, the smallest color screens are four to five inches and anything smaller is black-and-white.

If you don't plan to use the TV on picnics or in a vehicle, you might settle for a slightly larger set that operates only on household current. Sets with nine-, ten- and 12-inch screens are still portable, and they cost a lot less than most true minis.

Projection TV. The main types include front projection sets in two- and one-piece systems and one-piece rear projection sets.

• *Two-piece front projection systems.* These include the Kloss Novabeam, Sony's KP-7220 and KP-5020 models and Advent's Videobeam 225. They operate much as slide or movie projectors do, with separate projectors and screens.

The picture-projecting unit consists of a TV receiver and a set of three tubes that project separate green, blue and red pictures. The pictures converge on the screen to form the proper colors for viewing. The projection equipment is housed in a knee-high cabinet that also contains a speaker designed to bounce the sound off the screen into the room. The cabinet can double as a coffee table or knick-knack stand.

GIANT-SCREEN TV SETS: A SAMPLING

MAKE	MODEL	PIECES	TYPE OF PROJEC-TION	DIAGONAL SCREEN SIZE (INCHES)	APPROXI-MATE COST
ADVENT	Videobeam 225	2	front	72	$3,295
	Videobeam T-100	1	front	50	2,795
GE	Widescreen 4000	1	rear	45	3,700
KLOSS	Novabeam	2	front	78	3,150
	Novabeam (ceiling mount)	2	front	78	3,600
MGA/ MITSUBISHI	VS-505	1	front	50	3,400
PANASONIC	CT-4500	1	rear	45	3,300
QUASAR	PR 4800P	1	rear	45	3,750
RCA	PFR 100	1	front	50	3,200
SANYO	PV5080R	1	front	50	3,500
SEARS	5450	1	front	50	2,950
SONY	KP-7200	1	front	72	3,800
	KP-5040	1	front	50	3,800
	KP-7220	2	front	72	3,300
	KP-5020	2	front	50	2,850
SYLVANIA	Superscreen	1	rear	50	3,500
ZENITH	SN4545	1	rear	45	3,750

The screen comes with a stand, or it can be mounted on a wall. It is slightly concave, to concentrate the brightness of the projected picture and minimize glare from other light sources. The screen's surface is an aluminum-coated material that also enhances picture brightness. Most screens are washable, and they can also be used for showing movies and slides.

The picture produced by early projection systems often lacked brightness and sharpness, but the new systems are much improved. Their pictures are bright and sharp enough to be viewed comfortably in a normally lighted room at home. However, to produce the best-quality picture, the projection unit must be placed a specific distance from the screen and be properly aligned. Consequently, you should know where you're going to place the set before you choose which one to buy. The sets usually come with alignment devices and focusing controls.

• *One-piece front projection sets.* These normally have smaller screens, usually mounted atop the cabinet containing the receiver, speakers and projection tubes. To use the set, you pull out a panel or drawer, which contains a mirror angled to reflect the picture from the projection tubes up to the screen. Mitsubishi, RCA, Sanyo, Sears and Sony models work this way. Some have doors that close over the screen to hide it when not in use. When the set is closed, it resembles a piece of furniture. Advent has one that becomes a card table.

• *Rear projection sets.* These usually look like giant conventional TV sets, but what appears to be the picture tube is not. It is a special plastic screen. The TV picture is projected onto the screen from the rear by means of a mirror in the cabinet.

The cabinet dimensions of most brands are similar to those of a china closet. Some of the sets have doors to hide the screen when not in use; the screen on Zenith's model SN4545 lowers into the cabinet, which then resembles a buffet.

Projection TV systems usually have the same electronic tuning, remote control, and sound and picture control features available on conventional TV sets, but there are some potential problems. For example, there can be noticeable differences in picture quality among various brands of front projection TVs and between front projection and rear projection sets, especially when you are not seated with a straight-ahead view of the screen. Before you buy, compare sets in lighting and space conditions that match as closely as possible conditions in the room in which you plan to install the set. You might need as little as 4 by 5 feet of floor space or as much as 10 by 12 for best viewing.

CONVENTIONAL SETS

Most new TV sets are still of the conventional 19-inch to 25-inch screen size. Prices typically range from about $300 to $800 for color sets and start under $100 for black-and-white.

These are some of the features you'll find when you shop.

Automatic picture control. Most of the new sets automatically hold the picture's color intensity, contrast and detail in the setting you've selected. Many sets also have a light sensor that automatically adjusts picture brightness to changing light in the room.

THE MINIS: PLUG IN OR USE BATTERIES

MAKE	MODEL	DIAGONAL SCREEN SIZE (INCHES)	WEIGHT (POUNDS)	DIMENSIONS, W × H × D (INCHES)	OTHER EQUIPMENT AND FEATURES (SEE FOOTNOTES)	APPROXIMATE COST
JVC						
color:	CX-610	5	9½	9⅝ × 5⅜ × 10⅞	—	$395
	CX-500	4.5	16½	17¼ × 5⅜ × 13	*†	500
PANASONIC						
color:	CT-778	7	20	8⅞ × 10¼ × 13½	—	380
B&W:	TR-1000P	1.5	4	5⁵⁄₁₆ × 1½ × 6⁹⁄₁₆	*	320
	TR-5050P	5	15	9¾ × 5³⁄₁₆ × 13⅜	pop-up screen*	200
SANYO						
color:	MTC40	5	19	18 × 5⅞ × 11⅜	*†	600
	MTC50	5	26	20¾ × 7⅛ × 14¾	**†	700
B&W:	TMP 2000	2	25	5⅛ × 2 × 6⅛	*	270
	TMP 2100	2	25	5⅛ × 2 × 6⅛	LCD quartz clock/alarm*	300
SHARP						
B&W:	3T59	4	13⅛	17¾ × 5¼ × 11⅙	*†	315
	3S62	5	10	8⅝ × 9⁷⁄₁₆ × 11⁷⁄₁₆	—	160
SONY						
color:	KV-5200	5	13¼	6⅜ × 10⅝ × 13	—	550
	KV-4000	3.7	6⅔	4¾ × 4¾ × 11⅜	—	580
B&W:	FX-414	3.7	14⅛	16⅞ × 5½ × 11⅜	**†	400
	TV-515	5	7⅔	9 × 6⅛ × 9¾	clock/alarm*	215
TOSHIBA						
color:	CA-045	4.5	7½	8½ × 4⅘ × 10⁷⁄₁₀	—	475
ZENITH						
B&W:	Explorer	5	6	6 × 7¼ × 11⅛	digital clock/timer*	200

* AM-FM radio. ** Stereo AM-FM radio. † Cassette recorder/player. — No other features.

Electronic tuning.   The mechanical TV dial has largely been replaced by the digital keyboard. Electronic circuitry, activated by taps on the numbered keys, changes channels instantly and silently.

Remote control.   With a hand-held, battery-powered control unit, you can turn the set on and off, adjust the volume and change channels from anywhere in the room. Some controllers also have channel-scanning and sound-muting buttons.

Built-in cable capacity.   Many new sets can accommodate cable TV without a separate converter.

Beefed-up sound. With two or more amplifiers and speakers, the new TVs produce a quality of sound close to that of a stereo system. Actual stereo sound on TV is expected to be a reality in the U.S. in the near future.

Auxiliary jacks. Built into most new sets are panels of jacks that allow easy hookup of a VCR, videodisc player, remote speakers, even stereo sound equipment for "simulcast" programs, in which a TV show's sound track is broadcast simultaneously on FM stereo radio.

The chief measure of a good television set is still the picture you get on it. The experts agree that there is very little difference in picture quality among the top-of-the-line sets. The best way to judge is with your own eyes. And that's no problem, because most TV stores and departments have a wide range of brands tuned to the same channel.

COMPREHENSION TEST

1. List two new types of television sets that are discussed in the article.

   a) _____

   b) _____

2. Name two new features now available for conventional TV sets.

   a) _____

   b) _____

3. What is the price range for large screen sets? _____

   For small TV sets? _____

4. List two types of projection sets.

   a) _____

   b) _____

5. What is the chief measure of a good TV set?

   _____

```
┌─────────────────────────────────────────────────────────┐
│                                                           │
│   Flexibility Pretest 2:              1430 words          │
│                                                           │
│   Finishing Time:    _____  _____  _____               │
│                       HR.     MIN.    SEC.                │
│   Starting Time:     _____  _____  _____               │
│                       HR.     MIN.    SEC.                │
│   Reading Time:              _____  _____               │
│                               MIN.    SEC.                │
│   WPM Score:                 _____             │
│                                                           │
│   Comprehension Score:       _____  %              │
│                                                           │
│   Reading Efficiency Score:  _____                 │
│                                                           │
└─────────────────────────────────────────────────────────┘
```

Reading Flexibility Pretest 3

Complete the third reading flexibility pretest following these directions:

1. The following selection is taken from a reference book on botany — the study of plants. Assume you are completing a writing project on this topic and need to find the answer to a question. Read the following selection only for the purpose of finding the answer to this question:

    What is the name of the seventeenth-century scientist who studied the structure of plant cells?

2. Before you begin reading, record the time in minutes and seconds in the space marked Starting Time following the Comprehension Test. Then begin reading the selection. Read it only once. When you finish, record the time in the space marked Finishing Time.
3. Answer the question that follows the selection. *Do not look back at the selection to find the answer.*
4. Score your answer using the Answer Key. Record your score in the space marked Comprehension Score — 100 if you answer correctly, zero if you could not answer or if you answer incorrectly.
5. Use the words-per-minute conversion chart included at the back of the book to find the average number of words that you read per minute and record it in the space marked WPM Score.

READING FLEXIBILITY PRETEST 3
SECOND REVOLUTION: PLANT MIGRATIONS AND AGRICULTURAL IMPROVEMENTS

Watson M. Laetsch

The fifteenth and sixteenth centuries were an age of exploration, when ships built and equipped by such farsighted monarchs as Prince Henry the Navigator of Portugal ventured out on the uncharted oceans to discover whole new continents. Plants now were spread worldwide. Many new ones — maize, beans, tomatoes, and potatoes — were introduced to Europe by explorers who touched American soil. Some, like the potato and tomato, were then reexported to the Far East, which in turn supplied such flavorings as cumin, turmeric, black pepper, and that instant best-seller, tea. As trade in these plant commodities spread and flourished, plants began to influence the world economy and even politics, and nations competed fiercely for trade routes and markets. Transplanting the rubber tree from Brazil to Asia via England was to affect relationships of nations right down to the present.

Soon followed the age of colonization. As settlers migrated from continent to continent across the seas, plants went with them, and they sent new plants back to the mother country. Sugar came to the New World and became an economic staple in the West Indies. Pineapples migrated from Central America to Asia, Africa, and the South Pacific. One attempt at wholesale transfer of plants to a new habitat was the voyage of the British Navy's ship *Bounty*, sent to Tahiti to load a cargo of a thousand young breadfruit plants that could be grown as cheap food for slaves in the Caribbean Islands. The *Bounty*'s crew interrupted the botanical experiment with mutiny, as we know from the classic book by Charles Nordhoff and James Hall, as well as the popular movie renditions.

Some of these introductions of plants to new environments did not have their full effect until many years later. Strawberries, native to California and eastern North America, were not domesticated in Europe until the nineteenth century. The tomato, which some thought poisonous, did not come into its own until early in this century, by which time it had spread all across the globe. Soybeans were imported to Europe from China in the seventeenth century and then into the United States at the beginning of the nineteenth century. They have been an important crop here only since the end of World War II. But the hunt for new varieties of useful plants has never slackened, especially now as a growing world population demands more and more food and fiber. Intensive searches are also being made for plants useful to medicine.

Down through all the centuries since human beings planted the first crop, some kinds of food plants have always been more valued by one population than by others. These are the staple foods that are a people's basic diet. They may be plants native to the area, or they may have been imported and then proved indispensable. History shows how and why each of these has pushed the world's agricultural food supply to its enormous economic importance.

Improvements in agriculture since the Renaissance show a long slow rise through the sixteenth, seventeenth, and eighteenth centuries. Tribes of native Americans knew as much about irrigation in pre-Columbian times as Europeans did in the eighteenth century; the Incas in Peru built terraces as efficient as any in the Alps or the Apennines of later centuries, and it is probable that many Western Hemisphere Indians knew as much about the structure and function of the plant as most Old World scientists until Robert Hooke and others laid bare the structure of plant cells late in the seventeenth century by using microscopes. In all that time there was no great incentive to improve farming methods or add to knowledge handed down by peasant fathers to their sons. Populations were still small; the great, hungry, sprawling cities had not yet evolved; and few understood exhaustion of the soil by overcultivation.

But by late in the eighteenth century, pressures were beginning to be felt. A few large cities were asserting demands for food, colonization was opening vast new areas of the world to human habitation and plant cultivation, and new farms and plantations were growing beyond one family's ability to till the soil, sow the seeds, and harvest the crop. Improved varieties of farm animals, better cultivation, and an expanding labor market all contributed to new agricultural practices, particularly where the Netherlands and Belgium, England, and Scotland are today. These changes in agriculture were precursors to the revolution that really shook the world: the Industrial Revolution of the nineteenth century.

COMPREHENSION TEST

1. What is the name of the seventeenth-century scientist who studied the structure of plant cells?

_____

Flexibility Pretest 3:   746 words

Finishing Time: ____ HR. ____ MIN. ____ SEC.

Starting Time: ____ HR. ____ MIN. ____ SEC.

Reading Time: ____ MIN. ____ SEC.

WPM Score: _____

Comprehension Score: _____ %

Reading Efficiency Score: _____

INTERPRETING YOUR SCORES

Now that you have completed the pretests, you are wondering how well you have scored. However, you should be more concerned with what the scores reveal about *how* you read than how well you scored compared to other students. We will therefore not attempt to define an "average" score. Instead, this section will show you what the pretests reveal about your current reading skill.

Your Reading Efficiency Score

The reading efficiency score (RES) is a number that combines the two crucial factors — rate and comprehension — to determine efficiency as a single score. When you multiply rate by comprehension, you are computing a number that takes into account both factors. If you read fast, but get a low comprehension score, your RES will reflect that. For example, if you read at 300 wpm but comprehend only 50 percent, then your RES would be 150. On the other hand, if you read slower, at 200 wpm, but attain a higher comprehension score, say 90 percent, your RES would be higher: 180. Your RES, in any case, can never be greater than your word-per-minute score and never less than zero. If it is, check your arithmetic. In general, the higher your RES is, the more efficiently you read.

Your Reading Flexibility Score

The pretests consisted of three selections that were to be read for three very different purposes. The first was a textbook excerpt that you were to read carefully and thoroughly in preparation for an exam. The second was a magazine article, and you were directed to locate only the main, most important ideas in the article. For the third selection, taken from a reference source, you were to read only to locate one piece of information.

Since there were three different purposes for reading, and three different types of material, a skilled, flexible reader would have read each differently. He or she would have read the textbook excerpt more slowly and carefully than the magazine article because the textbook excerpt required very detailed comprehension, whereas the magazine article specified only recall of main ideas. He or she would have covered the reference material even faster, since all that was required was the answer to a particular question. A flexible reader should have a low rate and high comprehension on the first, a higher rate and adequate comprehension on the second, and an even higher rate on the third. He or she would have the lowest RES on the first passage, a medium RES on the second passage, and the highest RES on the third passage.

You should not be discouraged if you found very little difference between your three scores. Most adults do not vary their rate to suit their purpose for reading or the type of material they are reading. Since you are just becoming familiar with the concepts of flexibility, you should not expect to be already a flexible reader. As you work through the text, you will learn specific skills that will enable you to read certain materials faster than others, as well as to increase your overall efficiency.

You can get an idea of how flexible you are, at this point, by seeing how much difference there is in your RES scores for the three selections. List them in the Pretest Summary on page 33.

Using the Reading Progress Chart

You have an estimate of your present level of reading efficiency and flexibility. When you complete the posttests in Chapter 19, you will be able to compare those results with your pretest scores and see how much you have improved. However, before that time, while you are progressing through the text, you will want to know whether you are improving. For this purpose, as well as to provide regular, consistent practice, two reading selections are included at the end of each of the remaining chapters. By recording your results of each reading selection that you complete on the Reading Progress Chart on page 458, you will be able to keep track of your weekly progress.

Do not expect to see sudden, dramatic increases in rate, comprehension, or efficiency. Instead, your performance will most likely be somewhat irregular, with increases as well as slight decreases, but with a steady upward trend. Also, you can expect your rate and comprehension, in later chapters, to fluctuate as you apply new techniques for rate increase.

```
PRETEST SUMMARY

Reading Efficiency

    Reading Efficiency Score:        _____

Reading Flexibility

  Pretest 1

    Comprehension Score:        _____ %

    WPM Score:                  _____

    Reading Efficiency Score:   _____

  Pretest 2

    Comprehension Score:        _____ %

    WPM Score:                  _____

    Reading Efficiency Score:   _____

  Pretest 3

    Comprehension Score:        _____ %

    WPM Score:                  _____

    Reading Efficiency Score:   _____
```

Unit Two:
How to Read Efficiently

Many people think of reading as a simple mechanical process of moving one's eyes across a line of print. Actually, reading is very complex, and although it does involve the physical process of eye movement, it is also concerned with understanding, or deriving meaning, from what the eyes see. Reading, then, is both a physical and a mental activity in which these two aspects of the reading process are closely related. In this unit, you will see how the physical process of reading — what you do before and while reading — directly affects how well you are able to understand what you read, and you will see how certain mental activities, or mind sets, influence understanding.

The purpose of this unit is to present an initial group of techniques that can make an immediate, appreciable change in your reading efficiency. Some of the techniques will help you improve the physical aspects of eye movement to make comprehension easier. Others will develop the ease and speed with which you understand the author's message. Together, these techniques will give you a general foundation for increasing comprehension, retention, vocabulary development, interpretation and evaluation, and rate and flexibility.

Chapter 3:
Keys to Reading Efficiently

Efficient reading involves approaching your reading material in a way that will enable you to get the most out of it in the least amount of time. There are a number of factors that directly influence how efficiently you read. First, your efficiency is affected by your mind set as you begin reading. In the first section of this chapter you will discover how a specific purpose or mental set can increase your comprehension and enable you to retain more of what you read. Your awareness of various textual aids and your ability to take advantage of them also contributes to efficient reading. In the second part of the chapter we will present various types of textual aids and discuss their use in efficient reading.

Your efficiency is also affected by your ability to control eye movements and eliminate bad habits. The rest of this chapter discusses the physical process of reading and shows you how to become more efficient by reading in phrases and by eliminating habits that impair efficiency.

READING WITH A PURPOSE

When you order a hamburger, go to the bank, or make a phone call, you have a specific purpose for doing so. You are buying something to eat, making a financial transaction, or talking to someone. In fact, most of your daily activities are purposeful; you do things for specific reasons in order to accomplish something.

Reading should also be a purposeful activity. Just as you have a reason for all other things you do, you should also have a reason for reading each piece of material that you pick up. That is, before you begin reading any article, selection, or chapter, you should clearly identify what it is you want to find out by reading it. In some situations your purpose might be quite general, whereas at other times it might be very specific. You might read a magazine article on child abuse for the general purpose of learning more about the nature and extent of the problem of child abuse. On the other hand, if you were doing a research paper for a sociology course on the topic of child abuse your purpose might be quite specific: you would be looking for facts and figures about causes, effects, and extent of child abuse.

Establishing a purpose for reading will greatly improve your reading efficiency. If you know what you are looking for as you read, you will find that you are able to concentrate more easily and that you can remember more of what you read. With many articles that you are interested in reading, you automatically have a purpose for reading them. You are interested in the topic to be discussed and you want to know more about it. However, when you have to read material that is not inherently interesting, you often must create a purpose for reading. Although many students do so, it is not sufficient to read something because it is assigned. This purpose, though realistic enough, will not help you to keep your mind on what you are reading or to identify important ideas to remember. In these situations, then, it is most useful to develop questions that will guide your reading and focus your attention.

How to Develop Purpose Questions

One of the easiest ways to establish a purpose question is to turn the title into a question that you will try to answer as you read. For instance, for an essay titled "Three Steps to a Healthier You" you could form this question: What are the three steps that lead to a healthier person? Then, as you read the essay, you would look for the answer. Here are a few other examples of titles and questions that you might ask.

Title: Our Ten Contributions to Civilization
Question: What are the ten contributions?

Title: Classroom Without Walls
Question: What is a classroom without walls?

Title: Bringing Science Under Law
Question: How can science be brought under the law?

or

Why should science be brought under the law?

For material with internal headings, the simplest way to establish a purpose for reading is to turn each heading into a question. Then, as you read the section following the heading, you search for the answer. For instance, for a section with the heading "Aging: Psychological Aspects" you could ask, "What are the psychological aspects of aging?" Then, as you read that section, you would search for the effects. Here are a few more examples of headings and purpose questions that might be asked.

Heading: American Beliefs About Political Power
Question: What do Americans believe about political power?

Heading: Unequal Distribution of Income
Question: Why is income unequally distributed?

Heading: The Life Cycle of Social Problems
Question: What are the stages in the life cycle?

or

What social problems have a life cycle?

Heading: The Development of the Women's Movement
Question: How did the Women's Movement develop?

or

Why did the Women's Movement develop?

Asking the Right Questions

The effectiveness of this technique depends on knowing how to ask the right questions. Some types of questions are especially helpful, whereas other types may not lead you to a full understanding of the passage. Questions that begin with *what, why,* and *how* are useful because they usually require you to think or to consolidate information and ideas. As a result, they force you to read carefully to be able to answer them fully. Questions that begin with *who, when,* or *where* are less useful, because very often they can be answered in a word or two; they often refer to a specific fact or detail rather than to larger ideas or concepts. For a section titled "Treatment for Drug Abuse Conditions" you could ask, "Where does treatment take place?" or, "Who is treated for drug abuse?" But most likely these questions would not lead you to the main point of the section. However, a question such as "How is drug abuse treated?" would focus your attention on the main topic discussed.

EXERCISE 3-1

Directions: *For each of the following titles or headings, write a purpose question that would be useful in guiding your reading of the material that would follow.*

1.   We Ask the Wrong Questions About Crime

_____

2.   The Plight of the U.S. Hospital Patient

_____

3.   What College Did to Me

_____

4.   The Thinking of Men and Machines

_____

5.   Ghana and Rhodesia — A Study in Contrasts

_____

6.   Magnetic Fields and Lines of Force

_____

7.   Comparing X Rays and Visible Light

_____

USING TEXTUAL AIDS

A writer communicates and develops his or her ideas through words, sentences, and paragraphs, commonly called the "text" of a writer's message. However, writers frequently include within this text numerous aids to explain, clarify, emphasize, and organize their ideas. Some of the most common textual aids will be discussed in this section. Different aids are used in different types of writing; you should not expect to find all of these aids used in a single piece of writing.

Common Textual Aids

Italics. Italics, or slanted print, are used to make a word or phrase noticeable to the reader. A writer uses italics to direct the reader's attention to the word itself, rather than to the overall meaning of the sentence in which it is included. Often, then, new terminology or words that the author is defining or emphasizing are printed in italics. If you notice a word printed in italics you should pay special attention to it. Italics are a clue to you that the writer feels that this word or term is important. Read the following paragraph, and, as you read, notice how the use of italics allows you quickly to identify the two inventory systems introduced in the paragraph.

> There are two basic inventory systems that businesses use to keep records of their stock. One method is a *perpetual* system in which a record is made each time an item leaves the stockroom. This system is most often used when the inventory consists of large items, such as appliances. The other method is an *interval* system in which the entire stock is counted at regularly scheduled periods.

You can see, then, that italics can be used to help you to recognize what is important and sometimes to identify the writer's organization or development of ideas.

Enumeration. Writers often use numbers or letters to present facts or ideas in a list form within a paragraph. Again, their purpose in doing so is to present information in a clear, direct manner. Notice in the following paragraph, that the three factors that contributed to the growth of Italian nationalism are presented in list format using the numbers (1) . . . (2) . . . (3) . . . to emphasize that there are three separate factors and to make each clearly distinguishable.

> As early as the 15th century, Machiavelli, the Italian statesman, dreamed of an Italian nation. However, it was not until the 19th century that this dream came true. The growth of nationalism was encouraged by three common factors. (1) The growth of Italian nationalism was encouraged by a common history of which Italy was very proud. Its city-states contributed greatly to the Renaissance, and its language had been among the first of the widely-used languages. (2) Although the Apennine Mountains and the Po River served to divide the country, Italy was a peninsula, surrounded on three sides by water and cut off from the rest of Europe by the Alps (mountains on the north). These geographic features encouraged Italian nationalism. (3) In addition, it should be remembered that Napoleon conquered Italy and spread the spirit of nationalism.[1]

Headings. Earlier in this unit you were introduced to the use of headings in developing purpose questions. Now you will see that headings are equally useful while you are reading. Major headings function as labels, and they indicate the general topic of the section that follows. Subheadings also separate portions of an article from one another, alerting you to the major divisions of the content, to changes in directions of thought, or to movement to a new topic.

The following major headings were taken from a portion of a sociology textbook chapter on alcoholism. Notice that the headings suggest how the topic of alcoholism is divided, or broken down, in the chapter.

ALCOHOLISM
Explanations for Alcoholism
Effects of Alcohol Abuse
Types of Treatment[2]

Next, notice how the following group of subheadings, taken from an ecology text, guides the reader through the selection, indicating changes and new directions of thought.

THE PROBLEM OF CHEMICAL WASTE DISPOSAL
The Governmental Viewpoint
Opposition to this Viewpoint
The Environmentalist Viewpoint
Large Corporations' Objections to Environmentalists

Maps, Photographs, Charts, Diagrams, and Graphs. In addition to the text of a printed page, graphs, maps, photographs, charts or diagrams may have been included. These textual features are useful to the reader because they emphasize or clarify facts, ideas, events, processes or relationships. Each presents information in a visual format and enables you to easily understand the facts and ideas included. These aids are essential to efficient reading because they allow you to quickly grasp an idea or relationship or to locate a fact quickly. Many readers have fallen into the habit of skipping over these textual aids, assuming that the text itself includes all necessary information. You have heard the everyday expression, "A picture is worth a thousand words." This adage concisely states the value of all visual aids. Each replaces lengthy, repetitious descriptions, explanations, or presentations of facts. Let us look at the function of each of these graphic aids.

Photographs. A writer includes photographs, sketches, or drawings to add interest to his or her writing as well as to help the reader visualize or further understand an event, concept, or feeling. Often a photo is intended to create an emotional or empathetic response.

For example, in discussing the problem of overcrowding in American prisons, a writer may include a photo of overcrowded conditions to help the reader visualize those conditions and better understand the problem. Or, to create an appreciation of the complicated, yet beautiful, carvings discovered at an archeological site, a photograph of the carvings may be included. Be sure to take a moment as you read to study the pictures to determine what ideas or concepts they are intended to illustrate. Photos provide important clues to what the author feels is important.

Maps. A map describes geographic location or geographical features. It enables a reader quickly to grasp the location of a particular place in relation to surrounding places. A writer may include a map in order to simplify a description of a geographic location or to emphasize the location of a particular place. As you read, be sure to study all maps that are included in the text. You will find that they make the content of surrounding text easier to understand. For example, studying a map of Germany would make it easier to understand a passage discussing the problems of the city of West Berlin because you would immediately see that West Berlin, a part of West Germany, is surrounded completely by East Germany and is separated from other parts of West Germany.

Charts and Tables. The purpose of a chart or table is to present facts, figures, statistics, and other data in an orderly sequence for convenience of reference. That is, rather than to present figures on the projected job openings for various occupations for 1976–85 in paragraph form, a writer might organize the data into the following table.[3]

Table 3-1. PROJECTED ANNUAL JOB OPENINGS, 1976–85

Stenographers, secretaries	295,000	Bank clerks	36,000
Farm workers	200,000	Welders, arc cutters	33,800
Building custodians	160,000	Police officers	32,500
Retail trade, salespeople	155,000	Auto mechanics	32,000
Bookkeepers	95,000	Cosmetologists	30,000
Cashiers	92,000	Industrial-machine repairmen	30,000
Registered nurses	83,000	Social workers	25,000
Nurses' aides, orderlies	83,000	Lawyers	23,400
Cooks, chefs	79,000	Personnel workers	23,000
Foremen	79,000	Machine-tool operators	22,000
Lease truck drivers	73,000	Bank tellers	21,000
Waiters, waitresses	71,000	Medical lab workers	20,000
Assemblers	70,000	College teachers	17,000
Elementary school teachers	70,000	Drafters	16,500
Carpenters	67,000	File clerks	16,000
Typists	63,000	Secondary school teachers	13,000
Practical nurses	53,000	Electrical engineers	12,800
Private household workers	53,000	Civil engineers	8,900
Factory inspectors	52,000	Computer operators	8,500
Accountants	51,500	Chemists	6,300
Construction workers	40,000	School counselors	1,500
Receptionists	38,000		

This table enables you to look up projected annual job openings for any particular occupation easily and also allows you quickly to inspect the data to determine any overall pattern. In this table you can see easily that office positions (stenographers, secretaries, bookkeepers) are in high demand, whereas certain teaching positions (secondary and college teachers) are in low demand. To read a chart or table quickly and accurately, first read the title and then the headings for each column or grouping of data. As a purpose for reading, try to notice changes and patterns in the data. Finally, decide what general trend, if any, is evident.

Diagrams. A diagram explains an object, idea, or process by outlining, in visual form, parts or steps or by showing its organization. The purpose of a diagram, as for tables and charts, is to simplify and clarify the writer's explanation and to help you visualize the item diagrammed. For example, the following diagram[4] showing the organizational structure of a branch bank, presents a clear picture of the position and relative importance of the various officers of the bank.

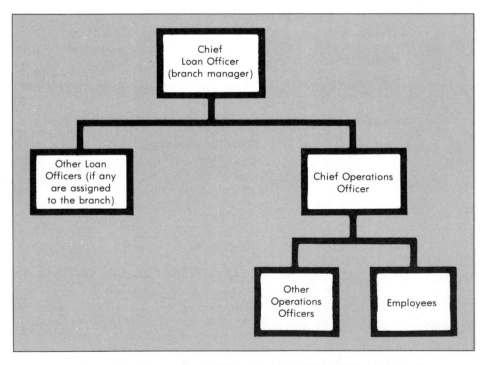

Figure 3-1. Simplified Organizational Structure of a Typical Branch Bank

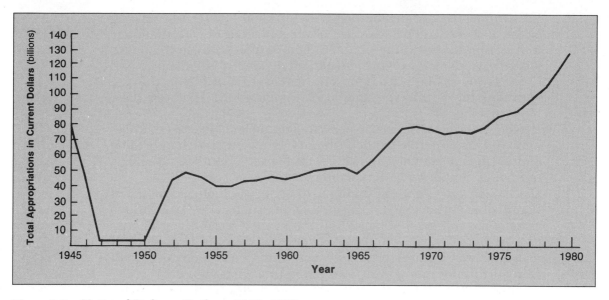

Figure 3-2. National Defense Outlays, 1945–1980

Graphs. The purpose of a graph is to clarify the relationship between two or more items. Graphs, then, usually compare one set of variables with another. For instance, the graph[5] above compares national defense spending from year to year. By studying the graph you are able to see that since 1950 there has been a general trend toward increased appropriations for national defense.

Textbook Learning Aids

In addition to the textual features already discussed, textbooks often contain aids not commonly found in other types of writing. Because a textbook is written to help you master a particular subject, the writer tries to offer as much guidance as possible. If you page quickly through a textbook chapter, you may notice chapter summaries, vocabulary lists, review questions, discussion questions, and chapter outlines. Each of these aids is intended to direct your attention and to guide your learning.

1. *Chapter summaries.* An end-of-the-chapter summary or conclusion serves several functions. First, it reviews the most important general ideas and concepts discussed in the chapter. Second, it draws the ideas together to enable you to see the relationships among them. Finally, by reviewing the important concepts, the summary helps you to recall what you have read.

2.   *Vocabulary lists*. Many textbooks include, either at the beginning or the end of each chapter, a list of vocabulary or new terminology that is introduced in the chapter. The purposes of the list are to identify words that are introduced and defined in the chapter and to focus the reader's attention on these words. In effect, this list identifies terms that you should be familiar with after you have read the chapter.

3.   *Review questions*. Some textbook writers include a series of questions that are intended to help the reader review the chapter. The review questions, when answered, form a list, or outline, of important ideas contained in the chapter.

4.   *Discussion questions*. In addition to or in place of review questions, some authors include discussion questions. These questions usually are intended to make you think; they require you to analyze, criticize, or react to the ideas presented in the chapter. It is useful to read through these questions and to use them as a point of departure for interpreting and evaluating what you read.

5.   *Chapter outlines*. Occasionally you may find a textbook that includes an outline of each chapter. Chapter outlines may appear at the ends of chapters or they may be grouped together at the end of the text. Again, their purpose is to emphasize what is important and to guide your reading and review of the chapter.

EXERCISE 3-2

Directions: *For one of the selections included at the end of the chapter, complete each of the following steps.*

1.   Write several purpose questions here.

_____

_____

_____

2.   Read the selection, and as you read, look for the answers to your questions. Briefly write the answer to each question you listed in step 1.

_____

_____

_____

3. Turn to the selection that you have just read and notice the various types of textual aids. List them here.

_____

_____

_____

EYE-MOVEMENT PATTERNS

In order to develop reading habits and patterns that can increase your efficiency, it is useful to understand a little about the reading process from a physical point of view. Specifically you should be aware of the physical features, characteristics, and limitations of eye movement. The following brief overview of the physical aspects of reading will familiarize you with eye movement and will help you to recognize habits that reduce your reading rate or comprehension.

What Happens When You Read

Your eyes are highly specialized and complicated instruments. They have the capacity to recognize words rapidly and to transmit them in the form of signals to the brain. Mental processes become involved as your brain attaches meaning to the signals it receives. As these two processes occur, you comprehend what you are reading. Training in the recognition of visual symbols began very early when you first learned to read. You learned letter shapes, letter-sound associations, word configurations (patterns), and letter-combination rules (phonics). As a result, most adults can recognize a large number of words. However, additional training and practice can greatly improve the efficiency of their eye movements and the speed with which they recognize words. To explain what occurs as your eyes move across a line of print, let us look at some physical features of the eye-movement process.

Left-to-Right Progression. Your eyes are already well trained to move in a left-to-right pattern across the page. This is a learned behavior, and not something that happens automatically. If you watch a young child learning to read, you may notice the child skipping about the page or even moving in the opposite direction, from right to left. Although your left-to-right progression is well established at this point, the speed of this progression is variable and can be significantly increased with practice and training.

Fixation. As your eyes move across a line of print, they move and stop, move and stop. When your eyes are in motion, they do not see anything. When your eyes stop, or focus, this is called a *fixation*. As your eyes move across a line of print, then, they make a number of stops, or fixations, and the number of fixations you make per line is directly related to your reading efficiency.

Eye Span. As your eyes stop, or fixate, while progressing from left to right across the line, they see a certain number of words or letters. The amount you see during each fixation is called your *eye span*. Some readers see only a part of a word in each fixation; others are able to see a whole word in one fixation. Still others may see several words in each fixation. Eye span is one commonly used measure to gauge reading efficiency.

You may find that your eye span varies greatly according to the type of material you are reading. For example, if you are reading a children's book to a child, you may be able to see several words at a time. On the other hand, when you read a chemistry textbook, you may need to focus on single words. Occasionally, when identifying an unfamiliar word, you may look at one part of a word and then another part.

Return Sweep. When your eyes reach the end of a line of print, they return to the beginning of the next line. This return motion is called the *return sweep*. Although your eyes are already trained to return automatically, the speed with which they make this return is variable. The efficiency of the return sweep, then, directly affects speed.

Regression. Normally, your eyes progress in a left-to-right direction, seeing each word in the order it was written. Occasionally, your eyes will, instead of moving to the next word, move backward, or *regress* to a word already read. This word may be on the same line or on a previous line. In the following line, each fixation is numbered consecutively to show a sample reader's regression pattern.

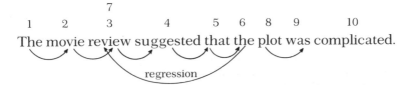

Notice that this reader moved from left to right through the sixth fixation. Then, instead of progressing to the next word, the reader

regressed to the word "review," reread it, and then continued from where he or she left off.

Regression is often unnecessary and slows you down. In fact, regressing may scramble, or mix up, the sentence order. As a result, you may have difficulty comprehending what you are reading. To illustrate, read the following sentence that is written as it would be read by a student who made two regressions in the sentence. The sentence is printed in correct order following the regression example:

Order as read
by student:

Then came the day when came the car payment was due and he was unable to payment meet it.

Correct order:

Then came the day when the car payment was due and he was unable to meet it.

Were you confused when you read the first version of the sentence? Did the sentence seem complicated? Regression commonly produces this type of confusion and complication. Many readers regress because they feel they are not understanding what they are reading or that they have missed something or misread a word. Regression can easily become a habit that a reader falls back on whenever the meaning is unclear.

Observing Eye-Movement Patterns

Most of the processes described so far can be readily observed by watching another person read. To get a better understanding of eye movement patterns, choose another person to work with and try the following experiments. Be sure to sit so that the other person is facing you and select sample pages from a book or text neither of you has already read.

Experiment 1: Observing Eye Movement
Ask the other person to hold up the book so that you can see his or her eyes as he reads. Then direct the person to start reading a paragraph. As he or she reads, notice how the eyes move and stop, move and stop. Also notice the return sweep to the beginning of the next line.

Experiment 2: Counting Fixations
As the person reads, count the number of eye stops or fixations made on each line. By counting the average number of words on the line and dividing it by the average number of fixations per line, you will be able to compute the person's eye span.

Experiment 3: Regression

   While observing the other person reading, ask him or her to deliberately regress to a word on a previous line. Notice the eye movement that occurs. Then have the person continue reading, and notice if he or she makes any regressions that he or she is unaware of.

   Now allow the other person to try each of these three experiments while you read.

   Now that you are familiar with the eye-movement process, you can begin to develop habits and eye-movement patterns that will increase your efficiency. First, it is important that you reduce or eliminate regressions; second, try to widen your eye span to encompass more than a single word at a time. Each of these techniques will be discussed in the sections that follow.

Reducing Regressions

   Although even very good readers occasionally regress, you will find that frequent regression interferes with your comprehension and slows you down. There are various mechanical devices used to reduce regression, but you can easily get the same results by using one or more of the following techniques.

1.   Be conscious of your tendency to regress and force yourself to move your eyes only from left to right. Do not regress in the middle of a sentence. Instead, if the meaning of a sentence is unclear after you have finished reading it, reread the entire sentence.

2.   Use a 5″ × 8″ index card to prevent regression to previous lines. As you read, slide the index card down the page so that it covers what you have already read. This technique will help you to eliminate regressions, because when you look back to a previous line, it will be covered up. Eventually, if you look back often enough and find the line is not visible, you will stop looking back.

3.   Use a pen, pencil, or finger to guide your eyes in a left-to-right direction across each line as you read. Move the object or your finger at the speed at which you normally read. You will find that the forward motion of your finger or the pen will force you to continue reading toward the right and will discourage you from regressing.

READING IN PHRASES

When   you   read   a   paragraph,   do   you
read   one   word   and   then   another   word
OR   does your eye   jump from   one group   of words to
another group   of words? Most adult readers read a word at a time,
as illustrated in the first half of the preceding sentence. Although most
are capable of reading more than one word at a time, they have not
developed the skill of doing so. Word-by-word reading is time consuming and, in many cases, actually distracts from understanding the
meaning a sentence expresses.

To understand how slow word-by-word reading can be, read the
following paragraph. It is written so that you will have to read it from
right to *left*, forcing you to read each word separately.

> spirits neutral of combination a is Vodka
> bring to added is water The .water and
> neutral Since .proof final its to vodka
> ,neutral equally much pretty are spirits
> but subtle for makes that water the is it
>   .differences appreciable

Phrase reading is the technique of seeing more than one word in
a single eye fixation. You recall that your eyes move and stop, move
and stop, as they proceed across a line of print. Phrase reading involves
widening your eye span so that you see several words in one fixation.

The development of your eye span from an early reading stage to
reading maturity suggests that eye span does increase gradually
throughout the learning-to-read process. For example, take the word
"automobile." A child just learning to read, when presented with this
word, would sound out one letter at a time — a-u-t-o-m-o-b-i-l-e — and
then attempt to blend the sounds together to form a word. Thus the eye
span at this point of development is the single letter.

As the child develops reading skill, he or she might approach the
word "automobile" by speech sounds, or syllables — au-to-mo-bile —
and, at this stage, would have an eye span of two to three letters. Even
later, the child may approach the unknown word by word parts (prefixes, roots, suffixes) — auto-mobile — and would have a four-, five-, or
six-letter eye span. As mature readers, of course, you recognize the
whole word by sight; no analysis is necessary, and your eye span is the
whole word: ten or more letter spaces. Since your eye span has already
developed from seeing only a single letter at a time to reading a whole
word at a time, it is possible to continue eye span development so that
you can see a two- or three-word phrase in one fixation — the phrase

"in the automobile" for example. These stages in the widening of eye span can be diagrammed as follows (a slash mark is used to separate fixations).

/a/u/t/o/m/o/b/i/l/e/
/au/to/mo/bile/
/auto/mobile/
/automobile/
/in the automobile/

You can see, then, that eye span widens from single letters to syllables, to word parts, then to whole words.

How to Phrase Read

Essentially, phrase reading involves widening your eye span to encompass two or three words in one fixation. To phrase read most effectively, however, you should try to group words together that naturally fit or go together. In both written and spoken language, words fall into natural groupings. Our language contains many words that carry little meaning alone, but when combined with others do express a thought or idea. For example, the words "in" and "the" have meaning mainly when combined with other words: for example, "in the house." The word grouping "in the house" is a meaningful phrase and could be read as a unit in one eye fixation. When you group words together in meaning units, you will find that it is easier to understand what you read. To illustrate this point, read both versions of the following sample paragraph; the same paragraph is divided up into phrases in two different ways. One version divides the paragraph into meaningful phrases; the other does not. Decide which version is easier to read.

Version 1
(By all) (outward appearances), (Ralph Nader) (should now) (be reaching) (the height) (of his power). (At 43), (the tall), (reedy, ascetic) (reformer has become) (the head of) (a loose organization) (of watchdog groups) (that resemble) (a corporate organization).

Version 2
(By all outward) (appearances, Ralph) (Nader should) (now be) (reaching the) (height of his) (power. At 43), (the tall) (reedy, ascetic reformer) (has become the) (head of a loose) (organization of watchdog) (groups that) (resemble a corporate) (organization).

You probably decided that the first version is easier to read because the words that belong together are grouped together.

Phrase reading can have a dramatic effect on your reading efficiency. By grouping words together into meaningful phrases, you make sentences easier to understand. Also, by widening your eye span, and thereby reducing the number of fixations per line, you are reducing the time it takes to read a line and are increasing your reading rate.

Learning to Phrase Read

For most students, learning to read in phrases requires considerable practice. It is not a skill that you can develop after a few trial reading sessions. Instead, you may find that it takes several weeks of continued practice to develop the habit. To develop the skill, try to read as many things as possible in phrases. Begin by reading easy material, such as newspaper and magazine articles, in phrases. Later, as you feel more confident about the skill, progress to more difficult types of material.

As you begin phrase reading, you may find that you frequently lapse back into word-by-word reading. This is a natural happening, as your attention focuses on the content of the material rather than the technique of reading. Once you realize that you have lapsed into word-by-word reading, just switch back to phrase reading and continue reading. As you become more skilled with phrase reading, you will find that fewer lapses will occur.

EXERCISE 3-3

Directions: *Choose one of the reading selections at the end of this chapter. Read the first five paragraphs, and, as you read, divide each sentence into meaningful phrase groups. Separate each phrase by using a slash mark (/) as has been done in the following example.*

Studying economics / is difficult / because it requires / careful attention / to facts and figures.

Then, reread the five paragraphs, trying to see each phrase rather than each single word.

EXERCISE 3-4

Directions: *Read the following passages that have been already divided up into phrases. They are designed to give you an idea of how it feels to phrase read. As you read, you should feel your eyes jumping from phrase to phrase in a rhythmical motion.*

1. When you   phrase read   it should feel   like this.
   Your eye should   move and stop,   move and stop.
   Each time   your eye stops,   or fixates   it should see
   a meaningful phrase.   Phrase reading   will improve
   your comprehension   and help you   read faster.

2. As a   used car shopper,   your first   task is
   to decide   what kind   of car   is going   to fill
   your needs.   Then   shop around   until you
   have a   good feel   for the market value   of that car.
   This way   you'll know   a bargain   when you   see one.
   You can   also check   the National   Automobile Dealers
   Association Used Car Guide   and the   Kelly Blue Book
   for prices   of used cars.   They'll give   you prices
   to work with,   *but they're   only guides*.
   Condition and mileage   will adjust   the price up
   or down.[6]

3. Anytime   you're told   that you   need surgery
   and it's   not an emergency,   it's a good idea
   to get a second   opinion from   a qualified specialist
   in the appropriate   field.   To find   this specialist,
   ask your   primary care physician   for a recommendation,
   or call   the nearest   teaching hospital   or an accredited
   hospital for   a recommendation.   You can   also consult
   the *Directory   of Medical Specialists*.[7]

4. Actually,   the common cold   is not   as simple
   as it seems.   It can   be caused   by any
   of 200 different   viruses,   and it can   bring misery
   eight ways: sore throat,   sneezing,   runny nose,
   watery eyes,   aches and pains,   mild fever,
   nasal congestion,   and coughing.   Thus
   the thinking behind   "combination" products: they
   supposedly contain   a little something   for the
   different symptoms.   One pill   or capsule,
   the advertisers say,   handles the   whole malady.
   A little like   one-stop shopping.[8]

5. Psychological principles   can be applied   by everyone.
   You can learn   to use   scientific psychology
   to help solve   your own problems.   There are
   a number   of important advantages   of do-it-yourself
   psychology.   One factor   is manpower.   For most people
   the major problem   a few   generations ago
   was physical   survival: now it is psychological   survival.

We seem to be tense,   alienated, confused.
Suicide, addiction,   violence, apathy,   neurosis —
are all   problems of   the modern world.
Psychological problems   are accelerating
and there   are not enough   professional psychologists
to go around.   Non-psychologists *must*   practice psychology
if psychology   is to be applied   to our problems.[9]

EXERCISE 3-5

Directions: *The following material has already been phrased. Practice reading each phrase with only one eye fixation. Move your eyes down each column, making only one fixation per line.*

1. There is   opportunity to
    no better way   try out
    to test   the fishing boat
    fishing boats   under the most
    than under   adverse weather
    actual fishing   conditions and
    conditions.   the most rapid
    Actual conditions   and unexpected
    provide the   passenger movements.

2. The purpose of   life insurance
    life insurance   by simply
    is to prevent   asking yourself
    financial difficulty   if your death
    for someone else   would put someone
    in the event   else in a tough
    of your death.   financial position.
    With that in mind,   If the answer
    you can determine   is yes,
    if you need   you need insurance.[10]

3. The job interview   Most employers
    is your best chance   will be impressed
    to sell yourself,   if you can
    so it pays   ask intelligent questions
    to be well-prepared.   about their company,
    First, rehearse   questions that show
    in your mind   you've done
    the qualifications   your homework.
    that would make   Your local librarian

you an asset
to the organization.
Second, learn
something about it.

can direct you
to a number
of reference books
that "profile"
business organizations.[11]

4. The most important
tool you have
in job-hunting
is your resume.
It's your calling card,
and it should reflect
what it is
about you
that makes
you eminently employable.
To put
the resume
in proper perspective,
think about
your potential employer.
He or she
is busy,
harassed, has a pile
of resumes
on the desk,

and has only
an hour
and a half
to read them.
All of them.
Then he hits
four pages
that follow you
from being
high school valedictorian
to shooting
the rapids of
the Congo.
Chances are
he'll shoot your resume —
rapidly —
into the wastebasket.
Many employers
spend only
15 to 30 seconds
on each resume.[12]

5. The best exercise
is the endurance type —
cardiovascular activities
that make you
breathe deeply,
elevate your pulse,
and make you sweat.
Dr. Kenneth Cooper,
expert on fitness,
lists the following
as the best activities
for physical fitness:
running, swimming,
cycling, walking or striding,
stationary running,
handball, basketball, squash.
Any activity that elevates
the heart rate

is beneficial.
The exercise should be
vigorous enough
to produce
a temporary feeling
of fatigue.
At this level
of intensity,
it strengthens the heart
and other muscles
and increases circulation.
Strenuous activity
should be scheduled
at least two
to three times
a week
for at least
a half hour each time.[13]

APPLYING WHAT YOU HAVE LEARNED

Directions: *Choose one of the selections at the end of the chapter and complete each of the following steps.*

1. Write several purpose questions here.

    _____

    _____

    _____

2. Read the selection, and as you read, try to read in phrases. Look for the answers to your questions as you read. After you finish reading, write the answers to your questions here.

    _____

    _____

    _____

READING SELECTION 1
MUSICAL SOUNDS

Difficulty Level: A

Paul G. Hewitt

NOISES AND MUSICAL SOUNDS

Most of the sounds we hear are noises. The impact of a falling object, the slamming of a door, the roaring of a motorcycle, and most of the sounds from traffic in city streets are noises. Noise corresponds to an irregular vibration of the eardrum produced by the irregular vibration of some nearby object. If we make a diagram to indicate the pressure of the air on the eardrum as it varies with time, the graph corresponding to a noise might look like that shown in Figure 1a. The sound of music has a different character, having more or less sustained tones — or musical "notes." (Musical instruments may make noise as well!) The graph representing a musical sound has a shape that repeats itself over and over again (Figure 1b). Such graphs can be displayed on the screen of an oscilloscope when the electric signal from a microphone is fed into the input terminal of this important instrument.

The dividing line between music and noise is not sharp and is subjective. To some contemporary composers, it is nonexistent.

Some people consider contemporary music and music from other cultures to be noise. Differentiating these types of music from noise becomes a problem of aesthetics. However, differentiating traditional music — that is, classical music and most types of popular music — from noise presents no problem. A deaf person could distinguish between these with the use of an oscilloscope.

Musicians usually speak of a musical tone in terms of three characteristics — the pitch, the loudness, and the quality.

PITCH

The pitch of a sound corresponds to frequency. A shrill high note is produced by rapid vibrations of the sound source, whereas a deep low note is from slow vibrations. We speak of the pitch of a sound in terms of its position in the musical scale. When middle C is struck on a piano, a hammer strikes two or three strings, each of which vibrates 264 times in 1 second. The pitch of middle C corresponds to 264 hertz.

Different musical notes are obtained by

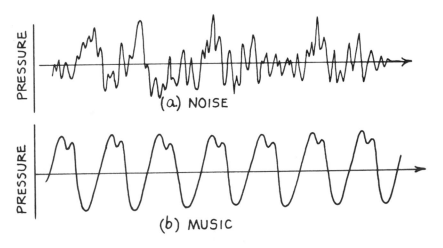

Figure 1.   Graphical Representations of Noise and Music

58

changing the frequency of the vibrating sound source. This is usually done by altering the size, the tightness, or the mass of the vibrating object. A guitarist or violinist, for example, adjusts the tightness, or tension, of the strings of the instrument when tuning them. Then different notes can be played by altering the length of each string by "stopping" them with the fingers. In wind instruments the length of the vibrating air column is altered to change the pitch of the note produced.

High-pitched sounds used in music are most often less than 4000 vibrations per second, but the average human ear can hear sounds up to 20,000 vibrations per second. Some people can hear tones of higher pitch than this, and most dogs can. In general, the upper limit of hearing in people gets lower as they grow older. A high-pitched sound is often inaudible to an older person and yet may be clearly heard by a younger one. So by the time you can really afford that high-fidelity music system, you may not be able to hear the difference.

LOUDNESS

The intensity of sound depends on pressure variations within the sound wave; it depends on the amplitude (more specifically, like any type of wave, intensity is proportional to the square of the amplitude). Sound intensity is a purely objective and physical attribute of a wave and can be measured by various acoustical instruments (such as the oscilloscope). *Loudness*, on the other hand, is a physiological sensation: it depends on intensity but in a complicated way. For example, if you turn a radio up until it seems about twice as loud as before, you would have to increase the power output, and therefore the intensity, by approximately eight times. Although the pitch of a sound can be judged very accurately, our ears are not very good at judging loudness. The loudest sounds we can tolerate have intensities a million million times greater than the faintest sounds. The difference in loudness, however, is much less than this amount.

The relative loudness of a sound heard by the ear is measured in *decibels,* a unit named after Alexander Graham Bell and abbreviated db. Some common sounds and their noise levels are compared in Table 1.

Table 1.

SOURCE OF SOUND	NOISE LEVEL (DB)
Jet airplane, 30 meters away	140
Air raid siren, nearby	125
Disco music, amplified	115
Riveter	95
Busy street traffic	70
Conversation in home	65
Quiet radio in home	40
Whisper	20
Rustle of leaves	10
Threshold of hearing	0

Decibel ratings are logarithmic , so that 60 decibels represent sound intensity a million times greater than 0 decibels; 80 decibels represent sound 100 times as intense as 60 decibels. Physiological hearing damage begins at exposure to 85 decibels, the degree depending on the length of exposure and frequency characteristics. Damage from loud sounds can be temporary or permanent as the organs of Corti, the receptor organs in the inner ear, are impaired or destroyed. A single burst of sound can produce vibrations in the organs intense enough to tear them apart. Less intense, but severe, noise can interfere with cellular processes in the organs that cause their eventual breakdown. Unfortunately, the cells of these organs do not regenerate.

From the earliest stages of human evolution we are subjected to a wide range of light intensities, and our eyes are now well adapted to the light we encounter in today's world. But not so with sound. Hearing loud and sustained sounds is something new for humans to contend with. Except for occasional bursts of thunder and the like, early people were not exposed to loud sounds and as a result we did not develop an adaptation to match the noise pollution we experience today. You know that you'll ruin your sense of sight if you stare into a source of light as bright as the sun. Please don't ruin your sense of hearing and blow the fine tuning in your ears by subjecting yourself to loud sounds.

Is hearing permanently impaired when attending concerts, discotheques, or functions that feature very loud music?*

Answer: Yes, depending on how loud, how long, and how often. Some music groups have emphasized loudness over quality. Tragically, as hearing becomes more and more impaired, members of the group (and their fans) require louder and louder sounds for stimulation. Hearing loss caused by loud sounds is particularly common in the frequency range of 2000 to 5000 hertz, the very range in which speech and music normally occur.

COMPREHENSION TEST 1

Directions: *Circle the letter of the correct answer.*

1. The three most important parts of musical sound are
   a) pitch, amplitude, harmonics
   b) pitch, aleatorations, and quality
   c) loudness, tone, and pitch
   d) pitch, quality, and loudness

2. Chance or "aleatory" music
   a) may seem like noise to some listeners
   b) is characterized by regular patterns
   c) is restricted to traditional forms
   d) is limited by the various sounds instruments can produce

3. Most forms of classical and pop music can be distinguished from noise
   a) only with great difficulty
   b) more easily by the composers than by listeners
   c) with relative ease
   d) using the oscilloscope

4. The oscilloscope records
   a) levels of noise
   b) level of pitch
   c) vibrations
   d) irregularities in sound

5. A decibel measures
   a) quality of sound
   b) variation in pitch
   c) frequency
   d) relative loudness

6. When the author says decibel ratings are *logarithmic,* he means that
   a) decibels equal intensity
   b) decibels increase faster than intensity
   c) intensity increases faster than decibels
   d) decibels are unrelated to intensity

7. If humans are continually exposed to loud noises over the next several thousand years, you might expect that they would
   a) continue to be highly sensitive to loudness
   b) become tone deaf
   c) react more sensitively to sound than to light
   d) develop the ability to adapt to loud noises

8. You can expect that the pitch of the sound of a bicycle wheel rotating
   a) increases as you pedal faster
   b) depends on your direction
   c) remains unchanged
   d) varies with the size of the wheel

9. If you worked in an industrial plant and experienced hearing loss in one ear due to a loud explosion you could expect
   a) the loss to be permanent
   b) to suddenly regain your hearing after several months

60

  c) to gradually regain your hearing
  d) to develop greater capacity in your other
     ear

10. Primarily, the author explains musical
    sound by
    a) comparing it to light and vision
    b) explaining its characteristics
    c) analyzing individual response to sound
    d) giving examples from particular musical
       pieces

Selection 1:   1055 words

Finishing Time: _____ _____ _____
                   HR.   MIN.   SEC.

Starting Time: _____ _____ _____
                   HR.   MIN.   SEC.

Reading Time: _____ _____
                           MIN.   SEC.

WPM Score: _____

Comprehension Score: _____ %

Reading Efficiency Score: _____

READING SELECTION 2
ELECTRONIC DATA PROCESSING

Difficulty Level: B

Robert A. Fleck and C. Brian Honess

The definition of data processing does not mention the computer. The computer is not needed for data processing. However, the phrase "electronic data processing" means that some electronic device, usually the computer, is involved in some capacity. Even adding the word "electronic" does not change the concept of data processing. A clear statement of the problem is still required; data must be collected; the processing method determined; and feedback established.

In any type of data processing, people are involved. People determine what problems are to be solved, what data are needed to solve the problem, how to transform the data into a problem solution, and whether the information generated by the process does solve the problem.

The computer is nothing more than a tool used to help transform data into information. It is incapable of deciding which problem to solve and which data or process to use to solve the problem. All these phases are under control of people.

The computer, since it embodies and typifies current technology, has often been made the scapegoat for problems attributable to people. Because it is inanimate, it is an easy and safe symbol to attack and has been blamed for social ills and job loss. Yet the computer was designed *by* people for the use of people for solving problems. Therefore, the more that you know about electronic data processing, the better you will be able to control and use the computer as a tool for problem solving.

COMPUTER PROBLEMS

What kind of problems then are best suited for using the computer as a tool? Among the characteristics of those problems usually solved by computers are:

1. High volume of input and output.
2. Need for rapid solution.
3. Need for great accuracy.
4. Repetitious tasks.
5. Complex or many calculations.

A firm with 20,000 hourly employees might be expected to use a computer for payroll. The firm would use the computer because of the large number of time cards to be processed and paychecks to be created. The time cards must be transformed into paychecks as soon as possible to reflect current pay periods. The calculations required for payroll must be accurate. If you have ever had trouble balancing a checkbook, which only involves addition and subtraction, imagine the problem you might have calculating payroll — with all the deductions for taxes, insurance, and other items. The advantage of the computer is that once you have correctly instructed it, it will carry out the calculations with much greater accuracy than you could, even with the aid of a calculator.

Payroll also involves doing the same type of calculations over and over for each employee each time a payroll is issued. Doing the same task over and over, even though the numbers may be different, involves repetition. Where repetition is boring to most people, the computer works best on simple, repetitious tasks. Again, once you have instructed the computer correctly, it will do a simple task the same way time after time. By using the computer for problems which require no creativity, people are freed to work on problems which require imagination.

To be able to use the computer as a tool, you must be able to do two things:

1. Carefully express the problem in terms that the computer understands; that is, quantify the data.
2. Communicate with the computer in a language the computer understands.

If you do not know how to solve a problem yourself, the computer is going to be of little use. You cannot ask the computer to predict the winner of a horse race unless you know how to do the computations yourself. The computer *must* be instructed in the solution technique by people. It does not have creativity. Someone must not only design the solution method, but must provide the feedback to make sure that the problem has been solved. Thus, for the computer to be useful in payroll, some person must know how to do all the calculations required. That person can then also check to see that the payroll is done on time and has used the correct time cards. By checking some of the payroll checks printed by the computer, feedback is provided.

We instruct the computer on how to solve problems via languages which we and the computer understand. Several common computer languages are shown in Table 1.1.

Table 1.1. COMMON COMPUTER LANGUAGES

```
BASIC
FORTRAN
COBOL
PL/1
Assembler
```

The computer is capable of communicating in many languages. Each language has special features which make it appropriate for certain types of problems. We will be discussing BASIC, FORTRAN, and COBOL later in this program.

COMPUTERS VS. . . .

Already you can see that computers are different from other business tools used in solving problems. The computer has limitations. The computer is the junior partner to people in solving problems, just as are the other tools found in a business enterprise: calculator, ledgers, filing cabinets, typewriters, and pencil and paper. Each of these is a tool that, when used properly, aids in solving problems. The computer electronically incorporates many of these other tools when it is used to solve problems. It is usually the magnitude of the problem that requires the use of the computer. However, the technology contained in the computer is also rather different from other tools such as the calculator.

The computer has often been called a giant brain or overgrown expensive calculator. It is neither a giant brain nor a calculator. The computer is not able to solve problems without human guidance. The calculator requires that humans intervene in the operations by entering data and instructions. The computer, once instructed and given the data, operates without human intervention. The computer also stores the instructions written in a language understood by you and the computer. This set of instructions in a computer language is called a *program*. The computer follows these instructions to operate on the data. The computer is an automated data processor. It has the function of manipulating the data under your control to create the output necessary for you to solve a problem. The computer is also capable of storing data like a filing cabinet, for future processing.

COMPREHENSION TEST 2

Directions: *Circle the letter of the best answer.*

1. The main point of this article is
   a) computers have revolutionized most business operations
   b) computers are tools for people to use in solving problems
   c) can understand one or more computer languages
   d) computers are best suited to computing repetitive tasks

2. Data processing always involves
   a) computers

b) people
c) print-outs
d) research

3. A program is
   a) a list of problems the computer is to solve
   b) the output sequence
   c) a written set of instructions the computer is to follow
   d) the manner in which data are entered

4. It is accurate to consider a computer as a
   a) sophisticated calculator
   b) giant brain
   c) tool for converting data into information
   d) means of defining problems

5. One of the main advantages of a computer over other types of business equipment is
   a) its high level of accuracy
   b) its ability to sort information
   c) its level of creativity
   d) its ability, once instructed and given data, to operate by itself

6. A *scapegoat* is someone or something that
   a) makes numerous errors
   b) is falsely blamed for mistakes
   c) solves problems
   d) is accused of making mistakes

7. A computer could be used to
   a) create a record-keeping file for library use
   b) keep records on tax-deductible expenses
   c) develop a system for filing and receipts
   d) plan a system for organizing driver's license renewals

8. A computer is well suited for all of the following tasks *except*
   a) keeping track of a store's inventory

b) recording orders for a mail-order company
c) scheduling classes into particular rooms in your college
d) determining the reasons for employee absence

9. Suppose that you go to the bank and deposit a check in your checking account. Several days later you find that the amount of the deposit was not credited to your account. Most likely, you can assume
   a) that the bank's computer made an error
   b) that the bank teller made an error
   c) the computer and the teller made errors
   d) the computer lost its memory

10. This article seems to be written for readers
    a) who are familiar with computers
    b) who will use computers in a business setting
    c) who think computers are to blame for errors in data
    d) who believe office machines are as efficient as computers

Selection 2: 1020 words

Finishing Time: ___ ___ ___ HR. MIN. SEC.

Starting Time: ___ ___ ___ HR. MIN. SEC.

Reading Time: ___ ___ MIN. SEC.

WPM Score: ___

Comprehension Score: ___ %

Reading Efficiency Score: ___

Chapter 4:
Prereading

There is general agreement that what you do *while* you are reading directly controls how much you are able to remember. Factors such as how well you are able to concentrate, how familiar you are with the vocabulary or terminology used, or how interested you are in the material all determine how effectively you read. However, most students do not realize that there is something they can do *before* they begin to read that also influences their efficiency. Specifically, before you begin reading, it is useful to familiarize yourself quickly with the organization and content of the material. This technique, called prereading, will enable you to read faster and remember more of what you read. You will find that it is one of the easiest techniques to use and one that makes a dramatic difference in your reading efficiency. Prereading involves getting a quick impression or overview of what you are going to read before beginning to read. It allows you to become familiar with the basic content and organization of the material before you read it. As a result, you will be able to read faster and follow the author's train of thought more easily.

GUIDELINES FOR PREREADING

The basic goal in prereading anything is to look only at those parts of the reading material that will tell you what it is primarily about or how it is organized. There are a number of steps you can follow that will make prereading easier. However, you will find that you may need to adapt these steps somewhat for different types of material. (Later in this chapter, you will be offered additional suggestions for prereading various types of materials.) Still, the following procedure provides a useful guide to prereading. As you follow each step apply it to the article beginning on page 66.

INTERLUDE

Hypnosis

Hypnosis has been defined as "an artificially induced state, usually (though not always) resembling sleep, but physiologically distinct from it, which is characterized by heightened suggestibility . . ." (Weitzenhoffer, 1963, p. 3). The sleepy, almost zombie-like behaviors common in hypnotized subjects are what gives hypnosis its name—*hypnos* is the Greek word for sleep. But it is *suggestibility*—a greater-than-normal willingness to accept the statements or suggestions of another person—that gives hypnosis its occult flavor. We have visions of an evil scientist controlling someone else's will, visions that have been dramatized in stories and movies. Suggestibility also gives hypnosis its important role in the history of psychology, as ". . . practically the beginning of the experimental psychology of motivation" (Boring, 1950, p. 116). In this interlude, we will focus on this aspect of hypnosis: how the study of hypnosis clarifies questions about the unconscious mind and human motivation in general.

MESMER

Although hypnosis has been practiced for centuries, it was Friedrich Anton Mesmer (1734–1815) who made hypnotic procedures famous. A Viennese physician, Mesmer believed that the sleeplike states he induced

226

were the result of magnetism; in fact, at first he induced hypnosis by stroking people with magnets. He soon found that this was unnecessary, that he could as easily hypnotize people without the magnets; his own body, he thought, provided the "animal magnetism." Mesmer used hypnosis to cure certain diseases, such as extreme nervousness, and he tried to interest the medical profession (without success) in what he called animal magnetism and others began to call mesmerism.

In 1778, the Viennese scientific academies forced Mesmer to flee to Paris, where he began a sort of group therapy. Having discovered that it was the subjects' *belief* in magnetism that made it work, he began using a number of gimmicks to help induce hypnosis. Patients sat around a "magnetized" oak chest; the therapy room was dimly lighted, and soft music was played. Mesmer himself often appeared in magician's dress, dancing around the room. He found that often all that was required for hypnosis was to look at someone and shout "Sleep!"

These shenanigans did little for Mesmer's reputation. He was investigated by a scientific commission, which concluded that animal magnetism was not at all like metal magnetism. But if it was not magnetism, then what was this mysterious force? The French government offered Mesmer 20,000 francs for the secret of hypnosis. Since Mesmer had no secret to disclose, he refused. He was denounced as a charlatan and forced to leave Paris; he died in disrepute in Switzerland in 1815.

HYPNOSIS AND PAIN

Dormant for 50 years, scientific interest in hypnosis was revived in the 1840s with the discovery that hypnotized patients, given the suggestion that they would feel no pain, could undergo painless surgery. (The chemical anesthetics—ether, chloroform—had not yet been discovered.) In 1842, an English physician named Ward amputated a leg of a hypnotized patient, who felt no pain. Unfortunately he was chastised by the national medical society: "Patients ought to suffer pain while their surgeons are operating" (Boring, 1950, p. 121). Another British surgeon named Esdaile was operating in India with patients under hypnosis; he performed about 300 major operations, with great success. But he, too, was criticized; his patients, it was said, were trying to please him by showing no evidence of pain.

I have personally witnessed the surgical removal of an appendix from a hypnotized patient, whose only anesthetic was an instruction to feel no pain. Anyone who could believe that he was trying to please the doctor has a greater capacity for belief than I. My impression was that I felt more pain, observing, than the patient did.

About the time hypnosis was beginning to find acceptance as a medical tool to lessen pain, the anesthetic properties of ether and chloroform came into use, and the somewhat suspect practice of mesmerism, now renamed "hypnosis," went into another decline. Then around 1885, Sigmund Freud began using hypnosis to treat mental disorders. He eventually discontinued it because it could not be used on all patients, and because he discovered what he considered a better technique—free association (see Chapter 10). Nevertheless, Freud's knowledge of hypnosis played a major role in his ideas about *unconscious motivation,* the concept on which his theory of personality—psychoanalysis—is based.

Putting someone into a hypnotic state—the *hypnotic induction* procedure—can be accomplished in several ways. Most commonly, the subject lies on a couch and gazes fixedly at some point on the ceiling. The hypnotist then gives instructions on how to enter the hypnotic state. These are mainly requests to relax—"You are getting very sleepy, very tired, very sleepy . . ."—and to pay attention only to the hypnotist and his or her suggestions—"Listen only to my words. Pay attention to nothing else but what I tell you."

Once the subject has been hypnotized, the hypnotist can suggest a number of experiences for the subject—imagine a fly buzzing around, for example. To demonstrate unconscious motivation, Freud used what is called a *posthypnotic suggestion*—an instruction given under hypnosis but to be carried out later, when the subject is awake. The hypnotist might give instructions something like this: "When you wake up, I will tap my desk with my pencil. When I do this, you will get up, walk to the phone on my desk, pick it up and say, 'Hello? Hello?' Then you will hang it up and sit down again. But you will not remember my telling you to do this, not until I say 'Now you can remember everything.' Then you will remember all that we said and did under hypnosis."

The subject is then awakened. After a few minutes of casual conversation, the hypnotist taps the desk, and, if the hypnotic subject is a good one, she will pick up the phone and say "Hello? Hello?" If you ask her why she did it, she will make up a plausible story—"I thought I heard the phone ring"—because she doesn't remember the real reason. Then the hypnotist gives the signal to remember—"Now you can remember everything"—and the subject recalls the suggestion given under hypnosis.

The phony explanation the subject gives when she is unconscious of her true motive is a particularly interesting aspect of human motivation. We cannot say, "I don't know why I did that." We have to rationalize it somehow, according to our individual whims.

229

PRESENT USES OF HYPNOSIS

Hypnosis today is used for a number of purposes, primarily in psychotherapy or to reduce pain, and it is an acceptable technique in both medicine and psychology. In psychotherapy, it is most often used to eliminate bad habits and annoying symptoms. Cigarette smoking can be treated, for example, by the suggestion that the person will feel nauseated whenever he or she thinks of smoking. Sufferers of migraine headaches treated with hypnotic suggestions to relax showed a much greater tendency to improve than sufferers treated with drugs; 44 percent were headache-free after 12 months of treatment, compared to 12 percent of their drug-treated counterparts (Anderson et al., 1975).

Other medical problems also can be treated effectively with hypnosis (Bowers, 1976). Most of these fall into the category of "psychosomatic illnesses," which means that although they are real physical disorders, they are believed to be induced or aggravated by tension, anxiety, and other psychological states. Asthma is an example. As with migraines, research suggests that hypnosis is more effective than known drugs at relieving the suffocating symptoms of asthma (Maher-Loughnam, 1970). But the most fascinating research involved warts (Sinclair-Gieben and Chalmers,

1959). Fourteen patients were given the hypnotic suggestion that their warts would disappear—but only on one side of their bodies! After a few months, nine of the patients were completely free of warts, or nearly so—on one side of their bodies.

The first medical use of hypnosis, to reduce pain, is probably still the most common. A Midwest obstetrician who prefers hypnosis (but keeps chemical anesthetics on hand) has reported on 1000 childbirths (Hilgard and Hilgard, 1974). He used the chemicals in 186 cases. In the other 814 cases, the babies were brought into the world—some by caesarean section —from a mother whose only anesthetic was an instruction, given under hypnosis, to feel no pain.

Research on reducing pain by hypnotic suggestion indicates that subjects carry out their instructions in a number of ways. One imagined that the hypnotist had injected him with a pain-killing drug. Another, told to experience no pain in her arm, imagined she was the Venus de Milo— with no arms! Cancer patients give similar reports. One imagined herself leaving her body and, thus, leaving the pain behind (Hilgard and Hilgard, 1974).

It is likely that hypnosis will become an increasingly frequent choice of treatments for the control of pain. Hypnosis has several advantages: It has no dangerous side effects. It is not addictive. It is inexpensive—free, in fact, if the patient can learn self-hypnosis. Practiced subjects can use their skills outside the laboratory to relieve pain, to put themselves to sleep at night, to study more effectively, and to bolster self-confidence (Hilgard and Hilgard, 1974). This, I think, is where hypnosis holds the greatest potential value: to help people deal effectively with the problems they face in life. These problems are largely psychological, not physical. Tension is a major factor, and hypnosis can be used to relieve tension in a far more satisfactory manner than a potentially addictive drug.

HYPNOSIS IN PERSPECTIVE

Psychologists who have worked with hypnosis generally do not consider it as unusual as most people do. Most of the things a hypnotic subject can do also can be done by people in the waking state (Barber, 1969). The typical report of a subject who has been hypnotized for the first time is that she doesn't believe it, because she felt "in control" at all times; she was expecting something that differed significantly from her usual state of consciousness, like a drug experience. But it's not so. Have you ever been tense and said to yourself, "Now, calm down!" You calm down because it suits you to comply with the instruction at that moment. Hypnosis is like that—ordinary.

Good hypnotic subjects experience some things that most of us cannot, but they also experience such things in everyday life (Hilgard, 1968). They are the types who get totally involved in a novel or a movie, and when you describe something to them, they actually see it. However, evidence indicates that hypnosis is a skill that can be learned; if you are not now susceptible to hypnosis, you can be taught how to allow yourself to go into a trance (Blum, 1961). How the good subjects learned their skills is still a mystery. Children, as a rule, are very easily hypnotized, so maybe it is the poor subjects who learn how *not* to be suggestible and, instead, to be critical, analytical, and reality-oriented.

A hypnotist does not hypnotize people. As one hypnotist puts it, "The subject enters the hypnotic state when the conditions are right; the hypnotist merely helps set these conditions" (Hilgard et al., 1975, p. 173). At first, the typical induction involves lengthy instructions, but subjects soon develop the ability to do it themselves. I used the phrase "Deep asleep," nothing more, for practiced subjects.

Hypnosis is really, in all cases, self-hypnosis, which in turn is essentially self-discipline. It's not magic; it's a demonstration of the power of the human mind.

SUGGESTED READINGS

Bowers, K. S. *Hypnosis for the seriously curious.* Brooks/Cole, 1976.
  An outstanding introduction to the scientific study of hypnosis.
Hilgard, E. R. *The experience of hypnosis.* Harcourt Brace Jovanovich, 1968.
  Hilgard has done a sizable proportion of the best research on hypnosis; this book contains a review of that work as well as the work of others.

Read the Title

Often the title functions as a label and tells you what the material is about. For example, the subject of a magazine article entitled "Living on an Island in Maine" is shown quite clearly by its title. You should realize, however, that all titles are not as descriptive and informative as this example. The same article mentioned above might be titled "An Exciting Week-Long Vacation in Maine." In this case you still get some idea of what the article is about, but you need further information. Still other titles may be designed to catch your attention or provoke interest in the article. If this is the case, this same article on Maine might be titled "Alone at Last." In any case, the title is only your first clue about the content of what you will read.

Check the Author's Name

It is always useful to know who wrote the material you're going to read. In many cases, you won't recognize the name. If information is available about the author in the form of a footnote, be sure to glance through it. If you do recognize the author, you can begin to build expectations about the content of the article. If, for example, you find that an article on politics is written by Jimmy Carter, you may expect the article to be based on his experiences and political perspective.

Read the Introduction

The first few paragraphs of a piece of writing are usually introductory. The author may explain the subject, outline his or her ideas or give some clues about his or her direction of thought. If the introduction is quite long, read only the first two or three paragraphs.

Read the Headings

If the selection contains any headings (often in dark print, called boldface), read through them in order. Headings, like titles, serve as labels and identify the content of the material they head. By reading each heading, you will be accumulating a list of the important topics covered in the selection. Together, the headings will form a minioutline of the content of the reading material. Notice how the headings contained in the sample selection form an outline of important ideas:

HYPNOSIS
Mesmer
Hypnosis and pain
Hypnosis and unconscious motivation
Present uses of hypnosis
Hypnosis in perspective

Read the First Sentence Under Each Heading

The first sentence following the heading often further explains the heading. Although the heading often announces the topic that will be discussed, the first sentence following the heading frequently states the central thought of the passage. In the sample selection, notice that many of the first sentences further explain the heading.

Notice Any Typographical Aids

Typographical aids include all features of the page that make facts or ideas outstanding or more understandable. These include italics (slanted print), boldface type, blank space (used to separate major portions or sections of the text), marginal notes, colored ink, capitalization, underlining, and enumeration (listing). Notice how, in each of the following examples, the typographical aid enables you immediately to locate the important information.

Example 1: Enumeration.

HOW TO MEDITATE

[STEP 1]   Go to a quiet room where you will be undisturbed and sit in a relaxed manner. Keep your back relatively straight and allow your head to tilt slightly forward. Place your hands in your lap.

[STEP 2]   Become passive and unresponsive in your thoughts. Let your thoughts move through you without reacting. The ideal is for your mind to become a room with open windows, through which your thoughts can move without becoming trapped.

[STEP 3]   Focus your attention on your breathing. You breathe in and out all day and night, but you are never mindful of it, you never for a second concentrate your mind on it. Now you are going to do just this. Breathe in and out as usual, without any effort or strain. Now, bring your mind to concentrate on your breathing in and out. When you breathe, you sometimes take deep breaths, sometimes not. This does not matter at all. Breathe normally and naturally. The only thing is that when you take deep breaths you should be aware that they are deep breaths, and so on. In other words, your mind should be so fully concentrated on your breathing that you are aware of its movements and changes. Forget all other things, your surroundings, your environment; do not raise your eyes and look at anything. Try to do this for five or ten minutes.

[STEP 4]   Note your daily progress. At the beginning you will find it extremely difficult to bring your mind to concentrate on your breathing. You will be astonished how your mind runs away. It does not stay. You begin to think of various things. You hear sounds outside. Your mind is disturbed and distracted. You may be dismayed and disappointed. But if you continue to practice this exercise twice a day, morning and evening, for about five or ten minutes at a time, you will gradually, by and by, begin to concentrate your mind on your breathing. After a certain period you will experience just that split second when your mind is fully concentrated on your breathing, when you will not hear even sound nearby, when no external world exists for you. This slight moment is such a tremendous experience for you, full of joy, happiness and tranquillity, that you would like to continue it. But still you cannot. Yet, if you go on practicing this regularly, you may repeat the experience again and again for longer and longer periods. That is the moment, when you lose yourself completely in your mindfulness of breathing. As long as you are conscious of yourself you cannot concentrate on anything.[1]

Example 2: Italics.

When you disclose your feelings and thoughts to others, you display your trust of them; and they, in turn, are encouraged to disclose their feelings and thoughts to you. You make a small disclosure; the other person makes a small disclosure. You then make a more personal disclosure; the other person often will reciprocate. In as little as an hour, two strangers can become intimate friends. The idea that disclosure begets disclosure is called *the dyadic effect: self-disclosure is usually reciprocated.*[2]

Example 3: Dark Print.

DEFENSE MECHANISMS

A normal way of coping with anxiety and frustration is to mobilize psychological defenses against the threat. These defensive tactics, though unconscious, are so common that they have been classified and named. You will recognize some of these defense mechanisms as ways you use to cope.

Repression is the forgetting of painful memories or frightening impulses. Material that is repressed is pushed out of consciousness so that the anxiety associated with it is lessened. If you have repressed the memory of your father's death, you cannot recall the details of the incident, although you may be aware that he is dead; you can thus avoid the pain and trauma you would experience in reliving the tragedy.

Displacement is the redirection of hostile feelings from an unsafe to a safe target. Anger that is displaced is anger that is directed toward, not the person who caused it, but a second party. A child who is spanked by a parent may displace the anger and kick, not the parent, but the cat — an innocent second party. If your day at school has been upsetting, you may come home and yell at your younger brother (displaced aggression).

Rationalization is a way of explaining away all your difficulties in a fashion that protects your ego and self-esteem. You rationalize your failures by inventing logical excuses for them. Suppose you tried to win a contest but failed; what could you do to feel better? You could say, "I didn't want to win anyway"; "the contest was rigged"; "I didn't really try"; or, "the contest actually wasn't worth the effort." Each of these rationalizations serves to defend your ego and self-esteem against the embarrassment of failure.

Projection is a way of denying your own feelings and attitudes and attributing them to others ("projecting" them onto other people). To admit that you feel angry may make you anxious; to defend yourself against this anxiety, you may insist that others are angry at you, rather than the other way around.

Emotional insulation is a way of defending yourself against hurt by withdrawing your emotional investment from your work and relationships. Rather than risk great disappointments, you are cautious and more reserved, and you are careful not to let your hopes get too high. If you take no risks, if you are careful not to put your ego on the line, no one can hurt you. You withdraw into a protective shell to ward off frustration and disappointment.[3]

Notice Any Graphs or Pictures

Graphs, charts, and pictures are used for two purposes. First, they emphasize important ideas and, second, they clarify or simplify information and relationships. Therefore, they are always important to notice when you are prereading. The easiest way to establish quickly what important element of the text is being further explained by the graph or picture is to read the caption.

Read the Last Paragraph

The last paragraph of an article often serves as a conclusion or summary. In some articles, more than one paragraph may be used for this purpose. In other types of writing, such as textbooks or journal articles, these last few paragraphs may actually be labeled "Summary" or "Conclusion." By reading the summary before reading the article, you will learn the general focus and content of the material. Notice that the last paragraph in the selection on pages 66–71 summarizes the entire article.

By applying these procedures to that selection, you have preread the selection. However, you were interrupted at each step by reading the explanation. Now preread the selection again, without interruption, and then try the following exercise. After you have completed it, check your answers with the answer key at the back of the book.

EXERCISE 4-1

Directions: *Complete this exercise after you have preread the selection on "Hypnosis." For each item, indicate whether the statement is true or false by marking T or F in the space provided. Answers are in the Answer Key at the back of the book.*

1. Hypnosis has been practiced for centuries. _____
2. Hypnosis is artificially induced and usually resembles sleep. _____
3. Hypnosis was *not* used to eliminate or lessen pain during surgery in the late 1800s. _____
4. Today, hypnosis is accepted as a legitimate technique in medicine and psychology. _____
5. Psychologists still regard hypnosis as a rare, unusual technique. _____

6. It is possible for a person to hypnotize him- or herself. _____
7. Placing a subject under hypnosis is called posthypnotic suggestion. _____
8. Hypnotism demonstrates the power of the human mind. _____
9. Hypnosis can be defined as a state of heightened suggestibility. _____
10. A physician named Mesmer is responsible for making hypnotic procedures famous. _____

Did you score 80 percent or higher on the exercise? You may have noticed that it did not test you on specific facts and details. Rather, the questions provided a fairly accurate measure of your recall of the *main ideas* of the selection. If you scored 80 percent or above, your prereading was successful because it acquainted you with most of the major ideas contained in the selection.

This exercise suggests that prereading does provide you with a great deal of information about the overall content of the article before reading it. It allows you to become familiar with the main ideas contained in the article and acquaints you with the basic structure of the material.

How to Preread Articles Without Headings

When available, headings are very useful in identifying topics that will be discussed in material you are about to read. However, not all written material uses headings as an organizational device. Prereading articles without headings is more difficult and time consuming than prereading with them. To get an overview of the content of an article without headings it is helpful to read the first sentence of each paragraph. As you have already learned, the first sentence of a paragraph often states the main idea of the paragraph. By reading first sentences, you will become familiar with most of the main ideas contained in the selection.

ADAPTING PREREADING TO VARIOUS TYPES OF MATERIALS

If the key to becoming a flexible reader lies in adapting techniques to fit the material, then the key to successful prereading is the same. By emphasizing some of the guidelines for prereading or by skipping others, you can easily adjust the way you preread to the type of material you must deal with. Here are a few suggestions to help you adjust your technique to a number of common types of reading material for which prereading can be useful.

Textbooks

Textbooks contain very specific features that are intended to help students learn their content. Chapters within textbooks also contain special features. These commonly include end-of-the-chapter questions, concise summaries, and vocabulary lists of key terms. It is useful when prereading to glance through each of these features.

When prereading a long textbook chapter that you do not intend to read in one session, do a very quick prereading of the entire chapter to get a general idea of its organization and content. Then more carefully preread the portion you intend to read.

Before beginning to read your first assignment in a textbook, you should use prereading to help you become generally familiar with the organization, content, and special features of the text. Be sure to look at each of these parts:

1. *The title and subtitle.* These tell you the general content of the book and give you a preliminary clue about its focus and approach.
2. *Preface.* The preface is the author's introduction to the text. It contains general information about the development, organization, and focus of the book. In a preface, an author presents information that you should have before you begin to read the book.
3. *Table of contents.* The table of contents is a listing or outline of the major topics included in the text. Prereading the table of contents will familiarize you with the basic content of the text.
4. *Appendix (Appendices).* Located at the end of a text, the appendix contains important materials and information that the author wanted to include but that were not appropriate to include in the text itself. Frequently, these materials are valuable aids to learning and it is useful to be aware of what the appendix contains. For example, an American history text might contain a chronological list of presidents, copies of the Declaration of Independence and

the Constitution, maps, or summary charts of significant historical events.

5. *Glossary.* A glossary is an alphabetical list of important terms used in the text along with the definition of each. It is located at the back of the text and serves as a minidictionary. By glancing through the glossary you can get an idea of how difficult the text is and how much new terminology you can expect to learn.

Newspapers

Prereading newspapers is a useful technique because it allows you to select articles to read and articles to skip. Often, after prereading an article, you may decide that you have enough information and do not need to read the article. Later in this book you will see that prereading, when used in this way, is a form of skimming.

The format and organization are different for newspaper articles than for other types of printed material, so they need to be preread differently. The title, of course, is extremely important because it is often a highly condensed summary of the article. The first paragraph of a newspaper article is not usually introductory. Instead, it often contains the most important facts or information in the article. The rest of the article, then, becomes progressively more detailed. The end of a news article often provides background information, or if it is a continuing news event, connects contents of the article with previous events. Notice how the following news story follows this organizational pattern.

ROYAL MONACO PAIR SEPARATED

Monte Carlo, Monaco (AP) A spokeswoman for Monaco's royal family said Saturday that Princess Caroline and her husband Philippe Junot, a French businessman, have separated, but no divorce proceedings have been initiated.

They were married June 28, 1978, amid reports that Caroline's parents, Prince Rainier and Princess Grace, the former American movie star Grace Kelly, disapproved of the marriage.

The decision for a formal separation came after a two-month period during which the 40-year-old Junot did not visit Princess Caroline, 23, according to the spokeswoman, Nadia Lacoste.

SEATED ALONE   Reporters had questioned the family after they noted that Princess Caroline was seated alone at a party for the International Red Cross Friday night at the Monaco Sporting Club.

Turkish newspapers said Junot arrived Friday in Istanbul, accompanied by a young Costa Rican woman, Facio Giannini, and told newsmen, "It's all over between Caroline and me. We are both free to do as we wish." He said Miss Giannini was his secretary and they had no romantic links.

Junot, speaking with reporters on July 15, had denied he and Caroline were separated and said their marriage was fine.

Their wedding was a quiet family affair, unlike the publicity-splashed entrance into royalty when Caroline's Philadelphia-born mother married Prince Rainier nearly 25 years ago.

Caroline does not succeed to her father's throne. Her younger brother, Prince Albert, is the heir.

Caroline met Junot in December 1975 while she was a philosophy student at the Sorbonne in Paris. They often were seen together at discotheques and on bridle paths and ski slopes before their marriage.

Junot, with offices in Paris and Montreal, is a financial adviser. His father, a former deputy mayor of Paris, is president of the French branch of Westinghouse Electric.

In prereading a news story, then, read the title, the first paragraph, and the headings throughout the rest of the article.

Tests and Exams

It is always useful to preread any test or exam you are taking. This includes classroom tests and exams as well as standardized tests, job placement tests, civil service exams, and graduate or professional school entrance exams. By prereading the exam, you will know generally what it contains and you will be able to budget your time effectively. When taking tests, too many students waste time on a relatively unimportant multiple-choice or true-false item because they do not know that there are several essays at the end of the exam for which they will need time.

To preread an exam, just page through it, noticing the number and type of items included in each section. Also notice the number of points each section is worth, if that is included. The point distribution will also help you to budget your time, allowing more for sections that count heavily.

Letters and Correspondence

Prereading business letters and memos enables you to read them faster, and, if your job requires you to handle large amounts of correspondence as part of your daily routine, prereading is a means of quickly identifying items that need your immediate attention. Figure 4-1 shows a sample business letter.

To preread a business letter, follow these steps:

1. Check the letterhead and typed signature to determine who wrote the letter.
2. Read the first paragraph. Often it contains background information or summarizes a previous contact, correspondence, or business arrangement. If you have had no previous contact with the person who wrote the letter, you can expect to find some form of introduction or reason for contacting you.
3. Read the first line or two of the second paragraph. Usually these first few lines state the purpose of the letter.

Novels

Prereading a novel, or any other type of fiction, is very different from prereading other prose material. To preread a novel, use the following steps:

1. Read the title.
2. Note the author. Read any biographical notes about the author. These notes will give you some information about what else the author wrote, when he or she lived, and so forth.
3. Read any summaries, comments, or review quotes that may appear on the book jacket.
4. Check the table of contents to see if the chapters are titled. If the chapters have titles, read through them.
5. Read quickly through the first chapter. It will give you a general impression of many features of the novel, including the place and time. Also you will get an idea of the author's style and his approach to characterization. In some novels, you may be introduced to the main character in the first chapter.

There is little else that you can check in prereading a novel, but these steps are often sufficient to guide you in further reading.

L E X O N

June 10, 1983

LEXON OIL COMPANY
P. O. Box 2743
DALLAS, TEXAS   77402

TRAVEL AND CREDIT CARD
MARKETING DIVISION

Dear Customer:

    We appreciate the opportunity to serve you as a LEXON Credit
Card customer, and we trust that you have found our service to be
convenient and reliable.

    Our current statement indicates that your account is seriously
past due. Of the two payment options shown on your statement, one
must be paid immediately:

    MINIMUM PAYMENT -- Includes the entire amount of your
    Regular balance plus any minimum amount due on your Time
    Chare Plan balance.

    FULL PAYMENT -- Includes full payment of both the Regular
    and Time Charge Plan balances. Payment of this amount will
    eliminate additional finance charges.

    Your prompt attention and remittance will reestablish your
credit and ensure uninterrupted credit card privileges. Please
accept our thanks if your payment is already in the mail.

                                        Yours truly,

                                        J.R. Smothers

                                        J. R. Smothers
                                        Manager, Credit

JRS/jaw

Figure 4-1.   A sample business letter

WHY PREREADING IS EFFECTIVE

As mentioned earlier, prereading is an effective technique that will help you read faster and remember more. It is effective for several reasons. First, prereading helps you to become interested and involved with what you will read. Through prereading you become familiar with the material; you acquire basic information about the organization and content of the article. In other words, prereading focuses your attention on the content of the article. Because you know what to expect in the article and your attention is already focused, you will be able to move along more rapidly.

Second, prereading provides you with a mental outline of the material you are going to read. With an outline already in mind, you are able to read more easily. You can anticipate the sequence of ideas, see relationships among topics, and follow the author's direction of thought. Also, reading becomes a process of completing or expanding the outline by identifying supporting details.

EXERCISE 4-2

Directions: *Select a chapter from one of your textbooks and preread it, using the guidelines included in this chapter. Then answer the following questions.*

Textbook Title _____

Chapter Title _____

1. What general subject does the chapter discuss?

    _____

2. How does the textbook author approach or divide the subject?

    _____

3. What special features does the chapter contain to aid you in learning the content of the chapter?

    _____

4.   List the major topics that the chapter covers.

_____

_____

EXERCISE 4-3

Directions: *Select a novel that you are planning to read or one that you would like to read when you have time. Preread the novel, using the guidelines included in this chapter. Then answer the following questions.*

Title of Novel _____

1.   Where and when does the novel take place? _____

_____

2.   Who do you think the main character is? _____

_____

3.   What style of writing does the author use? _____

_____

4.   What do you know about the overall subject or plot of the novel?

_____

APPLYING WHAT YOU HAVE LEARNED

Directions: *Preread each of the reading selections at the end of this chapter. Then answer the question below that pertains to each selection.*

Reading Selection 3
List the features (aspects) of weddings that are discussed in the article.

1.   _____

2. _____

3. _____

Reading Selection 4
List three possible causes of cancer.

1. _____

2. _____

3. _____

READING SELECTION 3
WEDDINGS, OLD AND NEW

Thomas F. Hoult and John W. Hudson

THE OLD IS STILL "NEW"

In an article titled "I Take Thee, Baby," *Time* magazine (4 July 1969) asserted that "More and more couples are breaking away from traditional marriage ceremonies to invent their own." *Time* apparently thought so-called "new weddings" represented a wave of the future. But *Time,* along with other observers, was badly misled by the wide press coverage given to a relatively few unusual wedding ceremonies.

The real truth, now as in 1969, is that a large majority of weddings are strictly in accordance with tradition, as suggested by the fact that in 1970 three-fourths of all marrying couples preferred a religious ceremony. In 1975, 86 percent of 38,000 teenagers surveyed by the editors of Scholastic Magazines expressed their opinion that a religious marriage ceremony is important (*Chicago Tribune–New York News'* Syndicate, 27 December 1975). In 1972, 80 percent of all first marriages were solemnized formally, and 87 percent of these brides wore floor-length gowns, 94 percent of which were white or ivory. Fully 96 percent of marrying couples have a reception, up from 85 percent in 1967. The interest in formal weddings is sufficient to make "The Bride Game" a perennial bestseller and to keep two mass-distributed bridal magazines in print (*Bride's Magazine* and *Modern Bride*). The Bride Game — "For the eight to fourteen set" — is played like Monopoly. Rolling the dice, players move from ring shop to card shop to florist to jeweler . . . to the aisle:

> The winner of The Bride Game is the first tot to reach the spot marked "Ceremony." Eight years old and she already *knows*, by God, that she must acquire her diamond and her garter and all her THINGS before she can get to the altar.

The cynical view is that most weddings are formal simply because such ceremonies have the biggest payoff in gifts. But the cynic does not see all. In addition to the obvious commercialism so evident in many modern weddings, they are important social–psychological events. Socially, they add a new family unit to society, and psychologically they call for fundamental role changes, both in the bridal pair and in those close to them. It is for these reasons, not for "payoff," that weddings are notable — and largely unchanging — phenomena in almost all societies. Only thus can there be some assurance that a young couple will be impressed with the significance of, and act appropriately on, their commitment and new responsibilities. The care of children that may result from the marriage is particularly important. Indeed, according to the Principle of Legitimacy as enunciated by anthropologist Bronislaw Malinowski, the main function of marriage has always been to give legitimacy to children. This function is so basic that marriage has been a celebrated institution even in societies — such as the Trobriand Islands — where it was not known that intercourse is related to pregnancy.

RITES AND RITES

Although marriage is everywhere celebrated, the rites marking or solemnizing it vary tremendously, ranging from the barely noticed to the so elaborate no one could fail to notice. When a young Trobriander couple decide they want to marry, they simply sleep together one night at the groom's parental home. In the morning, they share a meal prepared by the groom's mother. They are then considered married. It was even simpler, during the early days of the Israeli kibbutz, for a male–female pair to set up a marriage-like unit: the interested couple, having "fallen in love," just asked for permission to share a double room. Although the term "marriage" was not applied to such pair relationships, they were on the average more stable than American marriages. Despite this favorable experience with informal pairing, there has been a tendency in recent years for kibbutz residents to use a standard wedding ceremony.

The simplicity of early kibbutz and Trobriand "coupling" contrasts sharply with what one finds in middle echelon America. Here we are, as Seligson has put it, "deep in the heart of excess." Among the *nouveau riche* especially, weddings and the debuts which announce a young lady's marriage availability, tend to be a time for pulling out all the stops as those who want desperately to "arrive" assuage their feelings of unease. A startling example was provided by Henry Ford II on the occasion of the debut of his second daughter (*The Detroit Free Press*, 20 June 1961). For her, the "French provincial mansion" in which the family lived was not regarded as sufficiently grand for the ceremony. So, a Paris decorator was hired to design special backyard facilities; the result, at a cost of $280,000 (the equivalent sum today would be about $600,000), was a dance pavilion and two white summer houses, all three parquet-floored and outlined with sparkling fairy lights. At the end of the evening, the "set" was struck and another young lady was in the marriage market.

The weddings of such young ladies characteristically involve a "wedding consultant" whose every suggestion is taken as law. The consultant decides how long a veil should be, where the attendants should stand, what refreshments are "proper," what clothing is de rigueur, what to serve at a gift-viewing tea, what cards must be printed and how they should read, and so on and on. The main concern is that everything, everything should be *just so*, correct, without a flaw. As further insurance that all will be *right* there is typically a careful rehearsal, sometimes more than one, with all personnel present and performing in accordance with the wedding consultant's directions: He stands there, then hands the ring over when asked; she then makes a half turn to the right; the music swells; now step forward one pace; etc. If the wedding is at a church, then it must

be at the largest edifice possible, with at least twelve attendants and celebrated by a high-ranking dignitary. The reception is of course a catered affair; it begins with cocktails, followed by a sit-down dinner at the country club, culminating in a dance with music by a well-known "society" orchestra.

RITUALS, OLD AND NEW

The average American wedding is not nearly so carefully orchestrated as the catered affair described above, but even at the most humble ceremony the basic rituals and symbols are evident: fertility and good luck tokens, joyous feasting, attendants, and special events or colors to stand for virginity. Most of these can be traced back to their origins in magical beliefs and pagan rites. The word "wedding" itself is derived from the Anglo-Saxon *wed* which designated the material backing given by a prospective husband to the family of his intended bride to insure that he would carry through with his marriage promise. Some believe the wedding ring is properly interpreted as a symbol of bondage and can be traced back to the rope which was used to tie a woman when wives were obtained by capture. The color white, as used in the wedding dress, stands for the bride's supposed virginity, and her veil began with the practice of covering a woman's head when she had been spoken for and thus should no longer be viewed as having marriage potential. When fragile objects are destroyed, as in the stomping of a wine glass at a Jewish wedding, the wife's hymen is symbolically broken so the marriage can be consummated.*

The original function of such rituals was "to ease the transitions for the individuals concerned (and for society) by dealing with the psychic and social implications of the changes entailed." The rituals still function this way, at least to some degree. They seem to help some

---

* Authorities disagree on the meaning of this ritual; some say it commemorates the destruction of the Temple in Jerusalem during the first century of the Christian era; others claim it is meant to impress on viewers that as one step shatters a glass, so can one act of unfaithfulness destroy the holiness of a home.

couples act as such, yet not become totally separate from the social order. In Slater's words,

> The marriage ritual . . . becomes a series of mechanisms for pulling the dyad apart somewhat, so that its integration complements rather than replaces the various group ties of its members. . . . First of all, the ceremony is usually a sufficiently involved affair to require a number of practical social decisions from the couple in preparation for the occasion. Much of their interaction during this period will thus concern issues external to their own relationship, and there will be a great deal of preoccupation with loyalties and obligations outside the dyad itself.

One important implication of these observations is that it is probably fortunate there are relatively few quickie weddings performed by justices of the peace. Such weddings, with their inevitable brevity and perfunctory nature, cannot possibly fulfill the complex social and psychological functions effected by a full-fledged marriage ceremony when it is heartfelt and its meaning is not obscured by commercialism or undermined by keeping-up-with-the-Joneses rules of etiquette.

Commercialism and ordinary etiquette standards are notably absent in the "new" weddings. These ceremonies were first devised by idealistic youth during the 1960s. They are typically held outdoors, with a minimum of preparation and props, thus symbolizing the principals' desire to be at one with nature and to rid themselves of dependence on the tinsel and glitter of Western civilization. One part of the "glitter" that new weddings almost self-consciously eschew is the soap-opera-like expectations expressed in the traditional wedding rite: "Till death do us part," "Forever and ever," "Love, honor and obey." For such phrases, new weddings substitute "As long as love shall last," or "You do your thing and I'll do mine and it'll be cool when we overlap," or words from *The Prophet:* "Love one another but make not a *bond* of love." Despite the tentativeness of feelings expressed in the new weddings, those who have observed or participated in them characteristically testify that they are meaningful beyond all conventional understanding, more genuinely romantic and poignant by far than traditional ceremonies.

COMPREHENSION TEST 3

Directions: *Circle the letter of the best answer.*

1. The majority of modern-day weddings are
   a) breaking away from old-style ceremonies
   b) primarily nonreligious ceremonies
   c) still quite traditional
   d) held mainly for the gifts

2. The main purpose of the traditional type of wedding is to
   a) display the wealth of the parents
   b) ensure that enough gifts are received to give the couples a good start
   c) keep churches prominent in American life
   d) impress on the couple the importance of their commitment and responsibilities

3. According to this selection the wedding ring is regarded by some people as a symbol of
   a) bondage
   b) love
   c) eternity
   d) prosperity

4. One part of the marriage ritual that "new" weddings often change is the
   a) exchanging of rings
   b) presence of a minister, priest, or rabbi
   c) language of the vows
   d) the romantic feelings between bride and groom

5. The word "wed" comes from the
   a) Anglo-Saxon word "woo," meaning "to court"
   b) name for the money or property a man gave to the family of his intended bride
   c) term used to describe the typical feast held for the families of the bride and groom
   d) French word "oui," meaning "yes" — the typical response to marriage vows

6. The word "orchestrated" means
   a) planned and organized
   b) accompanied by music
   c) decorated
   d) attended

7. Typical wedding ceremonies for the "nouveau riche," such as Henry Ford's daughter, seem to have as their main purpose to
   a) display the wealth of the parents
   b) ensure that enough gifts are received to give the couple a good start
   c) keep churches prominent in American life
   d) impress on the couple the importance of their responsibilities

8. Marriages in the early days of the Israeli kibbutz
   a) were very formal compared to those of the Trobriand Islanders
   b) were usually traditional Jewish ceremonies
   c) lasted longer than the average American marriage
   d) involved a great deal of gift-giving

9. It is implied that marriages performed by justices of the peace are
   a) the most common type today
   b) complicated to plan
   c) not as meaningful as traditional ones
   d) the least expensive type of wedding

10. The writer uses the phrase "soap-opera-like expectations" in referring to the traditional vows, in order to suggest that
    a) young people today do not care for soap operas
    b) soap operas are the main reason for the wording of these vows
    c) they make the wedding seem too planned and artificial like a soap opera
    d) these promises may be quite unrealistic as a soap opera may be

Selection 3:		1678 words
Finishing Time:	——— ——— ———	
	HR. MIN. SEC.	
Starting Time:	——— ——— ———	
	HR. MIN. SEC.	
Reading Time:	——— ———	
	MIN. SEC.	
WPM Score:	———————	
Comprehension Score:	———————	%
Reading Efficiency Score:	———————	

READING SELECTION 4
WHAT CAUSES CANCER?

John Dorfman, Sheila Kitzinger, and Herman Schuchman

The question "What causes cancer?" has been asked for centuries. The short answer is: We still don't know. But a tremendous amount has been added to our understanding in recent decades. One major change in the way researchers view cancer is that they now rarely think in terms of a single, unitary cause. Rather, it appears that most cancers are caused by the interaction of several factors. In many cases, some or all of three factors may be involved: (1) viruses, (2) individual susceptibility, and (3) environmental irritants. Another major change in our contemporary view of cancer is that it is now regarded as the premiere example of an environmental disease — that is, a disease in which environmental factors are often crucial to the disease process.

VIRUSES

A number of viruses have been identified that induce cancer in laboratory animals. What about humans? As of the late 1970s, no virus had been shown conclusively to cause cancer in people. However, the scientific consensus was that it was probably only a matter of time before such a connection was proven.

Cancer, however, is not a communicable disease, like a cold or influenza. It is not "catching" in the ordinary sense of the word, and the mere presence of the suspect virus is apparently not enough, by itself, to produce the disease.

It appears that the process may work something like this: A carcinogenic virus enters a cell and insinuates itself amidst the cell's genetic material. (Viruses and genes are structurally similar.) The virus may then lie dormant for years, until it is triggered into action by some kind of environmental irritant, such as pollution or radiation. At that point, the reactivated virus causes changes in the genes,

altering the host cell permanently and also altering all the cells produced by the division of the original cell. The genetic program of these new — and now cancerous — cells calls for the unrestrained growth, dedifferentiation, anaplasia, and metastasis discussed earlier.

INDIVIDUAL SUSCEPTIBILITY

Some people may be more prone to develop cancers than others, for several possible reasons.

Heredity is one. Resistance to cancer, or susceptibility to it, is a quality for which laboratory animals can be bred. So, presumably, heredity may play some role in humans as well. Statistical evidence, however, shows only a minor tendency for cancers to run in families. Indeed, for most cancers no such tendency can be demonstrated. Cancers of the breast, lung, thyroid, colon, and rectum do seem to cluster in families, at least to some degree. If your family has a history involving one of these cancers, you and your physician may want to be especially vigilant for signs of such cancer during your periodic physical examinations.

Some researchers have proposed that personality characteristics may render some people more vulnerable to cancer. According to this theory, people are more likely to develop cancer, and more likely to die from it, if they have rigid, authoritarian personalities and suppressed inner conflicts about sexual and aggressive feelings. There have been many studies attempting to test this theory, and the results are thought-provoking. In one study, for example, doctors at the University of Rochester were able to predict with seventy-five percent accuracy whether women entering the hospital for a biopsy would have cancer or not, based on psychiatric interviews. However, this and many other studies linking cancer and psychological factors were performed on small samples. Well-controlled, large-scale, long-term studies are needed before the theory can be regarded as well established.

A third factor that might influence your susceptibility to cancer is the state of your immune system. When a person's immune system is weak, he or she has a heightened chance of developing cancer. The immune system can be weakened by a hereditary defect, by exposure to radiation, or by the action of immunosuppressive drugs (given, for example, to people who have organ transplants).

ENVIRONMENTAL IRRITANTS

You may have been surprised, in testing your knowledge about cancer earlier in this chapter, to learn that environmental factors play a role in from sixty to ninety percent of cancers. You may also wonder, how do we know?

We know, in large part, by studying the geographical patterns of cancer. Lung cancer, for example, is common in the United States and Britain, rare in Africa and most of Asia. Colon and rectal cancers are common in the West, rare in developing countries. Rates of various cancers also vary dramatically in various regions of the United States.

You might think that genetic or ethnic factors could account for these geographical differences. But careful studies of people who moved from one country to another showed that immigrant populations quickly lost the patterns of their country of origin and developed the cancer patterns typical of their new environment.

If more evidence is needed that environmental irritants play a major role in the development of cancer, it is abundantly supplied by the relationship between certain occupations and certain types of cancer. People who work with polyvinyl chloride have elevated rates of angiosarcoma of the liver, a rare type of liver cancer. People who work with asbestos have high rates of lung cancer; so do uranium miners and people who tend coke ovens at steel mills. People who work with aniline dyes or in the rubber industry have elevated rates of bladder cancer.

In some of these instances, it is possible to pinpoint a particular environmental irritant, such as asbestos or polyvinyl chloride, that is involved in the process of cancer development. In the population at large, however, it is a guessing game trying to ascertain which pollutants and other substances to which we are exposed — or which combinations of these substances — contribute to cancer. Are the major offenders in the water we drink? In the meat we eat? In the air we breathe? For the most part, we simply don't know. There are so many variables that analysis is extremely difficult.

COMPREHENSION TEST 4

Directions: *Circle the letter of the best answer.*

1. Research into the causes of cancer reveals that
    a) environment factors are solely responsible
    b) we are still unsure of its precise causes
    c) viruses are the main cancer causers
    d) cancer is primarily inherited

2. Family heredity is
    a) not a factor in cancer
    b) related to certain types of cancer

    c) a chief environmental cause of cancer
    d) a cause of all types of cancer

3. An individual's susceptibility to cancer is *not* influenced by
    a) age
    b) heredity
    c) personality characteristics
    d) weaknesses in the immune system

4. The link between viruses and cancer
    a) is expected to be proven soon

b) was proven in the late 1970s

c) has no possibilities of being proven

d) was disproved at the University of Rochester

5. Environmental factors are important
   a) only for certain types of cancers
   b) for a large percentage of all cancers
   c) only for certain geographic regions
   d) for a small percentage of all cancers

6. The best synonym for the word "dormant" as it is used in the passage is
   a) decaying
   b) altering
   c) weakening
   d) inactive

7. Which person is more prone to develop cancer than any of the others?
   a) a woman whose mother had breast cancer
   b) a child who has suffered numerous communicable diseases
   c) a worker in a factory that produces petrochemicals
   d) a salesman with a shy, recessive personality

8. The person with the highest risk of cancer would be
   a) a South American diamond miner
   b) a Mexican farmer
   c) a British fisherman
   d) an American steelworker

9. Which of the following statements best summarizes the present state of knowledge about the causes of cancer?
   a) some tentative causes have been identified, but further research is needed
   b) it is unlikely that the real cause of cancer will ever be identified
   c) until more cases of cancer are identified in their early stages, cures will be unlikely
   d) heredity will most likely prove to be the strongest link to cancer

10. The intent of the author in writing this passage was to
    a) frighten
    b) persuade
    c) inform
    d) entertain

Selection 4:	986 words
Finishing Time: _____ _____ _____	
HR.　MIN.　SEC.	
Starting Time: _____ _____ _____	
HR.　MIN.　SEC.	
Reading Time: _____ _____	
MIN.　SEC.	
WPM Score: _____	
Comprehension Score: _____ %	
Reading Efficiency Score: _____	

Unit Three:
How to Increase Your Comprehension

Reading is commonly thought of as a process in which the meaning of each word is understood successively and their meanings are added together to arrive at the overall meaning of sentences, paragraphs, and passages. Such a notion presumes that each word on a page is of equal importance and that each word performs the same function. Actually, reading involves much more than the cumulative addition of word meaning to word meaning. Words and groups of words vary in importance and in function. Reading involves not only the understanding of ideas, but also recognizing the relationship and structure among ideas. To read efficiently, you need to be able quickly to grasp each idea a writer expresses and then see how it relates to all the other ideas expressed in the same piece of writing. To grasp ideas and their relationships quickly, you must be familiar with the basic structure and organization of sentences, paragraphs, and passages or longer selections. Often, once you understand how material is organized, you can follow the author's train of thought much more easily and in a shorter period of time.

The purpose of this unit is to acquaint you with the basic structures and organization of sentences, paragraphs, and passages. In Chapter 5 we will discuss how to identify the key elements of a sentence as well as how to understand the relationship among various ideas expressed in a sentence. A procedure for understanding long, complicated sentences will also be presented. Chapter 6 will be concerned with the essential elements of the paragraph and will show how an awareness of this structure can increase your efficiency. Chapter 7 will present five of the most common patterns used to organize paragraphs and will show you how the recognition of organizational patterns can increase your retention of content. The last chapter in this unit will focus on reading passages and longer selections. You will see how various features such as titles, introductions, summaries, headings, transitions can help you to read the material more easily and efficiently.

Chapter 5:
Reading Sentences

The sentence is one of the basic vehicles of expression used in all types of writing. To read sentences effectively and efficiently, you must be able to identify the important ideas and sort or sift out the less important information. Also, you must see how the parts of a sentence are related.

Ordinarily, we think of a sentence as a simple group of words expressing a single idea, and in many types of written material a sentence is just that. However, in some textbooks or reference material, you may come across more complicated sentences such as this:

> Even though schools have helped create problems of teenage unemployment, drug abuse, and antisocial behavior, they have not helped to solve these problems.

This sentence is not simple, it is not very basic, and it contains a number of related ideas. Actually, this sentence could be broken down into two separate, simple or basic sentences.

> Schools have helped to create the problems of teenage unemployment, drug abuse, and antisocial behavior.

> Schools have not helped to solve these problems.

Also, many related facts are "packed" into this sentence. Here is a list of the separate pieces of information expressed in that sentence:

1. Teenage unemployment is a problem.
2. Drug abuse is a problem.
3. Antisocial behavior is a problem.
4. Schools have helped to cause teenage unemployment.
5. Schools have helped to cause drug abuse.
6. Schools have helped to cause antisocial behavior.
7. Schools have not helped to solve the problem of teenage unemployment.
8. Schools have not helped to solve the problem of drug abuse.
9. Schools have not helped to solve the problem of antisocial behavior.

You can see, then, that a sentence can express several related ideas and can contain a great deal of information. Also, you may have noticed in the original sentence that some of these facts seemed more important than others.

Beyond merely expressing a single thought, then, a sentence can express two or more related ideas and can include additional information of varying importance. The purpose of this chapter is to show you how to read sentences as accurately and efficiently as possible. It will focus on how to locate all the important parts of a sentence's message, how to recognize relationships between or among ideas, and how to read long, complicated sentences.

IDENTIFYING THE CORE PARTS

All sentences are built around one or more sets of essential elements or core parts. The core parts express the basic, unadorned meaning of the sentence. All other words and phrases in the sentences explain or describe these core parts. Each core part is made up of a subject and a verb. That is, the sentence must be about a person, place, idea, or concept, called the *subject,* and something must be said about the subject — it must perform some action or something must happen to it —called the *predicate*. In reading a sentence in which the core parts are not obvious to you, ask yourself these questions:

1.   Who or what is the sentence about?
2.   What is happening in the sentence?

Your answers to these questions will provide you with the core parts of the sentence. You can see how this works in the following example.

Mr. Ransom canceled our math class twice last week.

This sentence was about a person — Mr. Ransom; and the action he performed was the cancellation of the math class. Here are a few other sample sentences. The core parts have been underlined in each. First, read only the underlined words. Notice that by reading only the core parts you are able to understand the basic message of each sentence. Next, read each sentence completely, noticing the types of additional information included.

1.   Animals are frightened by loud noises.
2.   Animals who do not have to hunt for their food often get lazy.
3.   Children learn the meaning of many words by listening to adults.

96

Occasionally, a sentence may contain two or more subjects and/or two or more predicates. For instance, notice that each of the following sentences is about two persons, places, objects, or ideas.

Pete and Sam failed the philosophy exam.

Skiing and skating are fun in the winter.

Here are a few sentences containing two predicates. Notice that two actions occur in each.

Kate tripped and dropped her tray.

I locked the door and shut the window.

As you read sentences, especially long and complicated ones, be alert for compound subjects and compound predicates.

Once you have identified the core parts of a sentence, you will be able to determine how the other parts of the sentence relate to those core parts. Basically, the remaining parts of a sentence, called modifiers, provide further information about the subject or the verb. It is not necessary to learn various types of modifiers, but only to be able to see how each alters or affects the meaning conveyed by the sentence.

In the following sentence, the words enclosed in a box are modifiers that further explain or describe one of the core parts of the sentence. Notice how each modifier changes or adds to the meaning of the sentence.

My parents travel every summer.
    The modifier indicates *when* they travel.

Slowly and carefully, the team climbed the mountain.
    The modifier describes *how* the team climbed.

Sooner or later, we will be able to afford a new car.
    The modifier indicates *when* we can afford a new car.

William Faulkner, a popular American author, wrote about life in the South.
    The modifier tells *who* Faulkner was.

The World Trade Center, located in Manhattan, is one of the world's tallest buildings.
    The modifier describes by giving a location.

As you read sentences, then, be sure to notice how modifiers alter or complete their meanings.

EXERCISE 5-1

Directions: *For each of the following sentences, underline the core parts.*

1. Stress is defined as the rate of wear and tear on the body.
2. Political scientists are interested in finding out how society works.
3. In enforcing its decisions, the government may employ, allow, or prevent the use of force.
4. Power and authority, then, are central to politics.
5. In fact, the majority of reported cases of mental illness have no obvious physical cause.

RECOGNIZING RELATIONSHIPS AMONG IDEAS

Many sentences that you find in textbooks and reference material express two or more related ideas. Frequently a writer will combine closely related ideas into a single sentence to explain or emphasize the relationship among the ideas. In reading sentences of this type you should identify each idea and be sure that you understand how the ideas are connected. To do so, you will need to be familiar with the sentence patterns that can be used to show relationships.

There are two basic sentence patterns a writer can use to connect thoughts within a sentence. A writer can join the ideas in a structure that suggests that they are of equal importance, or in a way that indicates one idea's dependence on another, suggesting that one is more important than the other. Ideas of equal importance that are combined are referred to as *coordinate ideas*. When one idea is less important than another, the less important idea is said to be *subordinate*. The specific sentence patterns used for each will be discussed in this section.

Coordinate Relationships

When two or more ideas are of equal importance, an author may combine them into a single sentence. This type of sentence pattern is called a compound sentence. Here are a few sentences that combine two or more separate but related ideas.

My brother plans to become an accountant, and my sister is studying law.

Repetition is a key concept in advertising; a long series of short ads is more effective than one longer ad.

Many small towns try to protect their citizens by enacting town ordinances, but these are seldom enforced.

As you read sentences of this type be sure to recognize each major important idea and identify two or more sets of core parts. If you read too fast, or if you are not concentrating, it is easy to miss the second idea. The structure and punctuation of a sentence can often alert you to the fact that the sentence contains more than one idea. Separate ideas in a compound sentence must be joined in one of two ways. They can be connected with a semicolon or by a comma and a conjunction (words such as "and," "but," "or," "nor").

EXERCISE 5-2

Directions: *Each of the following sentences expresses a coordinate relationship. For each sentence, underline the core parts of each of the two ideas expressed.*

1. The professor summarized the plot of the short story and then he gave an assignment based on the story.
2. You can relieve tension through relaxation, but most people don't know how to relax.
3. The mind and the body are not separate, independent entities; any change in the body is accompanied by a change in mental or emotional state, and any change in the mind is accompanied by a corresponding change in the body.
4. Communication skill involves the ability to send the message you intend; listening skills involve the sensitivity to interpret the sent message properly so as to understand what was intended.

Subordinate Relationships

Sentences that contain subordinate, or less important, ideas are structured so that the meaning of the subordinate idea depends on the main part of the sentence. Subordinate ideas are never complete by themselves and make sense only when attached to a complete sentence. They also emphasize or further explain the more important idea with which they are combined. In the following sentences you can see that the underlined idea depends on the main part of the sentence.

<u>After it rained</u>, Peter cooked hamburgers on the grill.

<u>Although I had a sore throat</u>, I went to the party anyway.

<u>Because I forgot to bring my notebook home</u>, I couldn't study for the exam.

In each of these examples, the underlined information in some sense qualifies or further explains the more important part of the sentence. The first sentence tells *when* Peter cooked the hamburgers; the second explains a *condition* or circumstance of going to the party; the last offers a *reason* for not studying. Also, you can see that subordinate information is not as important as the remainder of the sentence. In the first sentence the fact that Peter cooked hamburgers is more important than the fact that he did it after it rained. When reading sentences containing subordinate information, be sure to notice the nature of the relationship between ideas. By the way information is arranged and structured, writers often provide additional information about ideas and their relative importance.

EXERCISE 5-3

Directions: *Each of the following sentences expresses a subordinate relationship between two ideas. Decide which idea is more important, the first or the second, and underline it.*

1. When a child throws a temper tantrum, the child usually receives attention.
2. After we fastened our seat belts, the pilot began to taxi down the runway.
3. As a piece of solid matter gains more and more energy, the molecules in that piece of matter move faster and further apart.
4. Though it may appear static and serene from telescopic observations, the universe is actually in constant motion.
5. Science does advance, producing an ever-growing body of knowledge, although there are occasional regressions and fanciful flights of the imagination.

UNRAVELING COMPLICATED SENTENCES

On occasion, you may find a sentence that is long, complicated, and confusing. When you encounter a sentence such as this, the best strategy to use is to unravel it, separating it into smaller, understandable pieces. Try to use the following steps in deciphering a complicated sentence.

1. Identify each separate, complete (coordinate) idea in the sentence, and find the core parts in each. If the vocabulary is difficult or technical, try to express the basic meaning of each coordinate idea in your own words.

2. For each coordinate idea, notice any modifiers that further explain the core parts and decide how each alters the meaning.

3. Identify any subordinate idea and decide which complete idea it explains and emphasizes; then determine how the meaning of the complete idea is affected.

4. Determine the relationship among the subordinate and coordinate ideas. Decide how each is related and what combined effect they produce.

5. Try to express the meaning of the entire sentence in your own words.

For example, in unraveling the following complicated sentence, you would first notice that it contains *two* separate complete ideas.

Although no single cause for it can be identified, inner cities have become overcrowded, and many well-to-do residents, including local businessmen, have moved to the suburbs.

One coordinate idea is that inner cities have become overcrowded; the other is that many residents have moved to the suburbs. Next, identify any modifiers that relate to either coordinate idea. The modifier "including local businessmen" provides further information about who has moved to the suburbs and emphasizes a particular group of people. Now identify any subordinate idea and determine its relationship to the main part. In this sentence, "Although no single cause can be identified," is a subordinate idea and explains that a single reason for inner city crowding cannot be identified. You can see that a cause-effect relationship is suggested. By combining the two coordinate ideas into a single sentence, the writer is suggesting that the overcrowding is causing well-to-do residents to move to the suburbs. The subordinate clause qualifies both ideas by explaining that no one cause has been identified for this overcrowding.

Finally, to restate the meaning in your own words, you might say that although a single cause for overcrowding in inner cities cannot be identified, it has forced people to move to the suburbs.

You can see that using the suggested steps can help you more fully to understand the sentence as well as to grasp the relationship among the ideas.

EXERCISE 5-4

Directions: *Read each of the following complicated sentences, using the procedure suggested. Underline the core parts of each sentence and, in the space provided, write the meaning of each sentence in your own words.*

1.   Often you don't realize you are tense; only later when you feel the ache in the back of your neck, the tightness around your eyes, or an unexplained tiredness, do you realize that you have been tense for some time.[1]

_____

_____

_____

2.   Modern urbanization and the rise of the nuclear family have removed many of the environmental supports and the kinds of help with marital problems that tend to be available in the extended family who live in a less hurried, less impersonal, more stable social network.[2]

_____

_____

_____

3.   Although "romantic" love is an established tradition in our time and a major preoccupation of the dreams of young men and women, poets, writers and singers, we have little scientific understanding of the phenomenon or of its actual importance in leading two young people to marry or in holding a marriage together.[3]

_____

_____

_____

4.   With all the variations among American families, it is apparent that they are all in greater or lesser degree in a process of change

toward an emerging type of family that is perhaps most aptly described as the "companionship" form.[4]

_____

_____

_____

5. Just when the management community had become disenchanted with the "human relations" approach, the applicability to management of a growing body of knowledge, based on research findings about human behavior, was increasingly recognized.[5]

_____

_____

_____

APPLYING WHAT YOU HAVE LEARNED

Directions: *Choose one of the selections included at the end of this chapter. Complete each of the following steps.*

1. Preread the selection.
2. Write some purpose questions to guide your reading.

_____

_____

3. After you have read the selection and answered the multiple choice questions, reread the article underlining the core parts of each sentence.

READING SELECTION 5
THE NON-RUNNER

Vic Ziegel and Lewis Grossberger

What kind of people are these non-runners? Who are these pathfinders bold enough to drop out of the faddish rat race? Are they weirdos? buffoons? sociopaths? naive sycophants? craven toadies? harmless eccentrics? perverts? trolls? Medicaid cheaters? brainwashed zombies? Red spies?

Not at all.

Surprisingly, non-runners are very much like you and me. They include people from every walk of life. And there are not only walkers. There are sitters, leaners, nappers, starers, procrastinators, TV-watchers, popsicle-lickers, readers, sneezers, yawners, teasers, stumblers, lechers, stamp collectors, static-electricity gatherers, and, of course, the totally immobile.

This amazingly versatile group comprises people of all ages, races, and sexes. Non-running is accessible to young and old, rich and fat, the famous as well as the depressed. Whether you're an android or an aborigine, you can take part. Or you can take all.

Many non-runners have been doing it all their lives. Others have only recently kicked the running habit to join the swelling ranks of the unrun. Together, these non-runners spend an estimated $665 billion annually on products totally unrelated to running in any way. Without them and their non-running-related expenditures, the U.S. economy would fold up in a minute.

But the economic gain from non-running is only part of the picture. There is also the spiritual side. Non-runners are linked by a common bond; they feel a kinship that expresses itself in innumerable ways. Non-runners will often wave to other non-runners they don't even know. Sometimes they will even invite them home to dinner and later go to bed with them.

And there is the well-known psychological lift that comes to non-runners. After the first half hour or so of not running, you become so elated by the realization that you are not out in the hot sun or in the rain pounding around a hard sidewalk or dusty track that you may find yourself uttering a restrained sigh. This indefinable sense of quiet satisfaction is one of the things that makes not running so pleasurable.

People find that once they start to not run, it's hard to stop. After just a small taste, the tyro non-runner finds his body demanding more and more until he is almost smiling with the sheer joy of not running. It is this "up" feeling that enables veteran non-runners to achieve the amazing feats about which you've undoubtedly read. These are the so-called marathoners who have attained the peak of the non-running experience. Some of them are capable of going twenty-four hours a day without a single running step. Even more astonishing, there are those who, by combining non-running with meditation, have achieved a mental state in which they don't even *think* about running for months on end.

Still another source of non-running's appeal is the surpassing ease with which it may be performed. As Dr. George Shoeshine, author of *Non-Running and Non-Being: The Totality of the Whole,* has eloquently put it, "The essence of not running — indeed, the beauty of it, as it were — is in its utter simplicity, if you know what I mean."

Non-running is so easy that it can be enjoyed at any time in any place: in city parks; alongside (or in) rivers, lakes, inland seas and oceans; atop mountains or supermarket shelves; on couches; inside roll-top desks; in the bath; out in the back; or over the rainbow. In 1972, the Russian cosmonaut Yuri Yugarin reported completing ten minutes of weightless non-running in space during the flight of Soyuz 12. He said it made him feel high.

And non-running is cheap. Sweatsuits, netted shirts, jockstraps, and German sneakers are not needed by non-runners. You can non-run in your street clothes, your formal wear, or in the nude. (While it's true that there are some non-runners who prefer special racing-stripe pajamas and leisure suits and who enjoy arguing the merits of hard slippers vs. soft, these are in the minority.)

Non-running gives the overstructured and overdirected life a needed sense of freedom and purposelessness. Life is, as we now know, totally meaningless, and artificial attempts to find goals and erect structures (like setting records or winning races) are doomed to fail and disappoint, ultimately leading to irreversible depression. The quicker you realize this, the happier you will be.

But some people never understand. Competitive, compulsive, indigestive, they become obsessed with crossing finish lines and counting laps. They wallow in linear thought. They begin to see life as a race. They have become running addicts, lured by the powerful metaphor of the race, with its false promise of getting someplace. They lose sight of the importance of staying in one spot and not moving for long periods of time. And they pay a fearful price in terms of curdled brains and the unnecessary provocation of untold thousands of innocent dogs that are rudely transformed into snapping curs with a morbid desire to taste the human ankle.

Non-runners do not have these problems. They truly understand the beauty and power of slow. They respect the concept of Take It Easy. They reject the pseudo-adventure of the road. They do not traffic in traffic. They know that wisdom can't be rushed. They know how to relax. Theirs is the way of the turtle and the snail. Theirs is the spirit of the glacier. The spirit of Walk, Do Not Run; of Haste Makes Waste; of Stop; and Halt; and Yield Right of Way. Grass grows under their feet and it tickles and that's nice. Baby ducks are not frightened by their passing. They are non-runners. And they know it.

COMPREHENSION TEST 5

Directions: *Circle the letter of the best answer.*

1. The purpose of this essay is to show that
   a) nonrunners are manic-depressive people who are obsessed with linear thought
   b) the sport of running has been overemphasized in the United States
   c) nonrunning is economically destroying and culturally dissatisfying
   d) running is generally bad for physical and mental health

2. According to the authors, nonrunners spend billions of dollars on
   a) other sports-related equipment
   b) passive entertainment
   c) nonrunning expenditures
   d) products to compensate for not running

3. "Nonrunners" get a psychological lift because they
   a) nonrun in weightlessness
   b) save money by not buying sweatsuits
   c) begin to see life as a race
   d) realize they are not out in the hot sun or on a dusty track

4. All of the following are reasons for nonrunning's widespread appeal *except*
   a) it is utterly simple
   b) nonrunners feel a bond of kinship
   c) nonrunners are obsessed with winning races
   d) the nonrunner feels happy because his body demands more nonrunning

5. In this selection runners are characterized as extremely
   a) competitive
   b) lazy
   c) depressed
   d) feeble-minded

6. A *versatile* group as used in this selection is one that is
   a) skillful or handy
   b) adaptable
   c) varied or diverse
   d) well organized

7. It is *unstated* but implied that runners
   a) are obsessed with crossing the finishing line
   b) outnumber nonrunners
   c) are happy individuals
   d) cause dogs to become aggressive

8. All of the following are probably true about runners, *except* that they
   a) spend large sums on equipment
   b) often become addicted to running
   c) see life as purposeless
   d) feel a "common bond"

9. Judging by this selection, the authors probably are
   a) nonrunners
   b) runners
   c) jealous
   d) sportswriters

10. The main method used by the writers to hold the interest of the reader is
    a) factual information
    b) personal experiences
    c) humor
    d) logical arguments

Selection 5:		924 words
Finishing Time:		
	HR. MIN.	SEC.
Starting Time:		
	HR. MIN.	SEC.
Reading Time:		
	MIN.	SEC.
WPM Score:		
Comprehension Score:		%
Reading Efficiency Score:		

READING SELECTION 6
CHILD ABUSE

Developing a peaceful, understanding, and supportive relationship between parents and children is not an easy task. Failures can and do occur at any age level, and at times the results are the abuse, neglect, and even death of children.

Child abuse has become a major topic in child development and an issue of much national concern. In the span of four legislative years, 1963–67, all fifty states enacted laws calling for the reporting of injuries inflicted on children. By 1973, the United States Congress passed the Child Abuse Prevention and Treatment Act (Public Law 93–247). This law not only reflected the mood of concerned citizens, but it also did much to clear up the confusion and disagreement over what is child abuse. In section 3 of the law, child abuse and neglect are defined as "the physical or mental injury, sexual abuse, negligent treatment or maltreatment of a child under the age of eighteen by a person who is responsible for the child's welfare under circumstances which indicate that the child's health or welfare is harmed or threatened thereby . . ."

How widespread are child abuse and neglect? Although the existence of state and federal laws provide general definitions of abuse, there is wide variation in how strictly the guidelines are interpreted. This in turn affects any attempt to determine how many children become victims of abuse and neglect. Estimates vary from 10,000 to 10 million cases a year. This rather dramatic difference in figures may be, in part, because of the degree of conformity to legally mandated reporting requirements. In all but six states, members of the medical profession are designated as the principal reporters of suspected abuse. In most states teachers, school administrators, social workers, law enforcement officials, coroners, attorneys, and psychologists are obligated to report suspected cases of abuse and neglect.

What is reportable? For a specific case of suspected abuse to be reported, there must be reason to believe that a child's injuries are not the result of an accident. Symptoms might include frequent complaints of abdominal pain, evidence of bruises, welts, wounds, cuts, or punctures, and cigarette burns. Indications of neglect could be tattered and unwashed clothing, evidence of hunger and improper nourishment, consistent early school arrival and staying after school has been dismissed, and poor hygiene and health care.

To whom to report a suspected case of child abuse varies from state to state. Most state laws specify a county or state department of welfare or a law enforcement division as the receiving agency.

The question "What causes child abuse?" has prompted much debate. The single most persistent myth which has plagued efforts to understand causes is the notion that parents who abuse children are mentally disturbed or ill. Although there is no specific psychiatric diagnosis which encompasses the behavior and personalities of abusers, they seem to share a common style of child rearing. Those parents demand high levels of child performance and they often use severe physical punishment to ensure the child's proper behavior. Abusive parents themselves were raised in similar family situations and their own childhood experience has a lasting influence on their behavior as adults.

Current research has suggested, however, that the "abuser is sick" hypothesis is too limited. A broader social, psychological approach recognizes that some personal problems are implicit but that psychological factors arise out of a social context. Social factors include unemployment, social isolation, and unwanted pregnancy. Moreover, findings that abuse occurs more frequently in larger families and families with low income, poor education, and low occupational status suggest that many such parents cannot withstand the twenty-four-hour-a-day responsibility to raise and care for their children. These problems aggravate the situation, especially when combined with the general approval in our culture of violence.

Both the social and the psychological approaches offer useful insights into the causes of child abuse. We can only develop a fuller understanding of this tragic phenomenon in our society by looking at both social and psychological factors.

COMPREHENSION TEST 6

Directions: *Circle the letter of the best answer.*

1. This selection suggests that child abuse is
   a) a problem in the United States, but a greater one in Europe
   b) caused primarily by the mentally ill
   c) a growing problem whose causes are not fully understood
   d) easily determined because of recent public laws

2. In most states all of the following persons are obligated to report possible cases of child abuse *except:*
   a) clergymen
   b) attorneys
   c) teachers
   d) psychologists

3. Abused children are protected by
   a) local agencies
   b) religious organizations
   c) federal laws
   d) the Constitution

4. The number of instances of child abuse in the United States each year is at least
   a) 10,000
   b) 100,000
   c) 1,000,000
   d) 1,000,000,000

5. The person who is *least* likely to be a child-abusing parent is one who is characterized as
   a) unemployed or socially isolated
   b) an abused child, him- or herself
   c) requiring high levels of performance from his or her child
   d) mentally ill

6. In the phrase "legally mandated reporting requirements" the word "mandate" means

   a) a legal strategy
   b) a misdemeanor charge
   c) a certificate of approval
   d) a command

7. A concerned teacher might be reluctant to report a case of suspected child abuse for all of the following reasons *except*
   a) lack of medical expertise
   b) inability to distinguish between poverty and neglect
   c) inability to determine causes of an injury
   d) fear of damaging the family reputation of the child abuser

8. Which *one* of the following persons has the greatest potential to become a child-abusing parent?
   a) a lawyer who was recently divorced
   b) a teacher who was laid off
   c) a widow
   d) an unhappy, pregnant woman whose religion forbids abortion

9. The author is most likely to agree with which *one* of the following statements?
   a) the media should not describe the details of child abuse cases
   b) medical doctors are largely to blame for unreported cases of child abuse
   c) violence on TV may contribute to child abuse
   d) violence in our society is acceptable unless children are victims

10. This selection would most likely be contained in a
    a) daily newspaper
    b) collection of essays
    c) weekly newsmagazine
    d) textbook

Selection 6:   757 words

Finishing Time: _____ _____ _____
                  HR.   MIN.   SEC.

Starting Time: _____ _____ _____
                 HR.   MIN.   SEC.

Reading Time: _____ _____
                          MIN.   SEC.

WPM Score: _____

Comprehension Score: _____ %

Reading Efficiency Score: _____

Chapter 6:
Paragraph Structure

When you shop you expect to find all the types of cereal displayed on the same shelf in a supermarket and all size 34 pants hung together on a rack. All items of a similar type are grouped together for convenience. Ideas expressed in written form should also be grouped together into paragraphs for the reader's convenience in understanding ideas that concern a similar topic. To illustrate further, notice what happens when ideas are *not* grouped together, as in the following sentences.

> Willow trees provide a great deal of shade, but it is difficult to mow the lawn underneath them. In the summer outdoor barbecues or corn roasts are enjoyable ways to entertain. When beginning college, many students are worried about whether they will know someone in each of their classes. The income tax structure in our country has been changed so that it does not discriminate against married couples who are both employed. Most people do not realize that tea and cola drinks contain as much caffeine as coffee.

This so-called paragraph is confusing and the train of thought is difficult or impossible to follow. It is not clear which idea or ideas the writer feels are important and which are less important. The reader has no sense of whether the ideas are connected to each other, and if so, how they are related.

To avoid the confusion demonstrated in that paragraph and to express written ideas in a clear, understandable way, writers adhere to a general pattern or structure in developing paragraphs. To read paragraphs in the most efficient manner, it is necessary to be familiar with their underlying structure. Then you will be able to follow the author's train of thought more easily, to anticipate ideas as they are about to be developed, and to recall more of what you read.

A paragraph is structured around four essential elements: the topic, the main idea, supporting details, and signal or linking words or

110

phrases. The function of each of these elements will be discussed in this chapter.

IDENTIFYING THE TOPIC

A paragraph can be defined as a group of related ideas. The sentences relate to one another in the sense that each is about a common person, place, thing, or idea. This common subject or idea is called the *topic*. Simply defined, the topic is what the entire paragraph is about. As you read the following paragraph, notice that each sentence describes information about one feature of investments — liquid assets.

> When an investment can be turned into money quickly, it is said to be *liquid*. This feature of an investment is desirable, for one may need money quickly to take care of emergencies. Suppose, for example, that you have $1,000 on deposit in a bank. If you need money right away, you can withdraw it from the bank. On the other hand, suppose that you own a piece of land which you bought for $1,000. The land may be a safe investment and may eventually return a satisfactory income; but if you need money at once, you may not be able to get it. You may have trouble selling the land, or you may be able to get only part of the price you paid for it, perhaps $700. In this case, you will lose $300, not because the investment was unsafe but because it could not be quickly turned into money.[1]

In this paragraph you could see that each sentence explains and provides examples about liquid investments and this topic is discussed throughout the paragraph. The first two sentences explain the term "liquid," and the next two give an example. The remaining sentences explain the desirability of liquid assets by offering an example of an investment that is not liquid. To identify the topic of a paragraph, ask yourself this question: "Who or what is the paragraph about?" Your answer to this question will be the topic of the paragraph. Now, try using this question as you read the following paragraph.

> People with normal vision need only the three additive primary colors to reproduce all the colors of the spectrum. People who are partially color blind need only two hues to reproduce all the colors they can see. The majority of partially color blind people can match all the hues they can see with combinations of only blue and yellow — they

cannot distinguish between reds and greens, which take on
a grayish appearance. (How many automobile accidents
could have been avoided if traffic engineers had taken color
blindness into account when stoplights were first designed?)
A few people are yellow-blue blind, and all the colors they
can see can be reproduced by combinations of red and
green. The very few individuals who are totally color blind
need but one color (any color at all — they all seem the
same) to reproduce all they can see. These few see no color
at all — their world appears as one black-and-white movie.[2]

In this paragraph, the question leads you directly to the topic — color
blindness. Each sentence in the paragraph describes or defines color
blindness or discusses its cause.

Now, try to identify the topic in the following paragraph.

Next time you fill up your tank, look at the price
schedule on the pump. There you will see that several cents
of each gallon's price is a federal tax. (In addition, most
states — and some cities — charge a tax on gasoline.) Most
of these federal tax collections flow into highway trust
funds, on the assumption that motorists should pay for the
construction and repair of the nation's highways. (If you
own a boat, you still pay the tax for gasoline. But you can
receive a rebate of the federal tax proceeds at the end of the
year. The reason, of course, is that boats don't need
highways.)[3]

The topic of this paragraph is gasoline taxes. Each sentence discusses
a type of or use for gasoline tax.

EXERCISE 6-1

Directions: *Read each of the following paragraphs and identify the
topic by writing it in the space provided.*

1. Coffee trees (actually they are more shrubs than trees) are
relatively fast-growing, bearing fruits three to four years after
planting. The fruits take another seven to nine months to mature.
It is from these that the beverage used by at least a third of the
world's people is produced. The mature fruits, or berries, are
harvested by hand and are processed by one of two methods. The
dry method is used in most of Brazil's coffee-producing regions:
the fruits are spread out to dry in the sun for fifteen to twenty-

112

five days and then hulled. The wet method calls for pulping the berries after picking to remove the outer layer and part of the fleshy inner layer of the fruit. The pulped fruit is then fermented in tanks, washed, and sun-dried for eight to ten days. The dry skin around the beans is removed by milling and polishing, leaving shiny blue or grayish blue beans. The characteristic brown color is produced by roasting.[4]

Topic: _____

2. Many long lists of emotional motives like security, curiosity, ego, comfort, recreation, emulation, pride, sex, and many others have been put forth. Any attempt to develop a complete classification of emotional buying motives is doomed to failure, however, because to make it both complete and mutually exclusive is impossible. One's emotions are such complex phenomena that it is presumptuous to attempt to single out and classify them. Two families may purchase the same model automobile for ostensibly the same commonly mentioned motive, "keeping up with the Joneses." Nevertheless, the exact motive-mixes underlying the purchase of the two cars may be different. One family may have bought its car because everyone else in the neighborhood had a new car. The other family may have acquired its new car because the husband felt his status in the community demanded that he drive a better car. Though both of these purchases would be lumped together in the broad category of "keeping up appearances," they were nevertheless made for different reasons.[5]

Topic: _____

3. It was a medieval custom to *swaddle* infants during their first year. Swaddling involved wrapping the infant in cloth bandages with arms and legs pressed closely to the body. Parents feared that infants might scratch their eyes or distort their tender limbs by bending them improperly. Swaddling also kept them from touching their genitals and from crawling "like a beast." However, De Mause, a historian who has studied concepts of childhood and child-rearing practices of the past, has found evidence that the main purpose of swaddling was adult convenience. Swaddled infants tend to be quiet and passive; they sleep more, their heart rate slows, and they cry less. Swaddled infants might be laid for hours "behind a hot oven, or hung on

pegs on the wall," and leading-strings were sometimes used to "puppet" the infant around for the amusement of adults.[6]

Topic: _____

4. Before we started radio communication in the last century, people had suggested ingenious ways of signaling our presence to other worlds in the solar system: huge bonfires in simple geometric patterns such as squares or triangles; planting a 16-kilometer-wide strip of pine forest in Siberia in the form of a right triangle; huge mirrors to reflect sunlight; a 30-kilometer circular ditch filled with water over which kerosene would be poured and set burning; a powerful concave mirror to focus sunlight on Mars and burn simple numbers on the desert sands of the planet; a network of large sunlight-reflecting mirrors strategically positioned in several European cities forming the shape of the Big Dipper in Ursa Major.[7]

Topic: _____

5. Too often, space exploration has been looked at only as a means of satisfying man's innate curiosity and as a stimulus in advancing his intellectual pursuits. This viewpoint overlooks many of the tangible benefits that we have derived from the exploration of our cosmic environment. The record of history is clear: witness the benefits to modern civilization in nearly all areas of human endeavor that have accrued from the work of the early astronomers. True, the past is no guarantor of the future; nevertheless, our present state of advanced technology and science augurs well that we shall reap even greater potential benefits to the human race from the exploration of space.[8]

Topic: _____

FINDING THE MAIN IDEA

In addition to presenting a topic, every paragraph must make some statement or express an idea about that topic. Each paragraph contains a broad, important idea that the writer develops throughout the paragraph. This general idea is called the *main idea*. The entire paragraph, then, explains, develops, and supports this main idea.

In the following paragraph, the topic is progressive tax, and the main idea expressed about the topic is that a progressive tax is one that increases in proportion to the amount taxed.

A *progressive tax* is one that increases the rate as the amount taxed increases. Our federal income tax is mainly a progressive tax. As taxable income increases, the rate also increases. For example, the tax on a taxable income of $20,000 may be almost three times the tax on a similar income of $10,000. The progressive feature of the federal income tax is generally accepted. It is generally believed that those with large incomes should pay a larger share of their incomes as tax than should those with small incomes.[9]

The first sentence defines the term "progressive tax," whereas the second indicates a type of tax that is progressive. The third offers a specific example, and the last two sentences state that it is accepted and offers a reason why it is accepted. To locate the main idea of a paragraph, first decide what the topic of the paragraph is, then ask yourself what the author is trying to express about the topic. Your answer will be a statement of the paragraph's main idea. Now, try using this question to find the main idea of the following paragraph.

The history of the treatment of the insane has been, until recently, a history of inhumanity and cruelty. Until the 1800s, there were no real mental hospitals. There were a few "zoos," such as the infamous Bethlehem asylum in London, where citizens could watch the antics of the inmates for a slight fee; the word "bedlam," meaning wild and disorganized activity, derives from the common pronunciation of Bethlehem. The theory of insanity most popular among both the educated and the uneducated was that mild forms of it were caused by moral inferiority, whereas particularly bizarre behavior was the result of possession by demons. (Roughly speaking, the mild forms would today be called neuroses and the more severe manifestations would be labeled psychoses.)[10]

The topic of this paragraph is "treatment of the insane." By asking what the author is trying to express about the topic, you can see that the author is saying that throughout history, mentally ill, or insane, persons were treated with cruelty and lack of understanding.

Here's another example. As you read it, look for the topic and main idea.

Analysis of individual consumer behavior begins with human needs. Everyone has basic needs, which when stimulated provoke action. Action leads to fulfillment, and the need is temporarily satisfied. Hunger, for example, is a basic biological need. You may be only vaguely aware of your hunger when you see a colorful billboard advertising hot cheese-and-pepperoni pizza. Then suddenly you're starved. You take action by stopping at a fast-food restaurant for lunch. Your need is satisfied, but it's still there, waiting for the next stimulus to start the cycle again.[11]

For this paragraph the topic is basic human needs, and the author is writing the paragraph to explain that everyone has basic needs and that these needs often cause certain actions and behaviors.

EXERCISE 6-2

Directions: *Read each of the following paragraphs, and then, in the space provided, write a statement that expresses the main idea of the paragraph.*

1. While love is private, marriage is public. And since dating often leads to marriage, parents are concerned about their sons' and daughters' dating partners. Although college students perceive that their parents have very little or no control over whom they date, parental influence on dating may be both direct and indirect. Parents who have resources (car, money) that their offspring want may make them available in exchange for compliance from their offspring or withhold them for noncompliance. Such withholding of resources is at considerable cost to the parent-child relationship since college students regard it as a threat to their independence. They also resent parental involvement in their dating relationships and regard it as a serious violation of their right to choose their own date and mate.[12]

Main Idea: _____

2. Earth is only one example of a planet. We must study different planets, each with its own complexity, to see how their differences have evolved from the same set of dynamic processes out of different initial conditions that led to their various structures. Earth does not exhibit all these processes. The planets are natural laboratories for observing phenomena beyond the range, in both time and processes, of our terrestrial limitations. To understand our own planet better, we must gain a perspective that can be acquired by a comparative study of other planets. The

global processes on Earth are now beginning to be understood in the light of processes on other planets.[13]

Main Idea: _____

3. One's self-concepts are not fixed. They constantly change with experiences and changes in attitudes, philosophies, and goals. It is a heartwarming experience to observe a young man in the process of upgrading his Ideal Self. Perhaps through a series of unfortunate academic selections he has been forced to conclude that he is a mediocre student at best: his Ideal Self requires only that he graduate from college. Then he encounters a subject area that appeals to him. His interest and grades soar. But at the same time the upgrading of his Ideal Self becomes perceptible. He may start thinking of graduate school. He starts making noises like a scholar instead of a playboy; he wants to alter his Real and Ideal Other. His consumption habits may also change; he may even rashly buy some nonrequired books.[14]

Main Idea: _____

4. Any discussion of sex among the Puritans would not be complete without reference to bundling, also called tarrying. Although not unique to the Puritans, bundling was a courtship custom which involved the would-be groom's sleeping in the girl's bed in her parents' home. But there were rules to restrict sexual contact. Both partners had to be fully clothed, and a wooden bar was placed between them. In addition, the young girl might be encased in a type of long laundry bag up to her armpits, her clothes might be sewn together at strategic points, and her parents might be sleeping in the same room.[15]

Main Idea: _____

5. While parents get the child first and provide the most pervasive influence, teachers represent a major source of influence outside the home. In a study of how and when preschool teachers spoke to the children in their classroom, the researchers observed that the teachers rewarded boys for being aggressive (by showing attention when they were rowdy), rewarded girls for being dependent (by showing attention when they were near), and gave more individual instruction to boys. And all of the fifteen teachers who were being observed were unaware that they were treating the sexes differently.[16]

Main Idea: _____

THE FUNCTION AND PLACEMENT OF THE TOPIC SENTENCE

Have you found it helpful when you make phone calls to make a general statement about the purpose of your call as you begin your conversation? For instance, have you found that in answering a help wanted ad, it is useful to begin by saying, "I'm calling about your ad in . . ." Or, in calling a doctor's office to make an appointment you might say, "I'm calling to make an appointment to see Dr. ———." You may have found that beginning with a general statement such as these helps your listener understand why you are calling and what you want. Also, it allows the listener time to focus his or her attention before you begin to give details of your situation. The general statement also gives the listener a chance to organize him- or herself or to get ready to receive the information.

Writers see a similar need to help a reader understand the purpose and follow the organization of a written message. Readers, like listeners, sometimes need assistance in focusing and organizing their thoughts and in anticipating the development of the message. Writers, therefore, often provide general, organizing statements to state the main idea of the paragraph. The sentence that most clearly states this main idea is called the *topic sentence*. The functions of the topic sentence are to express clearly the idea the paragraph discusses, to focus your attention on that idea, and to provide you with clues about the organization and development of the paragraph.

Depending on its placement within the paragraph, the topic sentence provides the reader with different clues. In this section several of the most common placements of topic sentences and the clues that each offers the reader about paragraph development and organization will be discussed.

Topic Sentence First

The most common location of the topic sentence is first in the paragraph. In this case the author states his main idea and then goes on to explain and develop that idea, as in the following paragraph.

> Communication is essential to any kind of social
> system. Even the apparently solitary male orangutan starts
> the day with a booming cry that tells other orangutans
> where he is. Sounds of this kind are common among the
> primates and many other mammals. Where primates live in
> social groups, communication is much more complicated.
> The animals must judge others' emotions, which are

conveyed by gestures and sounds. Bluffing is very important, and all the apes have biological structures adapted for bluffing. Gorillas, for example, pound their chests. Chimpanzees charge, hoot, and throw objects. In orangutans there are very large sacs connected with the larynx, and these make the territorial noises possible. When an ape and some monkeys are demonstrating aggressively, the hair on the heads and around the shoulders stands up. This has the effect of making the creature look two or three times its normal size, and being subject to a sudden bluff of this kind can be a scary experience.[17]

Notice that the author begins by stating that communication is an important part of any social system. Then, throughout the remainder of the paragraph, he explains the importance of communication by showing how it operates within the social structure of primates. When the topic sentence appears first in the paragraph, it, in effect, announces what the paragraph will be about. It tells you what to expect in the paragraph and provides a framework for the development of the ideas that support the main idea.

In informative writing, in which the writer states and then explains, proves, or describes an idea, you will often find the topic sentence first in the paragraph. In some paragraphs you may find the second sentence expressing the main idea. In this case, the first sentence often functions as an introduction or lead-in to the topic sentence.

Topic Sentence Last

The second most likely place for a topic sentence to appear is last in the paragraph. Most commonly, it is expressed in the very last sentence. However, on occasion you may find that it is expressed in the second-to-last sentence, with the last sentence functioning as a restatement or as a transition to connect the paragraph with what is to follow. When the topic sentence occurs last, you can expect the writer to build a structure of ideas and offer the topic sentence as a concluding statement. Commonly used in argumentative or persuasive writing, this structure uses sentences within the paragraph as building blocks that support the topic sentence. Notice in the following paragraph that the author leads up to the main idea and states it at the end of the paragraph.

We can measure the radioactivity of plants and animals today and compare this with the radioactivity of ancient organic matter. If we extract a small, but precise, quantity of carbon from an ancient wooden ax handle, for example, and find it has one-half as much radioactivity as an equal quantity of carbon extracted from a living tree, then the old wood must have come from a tree that was cut down or made from a log that died 5730 years ago. In this way, we can probe into the past as much as 50,000 years to find out such things as the age of ancient civilizations or the times of the ice ages that covered the earth.[18]

In this paragraph the author begins by explaining that radioactivity of plants and animals can be measured and can be compared with older organic matter. Then he uses an example describing how the radioactivity of an ancient ax head can be measured and how its age can be determined. In the last sentence the author states the main idea: that this procedure can be used to learn about the past.

Topic Sentence in the Middle

If it is neither first nor last, then, of course, the topic sentence will appear somewhere in the middle of the paragraph. In this case, the topic sentence in some way splits the paragraph into two parts: those sentences preceding it and those which follow it. Often, the sentences that precede the topic sentence lead up to or introduce the main idea. At other times, the preceding sentences may function as a transition, connecting the idea to be expressed in the paragraph with ideas in previous paragraphs. The sentences that follow the topic sentence usually explain, describe, or provide further information about the main idea. As you read the following paragraph, try to identify the sentence that expresses the main idea.

Economists have devoted much effort to finding ways of stabilizing the economy. We even have an act of Congress — the Employment Act of 1946 — which states that the federal government has the responsibility to promote maximum employment, production, and purchasing power. Reading these words in the 1970s and 1980s you will certainly be aware that our economists and our government haven't solved the problem of providing jobs and goods at stable prices. You probably know people who have been unemployed for long periods of time — perhaps even to the point of thinking that they will never find jobs again. You've also seen the prices of goods you buy increase faster than the money to pay for them. And you've heard TV newscasters say things like, "This has been one of the auto industry's worst years. Sales of new cars were 2 million less than in 1972."[19]

The paragraph opens with a very general statement about control of the economy. Then the second sentence mentions, as an example, a particular law enacted to improve the economy. In the third sentence the author states the main idea: that the problems of unemployment and stable prices have not been solved. The rest of the paragraph further explains the two problems. You can see that in this paragraph the author introduced the idea by discussing it within the context of our economy, then stated the idea, and finally explained it by illustrating the widespread nature of the problems.

Topic Sentence First and Last

Occasionally you may find a paragraph in which the main idea is stated at the beginning and again at the end. This structure is often used for emphasis or clarification. If a writer wants to emphasize an important idea, he or she may repeat it at the end of the paragraph. Or, a writer who feels an idea needs to be said another way in order to ensure that the reader understands it, may repeat it at the end of the paragraph. In the following paragraph notice that both the first and last sentences state, in different words, the same idea.

> The study of prehistoric humans is, of necessity, the study of their fossil remains. To begin to understand who our ancestors were and what they were like, we must be able to interpret the fragments of them that are coming to the surface in increasing numbers. Given fairly reliable methods to determine their age, we can now turn with more confidence to primate fossils for an answer to the all-important question: How do we tell monkeys, apes, and humans apart? For present-day species this is no problem; all have evolved sufficiently so that they no longer resemble one another. But since they all have a common ancestor, the farther back we go in time, the more similar their fossils begin to look. There finally comes a point when they are indistinguishable. The construction of a primate fossil family tree is essential if we are ever going to discover the line of descent from early hominid to modern human.[20]

In the above paragraph, both the first and last sentence state that the study of fossils enables us to study prehistoric man. The other sentences explain why fossils are important and how they can be used to distinguish stages in the development of man.

EXERCISE 6-3

Directions: *Underline the topic sentence in these paragraphs.*

1. Tobacco has affected both politics and economics in the New World. The Jamestown colony in Virginia could count on success when John Rolfe began cultivating tobacco there in 1612. Even in those days the demand for tobacco was endless — it was grown in the streets of Jamestown. Tobacco extracts large quantities of nitrogen from the soil, as planters in the southern colonies found when their soil was exhausted (the soils of George Washington's Mount Vernon plantation had used up their fertility by the time he died in 1799). The fertile soils of the east depleted, people demanded new lands west of the Appalachian Mountains, and pressure on the western frontier grew. Pressure for the hand labor necessary to tend the tobacco was a prime cause of slavery on southern plantations.[21]

2. The promotional device of offering free samples is generally used for products of relatively low cost — toiletries such as toothpaste and shampoos, for example. Trial offers are used for more expensive items — household appliances such as vacuum cleaners, perhaps, or items such as health-club membership and encyclopedias. Both devices have the advantage of cutting through the "noise level" of competing advertising claims and getting the consumer to personally test the product/service. *They seek to change attitudes by changing behavior* — an interesting reversal of the usual belief that you should change behavior by changing attitudes.[22]

3. Death and dying are sad, depressing subjects to most of us. No matter how prepared we are, or however strongly we may believe in a life after death, the loss of a close friend or relative is painful. The bereaved — those who have lost a loved one to death — are often faced with serious problems of adjustment, including coping with loneliness, sorrow, and the simple tasks of day-to-day living. There is a funeral, a will to be read and executed, expressions of sympathy to be accepted and responded to. These institutionalized aspects of the mourning period may help, as Freud once suggested, to spread the grief over several days. But soon they are over, and then comes the crying, the depression, the difficulty in sleeping, concentrating, and remembering, the lack of appetite for food and for life — the most common symptoms in a study of over 100 people who had lost a husband or wife.[23]

4. We have grown up in a society which stresses personal

freedom and alternative ways of doing things. An examination of these beliefs, however, may be revealing. Freedom is referred to as a quality or fact pertaining to individuals, who may make choices about certain ways of behaving in a situation. All cultures, to some degree, offer such behavioral alternatives in some areas. Ironically, we as individuals may choose only from a set of alternatives allowed by the culture. I may choose to be a Catholic or a Protestant. I may not, as an American, choose to be a cannibal, or to ritually kill sheep on my suburban front lawn. In fact, choices are *culturally constrained,* or defined, for us.[24]

5. But in spite of the richness of the combinations of gestures and sounds, all the nonhuman systems of communication are extremely limited. Other animals cannot communicate about the past or the future. Most communication (except for warning cries and territorial noises) is primarily gestural, and the animals must be able to see each other in order for communication to take place. An even greater limitation is that communication is confined almost entirely to emotions. All the primates can communicate fear, but only humans can say what they are afraid of. Some monkeys have sounds indicating danger from above (action, drop to lower branch) or from below (action, climb up), but they cannot indicate the nature of the danger.[25]

Paragraphs Without a Topic Sentence

Although most paragraphs do have a topic sentence, occasionally you will encounter a paragraph in which there is no one sentence that clearly expresses the main idea. This structure is used most commonly in descriptive writing and in narrative writing. In these paragraphs the reader must form his or her own statement or impression of the main idea. Although the paragraph contains numerous clues, the reader must piece together the information to form a generalized statement.

Here is a paragraph that does not contain a topic sentence:

For some people, carrying on the family name is important. Others want a child for its love or to prevent loneliness in old age. Some couples are curious about the result of their mixture of genes. Many of us have children because we want to give them opportunities that we never had or to treat them as we wish we had been treated: this may amount to living vicariously through our children. Some individuals have a child in order to hold their marriage together: this is unwise because it usually adds strain to an already failing relationship, and the child is often affected most.[26]

This paragraph discusses reasons why people have children. The first sentence offers one reason (carrying on the family name), and the second presents another (love or the prevention of loneliness), and so forth. Each sentence is concerned with a different reason for having children. You can see, then, that this paragraph lacks a topic sentence that explains what the paragraph is about. The main idea of this paragraph, however, is quite clear: "There are numerous reasons why people have children."

Here is another example:

Five and one-tenth million families and 5 million unrelated individuals make up a total of 25.5 million persons who are officially termed poor. They make up 13 percent of the population. As might be expected, certain categories of people are highly represented among the poor. These are women, children, minorities, the old, rural-farm workers, and the unemployed. People who fall into more than one of these categories are most likely to belong to the poor segment of the population: a minority child in a female-headed family or an aging female with no relatives is more likely to be poor than a white child in a male-headed family or a young female with family. Percentage-wise, 68 percent of the poor are children, school-age youths, and the elderly. Unrelated women and women family heads represent 13 percent of the poor. The remaining 19 percent consists of unemployed or underemployed males, as well as of a few males of working age who simply earn very little.[27]

In this paragraph each sentence presents a fact about persons classified as poor. The first two sentences explain how many people are considered poor. The next two sentences describe the types or categories that contain large numbers of poor people. The rest of the paragraph offers examples and lists percentages about types of persons who are considered poor. Again, there is no sentence that functions as a topic sentence, and it is left to the reader to draw together the facts presented. Taken together, the facts presented seem to suggest that there are large numbers of persons who are classified as poor and that there are various categories of people that contain the largest percentage of the poor. Overall, it seems as if the writer was intending to give the reader a general picture of the type of person who might be classified as poor.

From these examples you can see that in some paragraphs the topic sentence is not necessary and the reader can easily "add up" the facts and arrive at his or her own statement of the main idea. If you should encounter a paragraph in which the main idea is unstated and not immediately evident, first identify the topic, then ask yourself this question: "What does the writer want me to know about the topic?" In most cases, your answer will be a statement of the writer's main idea.

Once you have identified the main idea in a paragraph in which it is unstated, it may be useful to make a marginal note that summarizes the main idea of that paragraph. Then, when you are reviewing the material, it will not be necessary to reread the entire paragraph.

EXERCISE 6-4

Directions: *Read each of the following paragraphs, none of which has a topic sentence. For each, write your own statement of the main idea of the paragraph.*

1. Some physical anthropologists specialize in unearthing the fossil remains of our early ancestors. These *human paleon-tologists* dig in the earth for skeletons which they then reconstruct. They may also work with physicists and geologists, using various chemicals and radioactive substances, to determine the ages of the specimens removed from the earth. Other physical anthropologists are more closely related to biochemists in that they do the bulk of their work in laboratories, analyzing substances found in the bodies of primates, including humans. These scientists use microscopes and other laboratory equipment to study blood, urine, and other biochemicals. Their aim is to find variations in these substances —and the causes of the variations — among different human and nonhuman primates.[28]

Main Idea: _____

2. Today in America, $2 out of every $5 spent for food is spent eating away from home. In 1954 it was nearer $1 out of every $10. Based on these facts it is not difficult to see the tremendous opportunity that has existed in the foodservice industry during the past 20 years. Yet, from my vantage point as a keen observer of industry trends and events, I've seen hundreds of people and thousands of restaurants go broke. At the same time, I am personally aware of over 100 different people who have become millionaires in their endeavors in the foodservice field.[29]

Main Idea: _____

3. Overweight children are frequently rejected by their peer group because they do not do well in sports and because they

may be ungainly. A teen-age girl who is overweight, unless she has an unusual personality, may be ostracized by her peers. She is not asked to dance at parties and may not have dates. The results can be very serious, for these social activities are a normal part of growing up. Both men and women may become the butt of jokes by their friends because of their obese condition. Although they may appear to take it good naturedly, the sting remains.[30]

Main Idea: _____

4. Traffic is directed by color. Pilot instrument panels, landing strips, road and water crossings are regulated by many colored lights and signs. Factories use colors to distinguish between thoroughfares and work areas. Danger zones are painted in special colors. Lubrication points and removable parts are accentuated by color. Pipes for transporting water, steam, oil, chemicals, and compressed air, are designated by different colors. Electrical wires and resistances are color coded.[31]

Main Idea: _____

5. There can be no doubt that the reaction sought by the after-dinner speaker at a social banquet differs materially from that sought by a legislator urging the adoption of a bill, or that both of these desired responses differ from the response a college professor seeks when he addresses a class. The first speaker wants his audience to enjoy themselves; the second wants them to act, to vote "aye"; the third wants them to understand.[32]

Main Idea: _____

DEVELOPING EXPECTATIONS AS YOU READ

To be an effective reader you must become mentally active as you read. Rather than just taking in facts and ideas as you encounter them, you should be reacting to and thinking about what you are reading. In fact there are certain mental activities that should occur almost automatically as you read. For instance, you should be thinking about what you have just read, following the author's pattern of thought, and trying to relate the ideas. Also, as you read a paragraph you should be developing expectations about how the writer will develop his or her ideas, and what will come next in the paragraph. In other words, you should not only keep up with the writer, you should try to stay one jump ahead.

At the beginning of a conversation you can often predict in what direction the conversation is headed. If a friend starts a conversation with "I can't decide whether I can afford to quit my part-time job at Sears," you can guess what you will hear next. Your friend will discuss the pros and cons of quitting the job as it relates to his financial situation.

Similarly, as you begin to read a paragraph, often you will find sufficient clues to enable you to know what to expect throughout. Often, the topic sentence, especially if it appears first in the paragraph, will suggest how the paragraph will be developed. Suppose a paragraph were to begin with the following topic sentence:

> The unemployment rate in the past several years has increased due to a variety of economic factors.

What do you expect the rest of the paragraph to include? It will probably be about the various economic factors that cause unemployment. Now, look at this topic sentence:

> Minorities differ in racial or cultural visibility, in the amount of discrimination they suffer, in the character of their adjustment, both as individuals and as groups, and in the length of time they survive as identifiable populations or individuals.

This sentence indicates that the paragraph will contain a discussion of four ways that minority groups differ. Also, this topic sentence suggests the order in which these differences will be discussed. The factor mentioned first in the sentence (visibility) will be discussed first, the second idea mentioned will appear next, and so forth.

EXERCISE 6-5

Directions: *Assume that each of the following statements is the topic sentence of a paragraph. Read each sentence, then decide what you would expect a paragraph to include if it began with that sentence. Summarize your expectations in the space provided after each sentence. In some cases, there may be more than one correct set of expectations.*

1. Conventional musical instruments can be grouped into three classes.

    _____

    _____

2. The distinction between storage and retrieval has important implications for memory researchers.

_____

_____

3. When Charles Darwin published his theories of evolution, people objected on scientific and religious grounds.

_____

_____

4. Narcotics such as opium, morphine, and heroin are derived from different sources and vary in strength and after effects.

_____

_____

5. Not all factors that contribute to intelligence are measurable.

_____

_____

TYPES OF SUPPORTING DETAILS

In conversation there are a number of ways that you can explain an idea. If you are trying to explain to someone that you think dogs make better pets than cats, you could develop your idea by giving examples of the behaviors of particular dogs and cats. You could also explain by giving basic reasons why you hold that opinion, or you could present facts about dogs and cats that support your position. As in conversation, there are many ways a writer can explain an idea. In a paragraph a writer includes details that explain, support, or provide further information about the main idea.

Once you have identified the topic sentence, you should expect the rest of the paragraph to contain supporting information. However, not all details are equally important. For example, in the following paragraph the underlined ideas provide very important information about the main idea. As you read the paragraph notice how these ideas directly contribute to the overall meaning.

There are potential disadvantages to group therapy. <u>Many psychologists feel that the interactions in group situations are too superficial to be of much benefit.</u> A patient with deep-seated conflicts may be better treated by a psychotherapist in individual therapy; the therapist can exert consistent pressure, refusing to let the patient avoid the crucial issues, and she or he can control the therapeutic environment more effectively. <u>Another criticism of groups is that they are too powerful.</u> If the group starts to focus on one individual's defense mechanisms — which are used for a reason, remember — that individual might break down. If no trained therapist is present — which is often the case in encounter groups — the result can be disastrous.[33]

Each of the underlined details states one of the disadvantages of group therapy. Now look back at the details that were not. Can you see that they are of lesser importance in relation to the main idea? In a sense you can think of these as details that further explain details. For example, the third sentence further explains the disadvantage described in the second sentence. Also, the sentences that follow the second group of sentences explain what may happen as a result of a group becoming too powerful.

To find the most important or "key" supporting details, ask yourself this question: "Which statements directly prove or explain the main idea?" Your answer will lead you to the important details in the paragraph. Now apply this question to the following paragraph. As you read it, first identify the main idea, then try to locate those details that *directly* explain this idea.

We have seen that inequality has been a problem in human societies for a long time. Poverty has been explained several ways. The *personal view* blames the poor individuals for their poverty. Proponents of this view believe, in effect, that the poor are poor because they are morally or personally defective — lazy, apathetic, good for nothing. The *cultural view* also blames the poor individual for his poverty, but not directly. Rather, it blames the socialization process, which indoctrinates the children of the poor into a way of life that perpetuates their condition. In other words, the poor learn behavior patterns that prevent their upward mobility, patterns that are passed from generation to generation, in a vicious circle. Finally, the *economic view* is somewhat noncommittal: it maintains that the poor are poor because they have little or no money. They have little money because they are unemployed, underemployed, or kept in low-paying jobs. Consequently, they have little purchasing power and are underconsumers. The poor themselves are not at fault; our economic structure is.[34]

In this paragraph you should have identified the three views of poverty as key supporting details. Other sentences in the paragraph further explain each view and can be considered as less important.

EXERCISE 6-6

Directions: *Identify the main idea of each of the following paragraphs. Then underline the key supporting details in each. Underline only those details that directly explain or support the main idea.*

1. What is the study of politics? One thing you will notice about political science is that it's a lot like other social sciences such as history, economics, sociology, and psychology. Each studies aspects of the interactions among people. In any large group of people many social relations are going on. Each of these disciplines may look at the same group and ask different questions about the relationships going on there. This division of labor is partly traditional and partly a way of separating complicated human relations into more easily understood parts. Political science fits in by studying one type of interaction between people — that involving power and authority. An example may make the approaches of the other disciplines clearer and distinguish them from political science.[35]

2. The president is the symbolic head of *state* as well as the head of *government*. (In England the two positions are separate: the queen is head of state, a visible symbol of the nation, and the prime minister is head of government, exercising the real power.) As chief of state, the president has many ceremonial functions, ranging from declaring National Codfish Week to greeting foreign dignitaries. Because of this role, many people see the president as a symbol of the nation, somehow more than human, a fact that also gives him a political advantage. The difficulty in separating his ceremonial from his political actions is evident when, after President Reagan makes television broadcasts, the Democrats ask for equal time. Is he speaking in his role as a non-political chief of state, or as the head of the Republican party?[36]

3. The skin itself is the largest organ of the body, is composed of epithelial and connective tissue components, and forms a pliable protective covering over the external body surface. It accounts for

about 7 percent of the body weight and receives about 30 percent of the left ventricular output of blood. The term protective, as used here, includes not only resistance to bacterial invasion or attack from the outside, but also protection against large changes in the internal environment. Control of body temperature, prevention of excessive water loss, and prevention of excessive loss of organic and inorganic materials are necessary to the maintenance of internal homeostasis and continued normal activity of individual cells. In addition, the skin acts as an important area of storage, receives a variety of stimuli, and synthesizes several important substances used in the overall body economy.[37]

4. There are basically two types of computers — analog computers and digital computers. Analog computers operate on the principle of a parallel or analog between numbers and physical quantities. For example, a slide rule is an analog device with length representing numbers. Modern analog computers use electronic circuitry to represent physical processes with changes in electric current representing the behavior of the system being studied. Digital computers, on the other hand, are essentially based on counting operations. Most modern computers are digital computers, and it is usually digital computers which are referred to when the word "computer" is used. For this reason, the explanations in the chapters to follow apply only to digital computers.[38]

5. No part of the Earth's surface is exempt from earthquakes, but since the start of systematic recording many large areas have had only occasional shocks of small or moderate intensity. By contrast, several large tracts are subject to frequent shocks, both strong and weak, and are known as seismic belts. The most prominent, aptly called the Circum-Pacific belt, follows the western highlands of South and North America from Cape Horn to Alaska, crosses to Asia, extends southward along the eastern coast and related island arcs, and loops far to the southeast and south beyond New Zealand. Next in prominence is the broad east-west zone extending through the high mountains of southern Asia and the Mediterranean region to Gibraltar. A third long belt follows the Mid-Atlantic Ridge from Arctic to Antarctic waters, and a fourth runs along the Mid-Indian Ridge to unite with a belt in eastern Africa. Smaller seismic areas include island groups in the Pacific and Atlantic.[39]

There are many types of details that a writer can use to explain or support a main idea. As you read it, you should notice the type of details a writer uses as well as be able to identify which details are most important. As you will see later in chapters on evaluating and interpreting, the manner in which a writer explains and supports an idea may influence how readily you will accept or agree with an idea. Among the most common types of supporting details are illustrations and examples, facts or statistics, reasons, and descriptions. Each will be discussed briefly.

Illustration-Example

One way you will find ideas explained is through the use of illustrations or examples. Usually, a writer uses examples to make a concept, problem, or process understandable by showing its application in a situation or group of situations. In the following paragraph, numerous examples are provided that explain how various cultures carry labels or stereotypes.

> All of us live within a *culture,* one that is qualified by a label like "middle-class American," "Roman," or "Aztec" — a label that conjures up certain objects or behavior patterns typical of this particular culture. For instance, we associate hamburgers with middle-class American culture, and skin canoes with Eskimos. Romans are thought to have spent their time conquering the world, Sioux Indians wandering over the Great Plains. But such stereotypes are often crude, inaccurate generalizations. Though we think of American Indians as legendary, feathered braves, only a few Indian groups ever wore such head-dresses. In fact, the label "American Indian" includes an incredibly diverse set of peoples, ranging from family size hunter-gatherer bands to large, complex civilizations.[40]

In this paragraph the author uses examples from specific cultures — Eskimo, Roman, and American Indian — to illustrate that labels exist. As you read illustrations and examples, try to see the relationship between the example and the concept or idea it illustrates.

Facts and Statistics

Another way a writer supports an idea is by including facts and/or statistics that further explain the main idea. Notice how, in the following paragraph, the main idea expressed in the first sentence is explained by the use of statistics.

132

Compared with females, males have a great excess of crimes in all nations, all communities within nations, all age groups, all periods of history for which we have statistics, and all types of crime except those related to the female sex, such as abortion. In the United States, males are arrested approximately ten times as frequently as females, and they are committed to prisons and reformatories approximately twenty times as frequently as females. Of the cases coming before juvenile courts, about 85 per cent are boys. The official statistics are probably biased in favor of females, but even if correction could be made for the statistical bias, the criminal sex ratio probably would be well over 600 or 700.[41]

These authors used percentages and ratios to indicate that the crime rate is higher among males than females. When reading paragraphs developed by the use of facts and statistics, you can expect that these details will answer questions such as what, when, where, or how about the main idea.

Reasons

Certain types of main ideas are most easily explained by giving reasons. Especially in argumentative and persuasive writing, you will find that a writer supports an opinion, belief, or action by discussing *why* the thought or action is appropriate. In the following paragraph the writer provides reasons for the growth of public colleges and universities.

The growth in American higher education is taking place largely in the public colleges and universities. These colleges are usually more responsive than private colleges to state and local demands, and provide training for the increasingly numerous occupations that require advanced skills. They are relatively inexpensive, often easy to enter, and conveniently located to serve large numbers of students. The rapid expansion of college attendance among job-oriented young people of lower social origins is chiefly in these service-minded institutions.[42]

You can see that the writer offers numerous reasons for the growth trend, including response to local demands, cost, ease of entrance, location, and so forth.

Description

If the purpose of a paragraph is to help the reader understand or visualize the appearance, structure, organization, or composition of an object, then description is often used as a means of paragraph development. Descriptive details are facts that are intended to help you to visualize the person, object, or event being described. The following paragraph contains descriptive detail to enable you to create a visual image of a person.

> A newly married pair had boarded this coach at San Antonio. The man's face was reddened from many days in the wind and sun, and a direct result of his new black clothes was that his brick-colored hands were constantly performing in a most conscious fashion. From time to time he looked down respectfully at his attire. He sat with a hand on each knee, like a man waiting in a barber's shop. The glances he devoted to other passengers were furtive and shy.[43]

Notice how each detail, by itself, does not contribute much to your understanding of the bridegroom, but when all details are "added together" you are able to visualize him. Small details, such as sitting "with a hand on each knee," contribute to your overall impression and help you realize that the author is trying to suggest that the man was awkward and uncomfortable. In reading descriptive detail, you can see that you need to pay close attention to each detail as you try to form a visual impression of what is being described.

EXERCISE 6-7

Directions: *Read each of the following paragraphs and identify the type of supporting details the author provides to explain the main idea.*

> 1. The concept of insurance (sometimes called *assurance*) goes back to ancient times. Babylonian traders "insured" their caravans against loss. They financed them with loans that had to be repaid only if the caravans arrived safely. The rate of interest on the loans depended on the risk involved in the caravan journey. The Greeks applied a similar practice to their sea-borne trade. Romans developed burial clubs to provide funeral funds for members. Later, the clubs provided benefits to survivors of the deceased — the rudimentary beginnings of life insurance.[44]

Type of Details: _____

2. It is much easier to sell a person who possesses complete authority and is autonomous than to sell one having little authority. The bachelor responsible to no one buys whatever he wants without consulting anyone. The family man must usually consider his family and often must consult his wife, who frequently has a veto power over purchases, or at least is able to influence the buying decision markedly. The business executive who owns his own company and is in charge of operations will often buy things with little hesitation, in contrast to the junior executive not possessing such autonomy, who will usually be worried about what his superiors will think about a purchase. Anything new and startling he may resist tenaciously. The manufacturer of a new type of dictating system is wasting time attempting to sell middle-management executives; he must go directly to the top executives, because lower-echelon personnel usually are afraid to make decisions of such magnitude.[45]

Type of Details: _____

3. In the fall the war was always there, but we did not go to it anymore. It was cold in the fall in Milan and the dark came very early. Then the electric lights came on, and it was pleasant along the streets looking in the windows. There was much game hanging outside the shops, and the snow powdered in the fur of the foxes and the wind blew their tails. The deer hung stiff and heavy and empty, and small birds blew in the wind and the wind turned their feathers. It was a cold fall and the wind came down from the mountains.[46]

Type of Details: _____

4. The total number of Americans living in poverty has dropped from 39.5 million in 1959 to 25.0 million in 1976, a decrease from 22.4 percent to 11.8 percent. The poverty line went from $2,973 to $5,815, due to inflation. At the same time, however, the median income for all families rose from $5,417 to $14,958. In other words, in 1959 the poverty level was 55 percent of the median income, while by 1976 the government had reduced the figure to only 39 percent of median income. By making the poverty level proportionately lower, the government can theoretically eliminate as much poverty as it wants to. But those living with inadequate income levels are no better off just because government statistics say so.[47]

Type of Details: _____

5. In small societies, theft is uncommon, although it occasionally occurs. Under normal conditions in such societies, theft is generally unprofitable. Items of personal property are well-known to group members, making it impossible for a thief to keep and use what he might steal. Foods, which can be consumed quickly, are about the only items that can be stolen successfully. In preliterate societies, the actual basic needs of members are frequently provided for by informal charity or reciprocal giving. Thus, there is little necessity for theft which is made hazardous by the fact that people are under the observation of others most of the time in these societies.[48]

Type of Details: _____

DIRECTIONAL WORDS AND PHRASES

In listening to someone speak, you receive many clues about what is important, how the speaker feels about what he or she is saying, and what is to follow. The speaker's voice, gestures, facial expression, and body movements all are useful in following a speaker's train of thought. In reading a written message, none of these clues is available; all you have to work with are the printed words on the page. Recognizing that written language provides very few clues, writers deliberately include words and phrases to help the reader understand the message and to follow the train of thought. These words and phrases that provide clues about either the organization or content of a paragraph are called *directional words* because they provide clues about the direction or development of thought in the paragraph. You can think of directional words as signals or clues that a writer provides the reader. You might also think of them as words that connect ideas and lead from one idea to another. In the following paragraph the words "first" and "next" function as directional words.

Like the biological processes, the psychological processes make behavior possible. They are the ways we take in information, store it, and use it. First we will look at perception: how we become aware of our environment and how we construct internal representations of it. (Seeing is believing, isn't it? Or is it?) Next, the study of learning and memory deals with how we store information and how and when it comes out again in behavior. You will learn why it is hard to poison a rat, and how to improve your memory.[49]

Directional words or phrases perform four very important functions in a paragraph. They may mark important information, indicate a change or a continuation of thought, or they may show the relationship between ideas within a paragraph. Each of these functions will be discussed and some of the more common directional words and phrases of each type will be listed.

Markers for Important Information

Directional words are often used to mark or emphasize important information. In the paragraph below notice that the words "first" and "then" lead you directly to the two most important ideas in the paragraph.

> When most people think about memory, they consider only the way we retain facts. If you can remember many facts for a long time, then your memory is good; if not, it isn't. But memory is much more than just a mental warehouse cluttered with the experiences of living. First, it involves recognizing what we are experiencing; is it a horse or a deer, the letter A or the letter X, the sound of a voice or the sound of something else? This is a process that psychologists call *encoding*. Then there is the task of *storing* the information so we can get to it when we want it. This step is crucial since without adequate storage, our memory would be almost totally ineffective. Think of a library where a great many books are received, and then hurled over the librarian's shoulder onto an ever increasing mountain of items. When someone asks for a particular book, there would be no way to know if the library owned it unless you sifted through the pile, book by book, until you found what you were looking for or exhausted the search — or yourself. The problem is not that the book is not in the library; it may well be there. The problem is that there is no order to the way things are stored.[50]

In this paragraph the words "first" and "then" helped you to locate quickly the two steps in memory: encoding and storing information. Markers emphasize the facts and ideas that the writer feels are important and help you to locate them quickly.

DIRECTIONAL WORDS USED AS MARKERS

first	first
second	next
third	also
primarily	one
secondarily	another
	then

Change in Thought

When a writer moves from one idea to another, he or she often indicates this change by a directional word or phrase. In the following paragraph the word "however" suggests that the writer will switch to a discussion of an opposite or contrary idea.

> The body's preparation for activities like fighting or fleeing results in a number of physiological changes that indicate emotion. Many of these changes are internal happenings, providing information to no one but ourselves. Some, however, leak information to the outside world, enabling others to guess our emotional state more accurately than they would from our face and body configurations and the situation. The blush of embarrassment is such a case. Other people can also observe our hand tremors and irregular breathing, a shaky voice, or a nervous tic.[51]

The first part of this paragraph described internal events, and the word "however" was included to signal that the writer was going to change to a different idea — external or observable signs. You can see that directional words of this type announce that a new idea is to follow in the paragraph. They help you to get ready for this new direction of thought.

DIRECTIONAL WORDS INDICATING CHANGE IN THOUGHT

however	although
on the contrary	nevertheless
on the other hand	in contrast

Continuation of Thought

Directional words may also be used to indicate a continuation of thought. When used in this way, they suggest that the writer will continue to develop or further explain the same thought. In the following paragraph notice how the words "similarly" and "for example" connect ideas and indicate that the second idea is a continuation or further expansion of the first.

> All aspects of one's self-concepts are not harmonious with one another. The man who visualizes himself as an excellent golfer may have difficulty reconciling this concept with another that he is a good husband and spends a considerable amount of time with his family. Similarly, a

businessman may believe himself to be an exceedingly
shrewd person, able to extract the largest amount of profit
out of a given level of sales, and at the same time he may
consider himself a good man for whom to work. There are
many areas of business operation where these two concepts
would come into opposition. His union, <u>for example,</u> might
propose a substantial pension plan that he feels would
unduly lower profits but definitely provides his employees
with an attractive retirement system.[52]

DIRECTIONAL WORDS INDICATING CONTINUATION

also	for example
similarly	for instance
furthermore	to illustrate
in addition	moreover

Relationship Between Ideas

Directional words often are used to clarify the relationships between ideas. They commonly indicate cause-effect relationships, spatial
relationships, chronological relationships, or similarity or difference.
There are many directional words that fall into this category. However,
many of these directional words not only suggest relationships between
ideas; they also indicate the pattern of organization used throughout
the paragraph. Since Chapter 7 is concerned entirely with recognition
of these patterns, words that correspond to each pattern will be discussed there.

EXERCISE 6-8

Directions: *Read each of the following paragraphs and underline each
directional word. Then, in the space provided, indicate its type.*

1. The usual sequence by which memory is studied
experimentally has already been implied. First, the subject is
presented with a task to be learned, and usually some measure is
made of how much learning has taken place. Second, during
some length of time the subject is asked to engage in specified
types of activity (perhaps additional learning or perhaps some
time-filling task, like doing arithmetic problems, that simply
limits any thinking about the original task). Finally, the subject is
tested on what he or she is able to remember from the original
task, and this score is compared with the score that was obtained

at the end of the learning session. To measure the amount remembered, the investigator generally uses *recall* or *recognition*.[53]

Type: _____

2. The government may also intervene more directly in disputes among its citizens. For example, citizens of a town near a river may not be able to swim there because a paper mill dumps sewage into it. The citizens of the town or the owners of the mill may ask the government to settle the dispute. The appropriate part of the government may respond by passing a law or making a court ruling that decides whether the town or the paper mill will get the use of the river (the "valued thing").[54]

Type: _____

3. Nothing is quite so important in establishing personal contact with an audience as the simple device of looking at individuals directly. For this reason, reading a speech or even glancing at notes too frequently reduces this feeling of interpersonal communication and almost invariably detracts from a speaker's effectiveness. Obviously, it is impossible to look at each member of the audience at the same time. Therefore, do as you would in an informal conversation: pick out one person and talk directly to him for a few seconds, looking him in the eye as you do so; then shift to someone else. Be careful, moreover, to pick out people in various parts of the audience and to stay with each one long enough to avoid the appearance of simply wagging your head.[55]

Type: _____

4. Grief shared is grief reduced; disclosure relieves tension. When you feel upset or angry and talk to someone, or otherwise actively express your feelings, you feel better. Releasing strong emotions through crying also has healing effects. When some depressed persons express their feelings, they feel less depressed. And experiments have shown that anger can be reduced by talking it out. Furthermore, when you get things out in the open, you yourself can often see them more clearly and objectively. Additionally, those you talk with may be able to help you by contributing information or pointing out possibilities you have overlooked.[56]

Type: _____

5. Although the term "data processing" is of relatively recent origin, this does not mean that the activity itself is new. On the contrary, there is evidence that the need to process data originated as far back as the beginning of recorded history when man's activities first exceeded his ability to remember the details of his actions. Throughout history commercial and governmental activities have created the need for record keeping of one sort or another.[57]

Type: _____

APPLYING WHAT YOU HAVE LEARNED

Directions: *Choose one of the selections at the end of the chapter. Read the selection and answer the multiple choice questions. Then go back to the selection and complete the following steps for* each paragraph.

1. Circle the topic.
2. Place brackets around the topic sentence. (If the main idea is unstated, write a brief statement of the main idea in the margin.)
3. Underline the most important details that support the main idea.
4. Mark any directional words with an X in the nearest margin.

READING SELECTION 7
WHO'S AFRAID OF MATH, AND WHY?

Sheila Tobias

The first thing people remember about failing at math is that it felt like sudden death. Whether the incident occurred while learning "word problems" in sixth grade, coping with equations in high school, or first confronting calculus and statistics in college, failure came suddenly and in a very frightening way. An idea or a new operation was not just difficult, it was impossible! And, instead of asking questions or taking the lesson slowly, most people remember having had the feeling that they would never go any further in mathematics. If we assume that the curriculum was reasonable, and that the new idea was but the next in a series of learnable concepts, the feeling of utter defeat was simply not rational; yet "math anxious" college students and adults have revealed that no matter how much the teacher reassured them, they could not overcome that feeling.

A common myth about the nature of mathematical ability holds that one either has or does not have a mathematical mind. Mathematical imagination and an intuitive grasp of mathematical principles may well be needed to do advanced research, but why should people who can do college-level work in other subjects not be able to do college-level math as well? Rates of learning may vary. Competency under time pressure may differ. Certainly low self-esteem will get in the way. But where is the evidence that a student needs a "mathematical mind" in order to succeed at learning math?

Consider the effects of this mythology. Since only a few people are supposed to have this mathematical mind, part of what makes us so passive in the face of our difficulties in learning mathematics is that we suspect all the while we may not be one of "them," and we spend our time waiting to find out when our nonmathematical minds will be exposed. Since our limit will eventually be reached, we see no point in being methodical or in attending to detail. We are grateful when we survive

fractions, word problems, or geometry. If that certain moment of failure hasn't struck yet, it is only temporarily postponed.

Parents, especially parents of girls, often expect their children to be nonmathematical. Parents are either poor at math and had their own sudden-death experiences, or, if math came easily for them, they do not know how it feels to be slow. In either case, they unwittingly foster the idea that a mathematical mind is something one either has or does not have.

MATHEMATICS AND SEX

Although fear of math is not a purely female phenomenon, girls tend to drop out of math sooner than boys, and adult women experience an aversion to math and math-related activities that is akin to anxiety. A 1972 survey of the amount of high school mathematics taken by incoming freshmen at Berkeley revealed that while 57 percent of the boys had taken four years of high school math, only 8 percent of the girls had had the same amount of preparation. Without four years of high school math, students at Berkeley, and at most other colleges and universities, are ineligible for the calculus sequence, unlikely to attempt chemistry or physics, and inadequately prepared for statistics and economics.

Unable to elect these entry-level courses, the remaining 92 percent of the girls will be limited, presumably, to the career choices that are considered feminine: the humanities, guidance and counseling, elementary school teaching, foreign languages, and the fine arts.

Boys and girls may be born alike with respect to math, but certain sex differences in performance emerge early according to several respected studies, and these differences remain through adulthood. They are:

1. Girls compute better than boys (elementary school and on).

2. Boys solve word problems better than girls (from age thirteen on).
3. Boys take more math than girls (from age sixteen on).
4. Girls learn to hate math sooner and possibly for different reasons.

Why the differences in performance? One reason is the amount of math learned and used at play. Another may be the difference in male-female maturation. If girls do better than boys at all elementary school tasks, then they may compute better for no other reason than that arithmetic is part of the elementary school curriculum. As boys and girls grow older, girls become, under pressure, academically less competitive. Thus, the falling off of girls' math performance between ages ten and fifteen may be because:

1. Math gets harder in each successive year and requires more work and commitment.
2. Both boys and girls are pressured, beginning at age ten, not to excel in areas designated by society to be outside their sex-role domains.
3. Thus girls have a good excuse to avoid the painful struggle with math; boys don't.

Such a model may explain girls' lower achievement in math overall, but why should girls even younger than ten have difficulty in problem-solving? In her review of the research on sex differences, psychologist Eleanor Maccoby noted that girls are generally more conforming, more suggestible, and more dependent upon the opinion of others than boys (all learned, not innate, behaviors). Being so, they may not be as willing to take risks or to think for themselves, two behaviors that are necessary in solving problems. Indeed, in one test of third-graders, girls were found to be not nearly as willing to estimate, to make judgments about "possible right answers," or to work with systems they had never seen before. Their very success at doing what is expected of them up to that time seems to get in the way of their doing something new.

If readiness to do word problems, to take one example, is as much a function of readiness to take risks as it is of "reasoning ability," then mathematics performance certainly requires more than memory, computation, and reasoning. The differences in math performance between boys and girls — no matter how consistently those differences show up — cannot be attributed simply to differences in innate ability.

Still, if one were to ask the victims themselves, they would probably disagree: they would say their problems with math have to do with the way they are "wired." They feel they are somehow missing something — one ability or several — that other people have. Although women want to believe they are not mentally inferior to men, many fear that, where math is concerned, they really are. Thus, we have to consider seriously whether mathematical ability has a biological basis, not only because a number of researchers believe this to be so, but because a number of victims agree with them.

COMPREHENSION TEST 7

Directions: *Circle the letter of the best answer.*

1. The differences in boys' and girls' math performance are probably not due to
   a) differences in natural talents
   b) girls' having learned to not think independently
   c) differences in learning rates
   d) boys' having learned to take risks

2. People who have problems with math believe that
   a) if they keep working at it, they will succeed
   b) it is the fault of their teachers
   c) they will improve as they get older and more mature
   d) they lack natural talent to learn it

3. As boys and girls continue through school
   a) boys become more intelligent
   b) girls take more math courses
   c) girls become less competitive
   d) they both learn to hate math around the same time

4. Parents of girls often expect their daughters to
   a) do well in math
   b) be nonmathematical
   c) do well in all subjects except math
   d) be able to perform simple arithmetic

5. Most women enter college
   a) with a strong math background
   b) without the right academic advisement
   c) with sufficient math background
   d) without appropriate math preparation for certain majors

6. As it is used here the term "innate" behavior is a behavior that is
   a) unusual
   b) inborn
   c) expected
   d) learned

7. Girls perform better than boys in
   a) arithmetic
   b) algebra
   c) word problems
   d) calculus

8. A career that does not require a great deal of math ability would be
   a) economics
   b) research chemistry

   c) commercial art
   d) medicine

9. The reader can conclude from the selection that
   a) boys are more willing to take risks than girls
   b) girls are more willing to take risks than boys
   c) women with careers in the sciences take more risks than men
   d) men with careers in the humanities take fewer risks than women scientists

10. The content of this passage could best be described as
    a) critical
    b) descriptive
    c) persuasive
    d) humorous

Selection 7:	1095 words
Finishing Time: __HR.__ __MIN.__ __SEC.__	
Starting Time: __HR.__ __MIN.__ __SEC.__	
Reading Time: __MIN.__ __SEC.__	
WPM Score: _____	
Comprehension Score: _____ %	
Reading Efficiency Score: _____	

144

READING SELECTION 8
CHUCK BERRY:
FOLK POET OF THE FIFTIES

Carl Belz

Few artists in the history of rock have been able to produce high-quality records over a long period of time. The majority have been "one-shots" who disappear after their first or second hit record. There are notable exceptions: Fats Domino and Chuck Berry in the 1950's; or the Beach Boys, the Beatles, and the Rolling Stones in the 1960's. All of these artists produced music of a high quality for a relatively long period. Others — Elvis Presley, for instance, or the Supremes — have remained popular for an extended period, although the quality of their music has diminished.

Chuck Berry has not at the time of writing produced a top-selling record since "It Goes To Show You Never Can Tell," which appeared in the spring of 1964. Before that, however, he produced a string of hits which spanned almost a decade. Many of these — "School Day," "Sweet Little Sixteen," "Rock and Roll Music," "Johnny B. Goode," "Carol," and "Almost Grown," among others — originated in the years between 1957 and 1963. All of them, including the earlier "Maybellene," "Too Much Monkey Business" and "Roll Over Beethoven," are as powerful and immediate today as they were when they first appeared. But an interesting feature of these records is that they do not reflect stylistic change. Chuck Berry's style in 1964 was essentially the same as it was in 1955 and, from the evidence of his recent personal appearances, it is exactly the same today. Few artists have so consistently resisted the self-consciousness brought about by popular success.

Chuck Berry epitomizes the folk artist of the rock idiom. His style did not change because it did not have to; from the beginning it unconsciously expressed the responses of the artist and his audience to the ordinary realities of their world: to cars, girls, growing up, school, or

music. An ingenuous vitality pervades all of his songs. His subjects are never treated self-consciously, and his lyrics reveal no effort to find special "meaning" or "significance" in the activities they describe. The keynote of Chuck Berry's style is its open endorsement of happiness, fun, and good times: "School Day," for instance, describes the "burden" of being in class, the excitement which accompanies the three o'clock bell, and the pleasure of arriving at the "juke joint"; "Roll Over Beethoven" encourages the listener — and Beethoven — to feel the music, to "reel and rock" to its vital rhythm. The frankness, honesty, and naïveté of Chuck Berry's songs give them a continuing significance. The fact that their subject matter may be less immediate now than it was is irrelevant to the aesthetic experience of the records. Their attitude is their content. Its meaning is in the spontaneous, vital pleasure of creating music.

The lyrics of Chuck Berry's songs constitute some of the most exciting folk poetry in the rock field. They represent the folk artist's unconsciousness of art — particularly in his innocent notion that poetry should rhyme and that all rhythmic spaces should be filled, even if filling them necessitates the slicing of words or the creation of new ones. In "Too Much Monkey Business," for example, every verse rhymes, and, when words cannot fill the existing spaces, the artist fills them with a flexible "aah." Of course, the poetry in this song is *sung* poetry. Its quality cannot be duplicated by reading it or by writing it down. In Chuck Berry's breathless presentation, the "aahs" which conclude each verse change each time they are verbalized. In one case they imply a sigh of disgust and, in another, a type of sultry indignation. But the language of Chuck Berry's poetry is always ordinary. He employs it naturally and without sophistication. The impact of the Chuck Berry records suggests that naturalness came unconsciously to his music. Younger rock artists, Bob Dylan for instance, have been able to learn it. They have been conscious of alternative types of language and they have deliberately chosen to give their songs the flavor of the natural. But Chuck Berry did not make that choice because he was not aware of the alternatives. As a traditional folk artist, he created art unconsciously.

An important aspect of Chuck Berry's artistic power, one which enhances his relevance to the current rock scene, is his guitar style. His records are generally characterized by a piercing electric guitar which is played by Berry himself, and which is occasionally accompanied by drums and piano. In contrast to the majority of Rhythm and Blues artists of the 1950's, Chuck Berry did not rely upon the support of saxophones. Like Elvis Presley, he was "a man with his guitar." More than Presley, however, Chuck Berry played the guitar with a vitality that constituted an important element in the total effect of his records.

Here too, Chuck Berry's attitude was that of the folk artist. His songs repeatedly use an identical introductory phrase on the guitar, or a slight variation of it, and they rely internally on similar "favorite" guitar melodies and combinations. These elements hardly changed in a decade of record production. The artist intuited their aesthetic rightness, and he continued to use them because they remained expressively functional. His folk artistry, perhaps his genius, lay in the fact that he never tried to change them; he never felt the need to keep up with stylistic innovations, because he was never conscious of style itself.

Chuck Berry's relation to his guitar is intimate and loving, and this is evident in both musical and visual terms. Musically, the guitar penetrates the lyrics and frequently responds to one or two lines of a given verse, so that voice and guitar account equally for the total impact of the sound. Visually, the same close relationship is emphasized, between the entire person of the artist and his instrument. When Chuck Berry performs, he cuddles and caresses his guitar; he playfully teases notes from it, and he dances with it in the process. This display involves more than a virtuoso technique: it emanates from a folk convention that the guitar is human: Like a woman, whose body it obviously resembles, it must be loved before it will radiate its absorbing music.

Chuck Berry composed and wrote nearly all of the songs he recorded. In this, he further epitomized the traditional folk artist who, in comparison to popular art singers, created his own material instead of having it written for him. During the 1950's, the practice exemplified by Chuck Berry gradually became common, and it marked a major difference between rock and other musical styles which made up the Pop field. Like Berry, Fats Domino, Little Richard, and Ray Charles — as well as the more traditional blues artists like B. B. King — almost invariably wrote the music and lyrics of the songs they recorded. In the 1960's, this practice became even more characteristic of rock music. It has now become a standard feature of the most creative groups.

In the late 1960's, Chuck Berry has enjoyed a comeback. During 1967, his personal appearances in London and San Francisco were greeted with enthusiastic appreciation and standing ovations, reportedly to the amazement of the artist himself. This response is the consequence of the growing sophistication of rock artists and audiences, the emergence of a sub-style called "folk-rock," and a revival of the Rhythm and Blues tradition in both England and the United States. Rock has become aware of its past. In view of Chuck Berry's quality, this awareness is welcome. But it is also ironic, because he has only recently been recognized as the folk artist he has always been.

146

COMPREHENSION TEST 8

Directions: *Circle the letter of the best answer.*

1. The main point the writer makes about the music of Chuck Berry is that it is
   a) unimportant in the development of rock music
   b) as much folk music as it is rock and roll
   c) based on the work of classical musicians such as Beethoven
   d) filled with exciting poetry

2. Chuck Berry's musical style
   a) was influenced by Mick Jagger
   b) has not changed since the 1950s
   c) has been affected by his popular success
   d) is much different now than in the early days

3. Because of the length of time of his popularity and the quality of his music, Chuck Berry is most similar to
   a) Elvis Presley
   b) James Taylor
   c) Ozzy Osborne
   d) the Rolling Stones

4. A keynote of his style is
   a) its emphasis on happiness and fun
   b) the deep meaning of his lyrics
   c) its complete lack of guitar rhythms
   d) the importance of saxophones in it

5. A major difference between rock and other styles of music, like pop, is that
   a) rock artists usually write their own songs
   b) rock music is the only style that uses guitar rhythm
   c) rock music contains superior poetry
   d) adults do not appreciate it

6. The word "epitomize" as used in two places in this selection, most nearly means
   a) copy the style of
   b) ignore the style of
   c) offer the best example of
   d) make fun of

7. Which of the following is *not* a characteristic of folk artistry in rock music?
   a) rhyme is emphasized
   b) the electric guitar is the most common musical instrument used
   c) it deals with common, everyday events and experiences
   d) each musician has his own special introductory musical phrase

8. The writer implies that the music produced by most rock artists
   a) steadily improves after their first few hits
   b) is generally poorly written and performed
   c) is the most popular in the history of the recording industry
   d) does not maintain high quality very long

9. When we say that Chuck Berry is a "folk artist," we mean that
   a) the songs he did were mainly traditional ones passed down from generation to generation
   b) his music was created in cooperation with many other people
   c) he created music that was simple, spontaneous, and natural
   d) he had studied folk music at a prestigious music school

10. The central purpose of this passage was to
    a) analyze Chuck Berry's musical style
    b) offer a complete listing of Chuck Berry's recordings
    c) describe the history of rock from the 1950s to the present
    d) present the humorous side of Chuck Berry

147

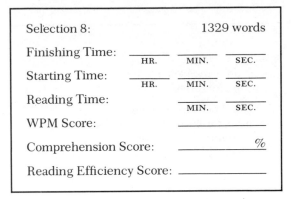

Selection 8:   1329 words

Finishing Time: _____ _____ _____
                  HR.   MIN.   SEC.

Starting Time: _____ _____ _____
                  HR.   MIN.   SEC.

Reading Time: _____ _____
                       MIN.   SEC.

WPM Score: _____

Comprehension Score: _____ %

Reading Efficiency Score: _____

Chapter 7:
Organizational Patterns

Many of our daily activities involve following a pattern or organizing principle. For instance, when you change a flat tire, bake a batch of cookies, assemble a toy, or write a term paper, do you do things in a particular order? Most likely you use some organized approach or method. Activities around you also have an organization or system. Think of a church service, a football game, or a meal in a restaurant. In each, things do happen in a particular order, and at any point you can predict what is to follow. Why do so many activities and events have a pattern? Of course many things, such as changing a flat tire, must, due to their nature, follow a particular order. You cannot, for instance, replace the flat tire with the new tire until you first take the flat tire off, and you cannot take it off until you remove the hubcap, and so forth. Other events, however, have no inherent order, yet they also follow a pattern. In these situations, the order often allows participants or spectators to know what to do or to expect next. Humans have a basic need to make sense out of things or to understand how things are done.

Paragraphs, like many other things, often follow a pattern, and for similar reasons. Many ideas or events that are recorded in written form have a natural order and this order is often followed as the idea is explained in the paragraph. For instance, in writing a paragraph that describes how to change a flat tire, the simplest way to arrange the details is in the order in which the task is done. In other cases, a pattern allows the reader to follow the ideas more easily, remember them more easily, and see the relationship between the ideas. In this chapter you will see how recognition of these patterns can improve recall and will look at the most common organizational patterns.

HOW RECOGNITION OF PATTERN IMPROVES RECALL

Which of the following phone numbers would be easier to remember?

876-5432
792-6538

Which of the following sets of directions would be easier to re-member?

After you pass two signals turn left. Then pass two more signals, and turn right again. Next, pass two more signals and turn left.

After you pass two streets, turn left. Then after you pass three more streets, turn right. Next, pass one more street, and turn right.

Which of the following shopping lists would be easier to remember if you forgot your list?

paint, brushes, paint remover, drop cloth

milk, deodorant, nails, comb

In each example, you probably selected the first choice as easier to remember. Now, let us consider *why* each is easier to remember than the other choice. The first choices each had a pattern. The items were connected in some way that made it possible to remember them together. The phone number consists of consecutive digits in reverse order; the directions consist of 2-left-2-right-2-left; the shopping list contained items related to a particular task — painting. From these examples you can see that items are easier to remember if they are related in some way.

Now try this experiment. Lists A and B each contain five facts. First, memorize list A and then memorize list B. Test your memory by writing a list of the facts on a piece of scrap paper. You should be able to remember each fact in the order in which it is presented. Record the amount of time it takes you to memorize each list.

LIST A
1. Cheeseburgers contain more calories than hamburgers.
2. Christmas cactus plants bloom once a year.
3. Many herbs have medicinal uses.
4. Many ethnic groups live in Toronto.
5. Fiction books are arranged alphabetically by author.

Time _____

LIST B
1. There are several characteristics of effective advertising.
2. An ad must be unique.
3. An ad must be believable.
4. An ad must make a lasting impression.
5. An ad must substantiate a claim.

Time _____

150

Most likely, you found list B easier and faster to learn. There was no connection between facts in list A; the facts in list B, on the other hand, were related. The first sentence made a general statement and each remaining sentence stated a particular characteristic of effective advertising. Together they fit into a pattern.

The details of a paragraph often fit a pattern and, if you can recognize the pattern, you will find that it is easier to remember the content of the paragraph. Once you establish how the details are related, you will be able to remember them as a unified whole rather than as independent pieces of information. Throughout the rest of this chapter you will learn the most common patterns for details in a paragraph. For each pattern, directional words that are commonly used will be presented. You will see how these directional words connect the ideas and make the pattern more easily identifiable.

COMMON ORGANIZATIONAL PATTERNS

The most common organizational patterns found in factual prose, including textbooks, magazines, and nonfiction are chronological order, statement-support, comparison-contrast, cause-effect, and listing of information. In this section we will discuss each of these patterns, offer examples, and list frequently used directional words in conjunction with each pattern.

Chronological Order

One of the most obvious patterns is chronological order, also called sequence of events. In a paragraph organized by chronology, the details are presented in the order in which they occur in time. That is, the event that happened first, or earliest in time, appears first in the paragraph; the event that occurred next in time appears next.

Chronology is used frequently in reporting current events and appears commonly in news articles and in magazines. It is also used to recount historical events or provide a historical perspective, and it is used in textbooks and reference sources. The following paragraph, taken from a botany text, is organized using chronology.

> Coffee drinking started in Arabia during the fifteenth century, and it is still very popular there. Native to the Old World, most coffee today is grown in South America, where Brazil produces 75 percent of the world's supply. Amazingly, much of the world's coffee is descended from a single coffee

151

plant obtained in Java in 1706 and sent to Amsterdam.
Seeds were later sent to the Dutch colony of Surinam.
Surinam coffee later spread throughout the New World.[1]

This paragraph describes, in chronological sequence, the development of the custom of coffee drinking.

One of the clearest ways to describe how to do something is to use steps that follow the order in which it is to be done. Chronological order, then, is often used to describe the steps in a process or to outline a method or procedure. The following paragraph uses steps to describe a method of solving the world's food supply problem.

To solve our critical food supply problem, we must take several steps. First, we must alter our place on the food chain. For most of the world's population in the less developed countries, eating less red meat would not change the diet greatly. But for beef eaters in the more affluent nations like those in the United States, Canada, Europe, Argentina, New Zealand, and Australia, the change would be drastic. We have seen the enormous waste in eating beef, a loss of about 99.98 percent between the energy beamed to earth by the sun and the energy derived by one of us eating a steak. This waste of energy can be decreased by moving down the food chain and eating plants or by using more efficient converters of energy such as hogs, fish, and chicken. Also, the amount of grain-fed meat will diminish in favor of grass-fed meat. Most food that cattle and sheep eat is forage like grass, clover, and alfalfa, which cannot be digested by people. Converting this unavailable matter and energy to meat and dairy products is an excellent way to use this vast source of energy.[2]

Paragraphs organized by chronological order use signal words to connect the events described or steps in the process. The most frequently used signal words are listed here.

DIRECTIONAL WORDS FOR CHRONOLOGICAL ORDER

first	next	finally	then
before	following	later	after
			last

When you realize that a paragraph is organized chronologically, you will expect that whatever event appears next in the paragraph will have happened next in time. You will find it easier to remember facts, details, dates or events because they are organized and connected by their occurrence in time.

Statement-Support

Another common way that details in a paragraph can be arranged is called the statement-support pattern. The topic sentence of the paragraph functions as a general statement and the details provide supporting evidence for this main idea. Various types of evidence may be used, including examples, definitions, statistics, and reasons or facts. Notice, in the following example, how the main idea of the paragraph is supported using examples.

> For many years Harry Harlow had been one of the most prominent and insightful investigators of animal behavior in this country. While he focused primarily on primate learning — how monkeys solved problems — he occasionally encountered intriguing behaviors that seemed unrelated to his stated research goals. For instance, after separating young monkeys from their mothers so they would not be exposed to disease, Harlow noticed that the offspring became physically healthy but seriously impaired socially. Another time Harlow noted that monkeys often became quite attached to soft cheesecloth diapers in their cages. Finally Harlow visited an institution where he saw human infants huddling pathetically in corners.[3]

In this paragraph, the author explains that Harlow has observed behaviors that seem difficult to understand by giving three specific instances of behavior.

In addition to examples or illustrations, statements that explain or provide more information about the main idea may be used. Usually the supporting details answer questions such as how, when, what, where, or why. Here is a statement-support paragraph developed using explanation.

> The lack of memory for past events is called *amnesia*. The kind of amnesia often encountered in novels or movies is the result not of brain concussions, but of active repression, a Freudian term meaning the inability to recall because, on some level, the person does not want to remember. This type of amnesia can usually be overcome by psychotherapy, and the repressed material is returned to

consciousness. Not so with *retrograde amnesia,* the kind
caused by a bump on the head. "Retrograde" means "acting
backwards," as if the concussion had gone back in time to
wipe out the memories as they were initially being formed.
This lack of memory is a true loss of information and
indicates that the bump has disrupted a process necessary to
establish permanent memory.[4]

The author explains his definition of amnesia by explaining that there
are two basic types, describing each, and discussing the cause of each.

The statement-support pattern is used in many types of materials.
It is particularly common in textbooks, essays, and factual articles.
Once you have identified the pattern of a statement-support paragraph,
again you can anticipate both the content and structure of the remainder of the paragraph. You can expect each detail to, in some way,
provide evidence in support of the main idea. Also, you can expect that
each detail will offer facts, examples, or some other form of evidence
that will support the main idea.

Directional words will often help you to identify the pattern as well
as to locate each important detail. The following directional words are
often used in conjunction with the statement-support pattern.

DIRECTIONAL WORDS FOR STATEMENT-SUPPORT

for example
to illustrate
for instance
such as
in this case

Comparison-Contrast

Often a writer will explain an object or idea, especially if it is
unfamiliar to the reader, by showing how it is similar to or different
from a familiar object or idea. At other times, it may be the writer's
purpose to show how two ideas, places, objects, or people are similar or
different. In each of these situations, then, a writer commonly uses a
pattern called comparison-contrast. In this pattern the paragraph is
organized to emphasize the similarities or differences between two or
more items. There are several variations on this pattern: a paragraph
may focus only on similarities or only differences or both. Here is a
paragraph on the physical differences between the sexes.

There are other physical differences between the sexes. Boys are generally superior in gross motor skills, girls in fine eye-hand coordination; after the age of six, boys are generally stronger. These differences are assumed to reflect sex differences in practice and motivation. Other differences have a physiological basis: boys are more likely to be color blind, because color blindness results from a sex-linked recessive gene — it is recessive in females but dominant in males. Females have greater sensitivity to tastes, odors, and sounds, especially for the higher pitches. Brain damage is more frequent in male infants, perhaps because the female is better able to tolerate changes in oxygen level during the fetal period. Hyperactivity, which has been attributed to "minimal brain damage" (alleged brain damage that is suspected from behavioral symptoms but is not detectable with physiological measures), is also more frequent in boys than girls, perhaps also reflecting the sex difference in fetal tolerance of environmental fluctuations.[5]

When you become aware that a paragraph seems to be organized by comparison-contrast, you should begin to look for similarities and differences. First, establish what is being compared or contrasted to what. Next, determine whether similarities or differences or both are presented. Often, the topic sentence of the paragraph will express the basic relationship between the items or ideas discussed. A topic sentence that states "It is important to make a distinction between amnesia and forgetting" indicates that the paragraph will be primarily concerned with differences. On the other hand, a paragraph that begins with a topic sentence that states "Although there are a number of similarities between the two authors, their approach to life makes them clearly distinguishable" will most likely be concerned with both similarities and differences. Finally, decide whether the comparison or contrast is the author's central purpose or whether it is used only as a means of support for a main idea.

You will find that directional words help you to identify the pattern as well as to decide whether the paragraph focuses on similarities, on differences, or on both.

DIRECTIONAL WORDS FOR COMPARISON-CONTRAST

in contrast	however
similarly	in comparison
likewise	to compare
on the other hand	

Cause-Effect

When a paragraph describes or discusses an event or action that is caused by another event or action, the pattern is called cause-effect. A cause-effect paragraph explains by describing why or how something happened. Its purpose is to show how two or more events are related. Some paragraphs describe a single cause producing a single effect (Unemployment is caused by inflation). Others may show how a single cause produced multiple effects (A snowstorm caused cars to get stuck, schools to be closed, and streets to be closed). Still other paragraphs may describe multiple causes that produce a single effect (Reading textbook assignments, careful study, and regular class attendance produce a good grade on an exam). Finally, multiple causes and multiple effects may be discussed within a single paragraph (Because you missed the bus and couldn't find your car keys, you missed your first class and did not meet your friends for coffee).

The following paragraph describes the cause of inflation.

> Inflation occurs whenever the demand for goods and services tends to be greater than the supply. In a period of prosperity when almost everyone has a job, many people become too optimistic. They spend their earnings freely and greatly increase their credit purchases, especially those made on the installment plan. As a result, the demand for goods of all kinds tends to increase rapidly. What happens? Prices rise.[6]

To read paragraphs using the cause-effect pattern, pay close attention to the topic sentence. It usually states the cause-effect relationship that is detailed throughout the paragraph. Then, as you read through the paragraph, read to find the specific causes and specific effects. Determine the connection between causes and effects: *Why* did a particular event or action occur? *What* happened as a result of it?

Directional words can help you to identify the pattern as well as to determine the exact nature of the cause-effect relationship. The following list contains directional words that most commonly indicate a cause-effect pattern.

DIRECTIONAL WORDS FOR CAUSE-EFFECT

for	consequently
because	hence
therefore	due to
as a result	

In the following paragraph, the directional words are underlined. Notice how they serve as markers for important causes discussed in the paragraph.

> <u>Because</u> of its small mass, the moon's history has been vastly different from the earth's. With a small mass comes a weak gravitational force; <u>as a result</u> the moon retains almost no atmosphere. It has no surface water, either free or chemically combined in the rocks (as in earth rocks), although some water may be trapped under its surface. Also, it has no general magnetic field, but its rocks suggest that a strong one existed in the very distant past. However, the moon is far from a simple, featureless satellite.[7]

Listing of Information

Many paragraphs are written simply to present facts. A paragraph may list important characteristics of an ancient culture, discuss three formulas for computing bank interest, or present four types of aggressive behavior. In each of these cases, there is no obvious way to arrange the details of the paragraph. Each is intended to inform the reader about the items presented. For paragraphs that list information, then, there is really no particular pattern or arrangement of details. Of course, the writer may choose to present the items in a way that is easiest to explain or that is easiest for the reader to understand, but even if this is done, there still is no obvious pattern that will help you to organize and remember the information. The following paragraph is an example of a paragraph whose only pattern is to list information.

> Cinnamon comes from the bark of *Cinnamomum zelyanicum,* an evergreen tree in the family Lauraceae. Others in the family are mainly aromatic evergreen trees and shrubs, among them camphor and avocado. Cinnamon is native to Ceylon, where all commercial production of the spice is still carried on; attempts to introduce it elsewhere have never been entirely successful. Cinnamon flavors desserts, cakes, and candy, and it is part of curry powder; its oil, distilled from the leaves, is used medicinally.[8]

As you can see, the paragraph listed information about cinnamon — its source, its origin, and its uses.

When you identify a paragraph as a listing of information, your primary purpose should be to identify each item in the list and to determine its relationship to the others. This is one type of paragraph in

157

which the details may be more important than the main idea. For instance, a topic sentence may state that there are four types of criminal behavior, and then the remainder of the paragraph would identify and explain each type. In most cases it is more important to know what the types of criminal behavior are than it is to know that there are four types.

Directional words are extremely useful in locating items in the list. Usually, as a writer moves from one item in the list to another, he or she will indicate the change.

DIRECTIONAL WORDS FOR LISTING OF INFORMATION

first	one
second	another
third	finally

EXERCISE 7-1

Directions: *Read each of the following paragraphs and identify the predominant organizational pattern used. Write the name of the pattern in the space provided. Choose from among the following patterns: chronology, statement-support, comparison-contrast, cause-effect, listing of information.*

1. Lions in the great grasslands of Africa are very fond of zebras. When a lion kills and feasts on zebra flesh, it is filled with new energy, which enables it to live, sire offspring, and hunt more zebras. For their part, the zebras find food in the grasses and other plants. Taking in energy from the plants, the zebras can live and multiply. But the lions limit the number of zebras by hunting and killing them; if they did not kill the zebras, there might be more zebras than grass to support the zebras. The quantity of grass limits the lion population, too, because the number of lions that can survive depends on the quantity of zebras available as food, as energy. And thus there exists, between lions, zebras, and plants, a balance of energy — a balance of life.[9]

Pattern: _____

2. The national government, as we have seen, is based on a system of dividing or *decentralizing* power. Political parties, on the other hand, are a means of organizing or *centralizing* power. The framers of the Constitution decentralized power in separate branches and a federal system partly to avoid the development of

powerful factions that could take over the government. This very decentralization of power, however, created the need for parties that could pull together or centralize that power.[10]

Pattern: _____

3. After the Constitution was ratified, the Federalist faction grew stronger and more like a political party. Led by Alexander Hamilton, secretary of the treasury under President George Washington, the Federalists championed a strong national government that would promote the financial interests of merchants and manufacturers. After Thomas Jefferson left President Washington's cabinet in 1793, an opposition party began to form under his leadership. The new *Democratic-Republican* party drew the support of small farmers, debtors, and others who did not benefit from the financial programs of the Federalists. Under the Democratic-Republican label, Jefferson won the presidential election of 1800, and his party continued to control the presidency until 1828. The Federalists, without power or popular support, gradually died out.[11]

Pattern: _____

4. *Homeostasis* refers to an organism's tendency to maintain a relatively constant internal environment. When we are well, our body temperature is approximately 98.6° Fahrenheit. Organisms, in order to stay alive, must maintain a somewhat constant internal equilibrium. Some departures from homeostasis are brief and not injurious — exercise, for example. But prolonged departure from homeostasis can mean illness and threaten the survival of the organism.[12]

Pattern: _____

5. Every day the mass media tell us in some new way that the American family is in trouble. The divorce rate is rising rapidly — in California it is supposedly already over 50 percent. And it is going up fastest among people who have been married 20 years or longer. About a million legal abortions are done each year, sending the birthrate below the replacement level. Almost 50 percent of all adult women work at least part time, a parameter that implies, among other things, many children are being cared for largely by people other than their parents. And the women's liberation movement seems to be putting down most traditional ideas about how men and women should deal with each other.

The family seems to be facing a major crisis and some observers think it may be so seriously weakened that it can never fully recover.[13]

Pattern: _____

APPLYING WHAT YOU HAVE LEARNED

Directions: *Choose one of the selections at the end of the chapter. Read the selection and answer the multiple choice questions. Then review the selection and identify the organizational pattern of each paragraph. In the margin next to each paragraph, write, in abbreviated form, the name of the organizational pattern. Underline any directional words that you notice.*

READING SELECTION 9
SURGICAL SEARCH FOR YOUTH

Difficulty Level: A

K. W. Schaie and J. Geiwitz

Cosmetic or esthetic surgery is a relatively new specialization of plastic surgery born out of the human's psychological fear and anxiety of aging. In its infancy, cosmetic surgery catered to the jet set and movie personalities, but today surgeons are seeing men and women from all walks of middle-class life. In less than ten years the number of individuals receiving cosmetic surgery has increased tremendously. New York, Miami, Los Angeles, Brazil, and Mexico have become the centers for cosmetic surgery. In the past women more frequently sought cosmetic surgery, but a consensus of leading plastic surgeons has indicated that the number of men seeking changes has tripled in the last five years.

There are no statistics on the exact number of people who obtain cosmetic surgery. Unless there is a definite health reason for cosmetic surgery, private insurance will not pay for it; therefore, insurance statistics are of limited use. In addition, a great many physicians who have limited their practice to cosmetic surgery perform their operations in private hospitals and clinics.

RATIONALE FOR SURGERY

Many reasons have been given for cosmetic surgery. Most of them deal with perceived physical and emotional inadequacies. The normal physiological changes in the skin do not begin to appear until generally around age 30, although variations may be seen in individuals. Young people who seek cosmetic surgery generally do so for changes in their noses or to remove facial scarring from severe cases of acne. In the mature adult we see that the image of grandma and grandpa has changed over the years. Today's older people retire earlier, and are ". . . living longer and maintaining good health longer, they're doing things that only young people used to do, . . . they feel good and want to look as good as they feel."

Job Security

Some cosmetic surgeries are related to job security. For example, one woman said that she wanted surgery because she did not want her employer to know her age so that she could keep her job. She was 70. A top executive showing premature signs of aging was incorrectly thought to be an alcoholic. Men feel that they fare better in daily job competition if they look young and fresh.

Marital Security

Martha was anxious and fearful that her husband was no longer interested in her. She was beginning to show signs of aging which bothered her. Her children were grown and had left home. Her husband, a college professor, was engrossed in his career and a female graduate assistant whom he described as "sharp and all fired up over teaching." His enthusiasm and constant talk about the graduate student only confirmed Martha's fears that her marriage was beginning to fail because she looked old. She sought and was refused cosmetic surgery from a trained medical specialist. As her frustration and anxiety mounted, she turned to a lesser trained physician who agreed to her surgery.

At first, her surgery seemed successful, but after several months her eyelids drooped unevenly and she looked far worse than before her surgery. At this point she finally admitted to her husband her fears about his interest in younger women. Martha's husband insisted that she was wrong and took her to meet the graduate assistant who turned out to be Martha's age. The graduate student told Martha that she had had the same feelings about her children's leaving home, her husband being busy with his career, and her own feelings about her age changes, and so she had decided upon a second career. With the support of her husband, Martha obtained help from a trained specialist to correct the botched surgery. She then reassessed her life and went back to school.

This is only one example. Hundreds of other surgeries are performed on both men and women because they fear loss of interest of a spouse and marriage failure because they are beginning to look older. Men who marry much younger women often seek cosmetic surgery in hopes of improving their marriage.

Societal Attitudes

Many adults fear the bags, sags, wrinkles, and double chins which often accompany age. As the gerontological literature points out, we seem to be currently living in a youth culture. Some obtain facial remodeling in order to conform to society's attitude toward being "young and beautiful." Undoubtedly, divorce rates are higher than ever before. In order to make a good "catch" for a second or third marriage, some feel they have to look younger.

PHYSICIAN CONCERNS

Medicare or private insurance will cover the expenses for cosmetic surgery if there are justifiable medical reasons for the surgery. Most generally, this includes such things as a divided nasal septum, impaired vision, or catastrophic injury. This means that the thousands of men and women who are having cosmetic surgery are paying for it themselves (Table 1).

Table 1. TYPES AND COST OF COSMETIC SURGERY

TYPE	DESCRIPTION	COST
Rhytidoplasty (Face lift)	The tightening and lifting of excessive skin which has lost its elasticity producing sags and wrinkles. Usually done under a general anesthetic. Most common type of surgery sought.	$1000–$5000
Blepharoplasty (eyelid lift, brow lift)	The tightening and removal of excessive skin on the eyelid or eyebrow.	$1000–$2000
Submandibular lipectomy	The removal of excessive skin from the neck and chin.	$1000–$2000
Full face lift	A combination of the rhytidoplasty, blepharoplasty, and submandibular lipectomy.	$2000–$5000
Full body contour	Removal of excessive fat from the hips and thighs.	$5000
Rhinoplasty	Removal of unwanted nasal bone and cartilage.	$1000–$1500
Hair transplants	Small plugs of hair growing skin are removed from the back of the head and reimplanted in the front.	$15 per plug
Mammoplasty	Reduction or enlargement of the breasts.	$1500, depending on whether there are complications

Source: Gertrude Lang, "Facing the Facts About Face-Lifts," *Retirement Living* (February 1978), 74. Matt Clark et al., "The Plastic-Surgery Boom," *Newsweek* (January 24, 1977), 26.

Most physicians are concerned about the physical and mental well-being of their patients. They obtain complete medical histories of their patients and discuss with them the reasons why they want to have cosmetic surgery. Most of the time a patient is refused surgery when one of the following situations exists:

1. Another person has encouraged the surgery.
2. No obvious problem exists.
3. The person feels that his or her marriage will improve.
4. The person is a surgery seeker.
5. The person feels that cosmetic surgery will solve his or her personal problems.
6. The person is under psychiatric care.

Perhaps the most serious concern of the physician is with breast enlargements using silicone. Physicians report that about 60% of the cases will develop one or several of the following complications:

1. Siliconomos (excessive scarring in fatty layers of breast tissue)
2. Silicone lumps
3. Migration of silicone to other parts of the body which results in disfigurement

4. Severe infection
5. Gangrene
6. Mastectomies

One physician in San Diego reported 400 breast complications between 1967 and 1974. Twenty percent of them resulted in breast removal.

For the most part, cosmetic surgery will not make a person look younger. What it does do is make an individual look less tired and more refreshed. Surgeons report that the effects of cosmetic surgery only last from five to ten years before excessive skin begins to show up again. Cosmetic surgery does not eliminate other characteristics of aging such as changes in body contour, hands, skin tone, voice, and posture.

One man had cosmetic surgery when his wife did. When he was asked if he would have it done again when it was needed, he said that he wouldn't because his original motivation for having it done was to carry him over into retirement and that had been fulfilled and because it would be too expensive on a retirement income. He also said, "Sooner or later we all reach an age where we're willing to *be* our age."

COMPREHENSION TEST 9

Directions: *Circle the letter of the best answer.*

1. A major use of cosmetic surgery is to
   a) correct facial deformities
   b) relieve the anxiety of aging
   c) make the patient happier
   d) eliminate telltale symptoms of stress

2. Cosmetic surgery
   a) has increased dramatically in less than ten years
   b) remains an extravagance of the wealthy
   c) has decreased due to health risks
   d) continues to be a major concern of the elderly

3. The type of cosmetic surgery that has a large percentage of complications is
   a) face lifts
   b) hair transplants
   c) eyelid lifts
   d) breast enlargement

4. A surgeon may refuse to perform cosmetic surgery on a person who
   a) is susceptible to cancer
   b) wishes to improve his or her marriage
   c) fears surgery
   d) is unable to face reality

5. Reasons for having cosmetic surgery include all of the following *except*
   a) job security
   b) fashion trends
   c) societal attitudes toward aging
   d) marital problems

163

6. The term "premature" in the phrase "premature sign of aging" means
   a) in a particular manner
   b) uncontrolled
   c) before the usual time
   d) slow

7. From this article you might infer that, in our society, aging is a
   a) desirable and respected occurrence
   b) stressful, negative experience
   c) natural, inescapable part of life
   d) scientifically controlled experience

8. The last sentence in the selection, "Sooner or later we all reach an age where we're willing to be our age," suggests that cosmetic surgery
   a) helps us to accept the reality of aging
   b) is an escape from being one's age
   c) discourages a positive attitude toward aging
   d) increases one's ability to admit that aging is inevitable

9. The author feels that cosmetic surgery
   a) is worthwhile
   b) helps people cope with the aging process
   c) is related to other, more deeply rooted emotional problems
   d) is a legitimate operation that should be covered by insurance

10. The author explains cosmetic surgery by
    a) giving examples
    b) comparing practices in the United States to those in other countries
    c) discussing long-range effects on society
    d) emphasizing its importance to the insurance industry

Selection 9:	1123 words
Finishing Time:	_____ _____ _____
	HR. MIN. SEC.
Starting Time:	_____ _____ _____
	HR. MIN. SEC.
Reading Time:	_____ _____
	MIN. SEC.
WPM Score:	_____
Comprehension Score:	_____ %
Reading Efficiency Score:	_____

164

READING SELECTION 10
AUTO INSURANCE

Denis T. Raihall

Because of the unpredictable nature of auto accidents, even a careful driver stands the chance of becoming involved, innocently or otherwise, in a collision. In addition to being subjected to accident risk, a person faces the threat of being held legally responsible for the injuries and damages caused by his auto. Given such uncertainties and the ensuing possibilities, an individual could be suddenly confronted with a lawsuit for a staggering sum. It is not unusual to hear that a jury has awarded a victim $100,000; $200,000; or even more for injuries sustained in an auto accident. Although there are a few people who could afford such a financial loss, most of us would find ourselves facing bankruptcy. Fortunately, we are able to protect ourselves against such a situation by purchasing auto insurance.

There are six basic kinds of coverage available for cars and their owners:

Bodily injury liability provides payment to those individuals, excluding you or your family, who are injured by your car.
Property damage liability covers you when your car causes damage to the property of others.
Medical payment coverage pays for medical treatment for yourself or your passengers for injuries sustained in an auto accident, regardless of who is at fault.
Collision coverage pays for repairs to your own auto if it is damaged by another auto or collides with an object like a wall or a telephone pole.
Comprehensive coverage reimburses you for losses from such hazards as malicious damage, theft, fire, wind and vandalism.
Uninsured motorist coverage pays for bodily injury to you caused by another driver whose own insurance is insufficient, or by a hit-and-run driver who is not apprehended.

In addition to these six kinds of coverage, many auto insurance companies offer towing and road service coverage.

BODILY INJURY LIABILITY

In order to protect against financial loss arising from auto accidents that result in injury or death to others, drivers should give top priority to the purchase of bodily injury liability coverage. The amounts of bodily injury coverage are usually quoted using two terms such as "ten, twenty" (10/20); "twenty-five, fifty" (25/50); or "one hundred, three hundred" (100/300). The first figure in each case refers to the maximum amount in thousands of dollars payable per injured person. The second figure represents the maximum amount payable per accident. Let's assume Harry Collins was careless and caused an accident which injured the driver of the other vehicle. Harry was responsible, therefore the injured party filed suit. The court awarded the injured party $40,000. Harry's bodily injury coverage amounted to 25/50. Under its obligation, the insurance company would pay the injured party $25,000 (maximum per injured person), and the remaining $15,000 would be Harry's responsibility. If Harry had injured three people and the court had awarded each victim $20,000, the insurance company would have only been liable for $50,000 (maximum payment per accident), paying each of the injured victims on a prorated basis of one third of $50,000 — or $16,667. Again, the difference between the court judgment and the insurance payment would have to be paid by Harry. Any court costs incurred would be paid by the insurance company.

The protection offered under this type of coverage is extended to you the policyholder, your family, and to anyone driving the insured auto with your permission. You and members of your family are also protected while driving other cars, provided permission is received from the owner.

PROPERTY DAMAGE LIABILITY

Property damage liability insurance provides coverage to property of any sort which was damaged by your auto and for which you were held legally liable up to the limits of the policy. For instance, if Alice Cooper had neglected to purchase property damage liability insurance, she would have been personally liable for the damage caused by her unattended auto when it rolled down the hill and crashed into a restaurant. Fortunately, the $25,000 worth of property damage coverage she had purchased proved to be adequate to cover the $20,000 worth of damages. If Alice had bought only $10,000 worth of property damage coverage, the insurance company would have paid their limit toward the damages, leaving Alice with the burden of providing the $10,000 difference. It is typical for an insurance company to write bodily injury and property damage liability insurance together as 10/20/10, 25/50/25, or 100/300/50.* This type of insurance is available in coverages ranging from $5,000 to $100,000, with costs depending mainly on an individual's age, the type and use of car, and the area in which the driver resides.

MEDICAL EXPENSE INSURANCE

Pat and Sue, college roommates, were eagerly awaiting the opening of the ski season. Pat arranged to borrow her father's car for transportation to the ski slopes. The season arrived, and the girls hit the slopes and enjoyed themselves. Unfortunately, as they prepared to return home a snow storm moved in and blanketed the roads with snow and ice.

---

* It is also very common to have single-limit coverage providing, for example, $300,000 per accident for all bodily injury and property damage and without per-person restriction.

166

Considering herself a poor foul-weather driver, Pat was concerned about the trip home. Since Pat knew Sue was more experienced at driving in inclement weather, she let her drive. Sue fought the miserable conditions for a few miles until the car slid out of control and collided with a tree. The damage to the car was minor, but the girls were not so lucky. Sue hurt her back and Pat suffered severe lacerations of her face and arms. The medical expenses incurred were quite high and had to be assumed by Pat's father. These costs could have been avoided if only Pat's father had purchased appropriate insurance coverage.

Automobile owners may purchase a policy whereby the insuring company agrees to pay, up to the limits of the policy, all reasonable medical expenses incurred within one year from the date of the accident — these include surgical, X-ray, dental, ambulance, hospital, private nursing and funeral expenses. Like liability coverage, medical expense coverage is extended to you and your family whether in your own or another auto and to other occupants of your car. In addition, it extends coverage to the insured even if he is struck by an auto while crossing the street. Payment is generally made regardless of who is at fault.

COLLISION INSURANCE

The auto owner who purchases collision insurance protects himself against the cost of repairing or replacing his auto if it is damaged in a collision, regardless of who was at fault. However, it doesn't cover the damage done to the other auto. If you were at fault, the other auto would be repaired under your property liability insurance. One unique feature of this type of insurance enables the insured to have his auto repaired before legal settlement is made.

For example, when Arnold Nicholas and Jack Palmer drove into each other at the hazardous intersection of Long Drive and Fairway Lane, each claimed that his actions were faultless. Although Arnold and Jack were not hurt, their cars suffered considerable damage. The decision as to who was legally responsible was left to the court. Both men carried collision insurance which covered the repairs to their cars prior to the legal settlement.

More people would carry collision insurance if the rates for this protection were not so high. This type of insurance is available on a deductible basis, which serves to reduce the cost of the insurance. It is normally available in $50-, $100-, and $250-deductible amounts. This means that the insured is responsible for the designated deductible amount, while the insuring company is responsible for the remainder.

COMPREHENSIVE INSURANCE

Like collision insurance, comprehensive insurance covers the policyholder's auto. Under this type of coverage, the insured's car is protected against all physical damage resulting from causes other than collision. This includes any damage done by fire, theft, vandalism, windstorm, etc.

For instance, if you are driving along the highway and a stone flies up and cracks your windshield, the windshield will be replaced if you have comprehensive insurance coverage. The coverage is written for the actual cash value of the car. The cost of this type of insurance generally depends primarily on the area in which the insured resides and the value of the auto.

In some of the larger cities the frequency of small claims is so great that some insurance companies have introduced a deductible clause into their comprehensive plans in order to reduce the number of claims by policyholders.

UNINSURED MOTORISTS' INSURANCE

This coverage protects the insured against financial loss from bodily injury sustained in an accident with an uninsured motorist or a hit-and-run driver. It must be determined that the accident was the fault of the other party and that he does not have insurance or the available financial resources to cover his liability in the accident. Coverage applies to the policyholder and his family in their auto, in someone else's auto, and even when walking. Coverage also applies to guests in the insured car. Ray Klarke was pleasantly surprised when his insurance company notified him that his uninsured motorists' coverage would pay for the medical expenses incurred when he and his girlfriend Alice were victims of a hit-and-run accident.

The policy is written in terms identical to those in bodily injury insurance, i.e., 10/20, 50/100, etc. As with bodily injury insurance, the first term refers to each individual in an accident, and the second term refers to the total amount payable per accident. The primary advantage of this protection is the immediate payment by the insurance company for hospital and other medical related costs. The cost of this protection is so small, you can hardly afford to be without it.

COMPREHENSION TEST 10

Directions: *Circle the letter of the best answer.*

1. Auto insurance can be purchased
   a) very cheaply today due to federal laws
   b) for the protection of licensed drivers only
   c) to cover nearly all auto accident situations
   d) only by adults over the age of 25

2. The type of insurance coverage that pays for repairs to your own car if it is hit while parked by another car is called

   a) property damage liability
   b) collision coverage
   c) comprehensive coverage
   d) uninsured motorist coverage

3. Individuals, other than you and your family, who are injured by your car are covered by
   a) medical payment coverage
   b) comprehensive coverage
   c) uninsured motorist coverage
   d) bodily injury liability

4. When an auto accident case goes to court, the court costs are usually paid by
   a) the person who caused the accident
   b) the insurance company of the responsible party
   c) a special legal fund financed by taxes
   d) the individual who is awarded damages

5. $250 deductible collision insurance pays
   a) $250 for the first occurrence and less for each after that
   b) completely for damages over $250
   c) any amount of damage up to $250
   d) the amount of damages that exceed $250

6. As it is used here, *designated* means
   a) selected
   b) stated
   c) smallest
   d) spurious

7. If you had bodily injury liability coverage that amounted to 40/80, and the court awarded the party you injured $100,000
   a) you would have to pay the additional $20,000
   b) you could borrow on other portions of your insurance to make up the difference
   c) most insurance companies would offer you an "extended rider" to cover all costs
   d) the injured party would only receive $80,000

8. Suppose you were driving your brother's car on a trip and a deer ran across the highway. As you braked to avoid hitting the deer, the car behind you struck your car. Both cars were damaged; you were not injured but the other driver was. What types of insurance would you need to avoid any expenses as a result of this accident?
   a) only collision
   b) comprehensive, property damage, and medical payment
   c) property damage, medical payment, and collision
   d) collision, bodily injury, and property damage

9. The author seems to feel that everyone should carry
   a) property damage liability unless they do not have assets that can be awarded in a lawsuit
   b) as much insurance as one can afford
   c) only the minimum insurance required by law
   d) collision insurance regardless of the type and age of car owned

10. To make his topic more interesting the writer uses
    a) exciting descriptions
    b) excellent comparisons
    c) numerous examples
    d) realistic conversations

Selection 10:		1625 words
Finishing Time:		
	HR. MIN.	SEC.
Starting Time:		
	HR. MIN.	SEC.
Reading Time:		
	MIN.	SEC.
WPM Score:		
Comprehension Score:		%
Reading Efficiency Score:		

Chapter 8:
Reading Articles
and Longer Selections

Most of the reading that we do on a daily basis involves neither single paragraphs nor whole books, but something in between in length. The type of reading we do in the course of an average day consists of such materials as newspaper or magazine articles, chapters from textbooks or other nonfiction books and other selections from longer works.

An awareness of the organization and wise use of the special features contained in these longer selections can be an important means of improving your reading efficiency. In reading articles and longer selections, your purpose is often to extract the essential information in the most expedient manner. To locate these important ideas and necessary supporting information, you need to recognize how the material is organized and learn to use the author's aids to organization.

Just as was true for individual paragraphs, most articles, reading selections, and textbook or nonfiction chapters follow a basic organizational pattern. Most are titled and most are concerned with one item or idea, called a *subject*. Also, each of the paragraphs in a piece of writing develops or supports one general idea about that subject, called a *thesis*. The paragraphs are linked through the use of words, phrases, and sentences known as transitions. Most articles contain an introduction, body, and summary or conclusion. Finally, some types of articles, selections, and chapters employ headings to divide the material into smaller, more manageable topics or subtopics.

IDENTIFYING THE THESIS STATEMENT

Just as a paragraph develops one broad thought, called the main idea, so an article or reading selection develops a single idea throughout.

The thesis, then, is the most important idea in the article, and all of the paragraphs in the article explain or support it. Writers usually express their thesis in one sentence near the beginning of the article. You might think of this thesis statement as a one-sentence summary of the whole selection.

It is useful to identify the thesis statement because it provides an overall view of the article. It helps you to focus on the ideas to be discussed in the article and enables you to begin to develop expectations about the content, scope, and purpose of the material. A thesis statement may also provide clues about how the article will be organized. Suppose an article contains the following thesis statement:

> There is a substantial body of research that indicates that cigarette smoking is harmful, yet people continue to smoke to fulfill a variety of needs.

From this statement you can predict that the article will first summarize the research evidence that indicates smoking is harmful and then will explain the needs that smoking fulfills.

If you have difficulty identifying the thesis statement, ask yourself this question: What is the one, most important idea that is developed throughout the essay? Now, read the following brief article; as you read try to identify the thesis statement. After you have identified it, check to see that each paragraph in the article supports or explains this statement.

SPACE SPEAKS

As one travels abroad and examines how space is handled, startling variations are discovered — differences we react to vigorously. Literally thousands of experiences teach us unconsciously that space communicates. Yet this fact would probably never have been brought to the level of consciousness if it had not been realized that space is organized differently in each culture. The associations and feelings that are released in a member of one culture almost invariably mean something else in the next. When we say that some foreigners are "pushy," all this means is that their handling of space releases this association in our minds.

"It's as much as your life is worth to ride the streetcars. They're worse than our subways. What's more, these people don't seem to mind it at all." As Americans, we have a pattern which discourages touching, except in moments of intimacy. When we ride on a streetcar or crowded elevator we "hold ourselves in," having been taught from early childhood to avoid bodily contact with strangers. Abroad, it's confusing when conflicting feelings are being released at the same time. Our senses are bombarded by a strange language, different smells, and gestures, as well as a host of signs and symbols.

Whenever people travel abroad they suffer from a condition known as *culture shock*. Culture shock is simply a removal or distortion of many of the familiar cues one encounters at home and the substitution for them of other cues which are strange. A good deal of what occurs in the organization and use of space provides important leads as to the specific cues responsible for culture shock.

The Latin house is often built around a patio that is next to the sidewalk but hidden from outsiders behind a wall. It is not easy to describe the degree to which small architectural differences such as this affect outsiders. American foreign aid technicians living in Latin America used to complain that they felt "left out" of things, that they were "shut off." Others kept wondering what was going on "behind those walls." In the United States, on the other hand, propinquity is the basis of a good many relationships. To us the neighbor is actually quite close. You can borrow things, including food and drink, but you also have to take your neighbor to the hospital in an emergency. In this regard he has almost as much claim on you as a cousin.[1]

In this article, the thesis statement is contained in the first paragraph. The first and second sentences indicate that the article will discuss the way space is handled; it will show that space and our reactions to it communicate a message. Each of the paragraphs in the selection offers an example of different uses of space, reactions to these uses, and messages that the use suggests to the unaccustomed.

THE FUNCTION OF TITLES

In paging through a magazine or newspaper, how do you decide which articles or advertisements to read and which to skip? Often you decide solely on the basis of the title. From the title you determine whether the article is about a subject, event, or issue in which you are interested. The title, then, is an important part of any piece of writing.

You will find that most articles, essays, selections, and textbook chapters begin with a title. For selections or excerpts (material taken from a longer piece of writing) the title may be the heading.

There are two types of titles. Some titles are accurate labels, intended to describe and provide an overview of content of the article; they function as a direct announcement about an article's content. Others are "catchy" — intended to provoke interest or to catch the reader's attention. You might think of this type of title as an advertisement that is intended to interest or motivate the reader. These two types of titles will be called descriptive titles and interest-getting titles and are discussed in the following sections.

Descriptive Titles

Descriptive or factual titles, of course, are more useful to the reader. Because they accurately announce or summarize the article, they help you decide whether you are interested in reading the material. However, descriptive titles are also useful once you have decided to read the article, whether you are reading it because you are interested in it or because it is an assigned reading.

Beyond announcing the subject of the article, the title may suggest the author's approach or attitude toward the subject. For instance, the title "A Volunteer Army — Is America Safe?" identifies the subject of the article as a volunteer army. However, it also suggests the author's approach toward the subject. From the phrase "Is America Safe?" you know that the author will consider whether the volunteer army can provide a suitable defense for our country. Further, although you cannot be certain, you might predict the answer to the question; by the way the title is written, you might suspect a negative answer. In raising the issue of America's safety, the writer seems to be suggesting that it is in question. Descriptive titles, then, in addition to identifying the subject of the article, may provide information about the treatment of the subject in the article. Here are a few additional examples of descriptive titles, along with the subject each announces and further information it provides.

Title	*Subject*	*Further Information*
How to Beat the Clock and Have More Time	time management	offers suggestions on how to manage and plan your time
Spying Devices: Is Someone Listening to Your Every Word?	listening-spying equipment	suggests that a great deal of surveillance occurs and that it is *possible* (although not likely) that someone can easily listen in on your conversations
Death by Injection — A Legal Question	death penalty using drug injections	presents facts about death by injection and examines whether such practice is legal

172

EXERCISE 8-1

Directions: *Read each title, underline the subject, and then, in the space provided, describe what you expect the article to be about, based on the clues provided by the title.*

1. Computers Come Home

    _____

2. Businesses Take Action on the Battle Against Booze

    _____

3. Vitamins — Miracle or Money Down the Drain?

    _____

4. Movie Ratings: Do They Work?

    _____

5. How Healthy Is a Vegetarian?

    _____

Interest-Getting Titles

Titles that are intended to catch your interest or to appeal to your curiosity tend to be of little value in anticipating the content of an article. However, this is not to say that they have no place in serious writing. Often a "catchy" title will spark your interest and encourage you to read an article that turns out to be interesting but that you might not have read if the title had been clearly descriptive.

Here are a few interest-getting titles. Notice that each sparks your interest, yet it does not define the subject of the article. The actual subject of each article is listed following each title.

Million-Dollar Baby	the birth of a whale in captivity
Ah! Wilderness	a family adventure in the Arctic
Not Cinderella, Just Highly Competitive	a teen-age tennis star wins a tournament

| The Danger of Being in Second Place | a city newspaper losing popularity |
| The Party's Over | the President's return to the White House after foreign travel |

READING INTRODUCTIONS, SUMMARIES, AND CONCLUSIONS

Many articles, chapters, and essays begin with an introduction and end with a summary or conclusion. Also, you will find that many textbook chapters are similarly organized. Both introductions and summaries are integral parts of any piece of writing, and each provides you with valuable assistance in reading the article.

Reading Introductions

In a rush to read what they feel is important, many students pay little attention to the opening paragraphs of articles or chapters. Actually, the introduction is an extremely important part of any piece of writing. An introduction may serve a number of purposes. However, its primary function is to identify the subject of the article and lead the reader into the rest of the article by directly stating the author's main point. In fact, you might think of an introductory paragraph of an article as being similar to the topic sentence of a paragraph. Both the topic sentence of a paragraph and the introduction to a longer piece of writing explain what the entire piece of writing will be about; the topic or subject is identified, and the writer's main idea is presented. The following is the opening paragraph taken from an article titled "Breathe Your Troubles Away." The title indicates and the introductory paragraph confirms that the subject is breathing.

BREATHE YOUR TROUBLES AWAY

When I broke my foot while running, I thought it would mean complete inactivity. About all I could do was some breathing exercises learned during earlier yoga and martial-arts training. Breathing in a controlled fashion to exercise my chest and strengthen my stomach muscles, I found my pain also eased. Fascinated, I did some reading and discovered that breathing has been helpful in a wide variety of activities — from acting and singing to sports and meditation. The more I read, the more I realized that

174

breathing is the missing connection for the integration and control of body and mind.[2]

The introductory paragraph often answers questions that you might pose about the title. From the above title you might ask:

1. How can you breathe your troubles away?
2. What kind of troubles can you breathe away?

You will see that the paragraph answers these questions. The writer, by describing a personal experience, suggests that it is through breathing exercises that troubles can be "breathed" away. Also, from his description of his personal experience, you learn the answer to the second question. Breathing eases pain and is helpful in a wide variety of activities such as acting, singing, sports, and meditation.

These questions and their answers are also useful in leading you to the thesis statement, which is often contained in the introduction. You will find that the thesis statement often answers at least one of your questions.

Functions of the Introduction. In addition to establishing the subject of the article and expressing the thesis statement, the introduction may perform several other functions.

Enhancing Interest. Writers take special care in writing the introduction because they are aware that a reader uses it to decide whether to continue reading the article. They may relate an exciting event, make a shocking statement, refer to a well-known person or event, or raise a controversial issue. Notice how, in the following introduction, the writer begins by relating an incident concerning racecar drivers to interest the reader, while introducing the subject of the article.

FIFTY-FIVE IS FAST ENOUGH

In 1972, the winning car in the Indianapolis 500 was clocked at an average speed of 162.962 m.p.h., a record that stands today. The car, which I owned, was driven by my friend Mark Donohue. Three years later, Donohue crashed and was fatally injured while practicing for the Grand Prix in Austria. He was not yet 39.

Professional race drivers deliberately accept the risks of high speed and the ever-present possibility of sudden death behind the wheel. But for thousands of ordinary motorists every year, death on the highway is all too often unnecessary.[3]

The first paragraph of this introduction is intended to capture your interest; the second paragraph relates the incident about racecars to the subject of the article — the fifty-five-mile-per-hour speed limit for highway driving.

Providing Background Information. Writers seldom assume that the reader is familiar with the subject he or she is writing about. Instead, they provide sufficient background information to enable a reader who is unfamiliar with the subject to be able to read the material without undue difficulty. At other times, depending on the subject, a certain amount of background information is necessary, regardless of the reader's familiarity with the subject. For example, if a writer is describing a particular event, any reader may need to know the surrounding circumstances. The following opening paragraphs provide a good example of how a writer uses the introduction to provide background information. As you read them, first try to identify the thesis statement and then notice the types of information the author provides.

IS IT WORTH THE RISK?

A day in early July, perfect for climbing. From the mesas above Boulder, a heat-cutting breeze drove the smell of pines up onto the great tilting slabs of Flatirons, one of Colorado's classic rock-climbing locales.

It was 1961. I was 18, had been climbing about a year, Gabe even less. We were about 600 feet up, three-quarters of the way to the summit of the First Flatiron. It had gone okay, despite the lack of places to bang in pitons.

It was a joy to be climbing. Climbing was one of the best things — maybe *the* best thing — in life. There was a risk, but I knew the risk was worth it.[4]

The subject of the article (mountain climbing) and the thesis statement (that it is one of the best things in life) are clearly presented in the third paragraph. The first and second paragraph established a time and a setting for the rest of the article.

Establishing a Context for the Subject. Again, depending on the subject, it may be necessary for a writer to provide a framework to establish the place of the subject within a larger context. To do this, a writer often explains why the subject is important or shows how it relates to or affects larger concerns. In the following paragraph the writer's subject is foreign dependence on nonfuel minerals. However, the writer begins by relating the mineral shortage to the current energy crisis and suggests that it is even a more serious problem than is energy.

STRATEGIC MINERALS: THE INVISIBLE WAR

While most Americans are worrying about the energy crisis, an even more serious resource crunch could bring the U.S. economy to its knees. Of the 36 non-fuel minerals essential to the United States as an industrial society, we are crucially dependent upon foreign sources for 22 of them. In 1980, we were obliged to import 91 percent of our chromium, 88 percent of our platinum-group metals, 93 percent of our cobalt and 97 percent of our tantalum and manganese. By contrast, we were only 42-percent dependent on imported oil.[5]

This introduction, then, presents the problem of mineral shortage within the perspective of the more widely known energy crisis.

EXERCISE 8-2

Directions: *Choose one of the reading selections at the end of the chapter. Read the selection and answer the multiple choice questions. Then answer each of the following questions.*

1. Read the introductory paragraph again carefully and list the types of information that it gives you about the selection.

    _____

    _____

2. What function did the introduction perform?

    _____

    _____

Reading Summaries and Conclusions

Unified pieces of writing are brought to a close through the use of summaries and conclusions. Each in its own way brings the ideas expressed in the article together or enables the reader to draw the ideas together.

Summaries. A summary is a review of the important ideas expressed in the article. Found most commonly in highly factual materials such as textbooks, reports, and reference material, a summary is an outline in paragraph form. It reviews important facts and ideas, usually in the order in which they are presented in the body of the material for the purposes of emphasis and clarity. The following chapter summary, taken from a sociology textbook chapter on environmental abuse, provides a clear outline of the topics covered in the chapter.

SUMMARY

Environmental abuse occurs as humans violate basic principles of ecology. Polluting the air and water, spreading radioactivity into the atmosphere, increasing levels of noise, creating numerous wastes, and consuming irreplaceable resources — all affect the global ecosystem. Since human beings are part of the ecosystem, we too are affected by these activities.

There are a number of major types of environmental abuse. Air pollution is known to have harmful effects on health and property. Pollution of water brings the threat of disease, shortages of clean water, and destruction of plant and aquatic life. Nuclear power poses dangers of radioactive contamination. Solid wastes, many of which are not biologically decomposable, accumulate. Noise and visual pollution are on the increase, the former affecting health and both harming the appeal of our environment. Land is being lost to misuse, often to the detriment of vegetation and wildlife. Finally, irreplaceable resources — e.g., energy-producing fuels and ores crucial to manufacturing — are facing rapid depletion. Conflict over scarce resources — many of which are located primarily in poor Third World countries — promises to emerge in the future.

There are different views on why environmental abuse is taking place. Some feel it is a result of human nature. Blame has also been placed on population growth, as well as on a loss of control over science and technology. Finally, the profit-seeking orientation of capitalism has been blamed. There is little consensus on causes.

Many problems stand in the way of eliminating environmental abuse. Ignorance is a serious problem. Cultural drives, apathy, economic considerations, and political hurdles seem to work against the elimination — as opposed to the slowdown — of environmental abuse. Possible solutions include imposing strict controls over what is produced in our economy and how. We must alter our lifestyles by directing our consumption patterns into ecologically sane pathways.[6]

OUTLINE

Environmental abuse = humans violate principles of ecology.

Types of Abuse
1. Air
2. Water
3. Radioactive
4. Solid
5. Noise & Visual
6. Land Misuse
7. Energy

Reasons for Abuse
1. Human Nature
2. Population Growth
3. Capitalism

Problems
1. Ignorance
2. Cultural, Economic, and Political Concerns
3. Control of Life Style Necessary

Summaries are useful to the reader, even though they present no new information, because the writer states, in very abbreviated form, what is most important to remember from the article or chapter. Especially with long or complicated material, it is easy to become so involved with each new idea that you are unable to understand the larger, more important points to which each idea leads. A summary brings you back to these larger points and provides you with an overview of the subject.

Conclusions. A conclusion is a final statement, or group of statements, about a subject that takes the thought developed throughout the article one or more steps further. A conclusion may introduce a new thought or direction of thought, or it may tentatively propose a solution to the problem discussed or present a contrasting viewpoint. A conclusion always introduces a new idea that has not been previously stated. It may also review ideas presented earlier, but only to lead to a new idea. The new idea may have been hinted at, or suggested earlier in the article, but usually it is directly stated for the first time in the conclusion.

The following brief article is concerned with classifying football players according to personality types. As you read the article, notice that the last paragraph, while effectively drawing the article to a close, introduces several new ideas.

YOU CAN'T TELL THE PLAYERS WITHOUT A PSYCHIATRIST

If you were coaching a professional football team, would you assign your players to their positions on the basis of personality types? Arnold J. Mandell, of the University of California School of Medicine, thinks you could. A few years ago, Mandell spent several weeks with the San Diego Chargers of the National Football League studying the players on the field and off. His conclusions: a player's basic personality type tells a great deal about his ability to run, kick, block, and call signals. On the basis of his observations, Mandell evolved the following NFL personality typology (1976):

Offensive players "like structure and discipline." The linemen are "ambitious, tenacious, precise, attentive to detail . . ." The guards are especially aggressive and loyal, but the wide receiver is at heart an actor, ". . . narcissistic and vain, and basically a loner." Running backs fall into two classes. The honest, tough, disciplined backs run straight ahead, while the zig-zaggers are quick, suspicious, and treacherous. The quarterback is "not bothered by the rules of other men [but] makes his own. He exploits the environment in a tough, tricky way with very little compunction."

Defensive players are "renegades," according to Mandell. "They attack structure, and they feel that little is gained by identification with the establishment. They are basically angry and rebellious, primed to explode." Mandell found considerable depression and rage among defensive backs — "They need controlled and timed brutality and anger." These men in particular are "committed to please out of a deep sense of self-criticism and a compulsion to undo the unnamed sins [they] haven't yet committed."

You don't have to take Mandell's typology too seriously. But you might want to apply it, as he did, to other kinds of celebrities. Mandell thinks of Charles de Gaulle as a quarterback-type, and Woody Allen as a defensive back who lives [in Woody's own words] "to endlessly fend off guilt." Truman Capote is a wide receiver, Kate Smith is a fullback, and Gerald Ford is a "natural offensive lineman." What position would you play? [7]

The concluding paragraph of this article introduces the notion that this type of classification may apply to celebrities as well as to football players. Then, in the last sentence, another new direction of thought is suggested by the question, "What position would you play?" The question encourages you to analyze your own personality type and the "position" you play.

Both summaries and conclusions, then, fulfill important functions in the organization of an article or selection. Be sure to pay attention to summaries and conclusions, both when prereading and reading. They focus your attention on the most important ideas of the selection and fix them firmly in your mind.

EXERCISE 8-3

Directions: *Turn to the same selection you chose for Exercise 8-2, and reread the last paragraph. Then answer the following questions.*

1. What thesis did the selection develop?

   _____

2. Did the last paragraph function as a summary or as a conclusion?

   _____

3. If the last paragraph is a summary, list the ideas it reviews. If the last paragraph is a conclusion, write the new thought or idea that it introduced.

   _____

   _____

   _____

THE FUNCTION OF TRANSITIONS

Transitions in an article or longer selection function as directional words do in a paragraph. A transition is a word, phrase, or sentence that connects ideas or smooths the change from one idea to another. Transitions are important to notice as you read because, often, they explain the relationships among ideas contained in the article. You might think of them as a master link without which the article does not make sense.

Now, read the following group of paragraphs. As you read, you may notice that the paragraphs do not seem to fit together. Try to discover what is missing.

Today, being single is common and respectable. Little or no stigma is attached; in fact, many single people are envied for their freedom. They have time to pursue personal interests and make the contacts necessary for professional advancement.

Independence is one, because single people can plan their own lives and have things their own way. There is no necessity to consider another person's emotional and social needs. Singles set their own daily schedule, eating, working, and sleeping as they wish.

One salary has more buying power when it supports one person than when two or more people depend on it. The old saying that two can live as cheaply as one does not apply in our current economy. Single people usually have a higher standard of living, dress well, and travel frequently.

You might have noticed that the first paragraph did not seem related to the second paragraph and that the third did not seem connected to the first and second. The reason this passage seemed unconnected was that it did not contain any transitions. Now read the same passage after underlined transitions have been added.

Today, being single is common and respectable. Little or no stigma is attached; in fact, many single people are envied for their freedom. They have time to pursue personal interests and make the contacts necessary for professional advancement.

There are several major advantages to singlehood. Independence is one, because single people can plan their own lives and have things their own way. There is no necessity to consider another person's emotional and social needs. Singles set their own daily schedule, eating, working, and sleeping as they wish.

A second advantage of singlehood is a financial one. One salary has more buying power when it supports one person than when two or more people depend on it. The old saying that two can live as cheaply as one does not apply in our current economy. Single people usually have a higher standard of living, dress well, and travel frequently.

Did you notice that the transitions seemed to tie the paragraphs together and define the relationships among the ideas? Specifically, the first transition announces that the remainder of the article will discuss advantages of singlehood, and the second indicates that a second advantage — financial — will be discussed.

EXERCISE 8-4

Directions: *Turn to the same selection you chose for Exercises 8-2 and 8-3. Reread the selection, looking for transitional words and phrases. Underline each transition that you find.*

APPLYING WHAT YOU HAVE LEARNED

Directions: *Turn to the reading selection in this chapter that you have not read. Read the selection and answer the multiple choice questions. Then answer the following questions.*

1. What information did the introduction give you about the selection?

   _____

   _____

2. What thesis did the selection develop?

   _____

   _____

3. What was the function of the last paragraph?

   _____

   _____

READING SELECTION 11
AN UGLY NEW FOOTPRINT IN THE SAND

A. B. C. Whipple

There were strangers on our beach yesterday, for the first time in a month. A new footprint on our sand is nearly as rare as in *Robinson Crusoe*. We are at the very edge of the Atlantic; half a mile out in front of us is a coral reef, and then nothing but 3,000 miles of ocean to West Africa. It is a wild and lonely beach, with the same surf beating on it as when Columbus came by. And yet the beach is polluted.

Oil tankers over the horizon have fouled it more than legions of picnickers could. The oil comes ashore in floating patches that stain the coral black and gray. It has blighted the rock crabs and the crayfish and has coated the delicate whorls of the conch shells with black goo. And it has congealed upon itself, littering the beach with globes of tar that resemble the cannonballs of a deserted battlefield. The islanders, as they go beachcombing for the treasures the sea has washed up for centuries, now wear old shoes to protect their feet from the oil that washes up too.

You have to try to get away from pollution to realize how bad it really is. We have known for the last few years how bad our cities are. Now there is no longer an escape. If there is oil on this island far out in the Atlantic, there is oil on nearly every other island.

It is still early here. The air is still clear over the island, but it won't be when they build the airstrip they are talking about. The water out over the reef is still blue and green, but it is dirtier than it was a few years ago. And if the land is not despoiled, it is only because there are not yet enough people here to despoil it. There will be. And so for the moment on this island we are witnesses to the beginning, as it were, of the pollution of our environment. . . .

Until the pollution of our deserted beach, it seemed simple to blame everything on the "population explosion." If the population of this island, for example, could be stabilized at a couple of hundred, there would be very little problem with the environment in this secluded area. There would be no pollution of the environment if there were not too many people using it. And so if we concentrate on winning the war against overpopulation, we can save the earth for mankind.

But the oil on the beach belies this too-easy assumption. Those tankers are not out there because too many Chinese and Indians are being born every minute. They are not even out there because there are too many Americans and Europeans. They are delivering their oil, and cleaning their tanks at sea and sending the residue up onto the beaches of the Atlantic and Pacific, in order to fuel the technology of mankind — and the factories and the power plants, the vehicles and the engines that have enabled mankind to survive on his planet are now spoiling the planet for life.

The fishermen on this island are perfectly right in preferring the outboard motor to the sail. Their livelihood is involved, and the motor, for all its fouling smell, has helped increase the fisherman's catch so that he can now afford to dispense with the far more obnoxious outdoor privy. But the danger of technology is in its escalation, and there has already been a small amount of escalation here. You can see the motor oil slicks around the town dock. Electric generators can be heard over the sound of the surf. And while there are only about two dozen automobiles for the ten miles of road, already there is a wrecked jeep rusting in the harbor waters where it was dumped and abandoned. The escalation of technological pollution is coming here just as surely as it came to the mainland cities that are now shrouded by fly ash.

If the oil is killing the life along the coral

heads, what must it not be doing to the phytoplankton at sea which provide 70% of the oxygen we breathe? The lesson of our fouled beach is that we may not even have realized how late it is already. Mankind, because of his technology, may require far more space per person on this globe than we had ever thought, but it is more than a matter of a certain number of square yards per person. There is instead a delicate balance of nature in which many square miles of ocean and vegetation and clean air are needed to sustain only a relatively few human beings. We may find, as soon as the end of this century, that the final $\boxed{\text{despoliation}}$ of our environment has been signaled not by starvation but by people choking to death. The technology — the machine — will then indeed have had its ultimate, mindless, all-unintended triumph over man, by destroying the atmosphere he lives in just as surely as you can pinch off a diver's breathing tube.

Sitting on a lonely but spoiled beach, it is hard to imagine but possible to believe.

COMPREHENSION TEST 11

Directions: *Circle the letter of the best answer.*

1. The best statement of the main idea of this essay is
   a) Pollution has reached even the remotest areas of the globe and will only worsen.
   b) The solution to pollution problems lies in controlling population growth.
   c) Outboard motors are the major culprits in the pollution of our oceans.
   d) We can only solve pollution problems when we stop all oil production.

2. The writer feels that the final destruction of mankind could very well come from
   a) overpopulation
   b) nuclear war
   c) air pollution
   d) starvation

3. The major cause of pollution of the author's beach is
   a) increasing numbers of cars being used
   b) overpopulation of the tiny island
   c) oil tankers cleaning their tanks at sea
   d) large numbers of tourists invading the island

4. Before the pollution on the beach, the main environmental problems of the island were being caused by
   a) overpopulation
   b) factories
   c) wood stoves
   d) commercial fishing

5. The author thinks that if there is pollution on his little island
   a) the cities will be next
   b) its inhabitants are at fault
   c) the federal government should clean it up
   d) almost every other island is polluted

6. The word "despoliation" as used here means
   a) destruction
   b) definition
   c) desperation
   d) destination

7. The pollution in our oceans may be causing phytoplankton to
   a) increase to a dangerous level
   b) be eaten by fish in place of their usual food
   c) gradually be destroyed
   d) poison important species of fish

8. The author would most likely agree with legislation that would
   a) restrict the travel of oil tankers
   b) limit commercial fishing
   c) require factories to report and control industrial wastes
   d) limit technological research

9. The writer sees that our greatest conflict today is between man and
   a) nature
   b) technology
   c) man
   d) religion

10. The tone expressed throughout this essay is one of
    a) panic and confusion
    b) gloom and despair
    c) enthusiasm and hope
    d) humor and lightheartedness

Selection 11:	864 words

Finishing Time: ___ ___ ___
HR. MIN. SEC.

Starting Time: ___ ___ ___
HR. MIN. SEC.

Reading Time: ___ ___
MIN. SEC.

WPM Score: _____

Comprehension Score: _____ %

Reading Efficiency Score: _____

READING SELECTION 12
CLONING: A GENERATION MADE TO ORDER

Caryl Rivers

Human reproduction begins with the merger of the sex cells, sperm and egg. Since each contains only half a set of chromosomes, the joining of sperm with the egg is the first step in the creation of a new and unique individual, with traits inherited from both parents. But this is not the only possible way for life to begin.

The other type of cells in the human body already has a full set of chromosomes. All the genetic information necessary for an organism to reproduce itself is contained in the nucleus of every cell in that organism. If body cells could be made to divide, the result would be asexual reproduction — the production of offspring with only one parent. Such a process is already being used with other species — it is called cloning. It has been tried successfully with plants, fruit flies — and more significantly, with frogs.

In 1968, J. B. Gurdon at Oxford University produced a clonal frog. He took an unfertilized egg cell from an African clawed frog and destroyed its nucleus by ultraviolet radiation. He replaced it with the nucleus of an intestinal cell of another frog of the same species. The egg, suddenly finding itself with a full set of chromosomes, began to reproduce. It was "tricked" into starting the reproductive process. The result was a tadpole that was a genetic twin of the frog that donated the cell. The "mother" frog contributed nothing to the genetic identity of the tadpole, since her potential to pass on her traits was destroyed when the nucleus of her egg was obliterated .

How would it work with human beings? Roughly the same way. A healthy egg could be removed from a woman's body, in the same way that Edwards and Fowler obtain eggs for their work. But instead of fertilizing the egg with sperm, scientists could destroy the nucleus of the human egg and replace it with a cell taken from the arm or anywhere of a donor we'll call John X. The egg would be reimplanted in the uterus of a woman. Although its identity would

be wiped out with the destruction of its nucleus, it could nonetheless start to divide, because it had received the proper signal — the presence of a full set of chromosomes. The baby that would be the result of that process would have only one parent — John X. It would, in fact, be a carbon copy of John X — his twin, a generation removed. (Or her twin, if the cell donor were female.)

In March of this year scientists announced major progress on the hunt for the substance that "switches on" the reproductive mechanisms of the cell. Gurdon's first experiments with the frog proved that such a mechanism exists and that all cells — not just sex cells — could be made to reproduce. Now, work done by Gurdon at Cambridge and by Ann Janice Brothers at the University of Indiana is moving science closer to discovering the identity of the "master switch."

Gurdon inserted the nuclei of human cancer cells into immature frog eggs, and the human cell nuclei responded in dramatic fashion, swelling in size to as much as a hundredfold.

Brothers, working with amphibians, axolotls, has observed that a molecule identified as the O+ factor appears to be the substance that signals the reproductive process to carry on. Eggs produced by axolotls that did not contain the O+ factor did not develop past very rudimentary stages until they were injected with O+ substance. Brothers and her colleagues at Indiana report that O+ appears to be a large protein molecule that is somewhat acidic. The scientists are working to isolate and define that molecule. The identification of the "master switch" would be a giant step toward understanding cancer and would bring the day of human cloning closer.

The consequences of human cloning are almost impossible to imagine. Widespread human cloning would alter human society beyond recognition. The family would no longer exist, sexuality would have no connection with reproduction. The idea of parenthood would be completely changed. The diversity of human beings provided by sexual reproduction would vanish. One could imagine entire communities of people who looked exactly the same, whose range of potential was identical. Some scientists have suggested that "clones and clonishness" could replace our present patterns of nation and race.

The misuses of cloning are not hard to predict. Would an aging dictator try to insure the continuance of his regime by an heir apparent who was his genetic double? Would women and men project their egos into the future by producing their own "carbon copies"? Would society choose to clone our most valued citizens? Artists? Generals? Members of elite groups? The capacity of our species to change and adapt may be rooted in the diversity of the gene pool. By tampering with that process we could be limiting our own ability to survive.

There are some who believe that current work in test-tube fertilization to extract eggs is a first step in the direction of cloning. There have been some estimates that human cloning will be a reality within the decade. Who will say where we draw the line?

COMPREHENSION TEST 12

Directions: *Circle the letter of the best answer.*

1. The main point of this essay suggests that
   a) cloning could adversely change the human gene pool
   b) scientists are on the verge of a breakthrough in cloning
   c) human cloning could be used for evil purposes
   d) science is capable of accomplishing anything

2. In asexual reproduction offspring are created
   a) through artificial insemination
   b) in the womb of a person other than the parent
   c) by just one parent
   d) that are new and unique individuals

3. An organism produced by cloning would look
   a) exactly like the donor organism
   b) similar to the female who gives birth
   c) unlike any other organism
   d) like a combination of the two parents

4. It is believed that the "master switch" for the reproductive process is a particular type of
   a) vitamin C +
   b) triglyceride enzyme

   c) acidic protein molecule
   d) ultraviolet ray

5. Cloning has been accomplished with all of the following *except*
   a) amphibians
   b) humans
   c) insects
   d) plants

6. The word "obliterated" means
   a) somewhat altered
   b) reproduced asexually
   c) carefully selected
   d) totally destroyed

7. Rivers believes that human cloning would
   a) cause a radical change in human activities and customs
   b) be an extremely expensive matter
   c) improve the human race
   d) strengthen human society

8. Widespread cloning could be harmful to mankind by
   a) increasing the percentages of mutations in each generation
   b) causing a third world war
   c) affecting our ability to adjust to change
   d) offering a cure for cancer

9. The author of this essay probably regards human cloning as
   a) a useful way to improve the human race
   b) completely immoral
   c) an innovation, the possible results of which should be carefully weighed
   d) a technique that is impossible to develop

10. The author's attitude toward cloning could be described as
    a) completely pessimistic
    b) mildly humorous
    c) extremely critical
    d) cautiously objective

Selection 12:   858 words

Finishing Time: _____ _____ _____
                 HR.   MIN.   SEC.

Starting Time: _____ _____ _____
                HR.   MIN.   SEC.

Reading Time: _____ _____
                       MIN.   SEC.

WPM Score: _____

Comprehension Score: _____ %

Reading Efficiency Score: _____

Unit Four:
How to Remember
What You Read

Now that you have developed skills to comprehend accurately and efficiently, your next concern should be to develop techniques to remember the information that you identify as important. Even though you may understand what you read, unless you can remember it later, you are not an efficient reader. Just as was true for comprehension, retention is a skill that can be developed and polished by learning and applying various techniques and shortcuts.

Throughout this section, then, you will learn techniques for remembering what you read. Chapter 9 will present ways to increase your concentration and to use review after reading to increase your retention. Other retention aids will be discussed and a systematic approach that features learning while reading will be demonstrated. In Chapter 10 you will learn three notetaking systems to use to identify, record, and remember important information. Specific techniques for underlining, taking marginal notes, and using summary notes will be described and their use in particular reading-study situations will be discussed.

Chapter 9:
Techniques for Remembering
What You Read

Have you ever read an entire page, or more, and remembered little or nothing of what you read? Do you have difficulty keeping your mind on what you're reading? Would you like to be able to remember more of what you read? Would you like to be able to learn more without increasing your study time? If your answer is yes to any of these questions, then the techniques and methods presented in this chapter should be useful to you.

In the previous unit, you learned how to locate important information by recognizing the structure of sentences, paragraphs and selections, chapters, and articles. Of course, identifying what to learn is the first, and most important, step in studying anything. However, once you have identified what is important, the next step should be to learn and remember the information most efficiently. This chapter will focus on techniques to increase your ability to remember what you read. As a first step, you must be able to control your concentration, to keep your mind on what you are reading. In the first section of this chapter we will discuss ways to eliminate distractions as well as to focus your attention. Then, in the next two sections, specific suggestions for improving your ability to retain information will be discussed. Finally, an effective system for reading and studying factual material will be demonstrated.

IMPROVING YOUR CONCENTRATION

CONCENTRATION QUIZ
1. Are you sitting on a comfortable chair or lying on a comfortable bed?
2. Is there a TV nearby? Is it on?
3. Are there friends or family in the same room who are not studying?
4. Do you wish you didn't have to read this chapter?
5. Are you reading this chapter only because it was assigned by your instructor?

6. Are you worried about anything or trying to make an important decision?
7. Are you tired, either physically or mentally?
8. Do you think about other things you have to do as you are reading?

If your answer is yes to any of the above questions, reading and studying this chapter will probably take you more time than it should. A yes answer indicates that you are not reading and studying under the most favorable conditions. In the sections that follow you will learn how to control those factors which directly influence your ability to keep your mind on what you are reading and studying. If you can control external distractions and focus your attention on the task at hand, you will see an improvement in your ability to concentrate.

Controlling External Distractions

Many factors other than your mental capacity and how well you read and study will directly influence how effectively you can concentrate. Many events happen around you, and often these can divert your attention from what you are reading. A phone ringing, a dog barking, friends arguing, or parents reminding you about errands can break your concentration and cost you time. Usually an interruption costs you more time than the interruption itself. Each time you are interrupted, it takes time to get back to what you were doing. If you were reading, you have to locate where you were, and you may have to reread part of a paragraph. Also, each time you are distracted it takes you a minute or two to refocus your attention.

Although you cannot eliminate all distractions, it is possible to control many of them through a wise choice of time and place for study. For a week or so, analyze where and when you study. Try to notice situations in which you seemed to accomplish a great deal as well as those in which you accomplished very little. At the end of the week, look for a pattern emerging. Where and when did you find it was easy to concentrate? Where and when was it most difficult? Then, use the information from your analysis along with the following suggestions to choose a regular time and place for study.

1. *Choose a place to study that is relatively free of interruptions.* It may be necessary to decide what type of distractions occur most frequently and then choose a place where you will be free of them. For instance, if your home, apartment, or dorm has many distractions such as phone calls, friends stopping by, or family members talking and watching TV, and so forth, it may be necessary to find

a different place to study. The campus library or a neighborhood library is often quiet and free of distractions.

2. *Choose a place free of distractions.* Although, for example, your living room may be quiet and free of interruptions, you may not be able to concentrate there. You may be distracted by noises from the street, the view from a window, the presence of a TV, or a project you are working on.

3. *Do not study where you are too comfortable.* If you study in a lounge chair or lying across your bed, you may find it difficult to concentrate. Reading and studying requires close attention, and placing your body in a relaxing position will do nothing to encourage concentration; in fact, it may have a negative effect. You may find that you feel more inclined to relax than to study or that you may become drowsy or fall asleep.

4. *Study in the same place.* Once you have located a good place to study, try to study in this place regularly. You will find that you will become familiar with the surroundings and will begin to build up associations between the place and the activity you perform there. Eventually, as soon as you enter the room or sit down at the desk, you will begin to feel as though you should study.

5. *Choose a time of day when you are mentally alert.* Give yourself the advantage of reading or studying when your mind is sharp and ready to pick up new information. Avoid studying when you are hungry or tired, because it is most difficult to concentrate at these times.

6. *Establish a fixed time for reading or studying.* Studying at the same time each day will help you fall into the habit of studying more easily. For example, if you establish, as part of a schedule, that you will study right after dinner, soon it will become almost automatic to sit down to study as soon as you have finished dinner. You will find that, if you follow a schedule, the routine will make it easier to concentrate.

Focusing Your Attention

In addition to controlling interruptions and distractions in order to increase your concentration level, you must also learn to focus your attention on the task at hand. Most people can keep their minds on one topic for a limited period of time; that is called their *attention span*. Your attention span varies from subject to subject, from book to book, and from speaker to speaker. It may also vary according to the time of day and place where you are studying. However, you can increase your attention span by using techniques that help you to sharpen and to control your attention. As you use these techniques you will find that you are able to keep your mind on what you are reading for longer periods of time.

1. *Set goals for yourself.* Before you begin to read or study, decide what you intend to accomplish during that session and about how much time it will take. You might write these on paper and keep it in front of you. By having specific goals to meet, you may find that you feel more like working and you will be less inclined to waste time thinking about other things. For an evening of reading or studying, you might write goals like this:
   a) Complete math problems.
   b) Write rough draft of English paper.
   c) Review psychology notes.

2. *Read with a purpose.* In Chapter 3 we discussed the importance of having a specific purpose for reading. It increases your comprehension and retention, but it also helps you keep your mind on what you are reading. If you are looking for specific information as you read, it will be easier to keep your attention focused on the material.

3. *Keep a distractions list.* As you are reading, often you will think of something you should remember to do. You might remember to call your sister or to buy a Mother's Day card. An item like this will often flash through your mind at various times, distracting you from what you are reading. An effective solution to this problem is to keep a distraction list, or you might call it a "To Do" list. Keep a piece of paper nearby, and whenever something distracts you or you are reminded of something, jot it down on the paper. You will find that once you have written the item on paper it will no longer keep flashing through your mind. Your distractions list might look like this:
   a) Call Sam.
   b) Buy lab manual for chemistry.
   c) Get tire fixed.

4. *Vary your reading.* Most people tire of reading about a particular subject if they spend too long with it. Of course, as you tire or become less interested in a subject, your concentration lessens. To overcome this problem, try to read parts of several assignments in an evening rather than finishing one assignment completely. For example, you might read part of a psychology assignment, then complete a short story assigned for a literature course, and then finish a math assignment. The variety in subject matter would provide needed change and prevent you from losing interest in your reading.

5. *Combine physical and mental activities.* Although your eyes move across lines of print, reading is primarily a mental activity. Because the rest of your body is not involved in the reading process, it is easy to become restless or feel a need to *do* something. Many students find it helpful to be physically as well as mentally involved with what they are reading. Activities such as highlighting, underlining, making marginal notes, or writing summary outlines provide an outlet for physical energy as well as serving as useful study aids. You will learn more about each of these aids in the next chapter.

6. *Take frequent breaks.* Because your attention span is necessarily limited, it is important to take frequent breaks while you are reading. For instance, never decide to sit down and read for a solid three-hour block. After the first hour or so, you will tire and begin to lose concentration, and you will find yourself accomplishing less and less. Although it may seem that taking a break wastes time, you will see that you "make up" that lost time in increased efficiency and higher levels of concentration after your break.

7. *Approach your assignment positively.* If you approach a reading assignment with the attitude that you are not interested in it and you feel that reading it is a waste of time, you can be certain that you will have difficulty concentrating. A negative mind set almost ensures poor comprehension and low levels of concentration. To overcome this, try to find some way to become interested in the subject. Try to question or challenge the author as you read, or try to develop questions.

EXERCISE 9-1

Directions. *Now that you are aware of the factors that influence your concentration, answer the following questions about where and how you are reading this chapter. Your answers will give you an idea of how well you are controlling the factors that influence concentration.*

1. Are you reading in a place relatively free of distractions and interruptions?

   _____

2. Are you reading in the same place in which you usually read and study?

   _____

3. Notice what time of day it is. Is this a high or low concentration period? Is it the same time as you usually study?

_____

4. What is your purpose for reading this chapter?

_____

5. How long do you expect to spend reading this chapter?

_____

6. How many times has your mind wandered while you were doing this exercise?

_____

THE IMPORTANCE OF REVIEW

Once you have established your powers of concentration, the next step in increasing your ability to remember what you read is to take advantage of two variables that largely control the ease, accuracy, and speed with which you are able to recall what you have read. These essential factors are review and repetition. Let us see how you can use these two variables to increase your retention of any reading material.

Using Review to Increase Your Recall

Review refers to the process of going back over something you have already read. There are two types of review: immediate and periodic. Both types can greatly increase the amount you can remember from a printed page.

Immediate Review. When you finish reading an assignment, your first inclination may be to breathe a sigh of relief, close the book, and go on to another task. However, you can significantly increase your recall of the material if you take a few minutes immediately after you finish reading to go back over the material, briefly reviewing the overall organization and important ideas presented. In fact, you might think of review as a postreading activity, similar to prereading. In reviewing you should reread the parts of the article or chapter that contain the most important ideas. In review, just as in prereading, you should concentrate on titles, introductions, summaries, headings, graphic material, and depending on the length of the material, topic sentences. Also review any notes you took and any portions of the text that you underlined.

The purpose of reviewing is to enable you to form a final overall impression of the material and to be reexposed to each major idea so that it sticks in your mind. Considerable research has been conducted on how individuals learn and remember. These experiments have demonstrated that review immediately following reading greatly improves the amount remembered. However, the review must be *immediate;* it will not produce the same effects if you take a ten-minute break or do it later in the evening. In order to get the full benefit, you must review while the content of the article or chapter is still fresh in your mind. Review before you have had a chance to forget and before other thoughts and ideas interfere or compete with what you have read.

Periodic Review. Although immediate review is very effective and greatly increases your ability to recall the information, it is not sufficient to ensure that you will be able to remember the material for long periods of time. In order to remember facts and ideas permanently, you should review them periodically. That is, you must go back and refresh your recall on a regular basis by doing a brief review. For example, suppose you have read a chapter on criminal behavior in your sociology text and you need to remember the material for a mid-term exam scheduled in four weeks. If you read the chapter, reviewed it immediately following, and then did nothing with it until the exam a month later, you would not remember enough to score well on the exam. To achieve a good grade, you would need to keep the ideas in your memory, by reviewing the chapter periodically. You might review the chapter once several days after reading it, again a week later, and once again a week before the exam. Then, when the time comes to study the chapter for the exam, you will find that you are still basically familiar with the chapter's content and will not need to spend valuable study time becoming reacquainted with the material. Instead, studying will be a matter of learning specifics and organizing particular information into a format in which it can be easily remembered during the exam.

Why Review Is Effective

One of the primary reasons that both immediate and periodic review are effective is that each provides a repetition of an article or chapter's content. Repetition is one important way that you learn and remember information. Think of how you learned the multiplication tables or why you know the phone numbers of your closest friends. In both cases, frequent use enables you to remember. Numerous repetitions of the numbers made them part of your memory. However, if you were to stop using the numbers, you would find that they would fade from your memory. For instance, you probably cannot remember the phone number of an old friend who has moved away or whom you no longer call regularly. So you can see that frequent repetition is just as important to maintaining information in your memory as it is to initially establishing it.

A second reason for the effectiveness of review is that it consolidates, or draws together, information into a unified whole. As you read a chapter, you are processing the information piece by piece. Review, both immediate and periodic, provides a means of seeing how each piece relates to each other piece and how each piece relates to the material as a whole.

EXERCISE 9-2

Directions: *Choose one of the reading selections at the end of the chapter. Read the selection, and review it immediately. Then, underline the parts of the selection that you reread as part of your immediate review.*

OTHER AIDS TO RETENTION

Although review and repetition are the most important methods of increasing the amount of material you remember, there are many other devices and techniques that also increase your recall. However, for several of the techniques you will find that the usefulness depends, to a large extent, on the type of material you are reading. Some of the techniques suggested in this section will be well suited to certain materials and difficult to apply to others; adaptations will be necessary.

Intent to Remember

Very few people remember things which they have no intent to remember. Do you remember what color clothing a friend wore last week? Can you name all the songs that you heard on the radio this morning? Can you remember exactly what time you got home last Saturday night? If not, why not? Most likely you cannot remember

200

these facts, because, at the time, you did not see the importance of remembering them. Of course, if you had known at the time that you would be asked these questions, you would have remembered the items. From this illustration, then, you can see that you must intend to remember things in order to be able to do so effectively. The same principle holds true for reading and its retention. In order to remember what you read, you must have a clear and strong intent to remember specific types of information. Unless you have defined what you intend to remember before you begin reading, you will find that it is difficult to recall specific content.

An intent to remember can actually be interpreted as a purpose for reading. In Chapter 3 we discussed the establishment of purposes or questions as a key to reading efficiency and showed how a purpose can help you keep your mind on what you are reading. Now you can see that establishment of purpose also contributes to your ability to recall what you read. In a sense, then, prereading also contributes to your ability to recall, because prereading provides the basis for establishing purposes for reading. That is, prereading acquaints you with the overall content and structure and suggests what is important to remember in the article or chapter.

Organization/Categorization

When you read about paragraph organization, you learned that it is easier to remember information that has a pattern or structure than it is to remember material that is randomly arranged. Now you should be skilled in recognizing organizational patterns for paragraphs. The next step is to develop skill in recognizing relationships between patterns within longer pieces of writing for the purpose of increasing your recall.

Some essays, chapters, and articles or portions of them use the same organizational patterns that are used in paragraphs. For instance, a group of paragraphs may follow a chronological or example-illustration pattern. Just as in paragraphs, recognition of the pattern will increase your recall of the material's content.

In other selections, essays, and chapters a pattern may not be evident, yet you may be able to organize the ideas into a structure. One effective way to organize information is to *categorize* it, to arrange it in groups according to similar characteristics. Suppose, for example, that you had to remember the following list of items to buy for a picnic when you go shopping: bottle opener, candy, 7-Up, Pepsi, napkins, potato chips, lemonade, peanuts, paper plates. The easiest way to remember this list would be to divide it in groups. You might arrange it as follows:

Drinks	*Snacks*	*Picnic Supplies*
7-Up	peanuts	bottle opener
Pepsi	candy	paper plates
lemonade	potato chips	napkins

By grouping the items into categories, you are putting similar items together. Then, rather than learning one long list of unorganized items, you are learning three shorter, organized lists.

Now imagine you are reading an article on the discipline in public high schools. Instead of learning one long list of reasons for disruptive student behaviors, you might divide the reasons into groups, such as behaviors related to peer conflicts, behaviors related to teacher conflicts, and so forth.

Associating Ideas

Association is a useful way to remember new facts and ideas. It involves connecting information that is new and unfamiliar to facts and ideas you already know. For instance, if you are reading about divorce in a sociology class and are trying to remember a list of common causes, you might try to associate each cause with a person you know who exhibits that problem. Suppose one cause of divorce is lack of communication between the partners. You might remember this by thinking of a couple you know, Aunt Pat and Uncle Lorne, for example, who never seem to understand what the other is doing. Or to remember lack of common interests as a cause, think of a couple who have few shared interests.

Using association involves stretching your memory to see what the new information has in common with what you already know. When you find a connection between the known and unknown, you can retrieve from your memory the new information along with the old.

Using a Variety of Sensory Modes

Your senses of sight, hearing, and touch can all be used to help you remember what you read. Most of the time, most of us use just one sense — sight — as we read. However, if you are able to use more than one sense, you will find that recall is easier. Activities such as underlining, highlighting, notetaking, and outlining involve your sense of touch and enable you to reinforce your learning. Or, if you are having particular difficulty remembering something, try to use your auditory sense as well. You might try repeating the information out loud, or you might listen to someone else repeat the information.

Visualization

Visualizing, or creating a mental picture of what you have read, often aids recall. This technique definitely depends on the type of material you are reading. In reading descriptive writing in which the writer intends to create a mental picture, visualization is an easy task. In reading about events, people, processes, or procedures, visualization is again relatively simple. However, visualization of abstract ideas, theories, philosophies, and concepts may not be possible. Instead, you may be able to create in your mind, or on paper, a visual picture of the relationship of ideas. For example, suppose you are reading about the invasion of privacy and learn that there are arguments for and against the storage of personal data on each citizen in large computer banks. You might create a visual image of two lists of information — advantages and disadvantages.

Mnemonic Devices

Memory tricks and devices, often called mnemonics, are useful in helping you recall lists of factual information. You might use a rhyme, such as the one used for remembering the number of days in each month: "Thirty days hath September, April, June, and November. . . ." Another device involves making up a word or phrase in which each letter represents an item you are trying to remember. If you remember the name Roy G. Biv, for example, you will be able to recall the colors in the light spectrum: red, orange, yellow, green, blue, indigo, violet.

EXERCISE 9-3

Directions: *Five study/learning situations follow. Decide which of the aids to retention described in this section — organization/ categorization, association, sensory modes, and mnemonic devices — might be most useful in each situation and list the aid after each item.*

1. In a sociology course you are assigned to read about and remember the causes of child abuse. How might you remember them more easily?

   _____

   _____

2.   You are studying astronomy and you have to remember the names of the nine planets: Mercury, Venus, Earth, Mars, Jupiter, Saturn, Uranus, Neptune, and Pluto. What retention aid(s) could help you remember them?

_____

_____

3.   You are taking a course in anatomy and physiology and must learn the name and location of each bone in the human skull. How could you learn these easily?

_____

_____

4.   You have an entire chapter to review for history and your instructor has told you that your exam will contain thirty true-false questions on Civil War battles. What could you do as you review to help yourself remember the details of various battles?

_____

_____

5.   You are taking a course in twentieth-century history and are studying the causes of the Vietnam War in preparation for an essay exam. You find that there are many causes, some immediate, others long term. Some have to do with international politics, others with internal problems in North and South Vietnam. How could you organize your study for this exam?

_____

_____

SYSTEMS FOR REMEMBERING WHAT YOU READ

Throughout this chapter you have become familiar with devices and techniques to improve your ability to remember what you read. You may be wondering how you will be able to use all these techniques and how to combine them most effectively. Many students have asked similar questions, and, as a result, systems have been developed and tested that combine some of the most useful techniques into a step-by-step procedure for learning as you read.

The most widely used system is called SQ3R; the letters stand for Survey, Question, Read, Recite, and Review. As you read about SQ3R, you will see that it incorporates many of the skills you have already learned into an organized, systematic way of reading, and that it can increase your reading efficiency.

The SQ3R Reading-Study System

Developed in the 1940s, the SQ3R system has been used successfully for many years. Considerable experimentation has been done, and the system has proven effective in increasing students' retention of prose material. It is especially useful for textbooks and other highly factual, well-organized materials. Basically, SQ3R is a way of learning or remembering as you read. Each of the steps in the system will be briefly summarized, and then you will see how it can be applied to a sample selection.

1. *Survey*. Become familiar with the overall content and organization of the material. You have already learned this technique and know it as prereading.
2. *Question*. Formulate questions about the material that you expect to be able to answer as you read. As you read each successive heading, turn it into a question. This step is similar to establishing purposes for reading discussed in Chapter 3.
3. *Read*. As you read each section, actively search for the answer to your questions. When you find the answers, underline or mark portions of the text that concisely state the information.
4. *Recite*. Probably the most important part of the system, "recite" means that you should stop after each section or after each major heading, look away from the page, and try to remember the answer to your question. If you are unable to remember, then look back at the page and reread the material. Then test yourself again by looking away from the page and "reciting" the answer to your question.
5. *Review*. Immediately after you have finished reading, go back through the material again, reading titles, introductions, summaries, headings, and graphic material. As you read each heading, recall your question and test yourself to see if you can still remember the answer. If you cannot, reread that section again.

Now that you are generally familiar with the SQ3R system, you can see that it incorporates such techniques as intent to remember (in survey and question), repetition (in recite), and immediate review (in review), into a usable approach.

One of the reasons that SQ3R is so effective is that it forces you to test your own recall of the material in the recite step and again in review. The method helps you identify what you have not learned and provides a useful review of material that you have learned. It is also useful because it does not permit you to move on to a new section until you have learned the previous section. This ensures that you understand what you are reading and prevents you from going too far before realizing that you have not concentrated on the reading material.

Now, to give you a clear picture of how the steps in the SQ3R method work together to produce an efficient approach to study reading, the method will be applied to a textbook chapter. Suppose you have been assigned to read the following article for a sociology class that is studying how mate selection occurs. Follow each of the SQ3R steps in reading this selection.

1. *Survey.* Preread the article, noticing introductions, headings, first sentences, and summary. From this prereading you should have an overall picture of what this article is intended to study and know the general conclusions the authors draw about mate selection.

2. *Question.* Now, using the headings as a starting point, develop several questions to which you expect to find answers in the article. You might ask such questions as:

    What procedures did the authors use to study mate selection?
    What type of questionnaire was used?
    What students were involved in the study?
    How does age affect mate selection?
    What number of children is preferred?
    What personal factors are involved in mate selection?

3. *Read.* Now read the selection through, keeping your questions in mind as you read. Stop at the end of each major section and proceed to step 4.

4. *Recite.* After each section, stop reading and check to see if you can recall the answer to your question. For instance, you should have found in answer to the question "What number of children is preferred?" that there is a trend toward fewer children and that women prefer more children than men.

5. *Review.* When you have finished reading the entire article, take a few minutes to reread the headings, recall your questions and check to see that you can still recall the answers.

CAMPUS VALUES IN MATE SELECTION: A REPLICATION

John W. Hudson and Lura F. Henze

In the mass media, college students are often depicted as having departed from the traditional values of the society. Thus, the youth of today are frequently charged with being less serious in mate selection than were young people a generation ago. Is this mass media image valid?

To compare values in mate selection held by college students today with those of earlier years, the literature was reviewed for relevant research. This review indicated that . . . [Two related studies, both done at the University of Wisconsin, were cited most often. The oldest, "Campus Values in Mate Selection," was done by Reuben Hill in 1939; the other, "Campus Values in Mate Selection: A Repeat Study," was done in 1956 by Robert McGinnis.*]. . . . These studies were selected for replication as they focused on personal characteristics related to mate selection and because the students who were the respondents in 1939 are the parental generation of today.

PROCEDURES

To broaden the base of this study, an investigation was conducted on four campuses located in widely separated geographic regions — three in the United States and one in Canada. The American colleges selected were Arizona State University, the University of Nebraska at Omaha, and the State University of New York at Stony Brook. The Canadian college chosen was the University of Alberta at Edmonton.

A copy of the "Campus Values" questionnaire, together with a cover letter explaining the nature of the study and a postage-paid return envelope, was mailed to each student in the sample. The original questionnaire had been prepared by Reuben Hill and Harold T. Christensen.

Description of the Questionnaire

Included in the questionnaire were the usual background items of age, sex, marital status, education, and family data. The evaluative section included preferences on age at time of marriage, age difference between husband and wife, number of children, and personal characteristics. The personal characteristics were 18 traits to be evaluated according to their degree of importance in choosing a mate. Provision was made for the respondent to add any further personal characteristics which he felt should be included.

Students were asked to assign a numerical weight of "three" to characteristics

---

* Reuben Hill, "Campus Values in Mate Selection," *Journal of Home Economics,* 37 (November 1945), Robert McGinnis, "Campus Values in Mate Selection: A Repeat Study," *Social Forces,* 36 (May 1959).

which they believed were indispensable, "two" to traits important but not indispensable, "one" to those desirable but not important, and "zero" to factors irrelevant in mate selection. Thus, respondents evaluated each trait and assigned an appropriate numerical weight to each; the investigators then ranked the traits on the basis of mean values computed from the numerical weights. For the purposes of this paper, the terms "ranked" and "evaluated" are used synonymously.

Description of the Sample

A one-percent random sample of full-time students at each of the four universities was drawn by the registrars' offices. Questionnaires were mailed to a total of 826 students; 566 (68.5 percent) were returned and usable.

The sample included 337 males and 229 females. The median age was 21.6 years for men and 20.4 years for women. Seventy-six percent of the men and 82 percent of the women were single.

FINDINGS

Age Factors in Mate Selection

College men and women in the 1967 sample indicated a preference for marriage at an earlier age than had been indicated in the previous studies. . . . The median preferred age at marriage for men in 1939 was 25.1 years and was 24.9 years for the 1956 sample. The age preference dropped to 24.5 years in 1967. The median age preference for women in 1939 was 24.0 years, and in 1956 and 1967, it declined to 22.9 and 22.5 years, respectively.

In all three studies, males and females agreed that the husband should be older than the wife but did not agree on the preferred age difference. Women preferred a greater age gap between spouses than did men.

Number of Children Preferred

In all three time periods investigated, women preferred more children than did men. The trend was toward more children wanted by men and women in 1956 (3.6 and 3.9) than in 1939 (3.3 and 3.5), and fewer children in 1967 (2.9 and 3.3) than in either of the earlier periods.

Personal Factors in Mate Selection

The data indicate that from one time period to the next, three of the 18 items, as evaluated by men, maintained the same rank and 11 did not vary by more than one place. . . . Males, in all three studies, evaluated dependable character as the most indispensable personal characteristic in a mate. Sociability and favorable social status consistently held their rank of twelfth and sixteenth place, respectively, in 1939, 1956, and 1967.

Chastity, as evaluated by men, declined to a greater degree than did any other characteristic. This was indicated by mean scores as well as by rank. In 1939 the mean score for chastity was 2.06, and in 1967 it was 1.28. In rank, the decline was from tenth place to fifteenth.

Greater emphasis was placed on good looks by males in 1967 than in either of the earlier studies. During the time period under study, health declined in importance from fifth to ninth place. The traits which moved consistently upward from 1939 to 1967 were mutual attraction, good cook-housekeeper, and similar educational background — each moved up two positions. The characteristic which fluctuated the most was similar religious background, which changed from thirteenth place in 1939 to tenth in 1956 and declined to fourteenth in 1967.

In the responses by women, no trait was consistently evaluated as more important in 1956 and 1967 than it had been in 1939. One of the 18 traits — good cook-housekeeper — ranked sixteenth in all three studies; the rank of eight other traits did not vary by more than one place. Emotional stability and dependable character ranked first or second in each time period studied. Women gave the least weight to good looks and similar political background.

For women, the evaluation of chastity declined to a greater extent than for any other characteristic. This was indicated by mean scores and by rank. The mean score for chastity was 2.0 in 1939 and .93 in 1967, while the rank in 1939 was tenth and in 1956 and 1967 it was fifteenth. Ambition, good health, and sociability moved downward with consistency. Fluctuation was greatest for education-intelligence, which ranked ninth in 1939, fourteenth in 1956, and seventh in 1967.

SUMMARY

While this study does not clearly and precisely add to theory construction, it does add substantive material which suggests generational stability in criteria used in mate selection. For although a child may rebel against domination, he cannot escape the ideas conditioned in him from his childhood.*

In 1967, compared to 1939, there have been changes in the behavior patterns of the college populations studied in terms of age factors in mate selection and in marrying while in college. However, this change is compatible with the high value placed on marriage by the parental generation — who were the college students of 1939 — and the younger generation who are the students today.

The charge that young people have departed from traditional values and are less serious about mate selection is not given support by the present study. Indeed, the findings suggest that youth's values regarding the importance of personal characteristics in mate selection are much the same today as they were a generation ago.

It might be said in conclusion that social change in the area of mate selection has not been as great as indicated by the press, feared by the parent, and perhaps hoped by the youth.

* Robert H. Coombs, "Reinforcement of Values in the Parental Home as a Factor in Mate Selection," *Marriage and Family Living,* 24 (May 1962), p. 155.

How SQ3R Improves Your Reading Efficiency

The SQ3R system improves your reading efficiency in three ways. It increases your comprehension, it increases your recall, and it saves you valuable time by encouraging you to learn as you read.

Your comprehension is most directly improved by the S and Q steps. By surveying or prereading you acquire an overview of the material that serves as an outline to follow as you read. In the question step, you are focusing your attention and identifying what is important to look for as you read.

Your recall of the material is improved through the recite and review steps. By testing yourself while reading and immediately after you have finished reading, you are building a systematic review pattern that will provide the necessary repetitions to ensure learning and recall.

Finally, because you are learning as you are reading, you will save time later when you are ready to study the material for an exam. Since, through recitation and review, you have already learned the material, you will find that you need much less time to prepare for an exam. Instead of learning the material for the first time, all you will need to do is refresh your memory and review difficult portions again.

APPLYING WHAT YOU HAVE LEARNED

Directions: *Choose one of the selections at the end of the chapter. Read the selection using the SQ3R method, following each of these steps:*

1. *Survey.* Preread the article to get an overview of the organization and content of the article.
2. *Question.* Write the questions you expect to be able to answer when you read the article.

    _____

    _____

3. *Read.* Read the selection, looking for the answers to your questions. As you find them, write them in the space below.

    _____

    _____

4. *Recite.* After each dark print heading, stop and recall your question and its answer.
5. *Review.* After finishing the article, quickly go back through the article, reviewing the major points.

READING SELECTION 13
THE BIOSPHERE

Difficulty Level: A

Watson M. Laetsch

Think of a basketball with a postage stamp glued to it. Picture next how thin the ink on that stamp is. The part of earth occupied by living things is equal to the thickness of the ink on the stamp on the ball, no more. We are, in a sense, creatures who live in a thin layer of green scum painted on a small rock whirling through space. Everything we earth-dwellers — plants, microbes, fungi, animals — need to sustain life we find within this layer, known as the *biosphere,* that part of the planet where life is found.

Part of the biosphere is solid land. Part of it is water, including all the world's oceans. Its third portion is a part of the atmosphere. Taken together, the biosphere is a thin layer

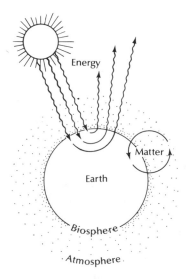

Figure 1 Energy enters and leaves the biosphere, forming an open system. This energy drives the cycling of matter within the biosphere. Matter does not enter or leave the earth, so matter is cycled within a closed system.

sandwiched between the *geosphere,* the mass of matter from which the earth is formed, and the *atmosphere,* the gaseous envelope that surrounds earth as it spins in space. Very uneven both in depth and in density, the biosphere extends upward to at most about 8 kilometers (5 miles) into the atmosphere. Eight kilometers up and 8 kilometers down (only in oceans) — those are the limits between which every form of life on earth exists.

MATTER AND ENERGY

Each living thing is a package of matter, made of chemical elements from the geosphere and atmosphere. These elements enter the biosphere and cycle through it in a complex fashion, the process we call living. When a living thing dies, the matter of which it was composed returns to the earth and the air, continuing in the eternal cycle between living and nonliving things. Earth's matter thus forms, for all practical purposes, a *closed system:* it is a *system* because a change in any part will affect all the other parts; it is *closed* because elements outside the system do not affect it significantly. Occasionally a few meteorites survive the fiery trip through the atmosphere and land on earth, but little matter enters the system that was not there before.

Earth's energy, in contrast to its matter, forms an *open system:* energy enters from outside the system, from the sun. In fact, if the only energy the earth had were that found within the biosphere, it would soon be exhausted, for two reasons.

First, energy can be neither created nor destroyed (this is known as the first law of thermodynamics), although it can be — and constantly is — transformed. Second, even though the amount of energy remains the same, the energy in the universe available to do *work* is

211

decreasing (this is the second law of thermodynamics). Why? When wind breaks a tree, when we cut a flower, when our muscles contract, when a cell divides, work is being done. All work requires the expenditure of energy; in fact, we can define energy as the "thing" that enables work to be done. When energy is used to do work, its form is changed, though the total amount remains constant. If you place buckets of water on top of a hill, the water has a certain energy (known as *potential energy:* because of its position, the water has the potential of doing work). If you then pour the water over the hill to fall on a waterwheel below, it makes the wheel turn. The potential energy is now transformed to an active form, which turns the wheel. Some of the energy will be converted into yet another form, heat, which happens whenever work is done. At both times the

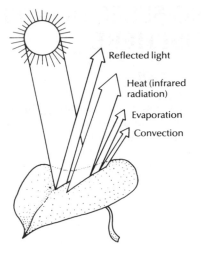

Figure 3 All organisms are fueled by light energy, which is transformed to chemical energy by photosynthesis. Only a small percentage, about 1 percent, of the radiation striking a leaf's surface is available for photosynthesis.

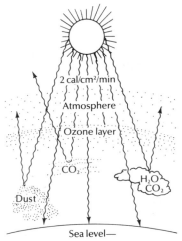

Figure 2 The atmosphere contains ozone (O_3), water (H_2O), carbon dioxide (CO_2), and dust, which either reflect incoming radiation or absorb it and reradiate energy back to space. As a result, about 40 percent of the sun's radiation received by the atmosphere is intercepted.

amount of energy is the same. But heat is a diffuse, disorderly kind of energy, frequently useless in itself for doing work (think of the steam venting from power plants: the heat in the steam represents energy, but it is too dispersed to do work). Thus some energy is always transformed into a useless form, and the amount of useful energy is decreased.

As work is done in the biosphere, most energy is lost as heat. Both this heat and that absorbed by earth and water are reflected from earth's surface as infrared rays, which are absorbed by clouds. On cloudy nights this radiation is reflected back by the cloud cover, giving us warmer nights. Eventually, though, this heat escapes to outer space, lost to earth forever; but as much energy comes in as goes out, so the biosphere's energy system is in a steady state. Nevertheless, the sun will cease to burn eventually, our earth will lose its energy, and the conditions of the second law of thermodynamics will be fulfilled.

212

THE SOURCE OF ENERGY

Within the biosphere itself several forms of energy are produced: hydraulic energy, created by water in motion (a river pouring over a dam, storm waves striking a shoreline); electrical energy (lightning); and geothermal energy (underground water converted to steam by hot rock formations). Powerful as these sources of energy can be, they are insignificant compared with the huge flow of energy that comes to earth from the sun.

The sun's energy begins with reactions like that of a hydrogen bomb. Nuclear fusion deep in the sun's core creates radiation, which makes its way to the sun's surface and is then radiated away — most of it as visible light, some as ultraviolet light and infrared light and X rays. This sunlight is the dominant form of energy in our world, one that primitive peoples recognized eons ago as the giver of life. All the energy humans produce in a single year from our many energy sources — coal, oil, hydraulic power, nuclear power — amounts, according to our present estimates, to only two ten-thousandths of the total energy coming to us each day from the sun.

Every minute of every day, every square inch of the earth's surface has beamed toward it an average of 2 calories (a calorie is the energy needed to raise the temperature of 1 gram of water 1°C). But as much as 40 percent of this energy never even reaches the ground because it is reflected back into space by clouds and dust. (Because of this reflection, the earth seen from outer space is as bright as the planet Venus, which we see as the brightest "star.") A small but significant amount of radiation is absorbed by the layer of ozone (O_3) that envelops the globe in the upper reaches of the atmosphere; carbon dioxide (CO_2) absorbs still more.

Even the sunlight that finally reaches a plant is not fully used. About 20 percent is reflected from the leaf's surface, allowing us to see the plant. Some of the solar energy is used for *evaporation* of water from the surfaces of leaves, which helps to cool the leaves and move water through the plant. Some energy is lost by *convection*, the transfer of heat by means of a circulating gas or liquid. (For example, on a warm summer day, the sun-warmed earth is hotter than the air above it and hence transfers heat to it, which sets the air in motion, resulting in a rising column of air in which hawks hover and sailplanes soar. In the same way a sun-warmed leaf transfers heat to the air around it.) The plant does not use some kinds of radiation at all, but it does use visible light. Of the total energy coming from the sun, most plants finally use less than 1 percent.

COMPREHENSION TEST 13

Directions: *Circle the letter of the best answer.*

1. Life in our biosphere could not exist without a constant cycle of
   a) meteorites
   b) convection
   c) rain
   d) energy

2. The largest amount of energy available on earth is
   a) hydraulic energy
   b) solar energy
   c) electrical energy
   d) geothermal energy

3. The continuing cycle of energy on earth is known as a(n)
   a) ozone system
   b) infrared system
   c) closed system
   d) open system

4. The postage stamp that the author describes as glued to the basketball is known as the
   a) geosphere
   b) biosphere
   c) atmosphere
   d) stratosphere

5. Human life on earth exists within a layer enveloping the earth that has a thickness of about
   a) one mile
   b) five miles
   c) thirty miles
   d) eighty miles

6. When it is said that "heat is a *diffuse, disorderly kind of energy,*" the word "diffuse" means
   a) concentrated
   b) confusing
   c) unusual
   d) spread out

7. Which of the following is *not* considered part of the biosphere?
   a) ocean coral
   b) gases
   c) one-celled animals
   d) plants

8. A ball balanced at the top of a flight of stairs possesses
   a) hydraulic energy
   b) kinetic energy
   c) potential energy
   d) electrical energy

9. When you start the engine of a car and begin to move forward you are
   a) using potential energy

b) converting energy from one form to another
c) introducing air pollution into a closed system
d) relying on hydraulic energy to move the car

10. The writer uses the description of earthly life as "a thin layer of green scum painted on a small rock whirling through space" to impress on the reader
    a) how we have polluted our environment
    b) the need for space exploration
    c) the importance of the sun in our solar system
    d) the insignificance of our world in the universe

Selection 13:	1345 words
Finishing Time: HR. MIN. SEC.	
Starting Time: HR. MIN. SEC.	
Reading Time: MIN. SEC.	
WPM Score:	
Comprehension Score:	%
Reading Efficiency Score:	

READING SELECTION 14

THE CREATIVE SIDE OF ADVERTISING

Frederick A. Russ and Charles A. Kirkpatrick

When advertising people refer to the "creative" side of advertising, they mean the activities involved in the actual preparation of advertisements: deciding how to appeal to the buyer, what specific headlines and illustrations to use, and what written copy will accomplish best the objectives. Seemingly small differences in an advertisement can have a dramatic impact on its effectiveness. As just one example, it has been shown that some ads are 150 percent more effective when placed on the back page of a newspaper than when placed on an inside page. Thus, choosing these elements and determining how they should be pulled together is a critical marketing activity.

The most important ingredient in an ad is the promise it makes. Why? Because the buyer responds favorably or not to what the advertiser claims its product or service will deliver. Remember, buyers do not buy products or services as such; instead, they exchange their money for what a product or service will do to or for them, for satisfaction of some sort. If consumers want a kitchen cleanser that will be gentle to their hands, that is what the product should offer and what the ad should promise.

VISUALIZATION AND LAYOUT

Once an ad's objective has been determined and its promise selected, the actual building of the ad can start. This calls for visualization and layout. Determining what elements or units an ad shall contain is called visualization. The common elements are headline, subheads, illustrations, and copy. Laying out the ad is a matter of position and relationships. Visualization decides *what* the ad will contain, layout decides *where* each of those elements will be placed. Should a retailer's name be at the top of a newspaper ad but a manufacturer's name at the bottom of a magazine ad? If several illustrations are to be included, where should each be placed? Well laid-out ads are sound and simple; their attractiveness invites reading. The expert selection and placement of illustrations can increase advertising effectiveness and the response the advertiser wants.

COPY

The most important element in an ad's copy message, the promise, is often expressed in the headline. The major jobs of headlines are to make contact with and attract the attention of the seller's prospects — also a responsibility of the ad's illustration — and to induce prospects to read the ad.

Most strong headlines have either news content or buyer-benefit — self-interest — content: "The K Cars are here," for example, a newsy headline from Chrysler, or "A better mileage rating than Audi 5000 for $1,699 less!" for the Pontiac Bonneville, stressing benefit to the buyer. Many headlines are a question — "What's Continental Telephone doing way out here?" — or a command: "Let Kelly work for you." Headlines may try to help prospects identify themselves as prospects by including such words as "motorists," or "students." Other words believed to be powerful in headlines include "free," "how to," "you," and "which."

Body copy is much like a salesperson's presentation in that it should expand on and explain the promise on which the ad is built. It should be built on a strong, persuasive sales idea. Product facts, product satisfaction, and product price are main ingredients. Body copy must be clear and believable, sincere yet interesting.

Ads should try to "close" just as salespeople do, and an ad's close is second only to its headline in importance. The close should urge some sort of immediate favorable action: "Fill out the coupon and mail it today"; "Visit your nearest dealer and ask for a demonstration"; or

215

simply, "Try it, you'll be glad you did." Words such as "go," "try," and "ask" are often found in closes. The advertiser's name and address or the brand name are often prominent in closes.

ILLUSTRATIONS

Illustrations — drawings, photos, or cartoons — share with headlines the assignment of attracting the attention of prospects . They can tell a story, make a point quickly and clearly, or prove a claim; "before-and-after" photographs are an example. Art directors are always debating illustration strategies. Should the ad contain a single, dominant illustration or several small illustrations? When should the product be shown, and when should some feature or part of the product be shown? Should people be included, perhaps using the product? Proven answers are rare for these questions; as in so much of advertising, experience is often the best guide.

THE ADVERTISING CAMPAIGN APPROACH

Much of manufacturers' advertising and some of retailers' advertising is planned and scheduled in the form of *advertising campaigns*. What is an ad campaign? It starts with planning aimed at avoiding hasty or ill-considered decisions. Erratic advertising, approved on a day-to-day basis, is far less productive than researched, coordinated advertising.

Each campaign consists of a group of related, organized, and rather similar ads, with a single sales goal or objective. It has a specific starting date, a schedule, and an ending date. For each campaign there is a single theme or keynote idea that runs through the entire campaign, that unifies and gives focus to it. The theme summarizes the substance of the campaign message or promise. Coca-Cola has used the theme "Coke adds life." Schlitz has said, "When you're out of Schlitz, you're out of beer." For decades Morton Salt promised, "When it rains it pours." The similarity between a keynote idea and a slogan is obvious, as is the similarity between a keynote idea and a buyer benefit. Campaigns vary in length. Each can

promote the image of the brand, the Chevy Citation, say, or the entire advertising firm, such as General Motors. Exhibit 1 discusses guidelines for successful advertising campaigns.

EXHIBIT 1
Keys to Advertising Success

Many times the business of advertising is so complex that students and advertisers alike wring their hands and cry, "Just give me a few simple rules for an effective ad campaign."

In 1972 in an advertisement (appropriately enough) in the *Wall Street Journal*, David Ogilvy of Ogilvy & Mather, one of the nation's top ad firms, listed thirty-eight pointers to the way of success in creating a good advertising campaign.

Here are a few that are common to all ads, regardless of the medium: *

- The most important decision you will have to make is how to position your product. Make that decision before you begin your campaign.
- Make your promises unique and competitive. Dr. Johnson once said, "Promise, large promise, is the soul of an advertisement."
- Don't be a bore. Nobody was ever bored into buying a product yet most advertising is impersonal, detached, and cold — and boring.
- Innovate. Start trends instead of following them.
- It pays to segment your market psychologically.
- Don't bury news.
- Boil down your strategy to one simple promise and go the whole hog in delivering that promise.
- It pays to give most products an image of quality, a first-class ticket. If your ads are ugly consumers will conclude that your product is shoddy, and they will be less likely to buy.
- Every advertisement should contribute to the complex symbol that is the brand image. The manufacturer that dedicates its advertising to building the most sharply defined personality for its brand gets the largest share of the market.

These are some of the rules Ogilvy uses in creating advertising for his clients. As his company has created more than $1.4 billion of advertising (that was before 1972), it seems safe to conclude that his formulas are successful.

* From an ad in the *Wall Street Journal*, June 14, 1972, p. 17. Reprinted by permission.

Advertising is not only the most familiar form of promotion; for many companies it is also the most important. Its best strategic use seems to be in selling many low-priced goods over a large area, which explains why most consumer-product companies depend on it so heavily. In this sense advertising seems to be almost the opposite of personal selling, which is best applied to the sale of expensive or complex goods to specifically identified customers. There are cases, however, in which neither personal selling nor advertising is precisely the promotional tool a marketer requires. In the next chapter we will turn to the tools that can be used for these other cases.

COMPREHENSION TEST 14

Directions: *Circle the letter of the best answer.*

1. The creative side of advertising is primarily concerned with
   a) selection of appropriate advertising media
   b) assessing buyer attitudes and motives
   c) designing the product to attract consumer attention
   d) designing and preparing the ad

2. The most important part of an ad's copy message is its
   a) promise
   b) tone
   c) closing
   d) delivery

3. An effective advertising campaign must have all of the following features *except* a
   a) specific ending date
   b) schedule of ads
   c) key illustration that captures the buyer's interest
   d) theme

4. The major function of a headline is to
   a) explain the illustration
   b) attract the buyer's attention
   c) suggest action
   d) describe the product being advertised

5. The layout of an ad is primarily concerned with the
   a) content of an ad
   b) promise it makes
   c) arrangement of its contents
   d) illustrations

6. As used in this selection the term "prospects" means
   a) prospective clients
   b) advertisers
   c) buyers
   d) copy writers

7. Suppose you had just developed a new soft drink, "Greatdrink," and wanted to develop an advertising campaign to market the product. Your first step would be to
   a) develop a slogan
   b) run a trial ad
   c) establish a sales objective and organize a schedule of ads
   d) identify a target buyer group most likely to purchase Greatdrink

8. An advertising slogan that states "Executive women hire temporary help from Kelly Girl" is designed to
   a) offer a promise
   b) help prospects identify themselves
   c) stress buyer benefits
   d) urge action

9. From the "Keys to Advertising Success" (Exhibit 1), it is reasonable to conclude that advertising
   a) is strictly logical and straightforward
   b) requires considerable artistic talent
   c) is based on a psychology of buyer attitude and response
   d) is hampered by buyer inconsistency and lack of sophistication

10. The last paragraph suggests that
    a) advertising is the only way to sell a product
    b) advertising is the best way to sell a product
    c) personal selling is an alternative to advertising
    d) personal selling is seldom as effective as advertising

Selection 14:	1407 words
Finishing Time:	___ ___ ___
	HR. MIN. SEC.
Starting Time:	___ ___ ___
	HR. MIN. SEC.
Reading Time:	___ ___
	MIN. SEC.
WPM Score:	_____
Comprehension Score:	_____ %
Reading Efficiency Score:	_____

218

Chapter 10:
Improving Your Long-Term Recall Through Notetaking

Regardless of how well you concentrate and how effectively you use various techniques to remember what you read, there will be times when there is such a high volume of information to be learned that you will be unable to remember it all. Also, you may find that you may be able to recall what you read shortly after reading but that you are unable to retain the information over long periods of time. In these situations, then, it is necessary to return to the material for review and study.

One of the best shortcuts to reading efficiency, in a study-review situation, is notetaking. As you read, you automatically sift and sort important from unimportant information. Once you have selected what is important to remember, very little additional effort is needed to underline or highlight, to make marginal notes, or to write a summary word or phrase in an outline. You will find that a little extra effort while reading can save you hours when you are ready to review and study the material. Unless you have in some way marked what is important, you will have to reread the material. Rereading is very time consuming, and for the amount of effort it requires you get little return in terms of increased recall. In fact, in rereading you waste time by reading again the facts and details that you do not need to recall. Your review time can be much better spent by organizing and learning facts, ideas, and concepts that you previously identified as worthwhile. This chapter will contain three approaches for recording important facts and ideas as you read and suggestions on how and when to use each.

UNDERLINING TECHNIQUES

When reading factual material, the easiest and fastest way to mark important facts and ideas is to underline them using a pen or pencil or a highlighter pen. Many students are hesitant to mark in their texts because they want to sell them at the end of the semester. However, underlining makes the book more useful to you, and you should try not to let your interest in selling the book stand in your way of reading and studying in the most efficient manner.

Underlining the Right Amount

If you underline either too much or too little, you will defeat the purpose of underlining. By underlining too little, you will miss valuable information and your review and study of the material will be incomplete. On the other hand, if you underline too much, you are not identifying only the most important ideas and eliminating less important facts. The more you underline, the more you will have to reread when studying, and the less of a timesaver the procedure will be.

Here is a passage underlined in three different ways. First, read the entire passage and then examine each version of the underlining. Try to decide which version would be most useful if you were rereading it for study purposes.

Version 1

ALCOHOLISM

<u>Alcoholism</u> is a <u>disease that requires medical treatment,</u> and <u>it is increasingly</u> common. It cuts across all age, class, and social strata. Contrary to stereotype, few alcoholics are skid row bums. Most are employed, married, respectable people; women are as vulnerable as men. Approximately seven percent of the population, or ten percent of all drinkers, are alcoholics.

Dr. E. M. Jellinek, <u>a leading researcher into alcoholism,</u> <u>divides the development of alcoholism into four stages:</u> (1) <u>the pre-alcoholic phase,</u> (2) the prodromal phase, (3) the crucial phase, and (4) the chronic phase. Perhaps most important for our purposes here is the pre-alcoholic phase, for it is hoped that some potential alcoholics, recognizing the early warning signals of alcoholism, will seek counseling or other help in time to prevent serious onset of the illness.

Some symptoms of the *pre-alcoholic phase* are (a) drinking used as a <u>mechanism to escape</u> from problems (in college students, usually academic or social problems); (b) drinking used to bolster courage, as before a test or job interview; (c) development of an increased tolerance for alcohol. There may also be (d) <u>feelings of guilt</u> associated with drinking or (e) feelings of urgency connected with downing the first few drinks. These <u>last two symptoms,</u> however, may not appear until the <u>prodromal phase.</u>[1]

Version 2

ALCOHOLISM

Alcoholism is a disease that requires medical treatment, and it is increasingly common. It cuts across all age, class, and social strata. Contrary to stereotype, few alcoholics are skid row bums. Most are employed, married, respectable people; women are as vulnerable as men. Approximately seven percent of the population, or ten percent of all drinkers, are alcoholics.

Dr. E. M. Jellinek, a leading researcher into alcoholism, divides the development of alcoholism into four stages: (1) the pre-alcoholic phase, (2) the prodromal phase, (3) the crucial phase, and (4) the chronic phase. Perhaps most important for our purposes here is the pre-alcoholic phase, for it is hoped that some potential alcoholics, recognizing the early warning signals of alcoholism, will seek counseling or other help in time to prevent serious onset of the illness.

Some symptoms of the *pre-alcoholic phase* are (a) drinking used as a mechanism to escape from problems (in college students, usually academic or social problems); (b) drinking used to bolster courage, as before a test or job interview; (c) development of an increased tolerance for alcohol. There may also be (d) feelings of guilt associated with drinking or (e) feelings of urgency connected with downing the first few drinks. These last two symptoms, however, may not appear until the prodromal phase.

Version 3

ALCOHOLISM

Alcoholism is a disease that requires medical treatment, and it is increasingly common. It cuts across all age, class, and social strata. Contrary to stereotype, few alcoholics are skid row bums. Most are employed, married, respectable people; women are as vulnerable as men. Approximately seven percent of the population, or ten percent of all drinkers, are alcoholics.

Dr. E. M. Jellinek, a leading researcher into alcoholism, divides the development of alcoholism into four stages: (1) the pre-alcoholic phase, (2) the prodromal phase, (3) the crucial phase, and (4) the chronic phase. Perhaps most important for our purposes here is the pre-alcoholic phase, for it is hoped that some potential alcoholics, recognizing the early warning signals of alcoholism, will seek counseling or other help in time to prevent serious onset of the illness.

Some <u>symptoms</u> of the *pre-alcoholic phase* are (a) <u>drinking used</u> as a mechanism <u>to escape</u> from <u>problems</u> (in college students, usually academic or social problems); (b) <u>drinking used to bolster courage,</u> as before a test or job interview; (c) development of an <u>increased tolerance for alcohol.</u> There may also be (d) <u>feelings of guilt</u> associated with drinking or (e) <u>feelings of urgency</u> connected with <u>downing the first few drinks.</u> These last two symptoms, however, may not appear until the prodromal phase.

This passage on alcoholism contains two important sets of information. It lists the four stages of alcoholism and it describes the symptoms of the prealcoholic phase. In evaluating the underlining done in version 1, you can see that it does not contain enough information. The four stages are not underlined and some, but not all, symptoms of prealcoholism are underlined.

Version 2, on the other hand, has too much underlining. Although all the important ideas are underlined, many less important details are also underlined. For instance, in the third paragraph examples of the various symptoms as well as the symptoms themselves are underlined, and appear to be of equal importance. In fact, nearly every sentence is underlined, and for review purposes, it would be almost as easy to reread the entire passage as it would be to read only the underlining.

Version 3, then, is an example of effective underlining. If you reread only the underlining, you will see that both the four stages of alcoholism and the symptoms of the prealcoholic phase are underlined.

As a general rule of thumb, try to underline no more than 20 to 30 percent of the passage. Once you exceed this range, you begin to lose effectiveness. Of course, there may be exceptions in which you feel that a particular section or passage is very factual or detailed and requires more detailed underlining. However, if you find that an entire assignment or chapter seems to require 60 to 70 percent underlining, you should consider using one of the other notetaking methods suggested later in this chapter.

How to Underline Effectively

Your goal in underlining is to identify and mark those portions of an assignment which are important to reread when you study that chapter. Here are a few suggestions on how to underline effectively.

1. Until you have become skilled in underlining, it is better to read a paragraph or section first and then go back and underline what is

important. If you underline as you read, you run the risk of underlining an idea that you think is important, only to find out later in the passage that it is less important than you originally thought.

2. Use your knowledge of paragraph structure to guide your underlining. Try to underline important portions of the topic sentence and any supporting details that you want to remember. Use signal words to locate changes or divisions of thought.

3. Be sure that your underlining accurately reflects the content of the passage. Incomplete or hasty underlining can mislead you as you review the passage and allow you to miss the main point. As a safeguard against this, occasionally test your accuracy by rereading only what you have underlined. Does your underlining tell what the paragraph or passage is about? Does it express the most important idea in the passage?

4. Use a system for underlining. There are a number of systems you can use. Some students use two or more different colors of ink or highlighters to distinguish between main ideas and details, or more and less important information. Others use single underlining for details and double underlining for main ideas. Still others place a bracket around the main idea and use highlighter to mark important details. Since there is no system that is most effective, you should try to develop a system that works well for you. It is important, however, to develop your own system and then use it consistently. If you vary systems, you will find that there is a greater chance for confusion and error while reviewing.

5. Underline as few words as possible in those sentences that you have decided are important. Very seldom should you underline a whole sentence. Usually, the core parts of the sentence along with an additional phrase or two are sufficient. Notice that you can understand the meaning of the following sentence by reading only the underlined parts.

<u>Fad</u> diets <u>disregard</u> the <u>necessity</u> <u>for</u> <u>balance</u> among the various classes of nutrients.

Now, read only the underlined parts of the following paragraph. Can you understand what the paragraph is about?

CIGARETTE SMOKING

The person who smokes <u>more than a pack</u> of cigarettes a day runs nearly twice the <u>risk of heart attack</u>, and nearly <u>five times the risk of stroke</u>, as does a nonsmoker. <u>Abstaining</u> from smoking <u>lowers</u> your <u>risk</u> of heart attack twenty-two <u>percent below the norm</u>. <u>Smoking more than a pack a day raises</u> your <u>risk to thirty-two percent above the norm</u>. <u>In addition</u>, as explained in other chapters of this book, smoking greatly <u>increases susceptibility</u> to lung <u>cancer</u> and to such lung diseases as <u>bronchitis</u> and <u>emphysema</u>.[2]

223

Most likely you were able to understand the basic message expressed in the above paragraph by reading only the underlined words. You were able to do so because the underlined words were core parts of each sentence or modifiers that directly explain these parts.

6. Use headings to guide your underlining. Earlier in this book you learned that headings could be used to establish a purpose for reading, and in the last chapter, you saw that turning headings into questions to guide your reading is the Q step in the SQ3R read-study system. A logical extension of these uses of headings is to use questions to help you identify what to underline. As you read, you should be looking for the answer to your questions; when you find information that answers the questions, underline it.

EXERCISE 10-1

Directions: *Choose one of the selections at the end of this chapter. Assume that you are reading it as part of a class reading assignment on which you will be tested. As you read, underline the important ideas.*

USING MARGINAL NOTATIONS

In addition to underlining important facts and ideas that you want to remember, it is often useful to make marginal notations. These may be symbols that mark particular types of information, or you may jot summary words in the margin. There are many types of information that you may need to mark for which simple underlining is not adequate. For instance, you may wish to emphasize important vocabulary, material you think will be on an exam, confusing ideas, or good discussion questions. At other times you may find that a few words or phrases can concisely summarize an entire paragraph. In such cases, writing a marginal note would be much more efficient than underlining large portions of the paragraph.

Using Symbols in Marking

Symbols can be used to distinguish types of information, to emphasize material to be studied, or to show relationships among ideas. They can be very convenient, for instance, in calling attention to examples or definitions, portions of an assignment that you feel are particularly important to study, or contrasting ideas and opinions.

As with underlining, there is no *one* correct way to mark. Instead, you should develop your own set of symbols and use them consistently. It does not matter what symbol you choose to represent a particular meaning, but it is important to use the same symbols once you have chosen them. Here is a sample list of commonly used symbols and their meaning.

Symbol	*Meaning*
ex	an example is included
def	an important term is defined
▭	unknown word to look up in dictionary later
T	good test question
?	confusing idea
✳	very important
sum	summary statement
↗	relates to another idea

Using Clue Words

When a word or phrase can accurately summarize several ideas or an entire paragraph it is useful to write a marginal note, avoiding lengthy underlining and saving time later as you review. Notice in the following passage how the clue words written in the margin *concisely* describe the content of the passage.

size of market depends of size and value of item

A *"market"* is a group of buyers with significant buying potential and unfulfilled needs or desires, who have the means to purchase, and whom the marketer can profitably serve. Let's take this definition apart.

First, a market must have significant potential. That is, usually the final amount of the sale will produce a current or future profit for you. Note that we did not specify market size. In the intermediate market the number of actual buyers may be small, but the size of the order may be substantial. The final market, however, can consist of many thousands or

millions of individual customers who purchase
fewer items. Thus, if you are marketing
consumer goods the sale of ten pairs of specially
designed athletic shoes to a basketball team
would not be significant. But the sale of one
atomic reactor with its power-plant complex to a
public utility company would represent billions
of dollars.[3]

Now, suppose that you did not know about clue words and that
you decided to use underlining; notice in the following illustration how
much you would have to underline in order to express the same idea as
was expressed using clue words.

A "market" is a group of buyers with significant buying
potential and unfulfilled needs or desires, who have the
means to purchase, and whom the marketer can profitably
serve. Let's take this definition apart.

First, a market must have significant potential. That is,
usually the final amount of the sale will produce a current or
future profit for you. Note that we did not specify market
size. In the intermediate market the number of actual
buyers may be small, but the size of the order may be
substantial. The final market, however, can consist of many
thousands or millions of individual customers who purchase
fewer items. Thus, if you are marketing consumer goods the
sale of ten pairs of specially designed athletic shoes to a
basketball team would not be significant. But the sale of one
atomic reactor with its power-plant complex to a public
utility company would represent billions of dollars.

You can see, then, that clue words are a time-saving device that is
useful when ideas are complicated and cannot be reviewed quickly by
underlining.

Clue words are intended to enable you to retrieve from your memory the complete idea to which the summary word refers. In a sense,
then, they function as clues or memory tags. Some students write clue
words and also underline, using the clue words as a quick way of
checking their recall of the ideas they underlined. They cover up their
underlining, reading only the clue words, and try to recall the underlined fact or idea to which the clue word refers. Marginal clue words,
then, can be used as a self-test as well as a convenient way of marking
important information.

226

TAKING SUMMARY NOTES

There are several situations in which writing summary or outline notes is more effective than either underlining or marginal notation. First, when you are dealing with theories, concepts, and ideas rather than with factual information, summary notes would be useful. In material of this type underlining often is ineffective because you cannot easily distinguish important from less important ideas. Instead each idea may relate to and support the next, providing a step toward a conclusion or statement of principle. Writing an outline forces you to determine the relationships among the ideas and provides an easy way for you to test your understanding. By writing an outline you will force yourself to express the ideas in your own words, and you will know if you do not fully understand an idea, because you will be unable to summarize it in outline form.

Summary notes are also useful for material that is complicated and difficult to learn and remember. Again, by writing an outline, you are forced to understand each idea in order to express it in your own words. Also, the process of expressing the idea in your own words and the physical act of writing it down will increase your ability to recall it.

Finally, summary notes are useful when you are using a book that you do not own. When reading library and other reference materials, using summary notes is the only possible way to record information for later study and review.

How to Take Summary Notes

Do not try to write summary notes while you are reading the material for the first time. Instead, read a section and then jot down notes. In taking summary notes, try to record all the most important ideas in the briefest form possible. Think of your outline as a visual representation of the main ideas and supporting details of a selection. However, your outline should not only record what is important but also show how the ideas are related and reflect the organization of the material.

To keep your outline as brief as possible, do not write in complete sentences. Use words and short phrases to summarize ideas. Also, be sure to put everything in your own words; do not copy sentences or parts of sentences from the selection. Finally, be highly selective in what you include. Unless you are sure that a fact or idea is important to remember, don't include it. If you are not selective, you will find that your outline is nearly as long as the selection itself, and you will save little time later as you review the material.

To be certain that your outline does contain sufficient information,

227

try to record the main idea of each paragraph and any supporting details that you will need to remember. Some paragraphs, however, are a repetition or further development of a previously expressed idea and may not need to be recorded.

Because an outline should show the relationships among ideas, an indentation system is used. As a general rule, the greater the importance of an idea, the further it is placed toward the left margin. Ideas of lesser importance are indented and appear more toward the center of the page. Also, ideas that are indented and appear underneath an item that is closer to the left margin are in some sense parts of or further explanations of that item.

A formal outline uses Roman numerals, capital letters, and numbers as well as indentation to distinguish the importance of ideas. For study and review it is seldom necessary to use formal outline unless you are already accustomed to outlining in that fashion. Instead, follow a simple system of indentation to separate main ideas and details. An outline might follow a format such as this:

THESIS STATEMENT
   MAIN IDEA
      Supporting detail
         fact
         fact
      Supporting detail
   MAIN IDEA
      Supporting detail
      Supporting detail
         fact
         fact

To illustrate further the technique of outlining, read the following passage, and then study the outline that follows it.

PROTEIN

Protein is essential for the repair and continuous replacement of body tissues and for growth. Proteins are a primary component of much body tissue, in particular of muscle. All enzymes are proteins, and protein is needed for making antibodies and hormones.

The body cannot store protein as it does fat; an adequate daily intake of protein is essential for well-being. A few Americans have diets deficient in protein, but most of us consume more protein daily than we need, as much as two or three times the necessary amount. For example, a woman who orders a twelve-ounce steak at a restaurant consumes about twice her daily protein requirement on the spot. For the average man, that same steak represents about 1.66 times the recommended daily allowance of protein. Although this is not in itself harmful (the excess protein is excreted), the extra calorie intake can lead to weight problems. Even in high-protein foods, such as lean meat or cheese, only twenty to thirty percent of the calories come from protein; the rest come from fat.

Proteins are the most complex molecules found in nature. They are built from smaller units called *amino acids*. Of these, there are two kinds: (1) those which the body cannot make, and which must be ingested, called the *essential* amino acids; (2) those which the body can make, ungratefully called the *nonessential* amino acids. The proteins our bodies use are made up of twenty-two amino acids; eight of these are those which the body cannot make.

Proteins that contain all of the essential amino acids, in such ratios as to make them usable by the body, are called *complete proteins*. Proteins which lack one or more of the essential amino acids, or which have them in proportions not usable by the human body, are called *incomplete proteins*. Animal proteins are generally complete, vegetable proteins incomplete.

However, it is possible to combine or supplement vegetable proteins in such a way as to obtain the amino acids of a complete protein. The science of such combinations is called protein supplementation, or protein complementarity. The complementary proteins must be eaten at the same meal in order for them to produce the equivalent of complete protein. Peanut butter and wheat products eaten together, for example, form a combination whose protein value approaches that of a complete protein. So do rice and dried beans. Vegetarian cookbooks include recipes geared toward providing complementary proteins. See, for example, *Diet for a Small Planet* by Frances Moore Lappe.

Should Americans eat more vegetable and less animal protein? A number of reasons may be put forward to suggest we should:

1. Although animal protein by itself is more complete than plant protein, its production is far less efficient in yield of edible protein per acre of land (because at least one extra step on the food chain is required). So, the

consumption of animal protein is wasteful in terms of
land use.
2. Animal protein is expensive.
3. Many of the foods high in animal protein are also high
in cholesterol, a fat-related substance that may have an
adverse effect on cardiovascular health. Plant foods
contain no cholesterol.
4. Some people have religious or ethical objections to
ingesting animal substances.[4]

Here is the outline for the above selection:

PROTEINS
essential for body tissue growth
— muscle
— enzymes
body cannot store protein
— most Americans consume too much
— can lead to weight problems
proteins build from 2 types of amino acids
1. essential amino acids
— body cannot make, must be ingested
2. nonessential amino acids
— body can make

By reading the passage and then reviewing the outline you can
see that it represents, in briefest form, the contents of the passage.
Reading an outline is an effective way to reacquaint yourself with the
content and organization of a chapter without taking the time that
reading, underlining, or marginal notation requires.

APPLYING WHAT YOU HAVE LEARNED

Directions: *Choose one of the selections at the end of this chapter.
Read it and answer the multiple choice questions. Then write a brief
outline of its content. Use the remaining space on this page to write
your outline. Be sure to show the relationship of ideas as well as to
record the most important ideas.*

READING SELECTION 15
THE APPRECIATION OF HUMOR

Difficulty Level: A

Mary J. Gander and Harry W. Gardiner

One example of the growing thinking capacity in middle childhood is children's appreciation of humor. Consider the joke: "Mr. Jones went into a restaurant and ordered a whole pizza for dinner. When the waiter asked if he wanted it cut into six or eight pieces, Mr. Jones said: 'Oh you'd better make it six! I could never eat eight!' "

Why do first graders who have just attained conservation of substance find this joke funnier than do nonconserving first graders or fifth graders who mastered this ability several years before? McGhee believes it is because this joke provokes a moderate amount of cognitive challenge, perfect for the conserving first graders.

Although many researchers have investigated children's humor, only Paul McGhee has conducted a longitudinal study of the development of humor. In his work at the Fels Institute, McGhee has proposed a fairly comprehensive theory of humor as part of his ongoing research on child development.

McGhee proposes that some incongruity (for example, something unexpected, absurd, inappropriate, or out of context) is usually the basis for humor. However, an incongruity in itself is insufficient; children must know enough about a situation so that the incongruity can be recognized, and they must be in a playful frame of mind. Incongruous events are funny to children precisely because these events are at odds with reality and they know it! Therefore, the kind of humor children appreciate depends on their underlying cognitive development.

When the father of three-year-old Paul put on a beard, glasses, and a large plastic nose, the child became frightened and began to cry, but his nine-year-old brother considered the disguise hilarious. The older boy had reached the concrete operational level and could imagine

his father as he was; moreover, he knew that the disguise had not really changed him.

Precursors of humor may be observed early. Laughter may be induced in four-month-old infants by tactile stimulation such as blowing against the baby's belly; at eight months, peek-a-boo; and at one year, Dad pretending to cry over a "hurt" finger.

McGhee proposes that true humor begins during the second year, or after the child has begun to be capable of fantasy and make-believe. It develops in an invariant sequence of stages related to cognitive development.

Stage 1: Incongruous actions toward objects.
Sometime between the ages of one and two years, toddlers begin to pretend that one object is another. Object number 1 somehow evokes their scheme for Object number 2, and they act on number 1 with the number 2 scheme, though fully aware that number 1 is *not* number 2. In a playful mood, they find it funny. For example, eighteen-month-old Sally put one of her blocks to her ear as if it were a phone, then "hung up" and laughed. She laughed too when her mother "ate" her toes and found their "taste" terrible.

Stage 2: Incongruous labeling of objects, events, people.
This stage usually begins around two years of age, or after children have developed some vocabulary. In it, the commonest type of humor consists of simply giving the wrong names to familiar objects, events, people, and parts of the body. A two-and-a-half-year-old girl told a visitor that she was going to a Winnie-the-Pooh movie. The visitor, trying to be funny, said, "Oh, Winnie-the-Pooh is an elephant, isn't he?" The child collapsed in laughter.

Stages 1 and 2 humor do not disappear as

the next stage begins, but become incorporated into it in more sophisticated ways.

Stage 3: Conceptual incongruity.   This stage may begin sometime between the ages of three and four and is heavily influenced by development of language and concepts. A distortion of a reality that children conceptually understand as a distortion is funny at this age; accordingly children may point and laugh at handicapped or deformed individuals because their strong egocentrism prevents consideration for others' feelings. Rhyming and creating nonsense words (Billy, pilly, dilly, silly, gilly) are considered great fun at this stage. So are puppets, such as a talking frog and a monster that devours cookies. Children also begin to find humor in taboo subject matter concerning toilets and physical differences between girls and boys. Within the context of a joke, such topics can release tension and excite much

laughter in preschoolers as well as older children.

Stage 4: Multiple meanings and the beginnings of adult-type humor.   This stage usually comes around ages seven and eight, when concrete operations and other cognitive skills permit appreciation of more sophisticated jokes. Concrete operational children can keep two ideas in mind at once and thus have no problem with double or multiple meanings, as long as they are familiar with the concepts involved. For example, eight- to ten-year-olds find this funny: "What did the man do when he stubbed his toe and broke it?" Answer: "He called a tow truck!" Riddles and "knock-knock" questions also gain popularity. According to McGhee, stage 4 humor can extend into adolescence and adulthood, although it usually becomes more complex and abstract.

COMPREHENSION TEST 15

Directions: *Circle the letter of the correct answer.*

1. Children's appreciation of humor
   a) is an area of child development that has not been studied
   b) develops along with their thinking ability
   c) does not occur until age seven or eight
   d) occurs earlier for girls than for boys

2. When children pass to stage 3 of humor, what they found to be funny in stage 2
   a) is no longer funny
   b) becomes incorporated into stage 3
   c) remains just as funny for them
   d) is forgotten

3. The basis for humor is usually
   a) one's fear of injury
   b) unusual sounding words
   c) a situation that is incongruous
   d) other people's weaknesses

4. "True humor" usually begins around the age of

a) four months
b) two years
c) four years
d) nine years

5. Around the age of three or four, children would most appreciate humor based on
   a) "knock-knock" jokes
   b) cartoon characters and animals
   c) double meanings
   d) nonsense words and rhymes

6. In the phrase "precursors of humor," "precursors" most closely means
   a) beginnings
   b) uses
   c) problems
   d) causes

7. A child that pretends that his or her dresser is a refrigerator is at least
   a) one year old
   b) six years old
   c) eight years old
   d) twelve years old

8. A child who enjoys calling his or her dog "Tommy Turtle" is operating at
   a) Stage 1: Incongruous Actions toward Objects
   b) Stage 2: Incongruous Labeling
   c) Stage 3: Conceptual Incongruity
   d) Stage 4: Multiple Meaning

9. The joke "What did the father chimney say to his son? You're too young to smoke!" would probably be funniest to a child of
   a) two
   b) four
   c) eight
   d) sixteen

10. The information in this passage is presented by
   a) describing the stages in their order of occurrence
   b) comparing and contrasting the stages with one other
   c) presenting the stages in the order of their importance
   d) listing problems with each stage and their solutions

Selection 15:	853 words
Finishing Time:	___ ___ ___
	HR. MIN. SEC.
Starting Time:	___ ___ ___
	HR. MIN. SEC.
Reading Time:	___ ___
	MIN. SEC.
WPM Score:	___
Comprehension Score:	___ %
Reading Efficiency Score:	___

ARCHAEOLOGICAL SITES

Brian M. Fagan

World prehistory is written from data recovered from thousands of *archaeological sites, places where traces of human activity are to be found.* Sites are normally identified through the presence of manufactured tools.

An archaeological site can consist of a single human burial, a huge rockshelter occupied over thousands of years, or a simple scatter of stone tools found on the surface of a plowed field in the Midwest. Sites can range in size from a huge prehistoric city like Teotihuacán in the Valley of Mexico to a small campsite occupied by hunter-gatherers 100,000 years ago. Sites available for study by archaeologists are limited in number and variety by preservation conditions and by the nature of the activities of the people who occupied them. Some, like Mesopotamian city mounds, were important settlements for hundreds, even thousands, of years. Some small sites were used only for a few hours, others for a generation or two.

Archaeological sites are most commonly classified by the activity that occurred there. *Habitation sites* are places where people lived and carried out a wide range of different activities. Most prehistoric sites come under this category, but habitation sites can vary from a small open campsite, through rockshelters and caves, to large accumulations of shellfish remains (shell middens). Village habitation sites may consist of a small accumulation of occupation deposit and mud hut fragments, huge earthen mounds, or communes of stone buildings or entire buried cities. Each presents its own special excavation problems.

Burial sites provide a wealth of information on the prehistoric past. Grinning skeletons are very much part of popular archaeological legend, and human remains are common finds in the archaeological record. The earliest deliberate human burials are between fifty and seventy thousand years old. Individual burials are found in habitation sites, but often the inhabitants designated a special area for a cemetery. This cemetery could be a communal burial place where everyone was buried regardless of social status. Other burial sites, like the Shang royal cemeteries in China, were reserved for nobility alone. Parts of a cemetery were sometimes reserved for certain special individuals in society such as clan leaders or priests. The patterning of grave goods in a cemetery can provide information about intangible aspects of human society such as religious beliefs or social organization. So can the pattern of deposition of the burials, their orientation in their graves, even family groupings. Sometimes physical anthropologists can detect biological similarities between different skeletons that may reflect close family, or other, ties.

Burial sites, especially those of important individuals, are among the most spectacular of all archaeological discoveries. Tut-ankh-Amun's tomb, the royal graves of Sumerian and Semitic nobles of Ur-of-the-Chaldees, and the sepulchres of Chinese nobles are justly famous for their remarkable wealth. People have buried their dead in cemeteries under stone pyramids in Egypt and Mexico, in great earthen mass burial mounds in the Midwest, in huge subterranean chambers in China, and in thousands of small, individual earthen mounds in western Europe. In each case, however, the features of the burials and their context in the sepulchre add valuable data to what the skeleton itself can tell us.

Kill sites consist of bones of slaughtered animals associated with hunting weapons. On the North American Great Plains, for example, the skeletons of eight-thousand-year-old bison are found along with stone spearpoints. The hunters camped by the carcasses while they butchered them, then moved elsewhere, leaving the carcasses, projectile heads and butchering tools where they lay for archaeologists to find thousands of years later.

Quarry sites are places where people mined prized raw materials such as obsidian (a volcanic glass used for fine knives and mirrors) or copper. Excavations at such sites yield roughed out blanks of stone, or metal ingots, as well as finished products ready for trading elsewhere. Such objects were bartered widely in prehistoric times.

Religious sites include Stonehenge in southern England, Mesopotamian mudbrick temples, known as *ziggurats,* and the great ceremonial centers of the lowland Maya in Mesoamerica, such as Tikal, Copán, and Palenque. Religious sites may be small shrines or huge public temples. Some are localities where religious ceremonies were conducted, often to the exclusion of any habitation at all.

Art sites such as the cave of Altamira in northern Spain, or Lascaux in southwestern France, are commonplace in some areas of the world, noticeably southern Africa and parts of North America. Many are caves and rockshelters where prehistoric people painted or engraved game animals, scenes of daily life, or religious symbols. Some French art sites are at least fifteen thousand years old.

Each of these site types represents a particular form of human activity, one that is represented in the archaeological record by specific artifact patterns and surface indications found and recorded by the archaeologist.

COMPREHENSION TEST 16

Directions: *Circle the letter of the correct answer.*

1. Archaeological sites are usually classified by
   a) the people who lived there
   b) the historical period during which they were occupied
   c) the type of activity for which they were used
   d) the degree of civilization of those who lived there

2. An archaeological site is defined as any place where
   a) some record of human activity is found
   b) humans bury beloved animals
   c) evidence of plant or animal life exists
   d) particular rock formations suggest the patterns of history

3. All of the following features of graves provide archaeologists with information about a particular society *except*
   a) the location of the grave
   b) the goods buried with the person
   c) the degree of preservation of the body
   d) the orientation of the body in the grave

4. Art sites often contain
   a) paintings showing scenes of daily life
   b) engravings of famous people
   c) paintings recording location of burial sites
   d) tools and primitive devices used for engraving

5. Quarry sites are places where
   a) game was slaughtered
   b) prized animals were buried
   c) raw materials were dug from the earth
   d) raw materials for burial sites were located

6. A "sepulchre" is a
   a) prehistorical tool used for burial
   b) type of grave
   c) form of preserving animal carcasses
   d) religious ritual

7. Which of the following items might you expect to find at a burial site?
   a) tools
   b) jewels
   c) bowls
   d) animal remains

8. The author suggests that cultural groups
   a) have similar methods of mixing raw materials
   b) reserve hunting grounds for specific tribes
   c) have specific sites for celebrations
   d) have different burial patterns

9. The author feels that archaeologists
   a) learn a great deal about early history
   b) locate valuable jewels and art
   c) disturb natural history by excavating
   d) prove man's natural superiority

10. This article was written to
    a) explain the different types of archaeological sites
    b) discuss archaeological excavation techniques
    c) explain why archaeology is important
    d) describe how to identify a habitation site

Selection 16:	794 words

Finishing Time: _____ _____ _____
                  HR.   MIN.   SEC.

Starting Time: _____ _____ _____
                  HR.   MIN.   SEC.

Reading Time: _____ _____
                     MIN.   SEC.

WPM Score: _____

Comprehension Score: _____ %

Reading Efficiency Score: _____

Unit Five:
How to Develop
Your Word Efficiency

Vocabulary development is crucial to the development of efficient and flexible reading skills. Your vocabulary, broadly defined, is the entire store of words that you recognize and understand. Over the years you have built up thousands of associations between particular groupings of letters and the object or idea that each represents. You have learned, for example, that the group of letters c-h-a-i-r stands for a four-legged object to sit on and that the combination of the letters s-h-o-e represents a foot covering. Vocabulary is at the core of communication, both oral and written. It is through words that it is possible to transmit meaning from one person to another. To communicate effectively, then, it is essential to have a broad, working vocabulary that will allow you to transmit and understand ideas.

There are two major ways to expand your vocabulary. First, you can learn the meaning of new, completely unfamiliar words. For example, you could learn the meaning of words such as "interregnum," "infusorian," "gemsbok," and "fennec." Some of these new words may be specialized terms used in particular fields of study; others may be general usage words that you have never encountered in your reading or listening. A second direction in which to expand your vocabulary is to learn new meanings or shades of meaning for words you already know. For instance, you may know what the word "card" means but you may not know that the word can be used to mean a circular piece of paper bearing the thirty-two points of a compass. You may discover that the words "recalcitrant" and "reluctant" both mean not giving additional effort or care but that "recalcitrant" suggests a stubborn resistance to authority or guidance whereas "reluctant" implies a hesitancy or unwillingness. Chapter 11 will contain techniques for learning new unfamiliar words as well as suggestions for expanding usages of already familiar words.

Given that there are two major directions in which you can expand your vocabulary, your immediate concern is *how* to expand both your technical vocabulary and your everyday vocabulary. Chapter 12 presents numerous suggestions for developing your vocabulary. First the chapter discusses the use of context, the words surrounding an unfamiliar word, as an aid to vocabulary development. Then, additional useful aids such as the dictionary and the thesaurus as well as a system for learning newly identified words is presented.

Chapter 11:
Expanding Your Vocabulary

Do you have an awareness for words? Are you constantly looking for new words that can expand your vocabulary? Do you notice how the meaning of a word changes, how certain subject areas use words in particular ways, and how words take on additional meanings? To provoke your "word awareness" try the following quiz. Answer each question in the space provided, then check your answers in the Answer Key.

1. How many different meanings can you think of for the word

    "run"? _____

    _____

2. What is an "island of poverty"? _____

    _____

3. All of the following words refer to a state of drowsiness and lack of energy. Which word would be most appropriate to use if you wanted to suggest that this state was caused by overwork or dejection?

    (a) apathy _____   (b) stupor _____   (c) lassitude _____

4. Precisely what is sodium hypochlorite? _____

    _____

5. If you wanted to describe someone as a lazy person who doesn't accomplish much, which word would you choose to create the most unfavorable image of the person?

    (a) lethargic _____   (b) lackadaisical _____   (c) laggard _____

6.   Do the following words have the same meaning?

irascible, meticulous, longanimous _____

_____

7.   Would you rather be the victim of a hoax, a fraud, or a flam? _____

_____

This word awareness quiz was intended to demonstrate some of the complexities of vocabulary development. It should have shown you that words have several meanings, that they can be used in specialized ways, and that words similar in meaning can create different or even opposite feelings or impressions. To read effectively you need to be aware of each of these aspects of word meaning and be able to adapt to each as you read.

MULTIPLE WORD MEANINGS

When you took the word awareness quiz, were you surprised to learn that the word "run" has a total of eighty-one meanings? You probably thought of meanings such as to *run* fast, a home *run,* a *run* in a stocking, but it is hard to believe that there are so many meanings for the word that the entry requires nearly an entire dictionary page. (See Figure 11-1.) As you glanced through this entry, you probably saw many meanings that you are familiar with but just did not think of when taking the awareness quiz. You certainly have heard the word used in the following ways: to *run* to the store, fish *run* upstream, to *run* a machine, to *run* a fever. On the other hand, you may not have known that a run is a term used in billiards meaning a series of uninterrupted strokes or that in golf "run" means to cause the ball to roll.

Actually, most words in the English language have more than one meaning. Just open any standard dictionary to any page and glance down one column of words. You will see that for most words, more than one meaning is given. Also, you can see that there is considerable opportunity to expand your vocabulary by becoming aware of additional meanings of words you already know.

More important, you can avoid misreading or having to reread a sentence if you are aware of the multiple meanings of words. As you read, you can use the meaning of the sentence in which a word is used to guide your choice of meaning. For instance, we ordinarily think of reservations as arrangements that you make with a hotel, restaurant,

240

run (run), *v.*, **ran, run, run·ning,** *n., adj.* —*v.i.* **1.** to go quickly by moving the legs more rapidly than at a walk and in such a manner that for an instant in each step all feet are off the ground. **2.** to move with haste; act quickly. **3.** to depart quickly; take to flight; flee or escape. **4.** to have recourse for aid, support, comfort, etc. **5.** to make a quick trip or informal visit for a short stay at a place. **6.** to go around, rove, or ramble without restraint. **7.** to move, roll, or progress from momentum or from being propelled. **8.** *Sports.* **a.** to take part in a race or contest. **b.** to finish in a race or contest in a certain numerical position: *The horse ran second.* **9.** to be or campaign as a candidate for election. **10.** to migrate, as fish. **11.** to migrate upstream or inshore from deep water to spawn. **12.** to move under continuing power or force, as of the wind, a motor, etc. **13.** (of a ship, automobile, etc.) to be sailed or driven from a safe, proper, or given route. **14.** to ply between places, as a vessel or conveyance. **15.** to move, glide, turn, rotate, or pass easily, freely, or smoothly: *A rope runs in a pulley.* **16.** to creep, trail, or climb, as growing vines. **17.** to come undone or to unravel, as stitches or a fabric. **18.** to flow, as a liquid. **19.** to flow along, esp. strongly, as a stream, the sea, etc. **20.** to empty or transfer contents. **21.** to include a specific range of variations (usually fol. by *from*): *Your work runs from fair to bad.* **22.** to melt and flow. **23.** to spread on being applied to a surface, as a liquid. **24.** to undergo a spreading of colors: *materials that run when washed.* **25.** to flow forth as a discharge, as a liquid. **26.** to overflow or leak, as a vessel. **27.** to operate or function. **28.** to be in operation. **29.** to elapse; pass or go by, as time. **30.** to pass into or meet with a certain state or condition. **31.** to get or become: *The well ran dry.* **32.** to amount; total: *The bill ran to $100.* **33.** to be stated or worded in a certain manner: *The minutes of the last meeting run as follows.* **34.** *Com.* to accumulate, follow, or become payable in due course, as interest on a debt. **35.** *Law.* **a.** to have legal force or effect, as a writ. **b.** to continue to operate. **c.** to go along with. **36.** to proceed, continue, or go: *The story runs for eight pages.* **37.** to extend in a given direction. **38.** to extend for a certain length. **39.** to appear in print or be published as a story, photograph, etc. **40.** to be performed or be played continually, as a play or movie. **41.** to pass quickly. **42.** to continue or return persistently; recur: *a tune running through the head.* **43.** to have or tend to have or produce a specified character, quality, form, etc.: *This novel runs to long descriptions.* **44.** to be or continue to be of a certain or average size, number, etc. **45.** *Naut.* to sail before the wind. —*v.t.* **46.** to move or run along (a surface, way, path, etc.). **47.** to traverse (a distance) in running. **48.** to perform, compete in, or accomplish by or as by running. **49.** to compete against in a race. **50.** to ride or cause to gallop. **51.** to enter in a race. **52.** to bring into a specified state by running. **53.** to trace, track, pursue, or hunt, as game: *to run deer on foot.* **54.** to drive (an animal) or cause to go by pursuing. **55.** to cause to ply between places, as a vessel or conveyance. **56.** to carry or transport, as in a vessel or vehicle. **57.** to cause to pass quickly: *He ran his eyes over the letter.* **58.** to get past or through: *to run a blockade.* **59.** to smuggle (contraband goods). **60.** to work, operate, or drive. **61.** to publish, print, or make copies of. **62.** to process, refine, manufacture, or subject to an analysis or treatment. **63.** to keep operating or going, as a machine. **64.** to keep (a motor) idling for an indefinite period. **65.** to allow (a ship, automobile, etc.) to depart from a safe, proper, or given route, as by negligence or error. **66.** to sponsor, support, or nominate (a person) as a candidate for election. **67.** to manage or conduct: *to run a business; to run one's own life.* **68.** to expose oneself to or be exposed to (a chance, risk, etc.). **69.** to cause (a liquid) to flow: *to run the water for a bath.* **70.** to give forth or flow with (a liquid); pour forth or discharge. **71.** to cause to move easily, freely, or smoothly. **72.** to cause stitches in (a garment or fabric) to unravel or come undone: *to run a stocking on a protruding nail.* **73.** to bring or force into a certain condition. **74.** to drive, force, or thrust. **75.** to graze; pasture. **76.** to extend (something) in a particular direction or to a given point or place. **77.** to cause to fuse and flow, as metal for casting in a mold. **78.** to draw, trace, or mark out, as a line. **79.** to cost (an amount or approximate amount). **80.** to cost (a person) an amount or approximate amount: *That dress will run you $30.* **81. run across,** to meet or find accidentally. **82. run afoul of, a.** *Naut.* to collide with so as to damage and entangle. **b.** to incur or become subject to the wrath or ill will of. **83. run down, a.** to strike and fell or overturn, esp. to drive a vehicle into (someone). **b.** to pursue until captured; chase. **c.** to peruse; review. **d.** to cease operation; stop. **e.** to speak disparagingly of; criticize severely. **f.** to search out; trace; find: *to run down information.* **g.** *Baseball.* to tag out (a base runner) between bases. **84. run in, a.** to visit casually. **b.** *Slang.* to arrest; take to jail. **c.** *Print.* to insert (text) without indenting. **d.** to break in (new machinery). **85. run into, a.** to crash into; collide with. **b.** to meet accidentally. **c.** to amount to; total. **d.** to succeed; follow. **e.** to experience; encounter. **86. run in with,** *Naut.* to sail close to (a coast, vessel, etc.). **87. run off, a.** to leave quickly; depart. **b.** to create or perform rapidly or easily. **c.** to determine the winner (of a contest, race, etc.) by a runoff. **d.** to drive away; expel. **88. run on, a.** to continue without interruption. **b.** *Print.* to insert (text) without indenting. **c.** to add something, as at the end of a text. **89. run out, a.** to terminate; end. **b.** to become used up. **c.** to drive out; expel. **90. run out of,** to exhaust a quantity or supply of. **91. run out on,** *Informal.* to withdraw one's support from; abandon. **92. run over, a.** to hit and knock down, esp. with a vehicle. **b.** to go beyond; exceed. **c.** to repeat; review. **93. run through, a.** to pierce or stab, as with a sword. **b.** to consume or use up recklessly; squander. **c.** to rehearse quickly or informally. **94. run up, a.** to sew rapidly. **b.** to amass; incur: *running up huge debts.* **c.** to cause to increase; raise. **d.** to build, esp. hurriedly. —*n.* **95.** the act, an instance, or period of running. **96.** a fleeing, esp. in great haste; flight. **97.** a running pace: *The boys set out at a run.* **98.** distance covered, as by racing, running, during a trip, etc. **99.** the act, an instance, or a period of traveling or moving between two places; trip. **100.** a quick trip for a short stay at a place. **101.** *Mil.* **a.** See **bomb run. b.** any portion of a military flight during which the aircraft flies directly toward the target in order to begin its attack: *a strafing run.* **102.** *Aeron.* **a.** the rapid movement, under its own power, of an aircraft on a runway, water, or another surface. **b.** a routine flight from one place to another. **103.** an interval or period during which something, as a machine, operates or continues operating. **104.** the amount of anything produced in such a period. **105.** a line or place in knitted work where a series of stitches has slipped out or come undone: *a run in a stocking.* **106.** onward movement, development, progress, course, etc. **107.** the direction of something or of its component elements: *the run of the grain of wood.* **108.** the particular course, order, or tendency of something. **109.** freedom to move around in, pass through, or use something. **110.** any rapid or easy course of progress. **111.** a continuous series of performances, as of a play. **112.** an uninterrupted course of some state or condition; a spell. **113.** a continuous extent of something, as a vein of ore. **114.** an uninterrupted series or sequence of things, events, etc. **115.** a sequence of cards in a given suit: *a heart run.* **116.** any extensive continued demand, sale, or the like. **117.** a series of sudden and urgent demands for payment, as on a bank. **118.** a period during which liquid flows. **119.** the amount that flows during such a period: *a run of 500 barrels a day.* **120.** a small stream; brook; rivulet. **121.** a flow or rush, as of water. **122.** a kind or class, as of goods. **123.** an inclined course, as on a slope, designed or used for a specific purpose. **124.** a fairly large enclosure within which domestic animals may move about freely; runway: *a chicken run.* **125.** the movement of a number of fish upstream or inshore from deep water. **126.** large numbers of fish in motion, esp. inshore from deep water or up a river for spawning: *a run of salmon.* **127.** a number of animals moving together. **128.** *Music.* a rapid succession of tones; a roulade. **129.** *Baseball.* the score unit made by safely running around all the bases and reaching home plate. **130.** a series of successful shots, strokes, or the like, in a game. **131. a run for one's money, a.** close or keen competition. **b.** enjoyment or profit in return for one's expense. **132. in the long run,** in the course of long experience; in the end. **133. on the run,** *Informal.* **a.** moving quickly; hurrying about. **b.** while running or in a hurry. **c.** escaping or hiding from the police. —*adj.* **134.** melted or liquefied: *run butter.* **135.** poured in a melted state; run into and cast in a mold. [ME *rinne(n)*, OE *rinnan*; c. G *rinnen*, Icel *rinna*; form. *run* orig. ptp., later extended to present tense]

Figure 11-1. Dictionary entry for the word "run" (*Random House College Dictionary, Revised Edition*, pp.1153–1154)

or airline to reserve a room or table, or a seat on a plane. Now read the following sentence:

The reservations we had about our trip were unfounded.

At some point, in reading this sentence, you realized that the word "reservation" was being used in a different sense than previously mentioned. Your first clue was the word "about"; usually you make hotel, restaurant, or plane reservations *for* rather than *about* a specific place. Then, as you finished the sentence, the word "unfounded" suggested that "reservations" as used in this sentence meant important concerns or qualifications about the trip.

Now, read the following pairs of sentences.

His <u>purple</u> coat was hand woven.

His <u>purple</u> language shocked everyone.

To <u>poach</u> an egg, you have to be sure the water is boiling.

To <u>poach</u> a deer, you must be quiet and make sure no one sees.

The chef placed some parsley on the plate as a <u>garnish</u>.

The judge placed a <u>garnish</u> on the man's paycheck.

In each group the first sentence used a common meaning of a word, and the second used a less familiar meaning. Did you find, in reading the second sentence in each group, that you had to make a mental switch in anticipated meaning? These examples were written to force you to make an immediate and obvious switch by providing you with strong clues that a different meaning was being used in the second sentence. However, in many reading situations, there may be little or no evidence that an unfamiliar meaning is being used; for example:

<u>Poaching</u> a chicken is a difficult task.
(In this case you would have to continue reading to learn whether "poaching," in this sentence, means cooking or stealing.)

There is general agreement that <u>scabs</u> are troublesome.
(Again you would have to continue reading to find out if "scab" means a crust on a wound, a person who refuses to join a union, a worker who refuses to strike, or a worker who takes the place of a striking worker.)

In some situations, then, it is necessary to continue reading beyond the sentence in which the word is used to determine its precise meaning. In most instances, you will have little or no difficulty determining the appropriate meaning of a word. However, if you are attentive to the unfamiliar or unusual ways a word is used, you will find that your vocabulary will expand dramatically.

EXERCISE 11-1

Directions: *Each of the following sentences uses a relatively uncommon meaning of the underlined word. After reading each sentence, write a synonym or brief definition of the underlined word. It may be necessary to check a dictionary to locate a precise meaning.*

1.   Investors should keep at least a portion of their assets <u>fluid</u>.

   _____

2.   The speech therapist noted that the child had difficulty with <u>glides</u>.

   _____

3.   The prisoner held a <u>jaundiced</u> view of life.

   _____

4.   The two garden hoses could not be connected without a <u>male</u> fitting.

   _____

5.   The outcome of the debate was a <u>moral</u> certainty.

   _____

TECHNICAL AND SPECIALIZED VOCABULARY

In the word awareness quiz at the beginning of this chapter you were asked two questions that pertained to technical or specialized vocabulary. These two questions, intended to illustrate the two types of specialized vocabulary, were:

1.   What is an "island of poverty"?
2.   Precisely what is sodium hypochlorite?

The first question illustrates the type of specialized vocabulary in which everyday words take on a very specific, specialized meaning for a particular subject area. You will recall from the answer key that the common, everyday words "island of poverty," in the field of economics, mean poverty that results from changes such as the decline or disappearance of an industry from a particular area. The second question is an example of specialized vocabulary: it is used only within a particular subject area and has no other meaning. This term refers to a specific chemical compound. Here are some examples of technical and specialized vocabulary taken from a botany textbook.

Everyday Words with
Specialized Meaning

Community — group of different organisms living together.

Cross — mating of two organisms.

Population — group of individuals of one species, capable of interbreeding.

Technical Terms

Biome — a region of climate.

Corolla — name for petals of a flower.

Rhizosphere — the part of the soil penetrated by roots.

As you begin to study any topic, you will soon discover that there is a set of words and terms that has meanings specific to just that field. Even hobbies, professions, and sports have, in a sense, their "own language," terms with specialized meanings. Think for a moment of the terms used among those who own CB radios. Also, consider a sport such as tennis. Words such as "love," "set," "ace," and "deuce" have very specific and specialized meanings.

Each academic discipline also has its own "language," so to speak, and in order to master the subject, you must first master its specialized terminology. For each course you are taking, then, it is very important to learn new terminology as it is introduced by instructors and in your textbooks. To illustrate, read the following passage, taken from a statistics textbook.

Multiple correlation provides an analysis of the relations among two or more predictor measures and a single criterion measure. One result of the analysis is an equation for predicting the criterion score of a subject from his known set of predictor scores. The complete test space in the analysis is p-dimensional, with $p - 1$ predictors plus the criterion variable. In our treatment we will partition a p-element vector variable so that the first $p - 1$ elements are the predictor elements and the pth element is the criterion element. As with all the prediction schemes developed in this text, the researcher requires a complete set of p scores for N subjects in what we may call the norming sample or estimating group. On the basis of what is learned about the interrelationships among the p elements of the vector variable as they are estimated from this norming sample it becomes possible to take the $p - 1$ predictor scores for new subjects, in a replication sample, and compute for each new subject a predicted score on the criterion element. This predicted score is also called a regressed score, and the formula that yields it is called a regression formula. The regressed score is a linear component of the predictor scores.[1]

Unless you have a strong academic background in multivariate statistics, this paragraph probably did not make much sense to you. It was difficult to understand because it used many specialized and technical terms, and without knowing their meaning, you could not comprehend the paragraph. You can see, then, that unless you learn the specialized terminology for a course, you can become hopelessly lost and confused. Learning specialized and technical vocabulary for a particular topic or subject area allows you to understand and communicate in a precise manner. You have already seen that most everyday words have more than one meaning and that, at times, confusion may exist. Thus you can see why specialized and technical terms are needed and widely used in most subjects.

To learn specialized terminology, mark or jot down each new term the first time you read or hear it. Then, use an index card system for learning the terms. (This system is explained in the next chapter.) Use the glossary at the end of your text instead of a dictionary to check the meaning of each term. The glossary lists the meaning of many of the specialized and technical terms commonly used in the particular subject area. Besides being more convenient than a dictionary, a glossary defines the terms as they are used in the subject area. You do not have to sort through numerous meanings that do not apply as you would when using a dictionary.

EXERCISE 11-2

Directions: *Select a chapter from one of your textbooks (you may choose a chapter that has been assigned to you already). Read the first three pages paying particular attention to specialized and technical vocabulary. List a few examples of each in the spaces provided.*

Specialized Terms	*Technical Words*
_____	_____
_____	_____
_____	_____
_____	_____
_____	_____

DENOTATIVE AND CONNOTATIVE MEANINGS

On the word awareness quiz, you were asked whether you would prefer to be the victim of a hoax, fraud, or flam. If you were to look these words up in a dictionary, you might find that each involves some sort of deception; however, they suggest varying degrees of seriousness. A hoax is often a joke or trick; a flam is a deceptive trick or lie; a fraud often suggests some sort of deception in which someone gives up property or money. Next, suppose you owned a jacket that looked like leather, but was not made out of real leather. Would you prefer someone to describe your jacket as fake, artificial, or synthetic? Most likely, you would prefer "synthetic." "Fake" suggests that you are trying to cover up the fact that it is not real leather, and "artificial" suggests, in a negative way, something that was made to look like something else. "Synthetic," however, refers to a product made by a chemical process. So you can see that in addition to their dictionary meanings, words may *suggest* additional meanings.

The meaning of a word as indicated by the dictionary is known as its *denotative* meaning, whereas its *connotative* meaning consists of the additional meanings a word may take on. Let's consider a few more examples to clarify the distinction between these two types of meanings. As an example, think of the word "walk." Its denotative or primary dictionary meaning is to move forward by placing one foot in front of the other. This meaning is easily understood and there is general agreement by everyone who uses the word that it has this meaning. Now, here are a few words that also, according to the dictionary, mean to move forward: stroll, swagger, lumber. Although the denotative meaning of each of these words is "to walk," each word has a slightly different connotation, or shade of meaning. As you read each word in a sentence the connotative meaning will become clear to you.

The newlyweds <u>strolled</u> down the streets of Paris.
("Stroll" suggests a leisurely, carefree walk.)

The wealthy businessman <u>swaggered</u> into the restaurant and demanded a table.
("Swagger" suggests walking in a bold, arrogant manner.)

The overweight man <u>lumbered</u> along, breathing heavily and occasionally tripping.
("Lumber" connotes a clumsy, awkward movement.)

Now let's consider another word — "mother." The meaning that everyone agrees on — its denotative meaning — is "a female parent." However, the word also has connotative meanings that may be different for different people. "Mother," to some, may suggest a warm, loving, caring person. To others it may suggest someone with control and authority. To still others mother may mean someone to confide in and to share problems with. The connotative meaning may suggest either a positive or negative reaction based on an individual's experiences and associations with the word and what it represents. For instance, listed below are a few words that describe a group of people. Notice that some are positive and others are negative.

crowd	gang	audience
mob	congregation	clique

When reading any type of informative or persuasive material, it is important to be aware of an author's use of denotation and connotation. From the examples you can see that it is possible to create very different impressions simply by selecting words with certain connotations. It is one thing to be said to be part of an audience and quite another to be part of a mob or gang. Often, then, writers communicate subtle messages or lead you to respond a certain way toward an object, action, or idea by choosing words with positive or negative connotations.

EXERCISE 11-3

Directions: *For each word listed, write another word that has the same denotative meaning but a different connotative meaning.*

Example: to drink <u>guzzle</u>

1. to eat   _____

2. to talk   _____

3. fair   _____

4. famous   _____

247

5. group   _____

6. to take   _____

7. ability   _____

8. dog   _____

9. fast   _____

10. to fall   _____

EXERCISE 11-4

Directions: *For each of the following groups of words, circle the word or phrase with a positive connotation and underline the word or phrase that carries a negative connotation.*

Example: write   <u>scribble</u>   (compose)

1.	clean	polish	decontaminate
2.	display	show	expose
3.	look at	stare	gaze
4.	encounter	meet	become acquainted
5.	throw	hurl	toss
6.	ask	request	demand
7.	relinquish	abandon	let go
8.	relegate	entrust	give
9.	overlook	forget	neglect
10.	joke	ridicule	tease

APPLYING WHAT YOU HAVE LEARNED

Directions: *Choose one of the reading selections at the end of the chapter. As you read, notice the author's choice of words. When you have finished reading the selection and answered the multiple choice questions, go back through the selection and underline the words that you feel have particularly strong connotations, either positive or negative.*

READING SELECTION 17
WINE LABELS

Difficulty Level: A

Richard George

The label on a wine bottle won't tell you whether you'll like it, but it'll give you some information that's worth having. Unfortunately, the *attractiveness* of the label is no measure of quality. Some of the greatest wines in the world have very simple labels.

Wines are usually named in one of two ways; either after pieces of real estate, or after the predominant grapes that go into the wine. Most European wines go the real estate route, and the general rule is: the smaller the piece of real estate, the more highly the wine is valued.

Take French wine. The right to use well-known place names, or *appellations*, is controlled by French law. Compliance with the law is indicated by the words *appellation contrôlée* on the label.

The rules differ a bit from one region of France to another, but here's how it works in Bordeaux, which many wine lovers consider the greatest wine-growing area in the world.

The broadest, and thus the lowest, designation is the regional *appellation* — Bordeaux. The *appellation* tells us that the wine can come from any part of Bordeaux. This doesn't mean that it isn't nice to drink, by the way — just that it's low in the hierarchy of Bordeaux wines.

Moving up the ladder: in the region of Bordeaux, there are two dozen districts, one of which is Médoc. And Médoc is divided into two areas, one of which is the Haut-Médoc, which in turn is divided into 28 municipalities, or communes. One of the best-known communes is Pauillac — you can see how our geography is narrowing down — and in the commune of Pauillac, one of the estates is Château Mouton-Rothschild, which is Baron Philippe de Rothschild's vineyard and which produces one of the world's most celebrated red wines. We don't recommend that you run right out and buy it, because it's very expensive. In this case the wine carries the name of the estate, which means the wine is a product of the baron's own vineyard.

A label may say that the wine was *mis en bouteilles au château,* which means it was "made and bottled at the estate." Estate-bottling is a mark of authenticity, like an artist signing his work. It doesn't always guarantee high quality; after all, Bordeaux has about 3,500 estates. Nevertheless, many wine experts think this phrase is worth looking for.

It's definitely a mark of higher quality than the phrase *mis en bouteilles dans nos chais,* that is, "bottled in our cellars." Every wine is bottled in some kind of cellar, so this phrase doesn't mean too much.

With France's on-again, off-again climate, the vintage date on the label is a matter of interest. Consult a reliable merchant or a vintage chart in a wine encyclopedia if you want to know whether the year is considered good, bad, or indifferent. Just don't go overboard about vintage, because some good wine is produced in the worst of years, and vice versa.

The United States is rapidly increasing its wine production. Most American wines come from California, but New York State and Ohio share a hefty slice of the market.

There are three terms used in discussing wine names. First is *generic,* which means the wine name or designation of class unrelated to the wine's origin, like rosé, sparkling, apéritif, and so on. Some American wines use "semi-generic" names, which come from old, traditional European place names that are considered to have become part of the public domain; for example, burgundy or chablis. This does not mean they taste the same as a French burgundy or chablis.

The second term is *proprietary,* used for wine blends with made-up names. Paul Masson's Emerald Dry is such a wine.

The third kind, *varietal* wines, are the aristocrats of American wine. They take their names from the variety of the ⌐predominant grape⌐, such as Pinot Chardonnay or Cabernet Sauvignon. By law, at least 51 percent of a varietal wine must come from that grape variety. The better vineyards use a higher percentage, to give more of the distinctive taste and aroma.

By the way, if you try a bottle of varietal wine and like it so much that you want a jug by the same maker, read the jug label *very* carefully. Sometimes there's less of the varietal grape in the jug than there is in the fifth. If so, there may be a telltale word added to the jug label: for instance, it may be "Cabernet Sauvignon" on the bottle, but "Mountain Cabernet Sauvignon" on the jug label.

"Produced and bottled by" is another phrase worth looking for. It means the winery must make at least 75 percent of the wine in the bottle. If the label says "made and bottled by," that percentage could be as little as 10 percent. In other words, the winery places more of its "signature" on the wine when it's labeled "produced and bottled by."

COMPREHENSION TEST 17

Directions: *Circle the letter of the correct answer.*

1. The central point of this article is that
   a) the careful wine buyer can find a wealth of information on wine labels
   b) the most expensive wines come from Bordeaux, but American wines offer better vintages
   c) sales of wines have declined in recent years due to the increasing popularity of generics
   d) the best wines are bottled in France and are usually your best choices

2. Which of the following correctly illustrates the Bordeaux district hierarchy as mentioned in the article?
   a) Pauillac, Château Mouton-Rothschild, Bordeaux, Médoc, Haut-Médoc
   b) Bordeaux, Médoc, Haut-Médoc, Pauillac, Château Mouton-Rothschild
   c) Château Mouton-Rothschild, Pauillac, Médoc, Haut-Médoc, Bordeaux
   d) Médoc, Haut-Médoc, Château Mouton-Rothschild, Pauillac, Bordeaux

3. Wine consumers should not go "overboard" in selecting wines solely according to vintage dates because
   a) only wine growers need to be particular about vintages
   b) the generic classification of the wine is more important than its vintage
   c) the vintage date on the label is often inaccurate
   d) good wine can be produced in the worst of years

4. Major American wine producing areas are located in all of the following states *except*
   a) Idaho
   b) New York
   c) California
   d) Ohio

5. A wine that takes its name from the name of the main grape used in it is known as a
   a) generic wine
   b) semi-generic wine
   c) varietal wine
   d) proprietary wine

6. In the phrase "predominant grape" the word "predominant" means
   a) vintage
   b) generic
   c) necessary
   d) major

7. A California wine labeled "burgundy" would most likely taste like
   a) a burgundy from New York
   b) other California red wines
   c) a French bordeaux
   d) a French burgundy

8. Your best choice for a bottle of fine French wine would probably be one that has printed on its label
   a) Haut-Médoc
   b) Red Bordeaux
   c) Châteaux Lafon-Rochet
   d) St. Estephe

9. If you wanted to buy a good bottle of American-made wine for a very special occasion, your best bet would be one labeled
   a) Cabernet Sauvignon
   b) Mountain Cabernet Sauvignon
   c) Emerald Dry
   d) made and bottled by . . .

10. The author of this article develops his main point by
    a) describing the tastes of various wines
    b) defining terms for various wines
    c) giving humorous examples
    d) comparing wine values

Selection 17:			829 words
Finishing Time:	___ HR.	___ MIN.	___ SEC.
Starting Time:	___ HR.	___ MIN.	___ SEC.
Reading Time:		___ MIN.	___ SEC.
WPM Score:			___
Comprehension Score:			___ %
Reading Efficiency Score:			___

READING SELECTION 18

TOUCHING — AND BEING TOUCHED

William H. Masters and Virginia E. Johnson

Long before sexual attractions exist as anything more than natural curiosity about anatomical differences, most little boys and girls sense that the mysterious feelings drawing them into the adventure of mutual exploration are wrong. They have absorbed from the adult world the idea that touching the human body is indecent.

"Don't touch!" is a childhood litany. Many parents set clear examples. Apart from an occasional perfunctory embrace, they do not so much as hold hands. The father will decide that his little son or daughter is too old to nestle in his lap or be kissed. The mother will stop giving baths to a still young child.

Such parents cannot permit the spontaneous physical expression of feelings — the stroking, snuggling and enfolding movements with which almost all living creatures seek the warmth and reassurance that is virtually indistinguishable from life itself. Thus, while still too young to understand why, children learn to restrain the impulse to reach out to someone of the opposite sex.

As they grow older, the impulse to touch is expressed by teasing. This leads to scuffling and wrestling, which, although ostensibly in conflict, give boys and girls a chance to experience close physical contact. By adolescence they realize that parental prohibitions are merely temporary restraining orders. Most then begin experimenting with kissing games, which escalate into necking and petting.

Now the girls become the ones who say, "Don't touch," echoing the lesson deeply ingrained in childhood: that sex is dirty, and touching means sex — so it's hands off. Reaching out, which has already been sharply limited as a spontaneous way of expressing affection and solidarity, is now stripped of all significance except that of sexual provocation.

Thus the use of touch as a natural, uncomplicated way to express goodwill or friendship is forfeited.

Later, at the age of sexual experimentation, girls are more inclined to let themselves be touched than to do the touching. This again is partly a result of cultural conditioning — passivity as the proper female role, and the deeply embedded feeling that sexual activity for her may be dishonorable. With the rationalization that the boy is the initiator, the aggressor, who must bear full responsibility for what takes place between them, she struggles to free herself from feelings of guilt or discomfort, to free herself from the tight, involuntary tensions of her body, to free herself to enjoy her natural, physical response to being touched.

Her reluctance to touch also may be based on a practical consideration. In her early encounters with a boy she is likely to find that he becomes too excited too soon — and additional stimulation seems not only unnecessary but inadvisable.

Boys think of touch — which, at this stage, is closer to groping or grabbing than to caressing — as a sexual starter, or trigger. The boy expects that once he places his hand on a girl's body, her sexual motor will automatically shift into high gear. Her failure to respond with an ardor to match his own may baffle him. He is likely to try all the harder to overcome the girl's resistance, believing that she is just afraid of being aroused by his touch, and that if he can force his way past her defenses, her resistance will melt.

When these first, fumbling encounters produce not the anticipated delight but dismay or disappointment, most young people question not their expectations but themselves — or each other. He decides she is uptight because she didn't let him touch her in the right place; she decides he is inept because he didn't know how to touch her in the right way. They believe that if they just try again — with a new partner — before too long they will surely master the trick of sex. And the search continues, on a trial-and-error basis.

In time, some young men and women find at least partial answers to their questions. But even for them, success is usually flawed by continuing inability to grasp the true function of touch. Many still think of it exclusively as a means to an end — touching for the purpose of having intercourse, a functional, wordless way to communicate a willingness, a wish or a demand to make love.

Meanwhile, for other couples, who also consider touching to be just a means to the same end, it becomes a means they enjoy almost as much as the end itself. They have advanced past the adolescent notion of touch-as-trigger to the more sophisticated notion of touch-as-technique. In essence, they have adopted the philosophy of the how-to-do-it sex manuals. Sex becomes a skill that can be learned, and then applied wherever desired. Men and women are taught not how to touch another human being but how to manipulate another body.

This is a dead-end approach to the sexual relationship. Preoccupation with manipulative technique turns persons into objects, and touching is turned into the science of stimulation. Instead of a sharing of private emotions, sex then comes perilously close to being an exchange of impersonal services.

For the man and woman who value each other as individuals and who want the satisfactions of a sustained relationship, it is important to avoid the fundamental error of believing that touch serves only as a means to an end. In fact it is a primary form of communication, a silent voice that avoids the pitfalls of words while expressing the feelings of the moment. It bridges the physical separateness from which no one is spared, literally establishing a sense of solidarity between two individuals.

Touch most often carries its own message. It can be asexual, used to represent personal attitudes or emotions, to give comfort, to reassure. It can be a sensual thing, exploring the texture of the skin, the suppleness of a muscle, the contours of the body, with no further goal than enjoyment of tactile perceptions. And yet such is the nature of the sense of touch, which can simultaneously give and receive impressions, that the very pleasure a woman experiences in stroking her husband's face, for example, is relayed back through her fingertips, giving him the pleasure of awareness of her pleasure in him.

This is the wellspring of emotion from which sexuality flows. In reaching out spontaneously to communicate by touch, a husband and wife reaffirm their trust in each other and renew their commitment. They draw on this emotional reservoir when one turns to the other with physical desire. Because their touching has a continuity, and is part of an intimate dialogue that does not begin and end in bed, they feel secure. Whoever makes an overture knows the other will understand and respond, and the partner is secure in the knowledge that his response will be accepted, no matter how limited the degree of erotic arousal may naturally be at that moment.

Where no such security exists, two individuals in a sexual encounter may touch physically but remain out of touch emotionally. When touch or submitting to touch takes place solely for the purpose of intercourse it can express neither warmth nor closeness. It is a signal without subtlety, a demand for service or a yielding to such a demand. And over the years the service deteriorates, until finally one of the partners can no longer, or will no longer, perform. In a sad and ironic echo of their childhood, a man and woman live out their later lives in married celibacy and "do not touch."

Today's young couples seem to be freer to express themselves, in words and physically. Perhaps they will succeed in incorporating into their sexual lives a new philosophy of touch. Perhaps they do understand that touching — like seeing, hearing, tasting and smelling — nourishes the pleasure of being alive; that touching another human being satisfies the profound creature need not to feel alone; that being touched by another human being satisfies the need to be desired as a physical presence;

and that in touching and being touched, one can experience not only the pleasure of being alive but also the joy of being a sexual creature — a joy that ultimately and inevitably, as a natural extension of life itself, expresses itself in the sexual embrace.

COMPREHENSION TEST 18

Directions: *Circle the letter of the correct answer.*

1. Touching is a means of communication that
   a) does not work for most people
   b) is unused or misused by many
   c) everyone understands
   d) is primarily sexual

2. The stage of life at which a person learns to restrain the impulse to touch another individual of the opposite sex is
   a) early infancy
   b) childhood
   c) adolescence
   d) adulthood

3. The "proper female role" at the "age of sexual experimentation" as ingrained by society was described as
   a) actively seeking the male's touch
   b) remaining passive because sex may be dishonorable
   c) avoiding any touching that may lead to sex
   d) guiding the male in his touching of her

4. In couples who have gained some experience in touching as a sexual technique, which of the following is *least* likely to be true?
   a) Touch is a learned skill.
   b) Touching is enjoyed almost as much as intercourse.
   c) Sex often becomes an exchange of impersonal services.
   d) The sharing of private emotions is deeply felt during sex.

5. Touching can be all of the following, *except*
   a) comforting or reassuring
   b) experienced only between married couples

   c) a simple enjoyment of tactile perceptions
   d) asexual

6. The word "prohibitions" as used in this passage refers to
   a) laws against alcoholic beverages
   b) restrictions or taboos
   c) freedoms
   d) actions

7. Due to the influence of parents, touching often becomes automatically connected with
   a) friendship
   b) marriage
   c) sex
   d) necking

8. In order to help their children learn that touching should not be frowned on, parents could
   a) touch each other, thereby setting an example for their children
   b) send their children to school at an early age so they can be taught to touch
   c) not touch their children, thereby encouraging the children to develop touching behavior among themselves
   d) set an example for children to learn that touching is not permissible anywhere except between members of the same sex

9. If a person were conditioned to think that touching is unhealthy or socially unacceptable, how do you think he or she would react if touched in a sexually inviting manner by a member of the opposite sex?
   a) He or she would welcome the touch.
   b) He or she would feel insecure.
   c) He or she would be passive and let the other person enjoy it.
   d) He or she would not feel dishonored.

10. The authors develop their main point by
   a) describing a number of general situations
   b) a series of personal examples
   c) showing problems and their solutions
   d) using strong persuasion

Selection 18:			1368 words

Finishing Time: _____ _____ _____
                    HR.   MIN.   SEC.

Starting Time: _____ _____ _____
                    HR.   MIN.   SEC.

Reading Time: _____ _____
                    MIN.   SEC.

WPM Score: _____

Comprehension Score: _____ %

Reading Efficiency Score: _____

Chapter 12:
Aids to Vocabulary Development

Most college students readily admit that they would like to possess a more extensive vocabulary. In fact, many college graduates, professionals, and even college instructors wish they had a better command of the words in our language. However, few people are able to find time in their already busy days to take a vocabulary improvement course or to devote a period of study solely to vocabulary development. Just because you might not have time specifically for vocabulary study, however, does not mean that you cannot improve your vocabulary. In fact, you can dramatically increase your word power by combining vocabulary improvement with other activities. For instance, whenever you read an assignment, an advertisement, or a magazine article there is an opportunity to broaden your vocabulary. In these circumstances you might encounter an unfamiliar word, notice a word used in a different way, or learn additional meanings for familiar words. Similarly, when you listen to your instructors, a news commentator, or a TV documentary you might meet new words or hear words used in different ways. As you write or speak, if you are aware of your word choice and make a conscious effort to select accurate and descriptive language, you will also find your vocabulary level expanding.

The purpose of this chapter is to suggest ways in which you can develop your vocabulary during the normal course of reading, studying, and completing class assignments. Specifically this chapter will offer you ideas on how to determine the meaning of unfamiliar words using their context, how to analyze word parts, how to develop an organizational system for learning new words, and how to use a dictionary and thesaurus to expand and diversify your vocabulary.

USING CONTEXTUAL AIDS

The following tests are intended to demonstrate an important principle of vocabulary development. Before continuing with this section, try these vocabulary tests. Complete *both* tests before checking your answers, which appear in the paragraph following test B. While working on the second test *do not* return to the first test to change any answers.

TEST A: WORDS WITHOUT CONTEXT

Directions: *For each item choose the word that is closest in meaning to the first word. Circle the letter of your answer.*

1. verbatim
   a) word by word
   b) using verbs
   c) idea by idea
   d) using abbreviations
   e) using an outline

2. sedentary
   a) very routine
   b) dull and boring
   c) quiet
   d) exciting
   e) involves sitting

3. thwarted
   a) initiated
   b) blocked
   c) controlled
   d) disagreed
   e) imposed

4. renounced
   a. gave up
   b) kept
   c) transferred
   d) criticized
   e) applied for

5. audacity
   a) patience
   b) boldness
   c) good sense
   d) courtesy
   e) understanding

6. disparaging
   a) encouraging
   b) questioning

    c) sincere
    d) logical
    e) belittling

7. capricious
    a) changeable
    b) dependable
    c) rational
    d) unusual
    e) puzzling

8. periphery
    a) outside
    b) focus
    c) inside
    d) edge
    e) middle

9. indigenous
    a) natural
    b) fertile
    c) native
    d) adaptations
    e) mutations

10. abject
    a) cruel
    b) most miserable and hated
    c) frightening
    d) difficult to commit
    e) illogical

Number Correct: _____

TEST B: WORDS IN CONTEXT

Directions: *For each item choose the word that is closest in meaning to the underlined word. Circle the letter of your answer.*

1. It is more efficient to take lecture notes in your own words than to try to record the lecture <u>verbatim</u>.
    a) word by word
    b) using verbs
    c) idea by idea
    d) using abbreviations
    e) using an outline

2. Office work is quite <u>sedentary</u>; while in factory work you are able to move around more.
   a) very routine
   b) dull and boring
   c) quiet
   d) exciting
   e) involves sitting

3. Joe's parents <u>thwarted</u> his efforts to get a student loan; they refused to disclose financial information, and refused to cosign for him.
   a) initiated
   b) blocked
   c) controlled
   d) disagreed
   e) imposed

4. Despite his love of the country, he <u>renounced</u> his citizenship when the war broke out.
   a) gave up
   b) kept
   c) transferred
   d) criticized
   e) applied for

5. The woman had the <u>audacity</u> to return the dress to the store after wearing it several times.
   a) patience
   b) boldness
   c) good sense
   d) courtesy
   e) understanding

6. Despite her husband's <u>disparaging</u> remarks, the woman persisted in her efforts to find a full-time job.
   a) encouraging
   b) questioning
   c) sincere
   d) logical
   e) belittling

7. As evidence of his wife's <u>capricious</u> behavior, the husband described how frequently she changed from one extreme to another.
   a) changeable
   b) dependable

   c) rational
   d) unusual
   e) puzzling

8. In certain societies, young children are always on the <u>periphery</u>, and never in the center, of family life.
   a) outside
   b) focus
   c) inside
   d) edge
   e) middle

9. Most types of pine trees are <u>indigenous</u> to North America, but many ornamental shrubs were brought here from other continents.
   a) natural
   b) fertile
   c) native
   d) adaptations
   e) mutations

10. Matricide, the killing of one's mother, is one of the most contemptible and <u>abject</u> crimes.
   a) cruel
   b) most miserable and hated
   c) frightening
   d) difficult to commit
   e) illogical

Number Correct: _____

Now score each test. The answers to both tests are the same. They are: (1) a, (2) e, (3) b, (4) a, (5) b, (6) e, (7) a, (8) d, (9) c, (10) b. Most likely, you had more items correct on test B than on test A. Why did your scores differ even though the words and the choices were the same on both tests? The answer is that test B was easier because in it the words were presented *in context;* the words around the italicized word provided clues to its meaning. Test A, on the other hand, had no sentences in which the words were used and it provided no meaningful clues at all.

The purpose of these tests, as you can see, was to demonstrate that you can often figure out the meaning of an unknown word by looking for clues in the sentence or paragraph in which it appears. In the rest of this section we show how to use the four most common clues that context can provide about the meaning of an unknown word.

Definition Clues

Many times a writer directly or indirectly defines a word immediately following its use. Usually, the writer does this when he or she suspects that some readers may be unfamiliar with the new term or concept. Sometimes a writer will include a formal definition of the type you might find in a dictionary. In these cases the meaning of the word will be stated directly. At other times a writer may informally restate the idea or offer a synonym, a word that means the same thing, and in this way provide enough of a clue so that you can grasp the meaning of the word. Here are a few examples of each type of definition clue.

FORMAL DEFINITION

1. **Horology** is the science of measuring time.
2. **Induction** refers to the process of reasoning from the known to the unknown.
3. **Metabolism** refers to the rate at which the body's cells manufacture energy from food or produce new cells.

Notice that in each example, the boldface word is clearly and directly defined (by the underlined part of the sentence). In fact, each sentence was written for the sole purpose of defining a term. This is the most obvious type of context clue, and you will have no difficulty determining the meaning of words explained in this manner. Almost as obvious as formal definition is the inclusion of a restatement or synonym as a means of defining a new word.

INDIRECT DEFINITIONS

1. **Hypochondria,** excessive worry over one's health, afflicts many Americans over forty.
2. There was a **consensus,** or agreement, among the faculty to require one term paper for each course.
3. Referring to the ability to "see" without using the normal sensory organs, **clairvoyance** is under study at the Psychic Research Center.
4. **Middle age** (thirty-five years to sixty-five years) is a time for strengthening and maintaining life goals.

In each of these examples, also, a meaning is provided for the boldface term. A complete definition is not given, but there is sufficient information (underlined) included to give you a general idea of the meaning so that you can continue reading without stopping to check a dictionary. Although indirect definitions are built into this kind of sentence, they are not the most important part of it. That is, the sentence's main function is *not* to define the word, but to express an idea that relates to or involves that term. Indirect definitions are usually set apart from the main part of a sentence by commas or parentheses or they are expressed in a phrase or clause that further explains the sentence's core parts.

EXERCISE 12-1

Directions: *In each sentence locate the part that gives a definition clue for the boldface term. Underline this portion of the sentence.*

1. **Chemical reactivity,** the tendency of an element to participate in chemical reactions, is an important concept in combining elements.
2. The **effectiveness adjustment,** the process by which an organism meets the demands of its environment, depends on many factors.
3. **Deductive thinking** involves drawing a conclusion from a set of general principles.
4. **Interrogation,** or questioning, can be psychologically and emotionally draining.
5. The boy was **maimed,** or disfigured, as a result of the accident.

Example Clues

A second way to determine the meaning of an unknown word is to look for examples that explain or clarify it. Suppose you do not know the meaning of the word "trauma," and you find it used in the following sentence:

Diane experienced many traumas during early childhood including injury in an auto accident, the death of her grandmother, and the divorce of her parents.

This sentence gives three examples of traumas, and from the examples given you could conclude that "trauma" means a shocking or psychologically damaging experience.

Here are a few other examples of sentences that contain example clues.

Toxic materials such as arsenic, asbestos, pesticides, and lead can cause permanent bodily damage.

Unconditioned responses, including heartbeat, blinking, and breathing, occur naturally in all humans.

Orthopterans, such as crickets, grasshoppers, and cockroaches, thrive in damp conditions.

You may have noticed in these sentences that the examples are signaled by certain words or phrases. "Such as" and "including" are used here. Other common signals are "for example," "for instance," and "to illustrate."

EXERCISE 12-2

Directions: *Read each sentence and write a definition or synonym for each boldface word or phrase. Use the example context clue to help you determine word meaning.*

1. Because of their **metallic properties,** such as thermal and electrical conductivity, luster, and ductility (ability to be shaped into thin pieces), copper and lead are used for electrical wiring.

    _____

2. Perceiving, learning, and thinking are examples of **cognitive** processes.

    _____

3. Many **debilities** of old age, including loss of hearing, poor eyesight, and diseases such as arthritis, can be treated medically.

    _____

4. **Phobias,** such as fear of heights, fear of water, or fear of crowds, can be eliminated through conditioning.

    _____

5. Humans have built-in **coping mechanisms;** we shout when we are angry, cry when we are sad, and tremble when we are nervous.

    _____

Contrast Clues

It is sometimes possible to determine the meaning of an unknown word from a word or phrase in the context that has an opposite meaning. Notice, in the following sentence, how a word opposite in meaning from the underlined word provides a clue to its meaning.

> During the concert the audience was quiet, but afterward the crowd became <u>boisterous</u>.

Although you may not know the meaning of "boisterous," you know that the audience was quiet during the concert and that afterward it acted differently. The word "but" suggests this. You know, then, that the crowd became the opposite of quiet (loud and noisy).

Here are a few additional examples of sentences containing contrast clues.

> I <u>loathe</u> cats even though most of my friends love them.

> Although the cottage appeared <u>derelict</u>, we discovered that a family lived there on weekends.

> Pete, through long hours of study, successfully passed the exam; on the other hand, Sam's efforts were <u>futile</u>.

In these examples you may have noticed that each contains a word or phrase that indicates that an opposite or contrasting situation exists. The signal words used in the examples were "even though," "although," and "on the other hand." Other words that also signal a contrasting idea include "but," "however," "despite," "rather," "while," "yet," and "nevertheless."

EXERCISE 12-3

Directions: *Read each sentence and write a definition or synonym for each boldface word. Use the contrast clue to help you determine the meaning of the word.*

1. Al was always talkative, whereas Ed remained **taciturn.**

    _____

2. The microwave oven is becoming **obsolete;** the newer microwave-convection oven offers the user more cooking options.

    _____

3. My brother lives in the **remote** hills of Kentucky, so he seldom has the opportunity to shop in big cities.

    _____

4. One of the women shoppers **succumbed** to the temptation of buying a new dress, but the others resisted.

    _____

5. Most members of Western society marry only one person at a time, but in other cultures **polygamy** is common and acceptable.

    _____

Inference Clues

Many times you can figure out the meaning of a word you do not know by guessing or figuring it out. From the information that is given in the context you can infer the meaning of a word you are not familiar with. For instance, look at the following sentence.

My father is a versatile man; he is a successful businessman, sportsman, author, and sportscar mechanic.

You can see that the father is successful at many different types of activities, and you could reason that "versatile" means capable of doing many things competently.

Similarly, in the following example the general sense of the context provides clues to the meaning of the word *robust*.

At the age of seventy-seven, Mr. George was still playing a skillful game of tennis. He jogged four miles each day and seldom missed his daily swim. For a man of his age he was extremely robust.

From the facts presented about Mr. George, you can infer that "robust" means full of health and vigor.

Sometimes your knowledge and experience can help you figure out an unknown word. Consider, for instance, the following sentence:

After tasting and eating most of seven different desserts, my appetite was completely satiated.

Your own experience would suggest that if you ate seven desserts, you would no longer feel like eating. Thus, you could reason that "satiated" means full or satisfied.

EXERCISE 12-4

Directions: *Read each sentence and write a definition or synonym for each boldface word. Try to reason out the meaning of each word using information provided in the context.*

1.   Although my grandfather is eighty-two he is far from **infirm;** he is active, ambitious, and healthy.

    _____

2.   My **unscrupulous** uncle tried to sell as an antique a rocking chair he bought just last year.

    _____

3.   My sister's life style always angered and disappointed my mother; yet, she **redeemed** herself by doing special favors for my mother's friends.

    _____

4.   The wind howling around the corner of the house that is rumored to have ghosts made an **eerie** sound.

    _____

5.   We burst out laughing at the **ludicrous** sight of the basketball team dressed up as cheerleaders.

    _____

EXERCISE 12-5

Directions: *Each of the following sentences contains a word or term whose meaning can be determined from the context. Underline the part of the sentence that contains the clue to the meaning of the boldface word. Then write a definition or synonym for the boldface word.*

1.   Tremendous **variability** characterizes the treatment of the mentally retarded during the medieval era, ranging from treatment as innocents to being tolerated as fools and persecuted as witches.

    _____

2.   A citizen review panel **exonerated** the public official of any possible misconduct or involvement in the acceptance of bribes.

    _____

3. The **tenacious** residents living near the polluted land fill responded vehemently to the court's recommended settlement while the chemical industry immediately agreed to the court settlement.

    _____

4. The economy was in continual **flux;** inflation increased one month and decreased the next.

    _____

5. The short story contained a series of **morbid** events: the death of the mother, the suicide of the grandmother, and the murder of a young child.

    _____

Limitations of Context

Although context clues are generally useful, there are two limitations to this approach. First, context clues seldom provide a complete meaning. Rather, they give you enough clues to allow you to continue reading without stopping to look up the word. The level of meaning you get from context clues is usually vague and very general. Context clues, then, are expedient, short-term aids to vocabulary development. You do not often learn a word or make it a permanent part of your vocabulary by determining its meaning from context. Therefore, as you encounter words while reading, even if you can figure them out from context, try to mark or underline them so you can return to them later. At that time, you can look them up in the dictionary and use one of the learning systems suggested later in this chapter.

Second, context, in determining word meaning, does not always work. You will find many instances in which you are unable to find a clue to the meaning of an unknown word. In such cases you will have to use other means of determining the meaning of the word. Various techniques will be suggested in the rest of this chapter.

Before concentrating on particular methods of vocabulary development, you should realize that you have several different vocabularies, each of which can be expanded in a slightly different way. Although most people regard vocabulary ability as a single entity, everyone actually has four distinct vocabularies: a reading vocabulary, a writing vocabulary, a speaking vocabulary, and a listening vocabulary. Although each has a common core of basic words, there are wide variations in the size of each and the types of words contained in each. For instance, there are words that you understand when listening to someone speak but do not use in your own speech or in your own writing. Similarly, there are words that you use in your speech but would not use in your writing. Also, there are words that you recognize when reading but never use in your own speech or writing.

As you expand your vocabulary, then, you will need to decide which vocabulary you are trying to expand and adapt the techniques accordingly.

OTHER AIDS TO VOCABULARY DEVELOPMENT

As you just learned, the use of context clues is a valuable, but immediate, approach to handling unfamiliar words as you are reading. However, the use of context contributes little to the long-term expansion of your vocabulary. This section of the chapter will contain several easy-to-use techniques for broadening your vocabulary.

Prefixes and Roots

Many words in the English language are made up of word parts called *prefixes, roots,* and *suffixes.* You might think of these as beginnings, middles, and endings of words. These word parts have specific meanings and when added together can provide strong clues to the meanings of a particular word. Of these three possible parts, prefixes and roots most consistently provide you with the basic meaning of many different words.

The prefixes and roots listed in the following tables occur in thousands of words. For instance, suppose that you do not know the meaning of the word "pseudonym." However, if you know that "pseudo" means false and "-nym" means name, then you would be able to add the two parts together and realize that a pseudonym means a false name that one assumes. Not all words are constructed as simply as this, though. They may be built in many combinations of prefixes, roots, and suffixes. For example the word "geology" (the study of the earth) is made up of two roots: "geo" and "logy," but no prefixes or suffixes. The word "insubordination" (the act of not being under another's authority) contains two prefixes: "in" and "sub"; one root: "ordin"; and one suffix: "ation." Several more variations are possible, but in most cases there must be one root upon which a word is built. By becoming acquainted with the prefixes and roots contained in the tables that follow, you will have a foothold in figuring out the meanings of thousands of words.

268

Table 12-1. COMMON PREFIXES

PREFIX	MEANING	SAMPLE WORD
ad	to, at, for	adhere
anti	against	antiwar
circum	around	circumvent
com/col/con	with, together	compile
contra	against, opposite	contradict
de	away, from	deport
dis	apart, away, not	disagree
equi	equal	equidistant
ex/extra	from, out of, former	ex-wife
hyper	over, excessive	hyperactive
in/il/ir/im	in, into, not	illogical
inter	between	interpersonal
intro/intra	within, into, in	introduction
micro	small	microscope
mis	wrong	misleading
mono	one	monologue
multi	many	multipurpose
non	not	nonfiction
poly	many	polygon
post	after	posttest
pre	before	premarital
pseudo	false	pseudonym
re	back, again	repeat
retro	backward	retrospect
semi	half	semicircle
sub	under, below	submarine
super	above, extra, above average	supercharge
tele	far	telescope
trans	across, over	transcontinental
un	not	unskilled

Before you begin to use these tables to figure out new words, however, you should realize that this approach, although very useful, has several exceptions. First, the roots may vary in spelling as they are combined with certain prefixes. (Many of these common variations are contained in the table.) Second, some roots are commonly found at the beginnings of words, others at the end, while still others can be found in either position. Finally, there are situations in which you may identify a group of letters, but find that it does not carry the meaning of prefix or root. For example, the word *internal* has nothing to do with the prefix "inter," meaning between, and the word *missile* does not mean wrong or bad. Despite these exceptions, you will find that these

Table 12-2. COMMON ROOTS

ROOT	MEANING	SAMPLE WORD
aud/audit	hear	audible
bio	life	biology
aster/astro	star	astronaut
cap	take, seize	captive
chron(o)	time	chronolog
corp	body	corpse
cred	believe	incredible
dict/dic	tell, say	predict
duc/duct	lead	introduce
fact/fac	make, do	factory
graph	write	telegraph
geo	earth	geophysics
log/logo/logy	study, thought	psychology
mit/miss	send	dismiss
mort/mor	die, death	immortal
path	feeling	sympathy
phono	sound/voice	telephone
photo	light	photosensitive
port	carry	transport
scop	seeing	microscope
scrib/script	write	inscription
sen/sent	feel	insensitive
spec/spic	look, see	retrospect
spect/spec	look at	spectacle
terr/terre	land, earth	territory
theo	god	theology
ven/vent	come	convention
vert/vers	turn	invert
vis/vid	see	invisible
voc	call	vocation

commonly used prefixes and roots can help you unlock the meaning of many new words.

EXERCISE 12-6

Directions: *Use the list of common prefixes in Table 12-1 to determine the meaning of each of the following words. Write a brief definition or synonym for each. If you are unfamiliar with the root, you may need to check a dictionary.*

1. misinformed _____

2. rephrase _____

3. interoffice _____

4. circumscribe _____

5. irreversible _____

6. substandard _____

7. supernatural _____

8. telecommunications _____

9. unqualified _____

10. subdivision _____

11. transcend _____

12. hypercritical _____

13. pseudointellectual _____

14. contraception _____

15. equivalence _____

EXERCISE 12-7

Directions: *Use the list of common roots (Table 12-2) and the list of common prefixes (Table 12-1) to determine the meaning of the following words. Write a brief definition or synonym for each, checking a dictionary if necessary.*

1. chronology _____

2. photocomposition _____

3. introspection _____

4. biology _____

5. subterranean _____

6. captivate _____

7. conversion _____

8. teleprompter _____

9. monotheism _____

10. exportation _____

Using the Dictionary

Although many students try to avoid using the dictionary, it is a valuable reference source and an important tool in vocabulary development. Repetitious dictionary drills and long lists of words assigned by well-meaning teachers may have created, for many students, a negative attitude toward dictionary use. However, the dictionary's uses are more general than most people realize.

Here are a few general principles to keep in mind:

1. Never spend time looking up long lists of words, even if you really want to learn each word on the list. By the time you finish the list, you will have forgotten the first ones you looked up. Instead, look up a few words at a time.
2. Do not interrupt your reading to check the meaning of a word in the dictionary unless the word is absolutely essential to the meaning of the sentence or paragraph. Instead, mark unknown words and look them up later.
3. Whenever you do look up a word, be sure to write down the word and its meaning. (A later section of the chapter on organizational approaches will suggest an effective way to do this.)
4. Whenever you look up a word, be sure to read through all the meanings and choose the meaning that suits the context in which it is used.

Types of Information to Find in the Dictionary. Although the dictionary, of course, is a source for definitions of words, it also contains other types of useful information that can significantly expand your vocabulary. Here are some types of information that we often overlook in using the dictionary.

1. *Word pronunciation.* Have you ever been unsure of how to pronounce a word? This situation most commonly arises when you attempt to use a word from your reading vocabulary in your speaking vocabulary. Rather than guess at the pronunciation of a word or avoid using it because you are unsure of its pronunciation, take a moment to look it up. Immediately following the word entry, you will find a pronunciation key. At first, this key may not appear very useful. Suppose you are trying to figure out how to pronounce the word "deign," meaning to agree in a condescending manner. After the word you would find the following: (dān). Although this phonetic spelling may not translate immediately into an easily pronounceable word or phrase, the key at the bottom of the page provides an easy way to interpret the phonetic symbols. For instance, the *American Heritage Desk Dictionary* lists the following key:

ă pat	ā pay	â care	ä father	ĕ pet	ē be	hw which	ĭ pit	ī tie	î pier	ŏ pot	ō toe	ô paw, for	oi noise
ōō took	ōō boot	ou out	th thin	*th* this	ŭ cut	û urge	zh vision	ə about, item, edible, gallop, circus					

    From the key you learn that the "a" sound in "deign" rhymes with the word "pay," and an accent mark ('), for words with two or more syllables, is included to indicate which part of the word should receive the greatest emphasis.

2. *Key to spelling.* The common complaint about using a dictionary as a spelling aid goes as follows: If I cannot spell it, how can I locate it in the dictionary? Generally, most spelling errors do not occur at the beginnings of words anyway (with the exception of words beginning with ph, mn, or ch-sh). Thus, it is possible to locate a particular word in a dictionary. In addition to the basic spelling of a word, the dictionary often shows how spellings change when the word becomes plural or an -ing ending is added to the word.

3. *Useful tables and charts.* Many dictionaries contain numerous tables and charts that make the dictionary a handy general reference book rather than just an alphabetical list of words and meanings. Commonly included among a dictionary's tables and charts are tables of weights and measures with metric equivalents, lists of abbreviations, lists of signs and symbols, a guide to punctuation, mechanics and manuscript form (also called a style manual), a table of periodic elements used in chemistry, and lists of famous people (dead and alive) and what they are noted for.

4. *Information on language history.* Actually, the dictionary functions as a brief history of the English language. For each word entry, information is given about the origin of the word. This ety-

mological information tells you the language or languages from which the word evolved. In the following entry (*Webster's New Collegiate Dictionary*) you can see that the word "establish" is derived from Middle English (ME), Middle French (MF), and Latin (L).

es·tab·lish \is-'tab-lish\ *vb* [ME *establissen,* fr. MF *establiss-,* stem of *establir,* fr. L *stabilire,* fr. *stabilis* stable] *vt* **1 :** to make firm or stable **2 :** to institute (as a law) permanently by enactment or agreement **3** *obs* **:** SETTLE7 **4 a :** to bring into existence **:** FOUND <~*ed* a republic> **b :** to bring about **:** EFFECT <~*ed* friendly relations> **5 a :** to set on a firm basis <~ his son in business> **b :** to put into a favorable position **c :** to gain full recognition or acceptance of **6 :** to make (a church) a national institution **7 :** to put beyond doubt **:** PROVE <~*ed* his innocence> ~ *vi, of a plant* **:** to become naturalized <a grass that ~ *es* on poor soil> **syn** see SET *ant* uproot (*as a plant or a practice*), abrogate (*as a privilege*) — **es·tab·lish·able** \-ə-bəl\ *adj* — **es·tab·lish·er** *n*

5. *Foreign expressions used in English.* Certain expressions from other languages have become widely used in the English language. These phrases often more accurately express an idea or feeling than do the English translations. The French expression *faux pas* is a good example, translated to mean a social blunder. Most dictionaries list foreign phrases alphabetically along with English words, although in some dictionaries you may find a separate list of foreign expressions. A few more examples of commonly used foreign expressions that are listed in most dictionaries are: *ad hoc, non sequitur, de facto, tête-à-tête,* and *bona fide.*

EXERCISE 12-8

Directions: *Use a dictionary to answer each of the following items. Write your answer in the space provided.*

1. What does the abbreviation *e.g.* stand for?

    _____

2. How is the word *deleterious* pronounced? (Record its phonetic spelling.)

    _____

3. From what language is the word *delicatessen* taken?

    _____

4. How many feet are in a *mile?*

   _____

5. What does the Latin expression *non sequitur* mean?

   _____

6. What is the plural spelling of *addendum?*

   _____

7. What type of punctuation is a *virgule?*

   _____

8. List a few words that contain the following sound: ī.

   _____

9. Who or what is a *Semite?*

   _____

10. Can the word *phrase* be used other than as a noun? If so, how?

    _____

Choosing the Appropriate Meaning. The crucial part of looking a word up in the dictionary is finding the appropriate meaning to fit the context in which the word is used. Since a dictionary lists all the common meanings of a word, you may have numerous possible choices but only one definition that is appropriate for the manner in which the word is used. For instance, suppose you were to read the following sentence and could not determine the meaning of "isometrics" from context. Since its meaning is crucial to understanding the sentence, you decide to look the word up in your dictionary.

The executive found that doing isometrics helped him to relax between business meetings.

The dictionary entry (*American Heritage Desk Dictionary*) for isometrics is:

i·so·met·ric (ī'sə-mĕt'rĭk) or **i·so·met·ri·cal** (-rĭ-kəl) *adj.*
1. Of or exhibiting equality in dimensions or measure-
ments. **2.** Of or being a crystal system of three equal axes
at right angles to one another. **3.** Of or involving muscle
contractions in which the ends of the muscle are held in
place so that there is an increase in tension rather than a
shortening of the muscle: *isometric exercises.* —*n.* **1.** A
line connecting isometric points. **2. isometrics** *(used with a
sing. verb).* Isometric exercise. [From Greek *isometros*, of
equal measure : *isos*, equal + *metron*, measure.]

Since there are five meanings listed, you must choose the definition
that makes the best sense in the sentence. You will notice that the
meanings are grouped and numbered consecutively according to parts
of speech. The meanings of the word when used as an adjective are
listed first, followed by two meanings for it as a noun. If you are able to
identify the part of speech of the word you are looking up, you can skip
over all parts of the entry that do not pertain to that part of speech. For
instance, in the sample sentence above, you can tell that "isometrics"
is a "thing" the executive does; therefore, it is a noun.

If you cannot identify the part of speech of a word you are looking
up, begin with the first meaning listed. Generally, the most common
meaning appears first, and more specialized meanings appear toward
the end of the entry.

Choosing the right meaning is basically a process of substitution.
That is, when you find a meaning that could fit into the sentence you
are working with, replace the word with its definition and then read
the entire sentence. If the definition makes sense in the sentence, you
can be fairly certain that you have selected the appropriate meaning.

EXERCISE 12-9

Directions: *Write an appropriate meaning for the underlined word in
each of the following sentences. Use the dictionary to help you find the
meaning that makes sense in the sentence.*

1. He <u>affected</u> a French accent.

    _____

2. The <u>amphibian</u> took us to our destination in less than an hour.

    _____

3. The plane stalled on the <u>apron</u>.

    _____

4. We <u>circumvented</u> the problem by calculating in metrics.

_____

5. The rising inflation rate has <u>embroiled</u> many consumers.

_____

Using a Thesaurus

Although a dictionary is a valuable tool in developing your vocabulary, there is another reference book that is more valuable than a dictionary in choosing precisely the right word to suit your meaning. This reference is called a *thesaurus,* and basically it is a dictionary of synonyms. It is written for the specific purpose of grouping words that are similar in meaning. A thesaurus is particularly useful when you have a word on the "tip of your tongue," so to speak, but cannot think of the exact word. It is also useful in locating a precise, accurate, or descriptive phrase to fit a particular situation.

Suppose you are looking for a more precise term for the expression "told us about" in the following sentence.

My instructor told us about an assignment that would be due next month.

The thesaurus lists the following synonyms:

.8 VERBS **inform, tell, speak,** apprize, **advise, advertise,** advertise of, **give word,** mention to, **acquaint, enlighten,** familiarize, brief, verse, wise up [slang], give the facts, give an account of, give by way of information; **instruct** 562.11; possess *or* seize one of the facts; **let know, have one to know, give one to understand;** tell once and for all; notify, give notice *or* notification, serve notice; **communicate** 554.6,7; bring *or* send *or* leave word; **report** 558.11; **disclose** 556.4–7; put in a new light, shed new *or* fresh light upon.

.9 **post** *or* **keep one posted** [both informal]; fill one in, bring up to date, put one in the picture [Brit].

.10 **hint, intimate, suggest, insinuate, imply, indicate,** adumbrate, lead *or* leave one to gather, justify one in supposing, give *or* drop *or* throw out a hint, give an inkling of, **hint at; allude to,** make an allusion to, glance at [archaic]; **prompt,** give the cue; put in *or* into one's head.

Right away you can identify several words that are more descriptive than "told us about." The next step, then, is to choose a word from the list that most closely suggests the meaning you intend. The easiest way to do this is to "test out" or substitute various choices in your sentence to see which one is most appropriate. Be sure to choose only those words with which you are familiar and for which you are aware of the "shades of meaning" they suggest. Remember, a misused word is often a more serious error than a wordy or imprecise expression.

The most widely used thesaurus was originally compiled by Roget and is known today as *Roget's Thesaurus;* inexpensive paperback copies are readily available. When you first use a thesaurus you will have to get used to how to use it. First, you have to look up the word in the back to locate the number of the section in the main part of the thesaurus that lists synonyms, then you must turn to that section.

A System for Learning New Words

In the normal course of reading textbook assignments and reference sources for your classes and while listening to your instructor's class presentations, you are constantly being exposed to new words. However, unless you make a deliberate effort to remember and use these words, many of them will probably fade from your memory. One of the most practical and easy-to-use systems for expanding your vocabulary is the index card system. It works like this:

1. Whenever you hear or read a new word that you intend to learn, jot it down in the margin of your notes or mark it some way in the material you are reading.
2. Later, write each word on the front of an index card, then look up the meaning (or meanings) of the word and write this on the back. You might also record a phonetic key for the word's pronunciation, if it is a difficult one, or a sample sentence in which the word is used. Your cards should look like the one on page 279.
3. Whenever you have a few spare minutes, go through your pack of index cards; for each card, look at the word on the front and try to recall its meaning on the back. Then check the back of the card to see if you were correct. If you were unable to recall the meaning or if you confused it with another word, retest yourself. Shuffle the cards after each use.
4. After you have gone through your pack of cards several times, sort the cards into two piles; separate the words you know from those which you have not learned. Then, putting the "known words" aside, concentrate on the words still to be learned.

FRONT

treachery

(trĕch′ ə rē)

BACK

1. betrayal of confidence
or trust

2. a disloyal (treasonous) act

5. Once you have mastered the entire pack, periodically review them to refresh your memory and keep the words current in your mind.

This word-card system is effective for several reasons. First, it can be accomplished in the spare moments that are often wasted waiting for a return phone call, waiting for a class to begin, riding a bus, and so forth. Second, the system enables you to spend time learning what you do *not* know rather than wasting time studying what you already know. Finally, the system overcomes a major problem that exists in learning information that appears in list form. If the material is in a fixed order, you tend to learn it in that order and are unable to recall the items when they appear in isolation or out of order. By shuffling the cards you are able to scramble the order of the words and avoid this problem.

Using Newly Learned Words

Although you may meet and learn new words daily, there is still no assurance that you will automatically use your newly acquired vocabulary in your own speech or writing. For this reason, listening and reading vocabularies tend to be much larger than writing or speaking vocabularies. It does require a conscious effort to begin to use new words. There is a saying that "If you use a word three times, it is yours forever." In a general sense, this saying appears to apply. It is important to use a word in order for it to remain a part of your vocabulary. The first time you use a new word you may be unsure if you are using it correctly. Try not to allow this element of risk to discourage you from trying new words and restrict your development of a speaking and writing vocabulary.

There are several situations in which you can begin to use newly learned words. Many of the new words you are learning are course-related: you have heard your instructor use them or you have encountered them in reading assignments. Therefore, the first place to use the new words is in course-related situations. For instance, when studying with a friend or when participating in a class discussion try to use these new words you have learned.

Another way to begin to expand your vocabulary is through the use of synonyms. There are many words and expressions that are overused and others that are so general that they fail to convey your meaning accurately. Here are a few examples of these types of words and phrases accompanied by synonyms that could be used to provide a more descriptive or precise meaning.

My sister is sad.
(Is she depressed? dejected? unhappy? sorrowful? gloomy? grief-stricken? mournful?)

I liked the movie we saw last night.
(Did you enjoy it? Were you amused? frightened? enthralled? fascinated?)

We had a good dinner at George's house.
(Was it pleasant? interesting? well prepared? unusual? plentiful? extraordinary?)

As you speak and write, then, try to be conscious of your word choices. Select words that most clearly and accurately convey the meaning you intend. Of course, selection of the most effective words is easier for writing than for speech. Speech is spontaneous and occurs immediately without allowing you time to give much thought to your choice of words. In writing, however, you do have the opportunity to revise and substitute more precise language. As a general rule, it is best to record your ideas first, without thinking about exact choices of words. Then, as you reread what you have written, try to think of words that express your ideas more accurately or that provide more complete information.

APPLYING WHAT YOU HAVE LEARNED

Directions: *Choose one of the selections at the end of the chapter. Read the selection and answer the multiple choice questions. Then complete each of the following steps.*

1. Review the selection and list any words whose meaning you determined from context.

    _____   _____

    _____   _____

    _____   _____

    _____   _____

    _____   _____

2. List any unfamiliar words for which you cannot determine a meaning from the context. Check the dictionary for the appropriate meaning of each and write it here.

    _____

    _____

_____

_____

_____

3.   Prepare an index card for each unfamiliar word you met in the selection. Review each periodically until you have learned the new word.

READING SELECTION 19
THE SINGING WHALES

David Attenborough

Dolphins produce a great variety of other noises quite apart from ultra-sounds and there has been considerable speculation as to whether these sounds constitute a language. Some workers have said that if only we were clever enough, we would be able to understand what they say and even exchange complex messages with them. So far, we have identified some twenty different sounds that dolphins make. Some seem to serve to keep a school together when they are travelling at speed. Some appear to be warning cries, and some call-signs so that animals can recognize each other at a distance. But no one yet has demonstrated that dolphins put these sounds together to form the equivalent of the two-word sentence that can justifiably be regarded as the beginning of true language. Chimpanzees can do so. But dolphins, as far as we can tell, cannot.

The great whales also have voices. Humpbacks, one of the baleen whales, congregate every spring in Hawaii to give birth to their young and to mate. Some of them also sing. Their song consists of a sequence of yelps, growls, high-pitched squeals and long-drawn-out rumbles. And the whales declaim these songs hour after hour in extended stately recitals. They contain unchanging sequences of notes that have been called themes. Each theme may be repeated over and over again — the number of times varies but the order of the themes in a song is always the same in any one season. Typically, a complete song lasts for about ten minutes, but some have been recorded that continue for half an hour; and whales may sing, repeating their songs, virtually continuously for over twenty-four hours. Each whale has its own characteristic song but it composes it from themes which it shares with the rest of the whale community in Hawaii.

The whales stay in Hawaiian waters for several months, calving, mating, and singing. Sometimes they lie on the surface, one immense flipper held vertically in the air. Sometimes they beat the water with it. Occasionally, one will leap clear of the surface, all fifty tons in the air, the ridging of its underside plain to see, and fall back with a gigantic surge and thunderous crash. It will breach in this way again and again.

Then, within a few days, the deep blue bays and straits off the Hawaiian islands are empty. The whales have gone. Humpbacks appear a few weeks later off Alaska. It is very likely that these are the Hawaiian animals but more studies will have to be made before we can be certain that they are.

Next spring, they reappear in Hawaii and once more begin to sing. But this time they have new themes in their repertoire and have dropped many of the old ones. Sometimes the songs are so loud that the whole hull of your boat resonates and you can hear ethereal moans and cries coming mysteriously, as from nowhere. If you dive into the peerlessly blue water and swim down, you may, with luck, see the singer hanging in the water below you, a cobalt shape in the sapphire depths. The sound penetrates your body, making the air in your sinuses vibrate in sympathy, as though you were sitting within the widest pipe of the largest cathedral organ, and the whole of your tissues are soaked in sound.

We still do not know why whales sing. Man can identify each individual whale by its song and if he can do so, then surely whales can do the same. Water transmits sound better than air so it may well be that sections of these songs, particularly those low vibrating notes, can be heard by other whales ten, twenty, even thirty miles away informing them of the whereabouts and activities of the whole whale community.

COMPREHENSION TEST 18

Directions: *Circle the letter of the correct answer.*

1. The main idea of this passage could best be stated as
   a) Whales and dolphins are less intelligent than man because they have not developed the two-word sentence.
   b) Whales always stay in the waters near Hawaii and continuously revise their "themes."
   c) Whales and dolphins have the ability to make noises or "sing," and people are just beginning to try to understand their meanings.
   d) Whales migrate to Alaska in the winter to compose new songs, mate, and to give birth to their young.

2. As stated in the selection, dolphin's noises may be *all* of the following *except*
   a) call-signs so animals can recognize one another
   b) two-word sentences expressing complete thought
   c) noises to keep a school of dolphins together
   d) warning cries

3. A whale's song may last as long as
   a) one-half hour
   b) ten minutes
   c) two hours
   d) twenty-four hours

4. After leaving Hawaiian waters, it is likely that humpback whales migrate to
   a) Alaska
   b) the Gulf of Mexico
   c) the Atlantic Ocean
   d) the coast of California

5. The low-pitched singing of whales is similar to the music made by a
   a) cello
   b) bass drum
   c) cathedral organ
   d) tuba

6. As it is used in this selection, the word "declaim" most nearly means

a) to deny
b) to give a loud speech
c) to compose a theme
d) to breach in the water

7. The animal that possesses a very basic form of "true language" is the
   a) dolphin
   b) humpbacked whale
   c) parrot
   d) chimpanzee

8. The themes of whales' songs
   a) change every season
   b) change every year
   c) remain unchanged until they find new mates
   d) remain the same for their entire lives

9. This article would be of most use to you if you were researching references for a paper on
   a) mating habits of animals
   b) animal communication
   c) migration of animals
   d) the feeding habits of whales

10. Through his wording of the fifth paragraph in this selection, the author is attempting to lead the reader to
    a) accept his theories about whale communication
    b) feel the sensation of experiencing a whale's "song"
    c) support the movement to "save the whales"
    d) be scientifically objective

Selection 19: 647 words

Finishing Time: ___ ___ ___
HR. MIN. SEC.

Starting Time: ___ ___ ___
HR. MIN. SEC.

Reading Time: ___ ___
MIN. SEC.

WPM Score: ___

Comprehension Score: ___ %

Reading Efficiency Score: ___

READING SELECTION 20
TIME IN THE CINEMA

Thomas Sobchack

Many art forms take place in time: dance is movement in time, music is sound in time, drama and prose fiction are actions in time. The moving image in film is an image in time, and — unlike the experience of looking at painting and sculpture — the experience of viewing a film requires the viewer to be in some way aware of the flow of time. This "flow of time," however, is not a simple thing, for there are several different kinds of time in the cinema.

Each film has a **running time,** an exact number of minutes during which it will occupy the space on the screen. Thus, running time is the time it takes for all the frames in the film to move past the lens of the projector at twenty-four frames per second (or sixteen to twenty-two frames if the film is silent). This time can range anywhere from a few seconds for an experimental short to many hours for some less than commercial narrative and documentary films. The original uncut version of Bernardo Bertolucci's *1900* (1977) has still not been released in the United States because its length — about six hours — created exhibition problems. Even the four-and-a-half-hour version shown here has had difficulty finding a large audience. Louis Malle's *Phantom India* (1968) runs six and a half hours, but it comes in the more acceptable form of a seven-part documentary.

Running time describes the length of the film, but **screen time** describes the time represented by the actions or events *within* the film. The running time of *2001: A Space Odyssey* (1968) is less than two and a half hours, but the screen time spans millions of years of human evolution. On the other hand, although the running time of *An Occurrence at Owl Creek Bridge* (Robert Enrico, 1961) is around a half-hour, most of the screen time of the film represents only a split second.

Finally, much more subjective and less controllable than either the running time or the screen time of a specific film, there is **psychological time.** Psychological time describes the viewer's sense of the pace and rhythm of the film, in other words, how long the film *feels*. A film running only five minutes may feel much longer, or a film might seem as if it were really quite short. We may feel that a film is swift because we are interested, or slow because we are bored, but we may also be responding to the way the film is constructed.

Although a film's running time is precise and specific (unless, of course, the film has been damaged or there are various versions of a particular movie in release — for example, movies edited for television), both screen time and psychological time can be manipulated in an almost endless variety of ways. When separate shots are joined together to represent an action, the time of that action can be compressed or expanded. For example, a shot showing a character entering an airport in New York can be joined to one showing him leaving an airport in California, thus compressing his trip. Or several shots of the details of a character involved in a car accident may be joined together to expand the action. Through this joining together of separate pieces of film, the process called editing, we can be made aware of simultaneous actions and sequential actions; we can enter a character's mind, we can see the past, we can be dislocated from any sense of "real" time and transported to a place where time seems not to exist or where it seems to operate in ways that defy logic. And the kinds of transitions the filmmaker uses to move us from one shot to another are also the result of choice; the editing may move us abruptly from one time to another or it may bridge time gracefully and slowly. All these manipulations of time , of both screen and psychological time, are the result of editing.

Editing, the joining together of separate pieces of film footage by various techniques to form an entire and cohesive film, establishes the order and rhythm of a movie. This chapter, examining the role of editing, will first deal with the simplest form of putting the shots together to form a coherent whole and will then go on to examine the more complex techniques which are used to create different sorts of time. Finally, it will examine the three major schools of editing.

COMPREHENSION TEST 20

Directions: *Circle the letter of the correct answer.*

1. The concept of time in cinema is so important because
   a) a film's running time can never be changed
   b) filmmakers have little knowledge of the "flow of time"
   c) time in a movie can be manipulated by editing
   d) films must all be less than two hours long

2. A film's "running time" can be measured
   a) only subjectively
   b) with a clock
   c) by a psychological "feel"
   d) depending on how the film is edited

3. The length of time a viewer feels during a film, or his or her sense of the film's rhythm and pace, is known as
   a) running time
   b) screen time
   c) psychological time
   d) editor's time

4. The most precise and specific way of measuring time in a movie is by means of its
   a) running time
   b) edited time
   c) psychological time
   d) spatial time

5. The art form in which it is most necessary for a viewer or audience to be aware of the "flow of time" is
   a) film
   b) novel
   c) sculpture
   d) painting

6. "Manipulations of time" means
   a) various categories
   b) changes for specific purposes
   c) losses
   d) events

7. You became very involved in a particular film, but it lasted for three hours. Psychologically, the length of the film would seem
   a) much shorter
   b) terribly long
   c) dependent on the running time
   d) highly edited or choppy

8. If, as an editor, you wanted to show the history of Galileo's life within the space of four hours, you would condense the actual time of his life best by
   a) limiting your screen time
   b) forcing your audience to alter their running time
   c) shortening the running time
   d) increasing your running time to approximate the length of Galileo's actual lifetime

9. From the author's statements in the passage you could conclude that time in a movie
   a) cannot change
   b) is not influenced by the editor
   c) can be manipulated
   d) is never considered when a film is made

10. The author of this selection uses as his main method of development
    a) vivid description
    b) conversation
    c) examples
    d) arguments and proof

Comprehension Test 20

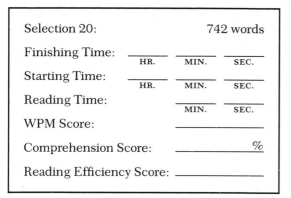

Selection 20:   742 words

Finishing Time: _____ _____ _____
                 HR.   MIN.   SEC.

Starting Time: _____ _____ _____
                 HR.   MIN.   SEC.

Reading Time: _____ _____
                      MIN.   SEC.

WPM Score: _____

Comprehension Score: _____ %

Reading Efficiency Score: _____

Unit Six:
How to Interpret and
Evaluate What You Read

Many college students and most adults accept everything they read at face value. Seldom do they sit back and examine the author's ideas, sources, evidence, or choice of words with a critical eye. In fact, many people still accept the adage, "If it's in print, then it must be true." Many opinions, beliefs, personal observations, misleading information, and unwarranted conclusions appear in print every day, however. To be an alert, informed, and knowledgeable person, you must approach everything you read with an open, questioning mind.

An essential part of efficient and flexible reading, then, is the ability to think about and react to what you read. To get a writer's full meaning, it is necessary to go beyond what the author *says* and to consider what he or she *means*. Also, it is necessary to evaluate or react critically to what the author says. These two skills — interpreting and evaluating — are the focus of this section.

In Chapter 13 you will see that it is necessary to make inferences to understand not only what the author says but also to consider what he or she has suggested. You will also learn more about the various levels of language available to a writer and see how an author can choose words carefully to influence the reader. Finally, you will see that identifying the author's purpose in writing will help you interpret what you read.

Chapter 14 is concerned with evaluating or reacting critically to an author's work. You will learn how to evaluate the source and the authority of an author, how to ask critical questions, how to evaluate supporting evidence, and how to recognize value judgments.

Chapter 13:
Interpreting What You Read

Up to this point, we have been concerned with the literal meaning of various units of prose — the sentence, the paragraph, and longer articles and selections. In each chapter, so far, we have discussed techniques that enable us to understand what the author *says* or to understand and retain the literal, factual content in the most efficient manner. However, in order to be an efficient reader, it is often necessary to go beyond what authors say and to be concerned with what they *mean*. Through their choice of words, descriptions, facts, arrangement of ideas, and suggestions, writers often mean more than they say. Although textbooks are written in a fairly direct manner, you will see that other materials, such as persuasive essays, advertisements, magazine articles, and editorials, often leave much for the readers to figure out by themselves. The purpose of this chapter is to present a foundation of skills that will enable you to interpret what you read as well as to understand what is directly stated.

Many skills are involved in interpreting what you read; three of the most useful will be discussed in this chapter. These are (1) making inferences, (2) recognizing types of language, and (3) identifying the author's purpose.

MAKING INFERENCES

Suppose you are ten minutes late for your psychology class, and when you arrive at the classroom you find that the room is empty. After a moment of puzzlement and confusion you might remember that your instructor has been ill and decide that your class has been canceled. Or you might recall that your instructor changed classrooms last week and decide that he or she has done so again. In this situation you used what you did know to make a reasonable guess about what you did not know. This reasoning process is called an *inference*. An inference is a logical connection that you draw between what you observe or know and what you do not know. All of us make numerous inferences in daily living without consciously thinking about them. When you wave at a friend and he or she does not wave back, you assume that he or she didn't see you. When you are driving down the highway and see a police car with its lights flashing behind you, you may infer that the police officer wants you to pull over and stop. When you see a friend behaving in a certain way you infer that he or she is unhappy.

Although inferences are reasonable guesses made on the basis of available information, they are not always correct. For instance, although you inferred that the friend who did not wave did not see you, it may be that he or she saw you but is angry with you and decided to ignore you. Similarly, the police car with the flashing lights may only want to pass you on the way to an accident ahead, and the friend you assume is unhappy may only be rehearsing for a play. Basically, an inference is the best guess that you can make given the available information and circumstances.

EXERCISE 13-1

Directions: *For each of the following items make an inference about each situation that is described.*

1. A woman seated alone at a bar offers to buy a drink for a man sitting several seats away.

   _____

2. A dog growls as a teenager walks toward the house.

   _____

3. Your three-year-old brother will not eat his dinner. A package of cookies is missing from the kitchen cupboard.

   _____

4. You have phoned your sister's apartment but there is no answer; later you drive over to the apartment and a police officer answers the door.

   _____

5. A close friend invites you to go out for pizza and beer on Tuesday. When you meet her at her home on Tuesday she tells you that

you must have confused the days and that she will see you
tomorrow evening.

Making Inferences as You Read

As in many other everyday situations, you make inferences frequently when you are reading. Applied to reading, an inference is a
reasonable guess about what the author does not say, based on what
he or she does say. You are required to make inferences when an author
suggests an idea but does not directly state it. For instance, suppose a
writer describes a character as follows:

> In the mirror John Bell noticed that his hair was
> graying at the temples. As he picked up the morning paper,
> he realized that he could no longer see well at all without his
> glasses. Looking at the hands holding the paper he saw that
> they were wrinkled.

From the information the author provides you may infer that the character is realizing that he is aging. However, notice that the author does
not mention aging at all. By the facts he or she provided, however, the
writer led you to infer that the character was thinking about aging.

Now, read the following description of an event.

> Their actions, on this sunny afternoon, have been
> carefully organized and rehearsed. Their work began weeks
> ago with a leisurely drive through a quiet residential area.
> While driving, they noticed particular homes that seemed
> isolated and free of activity. Over the next week, similar
> drives were taken at different times of day. Finally, a house
> was chosen and their work began in earnest. Through
> careful observation and several phone calls, they learned
> where the occupants worked. They studied the house,
> noting entrances and windows and anticipating the floor
> plan. Finally, they were ready to act. Phone calls made that
> morning confirmed that the occupants were at work.

What was about to happen in this description? From the facts presented, you probably realized that a daytime home burglary was about
to occur. Notice, however, that this burglary is not mentioned anywhere in the paragraph. Instead, using the information provided, you

made the logical connection between the known facts and the unknown about what was to occur.

How to Make Inferences

It is difficult to outline specific steps to follow in making inferences, since each inference entirely depends on the situation and the facts provided, as well as on your knowledge and experience with the situation. However, a few general guidelines for making inferences about what you read are offered.

Be sure you understand the literal meaning first. Before you can begin any form of interpretation, including inference, you must be sure that you have a clear grasp of the stated facts and ideas. For each paragraph, then, you should have identified the topic, main idea, supporting details, and organizational pattern. Only when you have an understanding of literal, or factual, content can you go beyond literal meaning and formulate inferences.

Ask yourself a question. To be sure that you are making necessary inferences to get the fullest meaning from a passage, ask yourself a question such as:

What is the author trying to suggest from the stated information?

or

What do all the facts and ideas point toward or seem to add up to?

or

For what purpose did the author include these facts and details?

In answering any of these questions, you will find that you are forced to add together the individual pieces of information to arrive at an inference. Making an inference is somewhat like putting together a complicated picture puzzle, where you try to make each piece fit with all the rest of the pieces to form something recognizable. In making an inference you take each piece of information and fit it together with all other available information to arrive at a general interpretation or inference about the situation described.

Use clues provided by the writer. A writer often provides numerous hints that point you toward accurate inferences. For instance, a writer's choice of words often suggests his or her attitude toward a subject. Try to notice descriptive words, emotionally charged words, and words with strong positive or negative connotations. Here is an example of how the choice of words can lead you to an inference.

> Grandmother had been an <u>unusually attractive</u> young woman, and she carried herself with the <u>graceful confidence</u> of a <u>natural charmer</u> to her last day.

The underlined phrases "unusually attractive," "graceful confidence," and "natural charmer" suggest that the writer feels positive about her grandmother. However, in the following example, notice how the underlined words and phrases create a negative image of the person.

> The <u>withdrawn</u> child <u>eyed</u> her teacher with a hostile disdain. When <u>directly spoken</u> to, the child responded in a <u>cold</u>, but carefully respectful way.

In this sentence the underlined words suggest that the child is unfriendly and that he or she dislikes the teacher.

Consider the author's purpose. An awareness of the author's purpose for writing is often helpful in making inferences. If an author's purpose, as in advertising, is to convince you to purchase a particular product, then as you begin reading, you already have a clear idea of the types of inferences the writer hopes you will make. For instance, a magazine ad for a stereo system reads,

> If you're in the market for true high fidelity sound, a prematched system is a good way to get it. The components in our system are built for each other by our audio engineers. You can be assured of high performance and sound quality.

You can guess that the writer's purpose is to encourage you to buy a prematched stereo system.

Verify your inference. Once you have made an inference, be sure to check that it is accurate. Look back at the stated facts to see that there is sufficient evidence to support the inference. Also, be sure that you have not overlooked other equally plausible or more plausible inferences that could be drawn from the same set of facts.

Why Writers Leave Ideas Unstated

You are probably wondering why writers, if their goal is to communicate ideas clearly, leave facts and ideas to be inferred by the reader. There are several situations in which a writer may have good reason to leave information unstated. First, writers leave some ideas unstated because they assume certain knowledge and sophistication on the part of the audience for whom they are writing. That is, some ideas are almost too obvious to state and if they were stated, might be regarded as too direct.

A second situation in which a writer may choose to leave inference making to the reader involves his or her purpose for writing. In writing humorous material, or in writing essays, stories, novels, or poems designed to entertain the reader, it is often necessary or to a writer's advantage to leave some things unsaid. As an example, think of any good joke you have heard recently. If in telling this joke you fully explained everything, including the punch line, the humor would be lost. Similarly, a James Bond spy movie or a murder mystery, if the full plot were revealed at the beginning, would not be very exciting or entertaining.

Also, in various types of persuasive writing the writer's purpose is to encourage the reader to accept a particular point of view or attitude. In such cases the writer intends to lead the reader to accept this attitude by providing only certain facts and ideas. Often, for a writer to clearly state an idea, rather than to merely suggest it, is too direct an approach and less effective than carefully prodding the reader along in forming this idea for him- or herself.

EXERCISE 13-2

Directions: *Read the following passage and then answer the questions. The answers are not directly stated in the passage; you will have to make inferences in order to answer them.*

One morning I put two poached eggs in front of Charlie, who looked up briefly from his newspaper.

"You've really shaped up, Cassie," he smiled. "A dreadful lady went to the hospital and a very nice Cassie came back. I think you've learned a lesson and, honey, I'm proud of you."

He went to work and I started the dishes, trying to feel thrilled at having shaped up for Charlie. *He sounds as though the hospital performed some sort of exorcism,* I mused, scraping egg off the dish with my fingernail. *Evil is banished, goodness restored. Then why don't I feel transformed?*

The dish slipped out of my hand and smashed into the sink, spraying chips over the counter. I looked down at the mess, then at the cluttered kitchen table, and beyond that to the dust on the television set in the den. I pictured the four unmade beds and the three clothes-strewn bedrooms and the toys in the living room and last night's newspaper on the floor next to Charlie's reclining chair and I yelled at the cat who was licking milk out of a cereal bowl, "What lesson? What goddamn lesson was I supposed to learn?"

I grabbed my coat and the grocery money and was waiting at the liquor store when it opened.

"You find a place where they give it away for free?" the man behind the counter leered. "We haven't seen you for weeks. Where you been?"

"Nowhere," I answered. "I've been nowhere." He gave me my bottle and I walked out thinking that I'd have to start trading at another store where the creeps weren't so free with their remarks.[1]

1. What problem is Cassie experiencing?

   _____

2. For what purpose was Cassie hospitalized?

   _____

3. How does Cassie feel about household chores?

   _____

4. What is Cassie's husband's attitude toward her problem? Is he part of her problem?

   _____

TYPES OF LANGUAGE

From your years of reading experience you have noticed that each author has his or her own style of writing; that each writes in a slightly different way. Depending on their purpose for writing and the audience for whom they are writing, authors control various features of their writing to make their writing clear and understandable. One important feature that writers adjust is the the kind of language they use. There are two basic types of language: objective and subjective. *Objective* language is factual, whereas *subjective* language reflects the individual's attitudes and feelings. A writer often chooses appropriate language to suit his or her purpose and audience.

Objective Language

Objective language counts, reports, and describes ideas and events without any personal involvement on the part of the author. Much of the material you read every day uses objective language; reference books, textbooks, contracts, job applications, phone directories, and news stories in newspapers all use objective language. In pieces of writing that use objective language the writer is attempting to present facts without coloring them with his or her own opinions and judgments. In objective writing, then, the writer remains impartial and removed from the ideas he or she is presenting. Here is an example of objective, factual language:

> Abortion is technically defined as the expulsion of a fetus from the womb before it is sufficiently developed to survive. Abortion was legalized in the United States in January 1973. The Supreme Court decision stated that prior to the end of the third month of pregnancy the decision to have an abortion was solely that of the pregnant woman and her physician. After that stage abortion is permissible if the mother's health is in danger.

In this passage you have no idea of how the writer feels about abortion. He or she is simply presenting facts about abortion without expressing an opinion or making a judgment about it.

Subjective Language

Unlike objective language, subjective language allows the writer to reveal attitudes and feelings toward his or her subject. Here is a second version of the passage on abortion, using subjective, rather than objective, language.

> Abortion can be defined as taking the life of another human being during its fetal development. The inhumane act of abortion was legalized in the United States in January 1973. The Supreme Court decided that killing a fetus prior to its third month of development was acceptable, but after that point only the self-interest of the mother for her own well-being should allow it to occur.

Notice that in this passage, you know exactly how the author feels about abortion. Through choice of words and selection of facts, a tone of moral disapproval toward abortion is evident in the passage. Words and phrases such as "taking the life," "inhumane," "killing," and "self-interest" all suggest that the writer is opposed to abortion.

Within the category of subjective language, there are several specific types of language that writers commonly use to reveal their attitudes. They are descriptive language, figurative language, and connotative language.

Descriptive Language. Descriptive language involves words that appeal to one or more of the reader's senses. Descriptive words enable the reader to create a mental or imaginary picture of the object, person, or event being described. Here is a paragraph that contains many descriptive words and phrases. As you read, look for words and phrases that help you to imagine what type of afternoon it was and to suggest that something is mysteriously wrong.

> I went out into the backyard and the usually roundish spots
> of dappled sunlight underneath the trees were all shaped
> like feathers, crescent in the same direction, from left to
> right. Though it was five o'clock on a summer afternoon, the
> birds were singing good-bye to the day, and their merged
> song seemed to soak the strange air in an additional
> strangeness. A kind of silence prevailed. Few cars were
> moving on the streets of the town. Of my children only the
> baby dared come into the yard with me. She wore only
> underpants, and as she stood beneath a tree, bulging her
> belly toward me in the mood of jolly flirtation she has grown
> into at the age of two, her bare skin was awash with pale
> crescents. It crossed my mind that she might be harmed,
> but I couldn't think how. *Cancer?* [2]

Did you notice the details that suggested something is wrong? Here are a few examples: Although it is only 5 P.M., the birds are saying good-bye to the day; there is a strange silence; only the baby *dared* to walk in the yard (others were afraid); the baby's skin was "awash."

Writers, by their choice of descriptive detail, can greatly influence the reader's response to an event, object, or individual. Here are two different descriptions of the same individual. The first is very positive, whereas the second is quite negative.

> Jean is an outgoing person who always seems to have a joke or amusing remark on the tip of her tongue. She has a carefree, fun-loving attitude, and she always looks at the good side of life.

> Jean is very independent, almost a loner. She has many friends, but they seem to exist as an audience for her constant jokes and off-color remarks. She always seeks a personal advantage in any situation.

299

You will often find that writers choose descriptive details in order to lend a particular impression or view. That is, the details often seem to "add up" to an overall feeling or image about the subject. The first description of Jean presents her as a happy, fun-loving person. The second description is quite different. Here she is seen as a self-centered person.

EXERCISE 13-3

Directions: *From the following list of people select four whom you feel you could describe. For each person, write a positive and a negative statement that accurately describes him or her.*

1. your mother or father
2. a friend
3. someone who lives in your neighborhood
4. a relative
5. a brother or sister
6. your boss
7. your instructor
8. a family friend

Figurative Language. Figurative language is a way of describing something that makes sense on an imaginative level but not on a literal or factual level. Notice in each of the following sentences that the underlined expression cannot be literally true, but that each is understandable and is effective in conveying the author's message.

An overly ambitious employee may find the <u>door to advancement closed</u>.
(There is no actual door that may close.)

The federal government is <u>draining</u> taxpayers of any accumulated wealth.
(Nothing is literally being "drained" or removed from the insides of taxpayers.)

The judge decided to <u>get to the heart</u> of the matter.
(Matters do not really have hearts.)

They <u>killed</u> a bottle of gin last night.
(A bottle of gin was not alive to begin with.)

In each of these expressions, one distinct thing is compared with another for some quality that they have in common.

Figurative language is an effective way to describe and to limit relationships. However, by their choice of figurative expressions writers can create either a positive or negative impression. For instance, this first statement is somewhat negative.

> The blush spread across her face like spilled paint.

Spilled paint is usually thought of as messy and problematic. However, this second statement creates a more positive image.

> The blush spread across her face <u>like wine being poured into a glass</u>.

Wine filling a glass is commonly thought of as a pleasant image.

As you can see from these examples, figurative language allows the writer a large amount of freedom of expression and judgment as he or she compares one item to another. When using figurative language, since it is in no sense factual, a writer is *not* restricted to direct, literal presentation of ideas. A writer's interpretation must be involved as he or she compares one entity to another.

As a reader, then, you should be aware that a writer's impressions and judgments are involved in all figurative expressions. As such, you should regard them as interpretations, as expressions of opinion and judgment rather than as factual information.

Connotative Language. Although descriptive language and the use of figurative expressions enable a writer to select and interpret information presented to the reader, a writer's choice of words is also a powerful vehicle of expression. Merely by choosing one word instead of another, a writer can color or shape your understanding and reaction to a particular subject or idea.

In Chapter 11, you learned that many words have connotative as well as denotative meanings and that connotative meanings are often either positive or negative. Through careful selection of words and consideration of their connotative meanings, then, a writer can influence the way you react to and interpret an idea.

Here are two sentences that create two very different impressions. As you read each, notice that it is through the use of word choice that you learn how Helen felt about the man across the room.

> Helen glanced cautiously at the man seated across the room.

> Helen stared enticingly at the man seated across the room.

Although both sentences describe the same general action — Helen looked at the man seated across the room — they express very different messages. In the first sentence Helen is seen as careful and shy, whereas in the second she is described as direct and bold. Notice that only two words in each sentence, and their connotations, established this very different image of Helen.

EXERCISE 13-4

Directions: *Read one of the selections at the end of the chapter, complete the multiple choice questions, and then answer each of the following questions.*

1. What inferences were you required to make?
2. Does the writer primarily use objective or subjective language?
3. List examples of descriptive language, figurative language, and connotative language, if used in the article.

Descriptive: _____

_____

Figurative: _____

_____

Connotative: _____

_____

IDENTIFYING THE AUTHOR'S PURPOSE

An important skill in reading all materials other than texts and references is the ability to identify the author's purpose for writing. Authors write for a variety of purposes: to inform or instruct the reader, to amuse or entertain, to arouse sympathy, to persuade the reader to take a particular action or accept a certain point of view. To be an effective reader you must be aware of the author's purpose. Sometimes the writer's purpose will be obvious, as in the following advertisements.

At Hair Design Salons we'll make you look better than you can imagine. Six professional stylists to meet your every need. Stop in for a free consultation today.

Puerto Rican white rum can do anything better than gin or vodka.

The first ad is written to encourage the readers to have their hair styled at Hair Design Salons. The second is intended to encourage readers to use rum instead of gin or vodka in their mixed drinks. In both ads it is clear that the writer is selling a product and trying to convince you to buy it. However, in many other types of reading material, even other advertisements, the writer's purpose is not so obvious.

For instance, in an ad for a particular brand of cigarettes, a stylishly dressed woman is pictured holding a cigarette. The caption reads "You've come a long way, baby." In this case, although you know that all ads are intended to sell a product or service, the ad does not even mention cigarettes. It is left up to you, the reader, to infer that stylish women smoke Virginia Slims.

You will often be able to predict the author's purpose from the title of the article or by your familiarity with the writer. For instance, if you noticed an article titled "My Role in Watergate," written by Richard Nixon, you could predict that the author's purpose is to defend his previous actions as president. An article titled "The President Flexes His Muscles but Nobody Is Watching" suggests that the author's purpose is to describe how the president is attempting to exert power, but also to indicate that the presidential action is having little effect.

How to Identify the Author's Purpose

To identify the author's purpose in articles where it is not apparent, first determine the subject and thesis of the article and notice how the writer supports the thesis. Then ask yourself questions to start you thinking critically about the article.

1. *Who is the intended audience?* Try to decide for whom or for what type or group of people the article seems to be written. Often, the level of language, the choice of words, and the complexity of the ideas, examples, or arguments included suggest the audience the writer has in mind. Once you have identified a potential audience, you can begin to consider what it is that the writer wants to communicate to that audience.

    A writer may write for a general interest audience (anyone who is interested in the subject, but not considered an expert on it). Most newspapers and periodicals such as *Time* or *Newsweek* appeal to a general interest audience. On the other hand, a writer may have a particular interest group in mind. A writer may write for medical doctors in the *Journal of American Medicine,* or for skiing enthusiasts in *Skiing Today,* or for antique collectors in *The World of Antiques.* Also, a writer may intend his or her writing for an audience with particular political, moral, or religious attitudes. Articles in the *Atlantic Monthly* often appeal to the conservative political viewpoint, whereas *The Catholic Digest* appeals to a particular religious group.

2. *How does the writer feel about the subject?* Determine whether the author is serious or whether he or she is trying to poke fun about the subject. If a writer is ridiculing or making light of a subject, he or she will usually offer clues that this is occurring. The writer may use exaggerations, describe unbelievable situations, or through choice of language and details, indicate that he or she is not completely serious.

3. *Does the writer treat the subject objectively or subjectively?* Decide whether the writer is attempting to discuss the subject in a factual, unbiased manner or is presenting only one point of view. For example, in an article on gun control, a writer may discuss both the advantages and disadvantages of gun control, or he or she may present only one point of view — that gun control would be ineffective in controlling crime. If a writer is presenting an objective view, usually it is quite clear that this is being done. Writers who approach their subject openly and objectively will want their readers to recognize that they are doing so. However, writers who are presenting a personal viewpoint or a one-sided viewpoint may not be as eager to reveal their subjectivity. Recognizing that a one-sided point of view is open to criticism, some writers may not directly admit, or may even disguise, their lack of objectivity.

4. *Does the writer try to prove anything about the subject? If so, what?* Try to determine if the article is written to persuade the reader to accept a certain idea or point of view or to encourage him or her to perform a certain action. For instance, a writer may write to convince you that inflation will cause a national disaster, or that abortion is morally wrong, or that the best jobs are available in health-related fields. Often, the beginning and the end of the article are the crucial parts that can help you to detect an argumentative or persuasive approach. Try to trace the author's train of thought; notice at what point the author begins and how the ideas progress toward the conclusion of the article. If an argumentative approach is used, then determine exactly what ideas the writer is encouraging the reader to accept.

To test the use of these questions, read the following passage and apply the questions to it.

I WANT A WIFE

Judy Syfers

I belong to that classification of people known as wives. I am A Wife. And, not altogether incidentally, I am a mother.

Not too long ago a male friend of mine appeared on the scene fresh from a recent divorce. He had one child, who is, of course, with his ex-wife. He is obviously looking for another wife. As I thought about him while I was ironing one evening, it suddenly occurred to me that I, too, would like to have a wife. Why do I want a wife?

I would like to go back to school so that I can become economically independent, support myself, and, if need be, support those dependent upon me. I want a wife who will work and send me to school. And while I am going to school I want a wife to take care of the children. I want a wife to keep track of the children's doctor and dentist appointments. And to keep track of mine too. I want a wife to make sure my children eat properly and are kept clean. I want a wife who will wash the children's clothes and keep them mended. I want a wife who is a good nurturant attendant to my children, who arranges for their schooling, makes sure that they have an adequate social life with their peers, takes them to the park, the zoo, et cetera. I want a wife who takes care of the children when they are sick, a wife who arranges to be around when the children need special care, because, of course, I cannot miss classes at school. My wife must arrange to lose time at work and not lose the job. It may mean a small cut in my wife's income from time to time, but I guess I can tolerate that. Needless to say, my wife will arrange and pay for the care of the children while my wife is working.

I want a wife who will take care of *my* physical needs. I want a wife who will keep my house clean. A wife who will pick up after me. I want a wife who will keep my clothes clean, ironed, mended, replaced when need be, and who will see to it that my personal things are kept in their proper place so that I can find what I need the minute I need it. I want a wife who cooks the meals, a wife who is a *good* cook. I want a wife who will plan the menus, do the necessary grocery shopping, prepare the meals, serve them pleasantly, and then do the cleaning up while I do my studying. I want a wife who will care for me when I am sick and sympathize with my pain and loss of time from school. I want a wife to go along when our family takes a vacation so that someone can continue to care for me and my children when I need a rest and change of scene.

I want a wife who will not bother me with rambling complaints about a wife's duties. But I want a wife who will listen to me when I feel the need to explain a rather difficult point I have come across in my course of studies. And I want a wife who will type my papers for me when I have written them.

I want a wife who will take care of the details of my social life. When my wife and I are invited out by my friends, I want a wife who will take care of the baby-sitting arrangements. When I meet people at school whom I like and want to entertain, I want a wife who will have the house clean, will prepare a special meal, serve it to me and my friends, and not interrupt when I talk about the things that interest me and my friends. I want a wife who will have arranged that the children are fed and ready for bed before my guests arrive so that the children do not bother us.

And I want a wife who knows that sometimes I need a night out by myself.

I want a wife who is sensitive to my sexual needs, a wife who makes love passionately and eagerly when I feel like it, a wife who makes sure that I am satisfied. And, of course, I want a wife who will not demand sexual attention when I am not in the mood for it. I want a wife who assumes the complete responsibility for birth control, because I do not want more children. I want a wife who will remain sexually faithful to me so that I do not have to clutter up my intellectual life with jealousies. And I want a wife who understands that *my* sexual needs may entail more than strict adherence to monogamy. I must, after all, be able to relate to people as fully as possible.

If, by chance, I find another person more suitable as a wife than the wife I already have, I want the liberty to replace my present wife with another one. Naturally, I will expect a fresh, new life; my wife will take the children and be solely responsible for them so that I am left free.

When I am through with school and have a job, I want my wife to quit working and remain at home so that my wife can more fully and completely take care of a wife's duties.

My God, who *wouldn't* want a wife?

The subject of this article is wives, and the author's thesis, at least on the surface, is that she wants a wife. You probably decided that the article was written for a general interest audience. The article is written simply, using everyday language and a direct style. In response to the question of how the author feels about the subject of wives, you should realize that she cannot be completely serious. Since the author is a woman, it is clear that wanting a wife is an unbelievable or seemingly impossible situation. Thus, you should suspect that the author's demands are not to be taken literally and that she is not completely serious about wanting a wife. Instead, the writer is using this demand as a means of demonstrating her feelings about the role of a wife in a marriage. You begin to see that Syfers feels that the traditional view of wives dictates that their primary function in life is to make their husbands happy and comfortable. From her tone throughout, you can tell that Syfers disagrees with this traditional view.

In considering the writer's objectivity, it is clear that Syfers presents only her own point of view; there is no mention of differing points of view. She does not, for instance, consider that some women may be completely happy as wives and find the role of a wife to be secure and fulfilling. Notice, though, that Syfers did not in any direct way indicate that she was presenting only one point of view.

Clearly the author tries to establish that the role of a wife is a subjugated position; a wife exists for the comfort and convenience of her husband. Through this line of questioning we thus arrive at the writer's purpose, which is to present a critical view of the role of a wife in our society.

APPLYING WHAT YOU HAVE LEARNED

Directions: *Briefly review the reading selection that you read for Exercise 13-4. Then answer each of the following.*

1. Who is the intended audience?

   _____

2. How does the writer feel about the subject?

   _____

3. Is the writer objective or subjective?

   _____

4. What, if anything, is the writer trying to prove about the subject?

   _____

5. Write a statement that describes the author's purpose for writing the article.

   _____

READING SELECTION 21
Difficulty Level: A

THE NIGHTMARE OF LIFE WITHOUT FUEL

Isaac Asimov

So it's 1997, and it's raining, and you'll have to walk to work again. The subways are crowded, and any given train breaks down one morning out of five. The buses are gone, and on a day like today the bicycles slosh and slide. Besides, you have only a mile and a half to go, and you have boots, raincoat and rain hat. And it's not a very cold rain, so why not?

Lucky you have a job in demolition too. It's steady work. Slow and dirty, but steady. The fading structures of a decaying city are the great mineral mines and hardware shops of the nation. Break them down and re-use the parts. Coal is too difficult to dig up and transport to give us energy in the amounts we need, nuclear fission is judged to be too dangerous, the technical breakthrough toward nuclear fusion that we hoped for never took place, and solar batteries are too expensive to maintain on the earth's surface in sufficient quantity.

Anyone older than ten can remember automobiles. They dwindled. At first the price of gasoline climbed — way up. Finally only the well-to-do drove, and that was too clear an indication that they were filthy rich, so any automobile that dared show itself on a city street was overturned and burned. Rationing was introduced to "equalize sacrifice," but every three months the ration was reduced. The cars just vanished and became part of the metal resource.

There are many advantages, if you want to look for them. Our 1997 newspapers continually point them out. The air is cleaner and there seem to be fewer colds. Against most predictions, the crime rate has dropped. With the police car too expensive (and too easy a target), policemen are back on their beats. More important, the streets are full. Legs are king in the cities of 1997, and people walk everywhere far into the night. Even the parks are full, and there is mutual protection in crowds.

If the weather isn't too cold, people sit out front. If it is hot, the open air is the only air conditioning they get. And at least the street lights still burn. Indoors, electricity is scarce, and few people can afford to keep lights burning after supper.

As for the winter — well, it is inconvenient to be cold, with most of what furnace fuel is allowed hoarded for the dawn; but sweaters are popular indoor wear and showers are not an everyday luxury. Lukewarm sponge baths will do, and if the air is not always very fragrant in the human vicinity, the automobile fumes are gone.

There is some consolation in the city that it is worse in the suburbs. The suburbs were born with the auto, lived with the auto, and are dying with the auto. One way out for the suburbanites is to form associations that assign turns to the procurement and distribution of food. Pushcarts creak from house to house along the posh suburban roads, and every bad snowstorm is a disaster. It isn't easy to hoard enough food to last till the roads are open. There is not much in the way of refrigeration except for the snowbanks, and then the dogs must be fought off.

What energy is left cannot be directed into personal comfort. The nation must survive until new energy sources are found, so it is the railroads and subways that are receiving major attention. The railroads must move the coal that is the immediate hope, and the subways can best move the people.

And then, of course, energy must be conserved for agriculture. The great car factories make trucks and farm machinery almost exclusively. We can huddle together when there is a lack of warmth, fan ourselves should there be no cooling breezes, sleep or make love at such times as there is a lack of light — but nothing will for long ameliorate a lack of food. The American population isn't going up

308

much any more, but the food supply must be kept high even though the prices and difficulty of distribution force each American to eat less. Food is needed for export so that we can pay for some trickle of oil and for other resources.

The rest of the world, of course, is not as lucky as we are. Some cynics say that it is the knowledge of this that helps keep America from despair. They're starving out there, because earth's population has continued to go up. The population on earth is 5.5 billion, and outside the United States and Europe, not more than one in five has enough to eat at any given time.

All the statistics point to a rapidly declining rate of population increase, but that is coming about chiefly through a high infant mortality ; the first and most helpless victims of starvation are babies, after their mothers have gone dry. A strong current of American opinion, as reflected in the newspapers (some of which still produce their daily eight pages of bad news), holds that it is just as well. It serves to reduce the population, doesn't it?

Others point out that it's more than just starvation. There are those who manage to survive on barely enough to keep the body working, and that proves to be not enough for the brain. It is estimated that there are now nearly 2 billion people in the world who are alive but who are permanently brain-damaged by undernutrition, and the number is growing year by year. It has already occurred to some that it would be "realistic" to wipe them out quietly and

rid the earth of an encumbering menace. The American newspapers of 1997 do not report that this is actually being done anywhere, but some travelers bring back horror tales.

At least the armies are gone — no one can afford to keep those expensive, energy-gobbling monstrosities. Some soldiers in uniform and with rifles are present in almost every still functioning nation, but only the United States and the Soviet Union can maintain a few tanks, planes and ships — which they dare not move for fear of biting into limited fuel reserves.

Energy continues to decline, and machines must be replaced by human muscle and beasts of burden. People are working longer hours and there is less leisure; but then, with electric lighting restricted, television for only three hours a night, movies three evenings a week, new books few and printed in small editions, what is there to do with leisure? Work, sleep and eating are the great trinity of 1997, and only the first two are guaranteed.

Where will it end? It must end in a return to the days before 1800, to the days before the fossil fuels powered a vast machine industry and technology. It must end in subsistence farming and in a world population reduced by starvation, disease and violence to less than a billion.

And what can we do to prevent all this now? Now? Almost nothing.

If we had started 20 years ago, that might have been another matter. If we had only started 50 years ago, it would have been easy.

COMPREHENSION TEST 21

Directions: *Circle the letter of the correct answer.*

1. The writer thinks that unless mankind changes its habits of energy use, we will
   a) eventually destroy ourselves through war
   b) soon be forced to live at a very primitive level
   c) be controlled by the Arab nations

   d) be required to develop nuclear power

2. In the world Asimov describes, the major hope for American fuel is
   a) oil
   b) coal
   c) wood
   d) solar energy

3. In the future, Asimov projects that life in the suburbs will be worse than city life mainly because of
   a) lack of automobile transportation
   b) roaming packs of dogs
   c) the high crime rate
   d) the crowded living conditions

4. Which of the following is *not* a high priority user of energy in Asimov's world of the future?
   a) railroads
   b) police vehicles
   c) farm equipment
   d) subways

5. The main means of travel in 1997 will be by
   a) foot
   b) automobile
   c) railroad
   d) airplane

6. In the phrase "infant mortality," "mortality" means
   a) humiliation
   b) murder
   c) virtue
   d) death

7. It is implied that in some countries the population is being controlled by
   a) the use of birth control devices
   b) voluntary sterilization programs
   c) mass killing of "undesirable" people
   d) the high suicide rate

8. According to Asimov if we begin now to deal with the growing fuel crises
   a) nothing can be done
   b) it will be easy to overcome
   c) life will be just as he has described it
   d) we still have a chance to solve it

9. During the next century life could eventually become much like it was during the
   a) prehistoric times
   b) 1700s
   c) 1800s
   d) 1900s

10. The author wrote this selection in order to
    a) present us with factual information
    b) show us the humorous side of life
    c) persuade us to take action
    d) depress us about the future

Selection 21:	1200 words
Finishing Time: ____ ____ ____ HR. MIN. SEC.	
Starting Time: ____ ____ ____ HR. MIN. SEC.	
Reading Time: ____ ____ MIN. SEC.	
WPM Score: _____	
Comprehension Score: _____ %	
Reading Efficiency Score: _____	

READING SELECTION 22
FLIRTATION —
THE SIGNALS OF ATTRACTION —
DECIPHERED

Maggie Paley

The art of flirtation is going out of style. I began to think about this the first time I heard Timothy Perper, Ph.D., discuss his work. We were both at his older sister's apartment for dinner. Perper, then a biologist at Rutgers University, with an interest in animal behavior, announced, by way of filling his sister in on his recent activities, that he'd been taking students with him to observe human flirtation at New Jersey singles bars. He'd discovered, he said, that most often women were the ones who chose the men. He hoped to get a grant to study the phenomenon further.

"You're going to get a grant to go to bars to prove that women choose men?" said Perper's belligerent sister. "You don't need a grant. Why don't you just ask me? Of course, women do the choosing. Any woman could tell you that."

At the time, Perper was thirty-nine and recently separated from his wife. His new line of research struck me as a peculiarly modern solution — in the self-help spirit — to the plight of the single scientist. In the old days, if a man wanted to watch people engage in "the first stages of becoming intimate," as Perper put it, he wouldn't have told anybody. In the old days, I could not have been lured into a singles bar, even to watch a behavioral scientist. Yet this was what, with some enthusiasm, I ended up doing a number of times recently.

It was a transition period in the history of the war between the sexes. Those women who'd been brought up to think you batted your eyes, smiled at a man, and then he made all your troubles disappear were beginning to see the flaws in this point of view. There were rumors that men were changing, and that some of them wanted equal relationships with women. These so-called "new men," instead of trying to amuse you, liked to talk about their feelings and health

habits ("Can I make you a hamburger?" "I say the faster an animal moves the less fat is on it. I won't eat anything slower than a chicken."). You paid your own way with them, and you were direct instead of demure.

To be direct and seductive at the same time took a discouraging amount of energy. I found it hard to flirt at all under these conditions. Everyone was so confused about the things that should be most natural — how to assert themselves, enjoy themselves, be themselves. What *was* correct flirtation behavior? I got tired of trying to decide. I phoned Perper.

By ignoring his sister's advice at that dinner four years ago, Perper had become an authority on flirtation behavior and was beginning his third year of research in singles bars supported by a grant from the Harry Frank Guggenheim Foundation.

He had now ventured far beyond his sister's area of expertise. As a biologist, he told me, he'd learned to watch people flirt in much the same way he'd once watched rats engage in "copulatory behavior." Using this method, he'd discovered that all human flirtation, like mate selection among rats, took place in the form of body movement. What others called "chemistry," or "sexual attraction," he referred to as "body-movement compatibility." In his opinion, everyone worried too much about good opening lines and clever conversation with strangers, when what they were really doing when they met was the human equivalent of sniffing each other out. Since no one could control such a process, he wished people would just relax and enjoy it.

We sat at a table at the Greenwich Village singles bar, One University Place. "I think there are a lot of unhappy people around," he said,

311

"who don't really know how to make contact. And I would have put myself in that category, before I learned to read signals."

Most of the people who didn't know how to make contact, he told me, were men, and he thought it was a matter of training: men were so *ignorant* about behavior that a man could easily be in the middle of a flirtation without even knowing it. Women almost always knew when they were flirting, and it was in this sense that they could be said to be the ones doing the choosing. He had confirmed his observations with interviews; most men didn't notice cues and signals, and they didn't understand what women meant with their languorous looks and graceful gestures, though women assumed they did. A man didn't have to be good-looking or smart to be successful with women under these circumstances, according to Perper; he just had to pay attention to what they were doing.

Flirting, which I liked to think of as light, graceful, and easy, Perper had broken down into a sequence with four parts. Every flirtation he'd watched so far, he said, went through "approach" (the couple acknowledge each other's presence and begin talking); "swivel" (they turn gradually to face each other); "synchronization" (their movements begin to match); and "touch." Perper said "synchronization" was the most important step and made people feel, when they reached it, that they had "good vibes" together. I asked him to take me with him to watch this mating dance that I, a lifelong flirt, presumably had many times performed, smiling, nodding, and batting my eyes, in a semiconscious state.

Most of the men and women at the bars Perper showed me appeared to be suffering from a failure of imagination. They were there, but pretending not to be. The men were just lolling around by themselves, drinking beer and watching television. The women, who traveled in pairs, or in packs of three or more, seemed to have dressed up and gone out to have a good gossip with each other. It was as if the courage it took to enter a bar, seeking the company of strangers, had exhausted their supply of enthusiasm for the opposite sex. The men looked frightened and the women exasperated,

and no one seemed capable of entering into a flirtation sequence.

I spent five nights with Perper, looking for a pickup to watch, and listening to his complaints about men — a welcome change from listening to my women friends' complaints about men. Perper spoke of men affectionately, as a high-school football coach might speak of a promising team that was always dropping the ball. During flirtation, he said, this happened particularly at what he called "escalation points," the moments when one partner, usually the woman, would act to move things forward — by turning to begin a "swivel," for example, or by putting a hand on the table where it could easily be touched. If the other partner, usually the man, didn't respond, the result would be "de-escalation." Perper hated to see a man de-escalate by accident.

With some agitation he would point out, say, a woman in a red dress, whom he'd refer to as "Red Dress." Red Dress would be sitting on a bar stool, facing "Check Suit" with adoration in her milk-chocolate eyes while Check Suit stood pivoting nervously back and forth. "That dumb jerk!" Perper would whisper to me. "If he doesn't turn towards her, she'll give up. You'd think he'd figure out that someone who's looking at him that way must like him."

Sometimes, Perper said, it was hard to stop himself from rushing to the aid of a floundering couple. "Once again now," he could imagine himself telling the man, "this time when she does that, take her hand." Check Suit looked to me like a man wracked by ambivalence — which was what most men and women seemed to feel for each other most of the time. Perper said he thought what women did when they flirted was absolutely beautiful, and he felt sorry for the men who couldn't see it.

Now, there are male flirts who know perfectly well what women do when they flirt, I can assure you; men who know how to laugh and bat their eyes in return. But few of any sex can have studied, with the absorption Perper has, the entire arsenal of the human gestures of flirtation. These are sure signs that the person using them is flirting — what else could he be doing? — and once Perper was comfortable in a bar, he liked to [mimic] them. Some of the gestures he showed me were as obvious as the "eye avert" — when a man who's been looking a woman up and down then casts his eyes sideways (Perper mimed looking demure); or "brushing" — when a woman brushes against a man as if by accident ("It's never by accident," Perper said, brushing my left leg). Other gestures were disturbingly indirect, and apparently unconscious. Flirting people, he pointed out, spend a great deal of time preening and caressing themselves: stroking the neck, massaging an arm or leg. Touching the hair is a giveaway. Perper explained this phenomenon as "displacement" — you do to yourself what you'd like to do to the other person.

In a bar, Perper was a man in an invisible lab coat. His eyebrows seemed perpetually raised above steel-rimmed spectacles and pale eyes that focused on the middle distance; his high-bridged, beaked nose probed the air as if searching for a decent smell. He wore calculatedly nondescript clothes: the technique he practiced, "participant observation," required that he blend in with his environment. He ordered his drinks according to what bar he was in, and for the sake of appearances, he told me, he always worked as a "mixed-sex couple," and flirted with his partner. At regular intervals, when we were out together, he would lovingly touch my arm; I'd remind myself this was for the benefit of the people watching us. No one was watching us, but it wasn't my business to disturb his equilibrium.

I did worry about the fact that there was nothing happening for us to watch. Then, on our fifth night, I saw synchronization. We were at a back table at The Mad Hatter of Second Avenue in Manhattan, a singles bar as cozy as home, with sawdust floors and mad hats hung from the ceiling beams. Perper had brought one of his regular partners with him, a bouncy anthropology graduate student named Marilyn Frasier.

Perper and Frasier were like hunters watching for lions. First they would scan the bar, where twelve men were lined up looking at the Yankee game and two women in jeans were talking to each other near the jukebox. Then they'd turn to the dining room which was crowded with young couples on dates, all of whom, according to Perper, were struggling through the flirtation sequence. Then, for a break, Perper and Frasier would flirt with each other. In the middle of my dinner, they located some action.

The couple at the table directly in front of us were engaging, Perper said heatedly, in "synchronization of drink-stirring behavior." This meant they'd stirred their drinks at the same time, and it didn't impress me. I continued to work on my filet of sole while Perper and Frasier gossiped about the couple.

"They're clasping their hands in unison."

"They're taking a drink. It's hard to see who's leading there."

"When you're really attracted to someone, you just seem to come towards each other at the same time, don't you?"

I thought something must actually be happening at that table. When I looked, a fluttering movement of the woman's right hand caught my attention. Almost at the same moment, the man made the same gesture with his right hand. Then the heel of his right hand went thoughtfully to his chin, and the heel of her right hand went to her chin, too. Next, he pulled his right earlobe. She pulled her right earlobe. Their gestures were light and graceful. She clasped both hands under her lower lip, and so did he. Both of them sipped from their drinks, causing Perper and Frasier to chortle. The lifting of glasses was apparently a well-known chorus in the ongoing dance of hands at the table. I felt like a voyeur.

No such reverence for privacy inhibited the gleeful Perper. "I'm waiting for the first touch," he said confidentially. "They have to get the ketchup out of the way, and then the drinks, so they can touch by accident."

To contemplate manifestations of the unconscious in people I'd never met was an unsettling experience. I thought the sheer amount of energy being concentrated on this couple would cause them to turn around and glare back at us. I looked away from them to find that Perper was in sync with Frasier. The two of them smiled, forearms on the table, right hands grasping left elbows. They didn't know what they were doing. "Sometimes I think this is more fun than sex," Frasier said.

That night none of us was to reach a climax. The unfortunate couple couldn't negotiate their next escalation point. When Perper said it was time for them to touch, they didn't. The woman caressed her glass (a "touch invitation"), and the man mistook the signal and lifted his glass to drink ("de-escalation"). The woman dropped her hands to her lap, giving up, and after that they gestured to each other in nervous jabs. They had lost the beat. "Dummy," Perper said in a small, pained voice as if he were the one who'd been de-escalated. "She made overtures, he did not respond, and he should have. It has an unhappy ending."

"Don't jump to conclusions," Frasier told him, "just relax." But the couple ate their dinner, paid their check, and left without ever synchronizing their body movements again.

By this time, the men at the bar were three-deep, watching the Yankee game. Two women in jeans sat on the jukebox. "The more I think about that, the more I think his inability to respond was absolutely classic," Perper said to Frasier.

"He got more and more uncomfortable," Frasier agreed. A man at the bar asked the two women to get off the jukebox. They stood by his side while he made his selections, but he didn't talk to them. He wore a T-shirt with a drawing of a molecule on it and the name of the male sex hormone, "testosterone."

Perper is writing a book about his findings. He says he thinks everyone should be "comfortable with their biology," and I hope he helps people to take it easy when they flirt. As for me, now that I've seen synchronization I can hardly gesture across a dinner table without checking to see what my partner is doing. I'm not sure all humans were meant to have their consciousness raised.

COMPREHENSION TEST 22

Directions: *Circle the letter of the correct answer.*

1. The main idea of this article could be stated as:
   a) men generally prefer females to de-escalate during the flirtation process
   b) flirtation is composed of several distinct steps of which most people are not conscious
   c) in all flirtation situations it is the female who begins conversation
   d) most people are highly skilled in the flirtation process and practice it at bars

2. The so-called "new men" would not prefer to
   a) have an equal relationship with a woman
   b) have women be direct with them
   c) tell women about their feelings
   d) discuss their health habits with women

3. During the scene that took place at The Mad Hatter of Second Avenue, the couple being observed have to move the ketchup and the drinks before moving on in the flirtation process because
   a) these items were a barrier to his de-escalation
   b) she felt intimidated by having a barrier between them
   c) these items were a barrier to their touching accidentally
   d) the author could not observe them with these obstructions

4. Men often found themselves in the middle of a flirtation without even knowing it because
   a) women were ignorant of this type of behavior
   b) men were ignorant of this type of behavior
   c) women had better opening lines and caught the men off guard
   d) men did not usually go to bars to flirt

5. The four parts of flirtation behavior are

a) approach, swivel, synchronization, touch
b) approach, synchronization, swivel, touch
c) approach, touch, swivel, synchronization
d) approach, swivel, touch, synchronization

6. As it is used here, the word "mimic" means to
   a) insult
   b) disturb
   c) imitate
   d) influence

7. In the case of the couple being observed at The Mad Hatter, the flirtation was ended due to the fault of the
   a) observers
   b) bartender
   c) woman
   d) man

8. Perper ignored his sister's advice because he
   a) needed to prove it scientifically
   b) believed she was wrong
   c) thought it would be fun to go to bars himself
   d) needed to spend the grant money

9. Judging by the author's experiences in singles bars, you can conclude that
   a) there are a great many examples of flirtation to be viewed there
   b) not as much flirtation goes on there as many people think
   c) men are really experts at flirtation
   d) women are very clumsy and inept flirters

10. When the author refers to Perper as "a man in an invisible lab coat," she means that
    a) it really was invisible
    b) he wore one made of clear plastic
    c) he was being a scientist but nobody knew it
    d) his clothes were nondescript

Selection 22:	2528 words
Finishing Time:	___ HR. ___ MIN. ___ SEC.
Starting Time:	___ HR. ___ MIN. ___ SEC.
Reading Time:	___ MIN. ___ SEC.
WPM Score:	_____
Comprehension Score:	_____ %
Reading Efficiency Score:	_____

315

Chapter 14:
Evaluating What You Read

Have you heard the expression "It's printed here in black and white" used to mean that something is true? This is a common misconception held by many people. Many readers assume that anything that appears in print is true and is to be accepted without question. Actually, just the opposite should be true. An effective reader should question and react to everything he or she reads. He or she should examine the truth, value, and usefulness of the ideas offered in any reading material; this is the essence of evaluation. You might evaluate the usefulness of an article, you might compare it to other materials written on the same subject, or you might, as a class assignment, write a reaction paper to the ideas presented. In this chapter are several criteria to aid you in assessing the value of a piece of writing.

EVALUATING SOURCE AND AUTHORITY

Two very important considerations in evaluating any written material are the source in which it was printed and the authority, or qualifications, of the author.

Considering the Source

There are numerous situations when you are asked to read something that is not in its original form. Many textbooks, such as this one, as well as various articles, essays, and reports include quotes, excerpts, or entire selections borrowed from another author. Instructors may photocopy materials and distribute them for you to read. A friend may hand you a magazine article that he or she thinks would interest you. In each of these situations, the source from which the material was taken is not immediately clear.

Your reaction to and evaluation of the material should take into account its source. Obviously, a reader cannot check or verify each fact that a writer provides; ultimately you have to trust that the writer has carefully researched his or her subject and has accurately reported or described the subject. However, there are times when either care in research or accuracy in reporting is lacking. Often the source of a piece of writing can indicate how accurate and how well documented you can expect an article to be. For example, in which of the following sources would you expect to find accurate, up-to-date information on the gas mileage of various cars?

an advertisement in *Time* magazine
a research report in *Car and Driver*
an article in the *Reader's Digest* on buying an economical car

The article in *Car and Driver* would be the most likely source to find information that is accurate and up to date. *Car and Driver* is a magazine devoted to the subject of cars and their performance and provides monthly information on these subjects. *Reader's Digest*, on the other hand, publishes selected articles and condensed writing from other periodicals and may not provide such timely information on a subject. *Time* is a weekly news magazine in which you can expect to find brief summaries of current information on a wide variety of subjects and paid advertisements which may not provide completely objective information.

Let's consider another example. Suppose you are in the library trying to find information on sleepwalking for a paper you are writing. You locate the following sources, each of which contains an article or section on sleepwalking. Which would you expect to be the most factual and report the most scientific information available?

an encyclopedia entry on "Sleepwalking"
an article titled "Strange Things Happen While You Are Sleeping," appearing in *Woman's Day*
an article titled "An Examination of Research on Sleepwalking" in the *Psychological Review*

Again you can see that from the source alone you can make predictions about the content and approach used. You would expect the encyclopedia entry to be factual but provide only a general overview of the causes and effects of sleepwalking. You might expect the article in *Woman's Day* to discuss various abnormalities that occur during sleep; sleepwalking would be only one of the topics discussed. Also, you might expect the article to be of general interest, relating several unusual or extreme cases of sleepwalking, rather than presenting a factual analysis of the topic. The article in *Psychological Review*, a journal that reports research in psychology, would be the one that contains a factual, authoritative discussion of sleepwalking.

In evaluating a source you might ask the following questions:

1. What reputation does the source have?
2. What is the audience for whom the source is intended?
3. For what type of material is the source noted?

Considering the Authority of the Author

In addition to assessing the source in which material is printed, it is equally important to consider the competency of the author when you evaluate a piece of material. If the author lacks expertise or experience with the subject, the material he or she produces will probably not meet the standards of scholarship and accuracy that may be important to you at this point.

Depending on the type of material you are using, there are several means of checking the authority of the author. In textbooks, the author's credentials may be described in one of two places. First, the author's college or university affiliation, and possibly his or her title, may appear on the title page underneath the author's name. Second, in the preface of the book, an author may indicate or summarize his or her qualifications for writing the text.

In nonfiction books, and general market paperbacks, a synopsis of the author's life may be included on the book jacket or the back cover. This summary usually outlines the author's background and suggests his or her experience and qualifications to write about the subject of the book. However, in other types of material, little effort is made to identify the author or his or her qualifications. In newspapers, magazines, and reference books, the reader is given little or no information about the writer. In effect, then, you are forced to rely upon the judgment of the editors or publishers to assess an author's authority.

ASKING CRITICAL QUESTIONS

As you evaluate the content of a particular piece of writing, always approach the material with a critical, questioning mind. Try to discover any errors in reasoning or any reasons why you should not accept the ideas as presented. There are many questions that a reader may ask about a given article or selection; here are some of the most useful.

318

What Is the Author's Basic Assumption?

Many writers begin by assuming that a particular set of facts or principles are true. Then, they develop their ideas based on that assumption. Of course, if the assumption is not correct, or if it cannot be proven, then the ideas that depend on that assumption may be incorrect. For instance, the following passage begins with an assumption that the writer makes no attempt to prove or justify. Rather, it is used as a starting point for the development of his ideas on the function of cities.

> Given that the older central cities have lost their capacity to serve as effective staging areas for newcomers, the question inevitably poses itself: What *is* the function of these cities? Permit me to suggest that it has become essentially that of a sandbox.
>
> A sandbox is a place where adults park their children in order to converse, play, or work with a minimum of interference. The adults, having found a distraction for the children, can get on with the serious things of life. There is some reward for the children in all this. The sandbox is given to them as their own turf. Occasionally, fresh sand or toys are put in the sandbox, along with an implicit admonition that these things are furnished to minimize the level of noise and nuisance. If the children do become noisy and distract their parents, fresh toys may be brought. If the occupants of the sandbox choose up sides and start bashing each other over the head, the adults will come running, smack the juniors more or less indiscriminately, calm things down, and then, perhaps, in an act of semi-contrition, bring fresh sand and fresh toys, pat the occupants of the sandbox on the head, and disappear once again into their adult involvements and pursuits.[1]

The assumption the writer makes is stated in the first sentence: that older cities have lost their ability to attract newcomers. The author offers no reasons or evidence in support of this statement; it is assumed to be true. This assumption is the base on which the author builds his argument that the city is a sandbox. As you read any type of subjective, nonfactual material, always begin to evaluate the ideas by examining the author's initial assumptions. Decide whether you agree or disagree with them and check to see whether the author provides any evidence that his or her assumptions are accurate. Once you have identified an assumption consider this question: If the assumption were untrue, how would it affect the author's development of ideas?

Is the Author Biased?

As you evaluate any piece of writing, always ask whether the author presents an objective view of the subject or whether he or she favors a particular point of view. You can determine if an author is biased by considering whether the author's feelings about the subject are evident. If the author reveals his or her attitude, then you know the author is biased. Once you have established an author's bias, then evaluating the material is an easier task. You know the direction in which the writer is trying to lead you and you can proceed cautiously.

Notice in the following passage that the author is clearly opposed to TV advertising for children.

TV ADVERTISING TO CHILDREN SHOULD BE BANNED!

Boston-based Action for Children's Television has led the fight to ban TV commericals from children's programming. In 1970 ACT sent three proposals to the Federal Communications Commission: All commercials should be banned from children's television. Children's show hosts, performers, and cartoon characters should not be used in commercials aired on other programs. And, to end the race for mass child audience appeal, each television station should program at least 14 hours a week specifically for children.

The broadcasting and advertising industry described the ACT petition as radical, unrealistic, and a bit kooky. Several interrelated arguments, however, support their contention that children's TV advertising should be banned:

Children are defenseless. Young children do not discriminate between program and commercial. They identify with commercial characters. And these characters, in turn, unfairly influence child viewers' requests for certain products.

Wants are created. A child can be induced to want something. Children know what they want, not what is good for them. TV may make them want candy, an expensive toy, or tasty vitamins. They may even want to fly like the commercial's trade character. The medium is supposed to entertain and educate, not pitch products to children.

> *Family tension results.* Children are bombarded by about 15 minutes of TV commercials per nonprime-time TV hour and 10 minutes per prime-time hour. Such exposure often sends them begging to parents. Their requests and the resulting parent/child conflicts would diminish if TV advertising were banned.
>
> *Children's TV commercials are deceptive.* Fast-action shots of toys in use and trick camera angles portray the product as bigger than life. Child models exaggerate reactions. Pressed paper parts look like metal when flashed over the screen. Expensive optional accessories, without which the toy would be meaningless, are said to be "available." Strength, vigor, and athletic ability from the use of certain products is implied. Emotional and psychological content, rather than communication of useful information, is relied on. These charges, and many more, have been made against advertisers.[2]

This passage is clearly biased against TV commercials directed toward children. This writer is fairly obvious in his or her bias; it is directly stated in the second paragraph that TV advertising should be banned. Notice that the writer presents only one side of the issue of advertising for children. Contrary arguments and viewpoints are not considered. For example, the author does not consider that children need to learn to be consumers and that early exposure to advertising may help them to understand its persuasive power.

As you read biased material, then, always keep these questions in mind: What is the other side of the issue? Are there stronger, more convincing facts and arguments that could be presented in opposition to the writer's stance?

Is the Writing Slanted?

Slanting refers to the process of selecting details that are, depending on the author's purpose, favorable or unfavorable to a particular subject. Slanted writing emphasizes certain details and omits or subordinates others to present a particular point of view. Suppose you had to describe a person you know. If you wanted your reader to respond favorably to the person you might include the following facts about him.

1. Sam is tall, well built, and carries himself well.
2. Sam is an easy-going person and seldom becomes angry or upset.
3. Sam wears neat casual clothing.

On the other hand, if you wanted to create a less positive image of Sam you might omit the above information and emphasize these facts instead.

1. Sam has a long nose and his teeth are crooked.
2. Sam frequently talks about himself and doesn't seem to listen to what others are saying.
3. Sam wears clothing that is two or three years out of date.

Much of what you read is slanted. For instance, advertisers do not tell you what is wrong with a product, and colleges do not explain the disadvantages of attending their institution in their college catalog. In the newspaper advice column, Ann Landers gives you her opinion of how to solve a reader's problem but she does not discuss all possible solutions. Help wanted ads describe the attractive features of a job, but seldom mention its more negative aspects.

As you read material that you suspect is slanted, be sure to keep the following questions in mind: What facts has the author omitted? How would the inclusion of these facts alter your overall reaction or impression?

EXERCISE 14-1

Directions: *Read the following passage and evaluate it using the critical questions that follow.*

This is a book about what happens to young people when they get out of high school.

It is about college only because college is where we put as many of them as possible to get them out of the way. It isn't about education, really, or the virtues of an educated citizenry. It is not about the value of college for those young people who love learning for its own sake, for those who would rather read a good book than eat. They are a minority, even at the big-name prestige colleges which recruit and attract the intellectually oriented. For them college is intellectual discovery and adventure.

But a great majority of our nine million postsecondary students who are "in college" are there because it has become the thing to do or because college is a pleasant place to be (pleasanter at least than the "outside," sometimes called "the real" world); because it's the only way they can get parents or taxpayers to support them without working at a job they don't like; because they can't get any job at all;

because Mother wanted them to go; or for some other reason utterly irrelevant to the courses of studies for which the college is supposedly organized.

It is dismaying to find, as I did, that college professors and administrators, when pressed for a candid opinion, estimate that no more than 25 percent of the students they serve are really turned on by classwork. For the other 75 percent, college is at best a social center, a youth ghetto, an aging vat, and at worst a young folks (rhymes with old folks) home, a youth house (rhymes with poorhouse), or even a prison. However good or bad it might be for the individual students, college is a place where young adults are set apart because they are superfluous people who are of no immediate use to the economy and are a potential embarrassment to the middle-aged white males who operate the outside or "real" world for their own convenience.

1. What assumptions does the author make?

   _____

   _____

2. Is the writer biased? What is her attitude toward college and college students?

   _____

   _____

3. Is the writing slanted? If so, what type of information is not included that would be necessary to present an objective view of college?

   _____

   _____

EVALUATING SUPPORTING EVIDENCE

As you learned in the chapters on paragraph development and on the organization of articles and longer selections, an author supports his or her ideas by providing facts, examples, and details that explain further or prove main ideas or thesis statements. Once you have established the relationship between the facts and main idea, as a critical reader, you must evaluate the accuracy and applicability of the support the author provides. Your overall purpose should be to decide whether the author provides sufficient information, or evidence, to adequately support the ideas offered. In other words, you must evaluate whether the author has given you sufficient reasons or has supplied sufficient facts to permit you to accept the ideas proposed. As you read critically, your overall purpose should be to judge the acceptability or worth of the author's ideas, in part, by evaluating the nature and quality of the supporting evidence.

Because judgment is involved, evaluating supporting evidence is always subjective. The supporting evidence that you regard as sufficient someone else may judge to be insufficient. For instance, in an article on the 55 mph speed limit, you may consider the supporting facts to be sufficient for your purposes, but a safety researcher might require additional facts and statistics before accepting the author's thesis.

To judge the quality of the support an author provides, you should consider several factors.

The Use of Generalizations

A generalization is a statement that is made about a large group or a class of items based on observation or experience with a part of that group or class. Suppose you interviewed a number of students on campus and asked each why he or she was attending college and each indicated that he or she was preparing for a career. From your interview you could make the generalization, "Students attend college to prepare for a career." Of course, you could not be absolutely certain that this statement is true until you asked *every* college student. Here are a few more generalizations. Some may seem very reasonable; you may disagree with others.

1. All college freshmen are confused and disoriented during their first week on campus.
2. Most parents are concerned for the happiness of their children.
3. Psychology instructors are interested in the psychology of learning.
4. College students are more interested in social life than scholarship.

As you evaluate the evidence a writer uses to support his or her ideas, be alert for generalizations used as facts. Remember that a generalization is not a fact and represents only the writer's judgment about a particular set of facts. Notice, in the following paragraph, how generalizations, not facts, are used to support the main idea.

> The wedding is a tradition that most young adults still value. Most engaged couples carefully plan their wedding and regard it as an important occasion in their life. Couples also are very concerned that their ceremony follow rules of etiquette and that everything be done "just so." Most give a great deal of attention to personalizing their ceremony, including their own vows, songs, and symbols.

Notice that the writer does not develop the paragraph using concrete, specific information. Instead, the author provides generalizations about how young adults feel about their weddings. If the writer is a sociologist who has studied the attitudes toward and customs of marriage, then the generalizations may be accurate. However, if the paragraph was written by a parent and based on experience with his or her children and their friends, then there is little reason to accept the generalizations since they are based on limited experience. You can see, then, that the expertise of the writer as well as the method by which he or she arrived at the generalizations influence how readily you should accept them.

When reading material that contains generalizations, approach the writer's conclusion with a critical, questioning attitude. When a generalization is unsubstantiated by facts, regard it as an opinion expressed by the author. Generalizations presented as facts are dangerous and misleading and may be completely false.

Use of Personal Experience as Evidence

Writers often substantiate their ideas about a particular issue or idea by using personal experience and reporting their observations. Although a writer's personal account of a situation may be interesting and provide a perspective on an issue, personal experience should not be accepted as proof. Suppose you are reading an article on drug use and the writer uses his personal experience with particular drugs to prove a point. Although the article provides an inside look into the life of someone who used drugs regularly, there are several reasons why the writer's conclusions about the effects of particular drugs should not be accepted as fact. First, the effects of a drug may vary from person to person. The drug's effect on the writer may be atypical. Second, unless the writer kept careful records on times, dosages, surrounding circumstances, etc., he will be describing events from memory. Over time, the writer may have exaggerated, recalled only selectively, or lost perspective on either positive or negative effects. As you read, treat ideas supported only through personal experience as *one person's experience,* and do not make the error of generalizing the experience.

The Use of Examples as Evidence

Examples are descriptions of particular situations that are used to illustrate or explain a principle, concept, or idea. To explain what aggressive behavior is, your psychology instructor may offer several examples: fighting, punching, and kicking. To illustrate how to score a spare or strike in bowling, a friend might describe the scoring of a particular game. Examples used for explanation are useful and effective. However, examples should not be used by themselves to prove the concept or idea they illustrate, as is done in the following sample.

> The American judicial system treats those who are called for jury duty unfairly. It is clear from my sister's experience that the system has little regard for the needs of those called as jurors. My sister was required to report for jury duty the week she was on vacation. She spent the entire week in a crowded, stuffy room waiting to be called to sit on a jury and never was called.

In this paragraph the writer was attempting to use her sister's single experience with jury duty as evidence that the system treats jurors unfairly. Actually, the writer has only managed to suggest that her sister was, in the writer's opinion, treated unfairly. The passage offers no evidence that this practice is widespread or that others have experienced similar inconvenient treatment.

The Use of Statistical Evidence

Many people are impressed by statistics — the reporting of figures, percentages, averages, and so forth — and assume they are irrefutable proof. Actually, statistics can be misused, misinterpreted, or used selectively to give other than the most objective, accurate picture of a situation. Suppose you read that magazine X has increased its readership by 50 percent while magazine Y made only a 10 percent increase. From this statistic some readers might assume that magazine X has a wider readership than magazine Y. However, if provided with complete information you can see that this is not true. The missing, but crucial, statistic is total readership of each magazine prior to the increase. If magazine X had a readership of 20,000, and increased it by 50 percent, its readership would total 30,000. However, if magazine Y's readership was already 50,000, a 10 percent increase (bringing the new total to 55,000), would still give it the larger readership despite the fact that it made the smaller increase.

The Assumption of Cause-Effect Relationships

A common error in reasoning is to attribute a cause to a particular effect or an effect to a particular cause because they happen within the same time frame. For instance, if you drove over broken glass on the highway and then, shortly afterward, you got a flat tire, you might assume that the broken glass caused the flat tire. Actually, a nail on the highway that you did not even see may have punctured the tire. If that were the case, then you would have falsely connected two occurrences because they happened in close proximity.

EXERCISE 14-2

Directions: *Briefly review the passage in Exercise 14-1. Then evaluate the author's use of supporting evidence by answering the following questions.*

1. What generalizations does the writer make?

    _____

2. Does the writer use personal experience as evidence?

    _____

3. Are examples used as evidence?

    _____

4. Is statistical evidence provided?

    _____

5. Are cause-effect relationships suggested? If so, do they seem logical?

    _____

RECOGNIZING VALUE JUDGMENTS

A writer who decides that an idea or action is right or wrong, good or bad, or desirable or undesirable is making a value judgment. That is, the writer is imposing his or her own judgment on the worth of a concept or action. Here are a few examples of value judgments.

> Divorces should be restricted to couples who can *prove* incompatibility.

> Abortion is wrong.

> Welfare applicants should be forced to apply for any job they are capable of performing.

> Premarital sex is acceptable.

You will notice that each statement is controversial. Each involves some type of conflict or idea over which there is disagreement. The conflicts are:

1. restriction versus freedom
2. right versus wrong
3. force versus choice
4. acceptability versus nonacceptability

You may know of some people who would agree and others who might disagree with each. When a writer takes a position or side of a "conflict," then, he or she is making a value judgment.

As you read, be alert for value judgments; it is important to recognize that they represent only one person's view and that there are, most likely, many other views toward the same topic. When you identify a value judgment, look "behind it," so to speak, to determine if the author offers any evidence in support of his or her position.

EXERCISE 14-3

Directions: *For each of the following statements, first decide if a value judgment is present. If it is, then write a statement that expresses an opposing point of view. The first item has been completed as an example.*

1. Statement: Required sex education class in the schools limits the parents' right to provide appropriate information.

Opposing View: <u>Required sex education classes provide</u>

<u>children with information that they have</u>

<u>a right and need to know.</u>

2. Statement: College students should not be allowed to receive low-interest government loans if their parents have the financial ability to loan them the money.

Opposing View: _____

_____

_____

3. Statement: The crime rate has been increasing steadily over the past ten years.

Opposing View: _____

_____

_____

4. Statement: Drivers convicted of driving while intoxicated should have their license suspended for one year.

Opposing View: _____

_____

_____

5. Statement: Smoke detectors have saved many lives by providing early warnings of fires.

Opposing View: _____

_____

_____

As you read you should always be alert for the presence of value judgments. The first step, of course, is to recognize them. Sophisticated writers may attempt to pass them off as facts or assumptions (something that is assumed to be true and is used as a starting point in an argument). Generally, if you disagree with a value judgment, you are more likely to recognize it. If, for example, you believe that the military draft should treat men and women equally, and you read a statement that defends the registration of only males, you are likely to react, disagree, and realize that the author is stating a judgment on the issue. On the other hand, if you read a statement that agrees with your own viewpoint, you are more likely to regard it as a statement of fact.

Because value judgments depend on a person's sense of what is right and wrong (one's set of values), they cannot be proved or disproved. When encountering value judgments in your reading, therefore, it is important to "look behind" the judgment to see if the writer offers reasonable, thoughtful evidence for the viewpoint assumed. In identifying and evaluating value judgments, you might apply the following questions:

1. Is there an opposite point of view that could be taken on the issue being discussed?
2. Are there enough reasons and evidence to allow you to accept the writer's point of view?
3. If you already agree with the writer, does he or she offer sufficient evidence to convince someone who might disagree?
4. Can you think of additional evidence in support of or in opposition to the author's position?

APPLYING WHAT YOU HAVE LEARNED

Directions: *Choose one of the selections at the end of the chapter. Read the selection and answer the multiple choice questions. Then review the article and answer the questions below.*

1. Does the author make any assumptions? If so, what are they?

   _____

2. Is the author biased?

   _____

3. Is the writing slanted?

   _____

4. What types of supporting evidence does the author use?

    _____

5. Does the author make any value judgments?

    _____

READING SELECTION 23
THE "FLICKERING BLUE PARENT": CHILDREN AND TELEVISION

Difficulty Level: A

Mary J. Gander and Harry W. Gardiner

Ninety-six percent of American homes have at least one television set which is turned on for an average of six hours each day. During the last three decades television has become a major agent of socialization, often competing with parents, siblings, peers, and teachers.

Kenneth Keniston, chairman of the Carnegie Council on Children, has referred to television as the "flickering blue parent occupying more of the waking hours of American children than any other single influence — including *both* parents and schools." Singer and Singer have characterized it as "a member of the family."

How much television and what kinds of programs do children watch? The answer depends on many factors, including children's age and season of the year. According to Winick and Winick, school-age children watch television between seventeen and thirty hours a week. For preschool children it is often as high as fifty-four hours a week. Nancy Larrick, a reading specialist and children's author, has pointed out that "by the time the child goes to kindergarten, he or she will have devoted more hours to watching television than a college student spends in four years of classes. . . . And by the time the youngster graduates from high school, he or she will have spent roughly 11,000 hours in school compared to more than 22,000 hours in front of television."

Children are not just watching so-called children's programs. On the contrary, according to figures released by the A. C. Nielsen Company, only 13 percent of television viewing among six- to eleven-year-old children occurs on Saturday between eight A.M. and one P.M. The largest portion of their viewing, 33 percent, takes place between eight and eleven P.M.

Monday through Saturday and between seven and eleven P.M. on Sunday.

Who selects the programs that children watch? According to Bower, when mothers and children watch together, the mother makes selections in 37 percent of the cases; joint decisions occur 27 percent of the time; 33 percent of the time children decide by themselves. In a study by Lyle and Hoffman, over 60 percent of mothers of first-graders reported that they placed no restrictions on the amount of time they permitted their children to watch television.

Teachers, schools, and parent associations have become increasingly concerned about the effects of television on school performance. Based on their classroom experiences, many teachers have reported mounting incidences of fatigue, tension, and aggressive behavior, as well as lessened spontaneity and imagination.

So what have schools been doing? At Kimberton Farms School in Phoenixville, Pennsylvania, parents and teachers have been following written guidelines for five years which include no television *at all* for children through the first grade. Children in second grade through high school are encouraged to watch no television on school nights and to restrict viewing to a total of three to four hours on weekends. According to Harry Blanchard, head of the faculty, "You can observe the effects with some youngsters almost immediately. . . . Three days after they turn off the set you see a marked improvement in their behavior. They concentrate better, and are more able to follow directions and get along with their neighbors. If they go back to the set you notice it right away."

As Fiske has pointed out, "In the final analysis, the success of schools in minimizing the negative effects of television on their (children's) academic progress depends almost entirely on whether the parents share this goal."

Many parents do share this goal and have been working with the National Parent-Teacher's Association in offering advice on choosing programs, setting time limitations, and helping parents and children develop critical attitudes. One of their publications, *PTA Review Guide,* periodically reports the collected opinions of 6,000 parents and teachers concerning current television programming. In addition, they have recommended guidelines which

include keeping a log of what programs and at what times children watch, helping in the selection of programs, setting reasonable limits, joining children in watching their programs, and asking and answering questions about the positive and negative content of them.

As Linda Lombardi has pointed out, "In the 1950s many parents felt they were depriving their children of something important if they didn't give them a TV set. Today, we're beginning to realize we're doing our children a favor when we take the TV set away, at least for a while every day."

COMPREHENSION TEST 23

Directions: *Circle the letter of the correct answer.*

1. A main point of this selection is that
   a) television is a better instrument of education than our public schools
   b) parents do not watch enough television
   c) television has helped children improve their imaginations
   d) children watch television extensively and their viewing habits need to be controlled

2. One thing that parents can do to improve children's viewing habits is to
   a) remove television from the home
   b) ask teachers to select appropriate programs
   c) view programs with them and discuss the ideas presented
   d) give them complete freedom in selecting programs

3. When an eighteen-year-old graduates from high school, he or she will have spent
   a) more hours attending school than in watching television
   b) less time watching television than he or she will spend studying in college
   c) more hours watching television than attending school
   d) more time watching television than he or she will spend studying in college

4. The largest portion of children's television viewing time is spent watching
   a) children's programs on Saturday morning
   b) adult programs during the evening
   c) game shows and children's programs
   d) educational programs

5. Many parents and educators feel that television has had
   a) a positive effect on student learning and behavior
   b) a negative effect on student learning and behavior
   c) a positive effect on student learning but not on behavior
   d) little effect on student learning and behavior

6. As used here, "restrictions" most nearly means
   a) reasons
   b) limitations
   c) values
   d) emphases

7. Television might be considered as a member of the family because
   a) children spend so much time with it
   b) children learn from it
   c) parents emphasize its importance by watching it at night
   d) children do exactly what they are told on television

8. By referring to television as the "flickering blue parent," the authors try to suggest that
   a) television exerts a strong influence on children that used to be exerted by parents
   b) television is able to teach and guide children toward acceptable behavior
   c) television is a member of the family
   d) parents use television as a substitute for talking to their children

9. Which of the following statements would best describe how the authors would control their own children's watching of television?
   a) They would not allow any viewing.
   b) They would allow unlimited viewing.
   c) They would permit carefully selected viewing.
   d) They would require the children to keep a log of what they watch.

10. Two adjectives that would best describe the authors' attitude toward their subject are
    a) serious and concerned
    b) outraged and upset
    c) indifferent and oblivious
    d) noncommittal and evasive

Selection 23:		723 words
Finishing Time:	HR. MIN.	SEC.
Starting Time:	HR. MIN.	SEC.
Reading Time:	MIN.	SEC.
WPM Score:		
Comprehension Score:		%
Reading Efficiency Score:		

READING SELECTION 24
VIOLENCE IN SPORTS

Robert C. Yeager

The evil of athletic violence touches nearly everyone. It tarnishes what may be our only religion. Brutality in games blasphemes play, perhaps our purest form of free expression. It blurs the clarity of open competition, obscuring our joy in victory as well as our dignity in defeat. It robs us of innocence, surprise, and self-respect. It spoils our fun.

For all these reasons, the shame of sports violence assumes epic dimensions, its sorrows seem even more consummate. The toll extends well beyond a small boy's vanished enthusiasms, though such boys — and girls — are many, and their collective loss large and important. The more tragic cost is physical, tallied in broken bones and torn flesh. From high school on, the careers of an alarming number of players end or are shortened because of crippling injuries.

Never before has the harming of athletes seemed more deliberate, its practice so widespread. Even those who have battled in the trenches of big-time, big-money sports sense a difference in attitude and tactics on the playing field. "When I came into pro ball, I don't think there were many guys who intentionally tried to hurt somebody," says Steve Owens, a Heisman Trophy winner and the first 1,000-yard rusher for the Detroit Lions. "But in the past few years I've seen enough to change my mind. They hit late, spear, and do unnecessary things when officials can't see it. They're trying to hurt people."

That the problem is neither exclusively American nor limited to the playing field provides little comfort. Canada's McMurtry report — an official government investigation of hockey violence prompted by the slaying of a teenage player — concluded that a "sick situation" existed at all levels of that country's favorite sport. The British athletic establishment was rocked by a recent finding that one in four male spectators has joined in soccer hooliganism, an epidemic of sports violence believed to include at least three murders. Elsewhere:

In Guatemala City, five persons are hacked to death at a soccer match when hometown loyalists, bitter in defeat, descend on the winning team with machetes.

In Florida, an argument at a high school football game ends when an assistant principal is shot and killed by the rival school's business manager. Seventy miles away, a boys' club football coach narrowly survives a beating by two dozen pipe-wielding spectators, mostly relatives of the losers.

In Italy, a rugby player emerges from a scrum with much of his left ear bitten off; newspapers in Rome call this the first instance of sports cannibalism.

In Florida, the facial bones of a major-league baseball manager are shattered in an attack by one of his own players during spring training. Successive World Series end in fan riots, with some of the violence so ugly that video crews are reluctant to film it.

From Toronto to Minneapolis, stick-swinging cheap-shot artists rule the National Hockey League. Players slam each other into the boards, brawl with officials and fans, and are let off by confused courts which cannot believe a proud sport has been taken over by plain, scofflaw thuggery. "Hooliganism must be eradicated," says one NHL executive, but after years of supposed cleanups and promised crackdowns, hockey violence today seems as bad as ever.

So it goes. Knifings, shootings, beatings, muggings, paralysis, and death become part of our play. Women baseball fans are warned to walk with friends and avoid taking their handbags to games because of strong-arm robberies and purse snatchings at San Francisco's Candlestick Park. A professional football coach, under oath in a slander case, describes some of his own players as part of a "criminal element" in his sport. The commissioner of football proclaims that playing field outlaws and bullies will be punished, but to anybody with normal eyesight and a working television set the action looks rougher than ever. In Europe and South America — and, chillingly, for the first time in the United States — authorities turn to snarling attack dogs to control unruly mobs at athletic events.

Sports officials, parents, and athletes themselves condemn the worldwide wave of bloodletting, but the ugly parade of savage spectator outbursts and player-maiming injuries keeps getting longer. We worry about our children viewing fictional mayhem on television; yet the camera's relentless athletic vigil presents, unexpurgated, every major act of sports viciousness, then endlessly replays it, in full view of millions of hero-worshipping youngsters.

Clearly, children are among the most unfortunate victims of sports violence. "Professional games are allegories," says Robert R. Luby, a health education and safety official for the Detroit public schools. "When overaggressiveness wins the day, it puts the wrong emphasis on the meaning of athletic competition."

We are only beginning to understand how much television magnifies such emphasis. According to a December 8, 1975, report in the *Journal of the American Medical Association,* the average youngster witnesses some 18,000 fictional video slayings by the time he or she is in the mid-teens. Televised acts of sports viciousness may add appreciably to that childhood exposure to violence, some experts believe. The mere televising — and replaying — of such acts in effect condones similar behavior in children who idolize athletes as incapable of wrongdoing. "Violence in hockey is appearing in younger and younger age groups," said a report by Canada's Royal Commission on Violence in the Communications Industry, "because

children are being shown on television the way professionals play the game."

What is sports violence? The distinction between unacceptable viciousness and a game's normal rough-and-tumble is impossible to make, or so the argument runs. This position may appeal to our penchant for legalism, but the truth is most of us know quite well when an act of needless savagery has been committed, and sports are little different from countless other activities of life. The distinction is as apparent as that between a deliberately aimed roundhouse and the arm flailing of an athlete losing his balance. When a player balls his hand into a fist, when he drives his helmet into an unsuspecting opponent — in short, when he crosses the boundary between playing hard and playing to hurt — he can only intend an act of violence.

Admittedly, violent acts in sports are difficult to police. But here, too, we find reflected the conditions of everyday life. Ambiguities in the law, confusion at the scene, and the reluctance of witnesses cloud almost any routine assault and battery case. Such uncertainties, however, have not prevented society from arresting people who strike their fellow citizens on the street.

Perhaps our troubles stem not from the games we play but rather from how we play them. The 1979 meeting between hockey stars from the Soviet Union and the National Hockey League provided a direct test of two approaches to sport — the emphasis on skill, grace, and finesse by the Russians and the stress on brutality and violence by the NHL. In a startling upset, the Russians embarrassed their rough-playing opponents and debunked a long-standing myth: that success in certain sports requires excessive violence.

Violence apologists cite two additional arguments. First, they say, sports always have been violent; today things are no different. But arguments in America's Old West were settled on Main Street with six-guns, and early cave-dwellers chose their women with a club. Civilizing influences ended those practices; yet we are told sports violence should be tolerated.

The second contention is that athletes accept risk as part of the game, and, in the case of professionals, are paid handsomely to do so. But can anyone seriously argue that being an athlete should require the acceptance of unnecessary physical abuse? And, exaggerated as it may seem, the pay of professional athletes presumably reflects their abilities, not an indemnification against combat injuries.

"Clearly we are in deep trouble," says perplexed former sportscaster and football player Al DeRogatis. "But how and why has it gotten so bad?"

COMPREHENSION TEST 24

Directions: *Circle the letter of the correct answer.*

1. Which statement best expresses the main point of this article?
   a) "That the problem is neither exclusively American nor limited to the playing field provides little comfort."
   b) "Admittedly violent acts in sports are difficult to police."
   c) "First, they say, sports always have been violent; today things are no different."
   d) "Never before has the harming of athletes seemed more deliberate, its practice so widespread."

2. The author believes that the most unfortunate victims of sports violence are
   a) spectators
   b) children
   c) players
   d) professional athletes

3. A major reason why the author thinks sports violence is on the rise is
   a) it makes sports more exciting
   b) it is important in democratic societies
   c) professional athletes are paid high salaries
   d) it is increasingly shown on television

4. In the viewpoint of the author, determining what is truly violent and what is a normal part of a sport
   a) is a relatively simple task
   b) requires a larger number of officials
   c) is nearly impossible because of differences of opinion
   d) should be decided by fans

5. In England about one out of four male spectators gets involved in violent acts connected with the sport of
   a) rugby
   b) soccer
   c) tennis
   d) cricket

6. In the phrase "the camera's relentless athletic vigil" the word "relentless" means
   a) unyielding
   b) fast-paced
   c) remarkable
   d) simultaneous

7. Acts of violence in sports are apparently uncommon in
   a) the United States
   b) Canada
   c) Russia
   d) Italy

8. The author feels that the way sports violence should be curbed is through
   a) taking legal action against offenders
   b) increasing the number of officials
   c) suspending athletes for violent acts
   d) fining club owners for these occurrences

9. The author's purpose in this selection is to lead the reader to see
   a) the values of sports
   b) a balanced picture of sports violence
   c) the ugly side of violence in sports
   d) the ridiculously high salaries of athletes

10. The tone of the writer as reflected in this selection is one of
    a) objectivity
    b) hopefulness
    c) disgust
    d) admiration

Selection 24:	1313 words

Finishing Time: _____ _____ _____
                     HR.   MIN.   SEC.

Starting Time: _____ _____ _____
                    HR.   MIN.   SEC.

Reading Time: _____ _____
                    MIN.   SEC.

WPM Score: _____

Comprehension Score: _____ %

Reading Efficiency Score: _____

338

Unit Seven:
How to Read Selectively

Before beginning this section it is essential that you agree with the following statement: Not everything in print is equally important and, depending on your purpose, some material is not worth reading at all. That is, in many situations reading material is important only if it contains information you need to learn or that you are interested in learning. Of course at times you may read for entertainment or enjoyment, in which case you are not concerned with importance. An efficient reader should be able to locate portions of material that fulfill his or her purpose and skip those portions which do not. For example, you may decide to read a newspaper movie review to get a general impression of the film. In that case, it would not be necessary to read detailed descriptions of particular scenes or of actors' performances. Or, you may read a magazine article to find out a specific piece of information. In that case most of the article would be unimportant and reading it would be an inefficient use of your time.

The purpose of this section is to present two very useful techniques, skimming and scanning, that will allow you to read selectively — reading what is important and skipping what does not suit your immediate purpose. Chapter 15 contains a technique for skimming, or locating only the most important ideas in any type of material. In Chapter 16 we will discuss scanning, the technique of rapidly locating particular types of information.

Chapter 15:
Skimming: Reading for Main Ideas

Suppose that you are browsing through magazines in the library, and, just before it is time to leave for your next class, you find a two- or three-page article that you are interested in reading. You cannot check out the magazine, and you do not have time to read it before class. You know that you will not take the time to come back later to find the magazine and read the article. What should you do?

One alternative is to forget about the article altogether and go to class. A second alternative is to *skim* the article, reading some parts and skipping others, in order to find the most important ideas. However, you would not read certain parts and skip others at random. Instead you would read the parts of the article that are most likely to provide the main ideas of the article and skip those which contain less important facts and details. *Skimming,* then, means reading selectively to get a general idea of what an article is about and to become familiar with the most important ideas in it.

In this chapter we will discuss the purposes, uses, and types of skimming, present a step-by-step procedure for skimming, and show how to adapt the technique to various types of reading material.

PURPOSES FOR SKIMMING

Throughout your years in school you have most likely been trained to read everything thoroughly. Think back to your high school years for a moment. You often were given entire chapters, articles, stories, or readings and were expected to read them completely. Everything was regarded as equally important, and usually it was not acceptable to skip any parts of these readings. Although, in many of these cases, complete reading *was* necessary, in others it was not. With the exception of textbook readings and course assignments, there are many situations in which complete reading is not necessary. In fact, there are some circumstances in which thorough reading may be an inefficient use of your time. Let's take a moment to consider a number of situations in which it might be appropriate to skim by reading certain parts and skipping others. Here are a few examples of material for which skimming would be the most effective technique to use.

1. *A Newspaper Report of a Fire in a Nearby Shopping Mall.* In reading this article, if you are only interested in the basic information such as the cause of the fire and extent of the damage, then skimming would be appropriate. You could skip sections of the article that give details such as the number of fire companies responding, the number of alarms, the time it began, and so forth.

2. *A Movie Review.* If you are reading the review to decide whether you want to see the movie, then you are probably looking for the writer's overall reaction to the movie: Was it exciting? Was it boring? Was it humorous? You could afford to skip in-depth descriptions of characters, of particular scenes, and of particular actors' or actresses' performances.

3. *Advertisements/Junk Mail.* In reading an advertisement or a letter from a company trying to sell you something, usually it is not necessary to read everything. Generally, you approach this type of material with two general purposes in mind: to find out what is being sold and to decide if you are interested in purchasing the product. If you are not in the market for the product, then you could skip the remainder of the letter or ad or throw it out.

Now, try to think of some other types of material that might be appropriate for you to skim. List them in the space provided.

1. _____

2. _____

3. _____

In each of the situations described earlier, as well as in the situations you listed, you should see that skimming was appropriate when complete information was *not* required. In each situation all that was needed was the basic information and the most important ideas or the "gist" of the article. You can begin to see, then, that your purpose or reason for reading is crucial in determining when it is appropriate to skim.

HOW TO SKIM

Throughout the book up to this point, you have developed a solid foundation of basic comprehension skills. Now you will begin to recognize that much of what you have learned about the structure and organization of paragraphs, passages, and longer selections has direct applications to skimming. You will see that many of the skills you have learned will enable you to skim effectively.

In skimming, your overall purpose should be to read only those parts of an article or selection which contain the most important information. Your goal is to read what is most important and skip what is least important. The basic task of skimming, then, is to identify those parts of any reading material which contain the main ideas. The type of material you are reading, will, in part, determine how you should adapt your reading techniques.

Authors use different patterns of organization and various formats, and skimming is a highly flexible technique that can be adapted to these varying structures and formats.

To acquaint you with the process of skimming, a basic, step-by-step procedure will be presented and applied to a sample article. Then adaptations of this general technique to specific types of reading materials will be discussed.

In general, then, use the following steps as a guide:

The Title. The title often announces the subject of the material and often provides clues about the author's approach or attitude toward the subject. (For a more detailed discussion of the function of titles, refer to Chapter 8.)

Subtitle or Introductory Byline. Some types of material include a statement underneath the title that further explains the title or is written to catch the reader's interest.

The Introductory Paragraph. The introductory paragraph often provides important background information and introduces the subject. It may also provide a brief overview of the treatment of the subject.

Headings. A heading announces the topic that will be discussed in the paragraphs that follow it. When read successively, the headings form an outline or list of topics covered in the material.

The First Sentence of Each Paragraph. From your experience with paragraph structure, you know that most paragraphs are built around a topic sentence, which states the main idea of the paragraph. Also, you already know that the most common position for the main idea is first in the paragraph. If you read a first sentence that clearly *is not* the topic sentence, you might jump to the end of the paragraph and read the last sentence. Your goal as you skim each paragraph should be to get an overview of its structure and content. The first sentence, if it functions

343

as a topic sentence, usually states the main idea and provides clues about how the rest of the paragraph is organized. Try to anticipate the organizational pattern.

The Remainder of the Paragraph. Quickly glance through the remainder of the paragraph. Let your eyes quickly sweep through the paragraph. Try to pick out words that answer who, what, when, where, or how much about the main idea of the paragraph. Also, notice any signal words; they will indicate continuation or change in thought pattern as you glance through the paragraph. Try to notice names, numbers, dates, or places, and capitalized or italicized words or phrases. Also notice any numbered sequences. This quick glance will add to your overall impression of the paragraph and will confirm that you have identified the main idea of the paragraph.

The Title or Legend of Any Maps, Graphs, Charts, or Diagrams. The title or legend will state concisely what the typographical aid depicts and suggest what important event, idea, or relationship it is intended to emphasize.

The Last Paragraph. The last paragraph often provides a conclusion or summary for the article. It might concisely state the main points of the article or it might suggest new directions for considering the topic.

Now that you are familiar with the procedure for skimming, you are probably wondering how fast to skim, how much to skip, and what level of comprehension to expect. Generally, your reading rate should be 800 wpm or above for skimming, or about three or four times as fast as you normally read. This rate is quite reasonable if you realize that when skimming you read approximately one-quarter of the material. It follows then that you should be able to cover the article four times as fast.

As a general rule of thumb, you should skip more than you read. Although the amount to skip varies according to the type of material, a safe estimate might be that you should skip about 70 to 80 percent of the material. Because you are skipping large portions of the material, your comprehension will be limited. An acceptable level of comprehension for skimming is approximately 50 percent.

To give you a better idea of what the technique of skimming is like, the following article has been *highlighted* to indicate the portions of the article that you might read when skimming. Of course, this is not the only correct way to skim this article. Depending on their purposes for reading, readers could identify different parts of the article as important. Also, readers might select different key words and phrases while glancing through each paragraph.

344

USED CARS: CAN YOU TELL WHEN THEY'RE REALLY GOOD BUYS?

Lillian Borgeson

Where to look, how to spot trouble, tips on the test drive

Back in the days when car styles changed more often than hemlines, the biennial trade-in was an essential middle-class status symbol, like the non-working wife. People bought new cars whether they needed to or not, and the used-car lots were jammed with immaculate cream puffs whose only sin was that they had last year's hood-line.

But that's no longer the case. Today automotive styling changes tend to be slow and relatively subtle; and with prices for new "family" models nudging $10,000, the typical owner feels a powerful incentive to hold onto a car until it shows signs of going sour. The inevitable result: *good* used cars are much harder to find than they used to be.

WHERE TO LOOK

Private-party transactions account for most used-car sales, and the reason is obvious: by eliminating the dealer and his markup, buyer and seller both can come out ahead. However, there are some drawbacks. Since often you'll be dealing with a stranger, it may be a good idea to bring along a friend as a safety precaution. You almost always have to pay the full price in cash, and you're buying the car "as is": there's no recourse if a major problem develops soon after you buy. Also, private sellers sometimes have exaggerated notions of value. The price in a private-party deal should never exceed the "retail" value of the car as shown in the *Kelley Blue Book* (which you can see in the car-loan department at your bank), and bargaining may make it considerably lower.

If you're prepared to pay full "retail" for a good late-model car, scout the new-car dealerships in or near high-income neighborhoods. In general, new-car dealers tend to keep and resell only the best of the cars they take in trade (the clunkers are wholesaled to used-car lots in low-budget neighborhoods); and since they generally have well-equipped service facilities, they may offer warranties for some or all of the used cars they sell.

You may also want to check the used-car lots maintained by the big car-rental companies. On the minus side, retired rentals tend to have many more miles on them than privately owned cars; on the plus side, they've been regularly and carefully serviced. Also, the big rental companies like Hertz and Avis do provide 12,000-mile/12-month warranties for the "power train" which includes the engine, transmission, drive shaft, and differential, thus covering most major repairs. To find out where they're selling in your area, call these toll-free numbers: Avis, (800) 331-1212; Hertz, (800) 654-3131.

STRAINING OUT THE LEMONS

No matter where you shop, don't buy a used car blindly. When you see one that appeals to you, take these steps:

Before you get in the car, look under it for leaks. Then sight along each side of the exterior; ripples in the metal or small differences in paint color may be clues that the car has been repaired after a major wreck. Check the condition of the tires; uneven wear usually means mechanical problems. And look for rusted-out areas, especially under the fenders and under any mats; rust that's gone all the way through the metal is always bad news.

Inside the car, first press your foot on the brake pedal and hold it down for about a minute; it should stop well above the floor and stay there without gradually sinking lower. Then turn on the ignition and make sure all the instrument-panel indicators work; check all the lights, inside and out, and don't forget the windshield wipers. If possible, start the engine when it's cold, with your ear cocked for weird sounds. After a brief warm-up, press the accelerator hard and look out the rear window for smoke: white smoke may just mean some water condensed in the exhaust system; black smoke suggests that the carburetor or choke needs work; but blue smoke is often a sign of major engine trouble.

Always test drive a car that passes your preliminary examination. Does it pick up speed smoothly? Accelerate reasonably well? Shift up and down smoothly and quietly? Do the brakes work smoothly and quickly, without pulling to one side or the other? Make at least a couple of right and left turns; the steering should feel neither too loose nor too tight. To check the suspension and shock absorbers, try to include a rough road or potholed street in your test run. And if possible, drive the car through a narrow alley or on a road with steep, high banks; engine and exhaust noises will be magnified, and you're likelier to hear anything abnormal.

As the final step before you buy, take the car to a mechanic you trust; or check local Yellow Pages under Automobile Diagnostic Service. You should be able to find someone who will check and test-drive the car for about $25. If your expert finds major flaws, you'll probably want to keep looking; if he finds minor problems, ask for an estimate of the repair costs, and use that figure as leverage in price bargaining for this car.

A few years ago a study sponsored by the Federal Trade Commission showed that one out of three used-car buyers is hit with substantial repair costs soon after making the purchase. This spring, the FTC will present to Congress a new regulation that, if passed, will require used-car dealers to reveal some facts about their wares via a "buyers' guide" window sticker. Though the regulation would not demand full disclosure, every little bit helps.

TYPES OF SKIMMING

Now that you are familiar with the steps involved in skimming, you should realize that it is very similar to a technique you learned much earlier in this book — prereading. Actually, prereading may be considered as a form of skimming. As you have seen throughout this book, it is necessary to adapt reading techniques to suit your purpose and the circumstances under which you are reading. Similarly, it is necessary to treat skimming as a flexible procedure that can be modified to meet your needs. Generally, there are three reasons for using skimming.

1. To become generally familiar with the organization and content of material *before* reading it. This is the type of skimming that is equivalent to prereading. Since an earlier chapter was devoted to prereading, no further discussion should be necessary here.

2. To get an *overview* of the content and organization without reading the material completely. Often referred to as skim-reading, this form of skimming is used when you do not intend to return to reading the material for a second, more thorough reading and when skimming alone meets your needs.

   Skim-reading is a means of covering material to get a "general picture" of the article's content. Overview skimming is a more thorough treatment of the material than is preread skimming. In preread skimming, since you will read the material thoroughly later, you can afford to miss some ideas. In skim-reading, on the other hand, you do not intend to read it later and cannot afford to skip over ideas.

3. To go back over material you have already read to review the main points of the material. Review skimming, then, is used only with material you have *already* read. Your purpose is to become reacquainted with the basic content and organization of the material. Chapter 9 treated review in detail, including various methods.

   The technique for review skimming is quite similar to prereading. By reading introductions, headings, first sentences, and conclusions or summaries, you are encountering, once again, the most important ideas contained in the material.

Limitations of Skimming

Whenever you skim, it is important to be aware that this technique has its limitations. Since skimming involves skipping large portions of the material, your comprehension will be restricted to the larger, more important ideas. You should not expect to retain the less important facts and details. You may even miss some of the main ideas in the selection. As a general rule, you can expect a comprehension level of about 50 percent when skimming. It is important, then, to skim a passage only when a relatively low comprehension level is compatible with your purposes.

The effectiveness of skimming is also limited by the type of material to be skimmed. In particular, the content and organization of the material, as well as your knowledge and experience with the subject matter, largely determine how effectively you will be able to skim it. For instance, an article that contains many headings would be easier to skim than one that contains no headings. Similarly, an article written about an everyday, general-information topic might be easier to skim than a selection from a technical report or scientific textbook. On the other hand, for a technical report on a subject you have studied and are quite familiar with, skimming may be a very simple task. In deciding to skim a piece of material, be sure that it appears sufficiently well structured and that you will be able to understand the subject without reading the entire passage.

SKIMMING VARIOUS TYPES OF MATERIAL

Effective skimming hinges on the reader's ability to recognize the organization and structure of the material and to use that awareness to locate the important parts that convey the main ideas of the selection. You can see, then, that the procedure for skimming outlined in the earlier section "How to Skim" is a general guide that must be adapted to the material.

Slight adjustments in the basic technique can allow you to apply it to a number of common types of reading material. The following suggestions should help you become more versatile and flexible with the technique of skimming.

Newspaper Articles

The title is particularly important in news articles because it may, in the briefest possible way, present a summary of the article. However, other titles may be misleading, intended only to catch the reader's interest. Many news stories follow a particular organizational pattern. The main idea, event, or problem is stated in summary form at the beginning of the article. Then the most important details are provided. The rest of the article then contains related information and background facts and details to provide a context for the story. A news story, then, is developed using a "most-to-least-important" order of information.

To skim a news article, pay attention to the title, read the first few paragraphs completely, then read only the first sentences of the remaining paragraphs. If you are already familiar with the background details of the news item, you might skip entirely the last few paragraphs of the article.

Now, try skimming the following news article, noticing the pattern of development.

MONEY + MYTH = DISNEY

David Nyhan
THE BOSTON GLOBE

KISSIMMEE, Fla. The Sunbelt's best example of the development ethic — creating wealth out of raw land and nothing else but sun, sand and water — is Disney World.

It's probably the safest community of its size in the world, yet the psychological overtones can be rather scary. It can be exciting on one level, or unrelentingly boring. It's very expensive, and very 1984. It's the wave of the future, a nostalgia-drenched tide from the past.

Almost 14 million people visited this place last year. That's the equivalent of one out of every 16 Americans. Disney World "is the No. 1 destination in the world," boasts a heavyweight claque of civic boosters, though a contention such as that is hard to measure. It's hard to compare anything to Disney World.

The profit figures are buried in corporate balance sheets, but the flow of people is staggering. It has become a way of life, a myth created out of a central Florida swamp, one of the wonders of the modern world, but a wonder you have to wonder about.

Big Brother Walter's awesome power is everywhere. The electronic signals that begin programming your behavior (it will be correct) and outlining your choices (they are limited) come over the car radio as you join a queue of cars and campers and buses crawling patiently into the Magic Kingdom's 40,000-odd acres. Parking is only 50 cents a car. That is the last real bargain of the day, unless you are thrilled by re-creations of images you've seen in Disney entertainment over the decades. A typical family of four can easily drop $70 or $80 for the day, a day that will seem more memorable the younger you are.

You get shuffled into one of the huge satellite parking lots, named after the cuddly animal figures that serve as corporate logos for the Disney fantasy. You get directed to a waiting area for a tractor-pulled tram train, and the first of hundreds of loudspeakers you will encounter this day begins assaulting your ears.

Uniformed young attendants, relentlessly courteous, recite their mechanical greetings and cautionary notes. By the end of the day you will feel as though you've been through boot camp, Disney style.

Cash is extracted beginning at the ticket gates, where a typical admission for the day is about $10 per head. Human behavior is modified by tremendously complex and shrewd engineering. Rare is the parent who can withstand the power of a kid who's just seen Mickey Mouse lead a band down Main Street and wants something from a shop or a souvenir stand or a fast-food concession. The coercion is based on

349

kid fantasies, and as every parent of a child exposed to televised images knows, that power is considerable.

A day at Disney is a programmed experience. Last year people went through at the rate of almost 38,000 a day. What other city of 38,000 people, which employs probably 50,000 people, has had only one armed crime in its history?

That came last March. A tourist's wallet was heisted at gunpoint on the Monorail. Park officials invited the victim and his family back, with free passes. He said thanks anyway, he'd just spend the rest of his Florida stay by the motel pool.

From the ticket pavilion you ride the famous circle-route monorail or take a large ferry across a huge man-made lagoon. Huge motels dot the complex. The lines in mid-March were incredible. My over-all feeling after a day was of waiting and walking amidst a faceless throng. It feels strange when someone is not treading on your heels. You can't do half of it in one long day. Through it all runs the seamless web of illusion.

The customers are skillfully shunted from one place to another. There is artful landscaping, but the peaceful lagoon, with its crescent of white, sandy beach, is scrupulously bare of people. You can't walk out there. Places to go off a bit and get away from the crush are for looking, not for walking.

The underwater ride in a replica of Capt. Nemo's submarine is totally ersatz. The flora and fauna, the underwater wrecks and effects, are all imitation, as they would have to be. Animals are statues, the sound effects and the visuals are all out of a Hollywood set. Not till you get back to your car after an endless day of walking is it quiet and peaceful. Your identity was stripped on the way in, you get it back when you leave.

And yet it was safe, it was wholesome, it was clean. The janitors come in at night and hose down the whole Magic Kingdom. The trash is trucked away through underground viaducts. It is some kind of triumph of human engineering, though George Orwell would question the cost in terms of spontaneity.

"They've set up their own separate country over there at Disney," said an Orlando civic leader. "They could conduct their own nuclear tests, and we wouldn't know about it. They've been good corporate citizens, their planning is comprehensive and efficient. They can move people around better than anyone, they have a real knowledge of how to move people. But they think they are only answerable to Walt, and he's in heaven."

The incredible complex of 45 square miles, "twice the size of Manhattan," is 25 miles southwest of Orlando, sprawling over parts of two counties. It is a virtually self-contained city created out of swampy wilderness. When the late Walt Disney conceived the notion, he had been dismayed at what happened to Disneyland, his original theme park in Anaheim, Calif.

That project was besieged by neighbors who crowded in, wanting to share the prosperity and latch onto the crowd that he drew. This time, he wanted his own enclave, with buffers of space to protect him from the camp followers who envisioned profiting with their own tourist attractions.

"Disney was given almost total carte blanche when Walt decided to build," said a local expert. "He felt it was required because of the horrors around Anaheim, the hotels and motels and fast-food joints across from that theme park. He made sure that would not occur in Florida."

The Disney empire is now run by the founder's son-in-law, Ron Miller, the president and chief operating officer of Disney Productions, who married Walt's daughter, Diane.

Disney lawyers negotiated with the state of Florida, which was eager to provide virtually all the legal help Disney wanted. The lawyers came up with a creature called "The Reedy Creek Improvement District." It gives Disney World virtually its own government, except taxing powers. Disney has its own government, utility company, phone network. The Magic Kingdom, centerpiece of the park, is built over its own subterranean network of roads and storage facilities.

The only people allowed to live there are two or three dozen key employees who are elected to office to man the shadow government. Disney can operate as an omniscient licensee regulating all commerce in the park. It can apply for government grants. At peak periods there are 14,000 employees, most of them in near minimum-wage jobs. (Last month, as Disney World passed its 10th anniversary, several of those employees complained about working conditions to the New York Times, in unauthorized interviews which they said could have cost them their jobs.)

And yes, the enabling legislation passed by the state allows Disney the right, under certain controls, to build a nuclear power installation, though that is subject to federal regulation now.

The latest wrinkle is something called EPCOT: experimental prototype city of tomorrow. It will provide something like 10,000 more jobs, local tourism experts claim. It is designed to bring paying customers back. The original dream of some kind of experimental community has been modified to more of an international trade fair, on various themes, to be opened in another year. Work is already under way. The whole of central Florida's business establishment seems convinced that Disney must top Disney World with EPCOT.

"If you turned Disney into a democracy, your 45-minute wait to get into Space Mountain would be eight hours, there'd be six fist fights — and people would be killing each other to get on," says a local community leader. "That courtesy and good humor and aggressive organization and enthusiasm is an unnatural act. It's forced. Everyone has bad days. But you can't do that over at Disney. Disney looked at human nature, he took the good traits, and he banned the bad ones. You're only allowed the best of mankind over there."

Magazine Articles

As is true of news stories, the title of a magazine article is often very descriptive and identifies the subject of the article. Magazine articles, too, have their own organizational pattern. A magazine article often begins with several paragraphs that express the author's central thoughts, which will be developed throughout the article. The rest of the article, then, provides facts, information, or arguments that support the author's central thought. The last several paragraphs often contain a summary or concluding statement about the subject.

In skimming a magazine article, the first several and last several paragraphs are most important and require more careful skimming than do those in the middle. As you skim, try to identify the author's central thought, check to see how that thought is developed and supported in the body of the article, and look for the author's final statement or suggested directions for further thought given in the summary or conclusion.

Notice that in the following short magazine article the title and subtitle clearly identify the subject of the article. Now skim-read the article to find out what the fast method of reducing stress is and how it works.

CALM DOWN IN SIX SECONDS
How to Handle Stress with Fast Method

Barbara Lang Stern

Do you have an effective technique that you use regularly to reduce your level of stress? If not, you may be among the many people who intellectually recognize the dangers of chronic stress — perhaps even have benefited from relaxation exercises — but somehow haven't made stress reduction part of their daily schedule. And you may be especially fascinated by a unique six-second exercise conceived and developed by Charles F. Stroebel, M.D., Ph.D., director of research at The Institute of Living in Hartford, Connecticut, and professor of psychiatry at the University of Connecticut Medical School.

"The difficulty most people experience in maintaining relaxation routines over the long haul was one major reason we wanted an alternative to existing stress-reduction techniques," commented Dr. Stroebel. "Our other goal was to have people practicing a reversal of the emergency fight-or-flight response at the very *scene of the crime of stress,* not in a quiet clinic or room at home.

"What we did was to analyze closely the first six to ten seconds of the emergency startle response," Dr. Stroebel explains. "The first thing that happens is the activity of the sympathetic nervous system increases. You can actually measure the pupils of the eyes dilating, trying to collect more information on what there is to be afraid about.

"The second reaction is increase in muscle tension, initially in the face around the eyes and mouth, and then extending gradually over the entire body. You can observe it in yourself when you're driving and catch yourself clenching the steering wheel.

"The third *typical* response is a catch or hold in the breath — although a few people will over-breathe or hyperventilate.

"Fourth is a clamping down of the blood flow in the hands and feet. The body is redirecting the blood to the deep muscles that would be used for running or fighting. This is one reason why many people who are in a chronic activation of the fight-or-flight response have constantly cold hands or feet.

"The final thing we observe within the initial six-to-ten-second period is actual clenching of the jaw. It's equivalent to the dog's baring his fangs going into battle, although more subtle. Jaw-clenching, called bruxism when it happens during sleep, is probably affecting close to 30 percent of our population today, and it's thought to be one factor behind the greatly increased amount of periodontal or gum disease," adds Dr. Stroebel.

In fact, the list of stress-related maladies is overwhelming and still growing, as research shows that chronic stress affects every system and organ in our body and may well be implicated in almost all physiological and many emotional problems we suffer from.

"What we have developed," continues Dr. Stroebel, "is a six-second exercise called the 'quieting reflex,' or 'QR'. This is a set of behaviors incompatible with the emergency response that you initially perform consciously but, with practice over a four- to six-month period, will become an *automatic reflex*.

"Step one is to become aware of whatever is annoying you or getting on your nerves. That's your cue.

"Now we ask you to give yourself the suggestion, 'Alert mind, calm body.' The idea is that most of the stresses and strains we encounter in daily life cannot be helped by getting our bodies ready to fight a saber-toothed tiger! The six-second quieting reflex provides a pause during which you can decide whether to shift into passing gear because your body *can* help you, or whether to leave your body out of it, which is appropriate most of the time.

"Third, we ask you to smile *inwardly* with your eyes and your mouth, to reverse the tendency of the eyes and mouth to go into a grim set. You can experiment and get this *feeling* — nothing obvious to observers.

"The last step is to inhale a breath easily to the count of about three, imagining that it comes through pores in the bottoms of your feet. When you give the brain that image, you actually get the sensation of flowing warmth and flowing heaviness coming up through the middle of your legs. It's identical to what people learn through biofeedback techniques. Then, as you exhale your breath back down through your legs and out those imaginary pores, let your jaw, tongue, and shoulders go slightly limp, feeling that wave of heaviness and warmth flowing to the toes. And then resume normal activity!"

When Dr. Stroebel developed QR in 1974, he worked only with professionals and patients. Subsequently, a classroom program for elementary schoolchildren was developed, recommended by the National Education Association, and has been used since October 1980, with about half a million students nationally. Currently, audio tapes for the lay public are being recorded (BMA Audio Cassettes), and a book, *QR, The Quieting Reflex,* is scheduled (Putnam) for spring, 1982.

Says Dr. Stroebel, "Most people notice that the quieting reflex feels good the very first time they run through it. And about 80 percent of individuals *will* develop an automatic skill if they practice the technique each time they feel annoyed or stressed — which is certainly fifty times a day if you live in a busy city."

Dr. Stroebel adds the caution that anyone who takes medication for diabetes, high blood pressure, epilepsy, or a thyroid condition should consult his or her physician before beginning QR.

353

The first paragraph of this article introduced the topic, stress reduction, and stated the thesis: that there is a unique six-second exercise designed to reduce stress. Then, the writer explained that the exercise was developed by studying the emergency startle response. Next, the four steps in the exercise were explained, and finally, the article concluded with some general comments about its use and effectiveness.

Nonfiction Books

Popular bookstores and bookracks in large stores carry numerous nonfiction paperbacks, many of which become best sellers, on a wide variety of general interest subjects. These include such books as the "how-to" books (*How I Made a Million Dollars in Real Estate*), the popular psychology books (*Looking Out for #1*), books on currently popular areas of interest such as types of music, political figures, diet and exercise, sports, and hobbies. Skimming is a very useful way of becoming familiar with the general content of nonfiction books and allows you to keep current with books in your area of interest or with current best sellers. Generally, you can skim a nonfiction book in an hour or less and become quite familiar and conversant about the focus, approach, and general content of the book.

To skim a nonfiction book, use the following steps as a guide, adapting them, as necessary, to suit the characteristics of the book you are skimming.

1. Read the title, subtitle, and the front and back of the book jacket. Often non-fiction books include brief summaries or descriptions of the book on the front or back cover.
2. Check the author and try to establish the author's credentials for writing the book.
3. Carefully read the table of contents. If chapter titles and subdivisions are included, then this is one of the most useful parts of the book to use in skimming. The table of contents is an outline of the book and from it you can learn the author's approach to the subject and the overall organization used. You can also identify individual chapters that may be most important to skim.
4. Read the introduction or preface. The author normally details there his or her reasons for writing the book, explains its focus and overall content, and describes its organization. You can see, then, that the preface or introduction, along with the table of contents, provides considerable information about the content and organization of the text.

354

5.   Skim each chapter. After skimming the first several chapters you will quickly discover how the chapters are organized and where the most information is contained. Until you discover the author's particular format, read the first few and last paragraphs completely. Read all headings and notice any maps, pictures, charts, or graphs that may be included. If there are no headings or if you feel that you still do not have a grasp of what the chapter is about, then read the first sentence of each paragraph or of several paragraphs on each page.

As soon as you realize that a section is unimportant, repetitious, or provides only examples or explains ideas that you are already familiar with, you should skip over it, even if it is a major part of a chapter.

The chapters to which you should pay most attention are the first and the last, as well as any that you have identified as especially useful during your study of the table of contents. You can expect that the first chapter will lay out the plan for the book, explain its purpose or focus and reveal the author's general attitude and approach toward the subject. In the final chapter, you can predict that the author will summarize his or her ideas or present future directions, solutions, related problems, or concerns about the subject.

Textbook Chapters

When you are using textbook chapters as additional sources, references, or supplementary materials, it may be appropriate to skim a textbook chapter. Normally, however, for textbooks used as a regular part of a course you should plan to read chapters thoroughly, preread skimming them prior to reading and review skimming after reading.

To skim a textbook chapter, be sure to use end-of-chapter aids as well as in-chapter features as a guide to important content. Recall and discussion questions, vocabulary lists, and outlines are all useful in locating important ideas in the chapter. Within the chapter pay attention to introductions and summaries, titles, headings, typographical aids, and graphic material.

EXERCISE 15-1

Directions: *Skim-read the following newspaper article. Be sure not to spend more than one minute. After you have finished, answer the questions below.*

MACOMBER ANIMAL FARM WITH A MISSION

Emilie Tavel Livezey
THE CHRISTIAN SCIENCE MONITOR

FRAMINGHAM, Mass. Three curious Canada geese swoop low over the Macomber Farm and Education Center and splash to a noisy landing in the pond — honk-honking as if to ask: "What's going on here now?"

These geese have reason to be perplexed. For generations the birds have fed on corn spread out for them here at what was once Raceland, the 46-acre estate of late Boston financier George R. Macomber. But the site was recently converted into what may be the only facility of its kind, to explore an issue rarely presented to the public: humane treatment for farm animals.

A "goose's eye" view reveals that in place of Mr. Macomber's private steeplechase and racetrack is a brand new farm, so manicured and perfect in every detail that it looks like a child's play set of handsome barns, freshly erected fences, grazing horses, mooing cattle and crowing roosters.

In every barn and winding path, schoolchildren squeal with delight at the animals they are seeing and petting — often for the first time.

Macomber Farm is the dream of David S. Claflin, president of the Massachusetts Society for the Prevention of Cruelty to Animals (MSPCA). The land was bequeathed by Macomber — a 38-year trustee of the non-profit, non-tax supported society. But it has taken the MSPCA five years and $7 million in private contributions to put together this unique learning center, designed to show how farm animals can be raised efficiently in an atmosphere of warmth, serenity and loving care.

Why farm animals? Because the MSPCA believes that today — unlike earlier eras when food animals were grown on private farms — this is the class of animal which is suffering the most from human abuse. The principal culprit: "factory farming."

This relatively new method of mass-producing food and fiber products from animals treats sentient creatures as if they were unfeeling bio-machines. Lifelong confinement completely restricts their normal movements, social interaction and natural way of life.

Nancy Ann Payton, the MSPCA's humane issues analyst, says, "If we were keeping dogs and cats in the same condition that we are keeping calves, swine, chickens and all these food animals, the public would be appalled, the outcry would be tremendous. We would have laws to protect them as we have laws to protect pets and zoo animals."

But, she says, few consumers have any idea of how animals that eventually wind up on the dinner table are treated while alive.

For example, Miss Payton reports that to satisfy the gourmet trade's demand for "white" (extremely tender) veal, on most factory farms calves are confined in stalls measuring one foot 10 inches wide by four feet six inches long, to prevent them from exercising and developing muscles. Similarly, 90 percent of all chickens are raised in layered cages so crowded that three or four must share a space no larger than a folded daily newspaper. Kept indoors, they never see the light of the sun.

It is against this background of mistreatment that Macomber Farm was established. According to Macomber's director, Robert A. Johnson, the farm's impact can be compared to "hitting the public over the head with a velvet hammer, to attract its attention and to kindle a spark of interest in and appreciation of farm animals — and concern for their welfare."

At Macomber, every animal is clean and in perfect condition — unafraid, contented, playful, showing forth the kind consideration it is receiving. Each candidate has been carefully "interviewed" to make sure it is friendly enough to enter public life at the farm. And each of the six animal barns has been designed to provide maximum comfort for the different species.

Macomber's large staff of well-trained young tour guides has already dubbed one barn the "Horse Hilton." Amenities include: box stalls large enough to move around and lie down in; a special shower stall for hosing down; plenty of good ventilation, plus a fire alarm system. And windows so horses can look out at the landscape. Meanwhile, goats can cavort on their own manmade hill. And dairy cows take delight in the latest equipment in their gleaming milking parlor.

Pigs — often mistakenly thought to be naturally dirty — are understood at Macomber to be smart and clean. When they roll in mud it is only to cool their bristly hides, because they have no sweat glands. Here a sprinkler system eliminates that need by protecting them from the heat. There are even toys to play with. When piglets want water, they push a valve with their tiny snouts to release water into their drinking trough.

The animals are the stars of this barnyard — but every performer needs an audience. Since Macomber opened early in May, several thousand schoolchildren have arrived by the busload helping to fill this role. Every exhibit in each of the eight barns invites visitors to play games in order to learn facts about farm creatures.

At one exhibit, you can pretend to be a horse. Feel for yourself what it's like to stride with a horse's gait or strain to pull a miniature milk wagon along a track. Then put on a fiberoptic sight mask and learn that a horse sees in almost a complete circle, but nothing at all directly in front of him.

Is your sense of smell as acute as that of a pig? Try sniffing your way out of a scent maze — hogs are masters at it.

In every animal barn, computer games — played by pushing keys — flash slow-motion drawings of animals onto a screen, ask questions, and give answers.

While having fun, children begin to get the idea. They crowd around this reporter's tape recorder: "I learned that animals need shelter, that they like being with their own species, and that they help people survive, like cows give milk," says one third-grader.

Chimes in another: "I learned that animals used to be wild a long time ago and now they aren't wild, and so we have to take care of them."

That is precisely the message Macomber Farm is intended to convey. "What we have got to get across to the public," says Miss Payton, "is that if you are going to eat and use animal products, you have to take responsibility to insure that they are raised, maintained, and killed in the most humane conditions possible."

As the trend towards factory farming in America intensifies, concern about the conditions it creates is also rising among humane groups. MSPCA and its sister organization, the American Humane Education Society (whose headquarters are also at the farm) are in the vanguard.

Miss Payton says the public's current attitude is that it is all right to treat farm animals differently from pets and zoo residents, because they are sources of food. "But that makes them second- or third-class animals. We feel that a calf is just as deserving as a dog in a kennel."

As a first step, the public must be informed and sensitized to what the humane community regards as the six basic rights of farm animals — freedom to turn around, get up, lie down, stretch their limbs, groom themselves, and enjoy the companionship of their own kind. Until awareness grows, Miss Payton says lobbyists cannot bring effective pressure upon lawmakers to introduce humane legislation. One Massachusetts legislator expressed a common viewpoint by exclaiming, "Don't even talk to me about chickens!"

At present, MSPCA reports "there are no federal laws that regulate the treatment of farm animals during the rearing process." Most states, including Massachusetts, have anticruelty statutes. Yet in this state, as in most others, such laws do not specifically protect farm animals.

With the help of Macomber Farm and other projects, MSPCA hopes eventually to win clear legal rights for livestock. As Miss Payton writes in *Animal*, the MSPCA magazine:

"Humane societies have avoided the intensive-farming issue, citing a myriad of rationalizations for not actively opposing this blatant cruelty. It is about time we changed our perspective. Instead of thinking of reasons why not to act, let us concentrate on the one reason why we must act — the animals are suffering!"

1. What is the MSPCA?

    _____

2. What is its purpose?

    _____

3. How are animals treated at Macomber Farm?

    _____

4. Are visitors allowed? If so, what is available to them?

    _____

EXERCISE 15-2

Directions: *Skim-read the following article. Be sure not to spend more than three minutes reading the article. After you have finished skimming, answer the questions that follow.*

JOBS FOR NEW COLLEGE GRADS

New engineers and computer scientists are still at the top of corporate recruiters' hiring lists, but prospects are pretty good for other disciplines as well. The survey sampler gives you a taste of the full report.

Despite a still-sputtering economy, the job market for 1982 college graduates promises to be at least as strong as it was for last June's class. Competition for jobs will be keen, and once again engineering and computer science graduates will be most in demand. This is the general picture that emerges from the latest annual *Changing Times* survey of jobs for new graduates.

Our survey of corporations and government agencies that provide starting jobs for new college grads has turned up descriptions of hundreds of specific job openings with 128 different employers. Three-quarters of survey participants said they would be hiring the same number of new graduates as they did last year or more. Nearly 70% reported shortages of candidates for certain kinds of jobs — mostly engineers and computer scientists, but also in fields as diverse as actuarial science, marketing and sales, dairy and agricultural science, health care and patent examining.

Some 77% of survey participants seek starting engineers, and 64% want computer science grads. Demand for accounting majors is close behind at 55%, and graduates in business, marketing and economics are being sought by 45% of the surveyed employers. Twenty-nine percent want physical sciences graduates, 23% are looking for math majors and 16% anticipate openings for liberal arts grads.

WHO GETS HIRED

Besides specific academic backgrounds, campus recruiters say they are looking for students with good grades, some work experience and a record of participation in extracurricular activities. These qualities are also mentioned frequently:

• *A good attitude toward work.*   One recruiter says he looks for students displaying good common sense, a good personality and a willingness to work: "Students who think industry owes them a living will get a rude awakening."

• *Communications skills.*   Whatever the job, employers value the ability to correspond and converse intelligibly.

• *Self-confidence.*   Recruiters are impressed by applicants who have a good idea of where they want to go in life and have made a realistic appraisal of how to apply their backgrounds to the career path that will get them there.

• *A businesslike appearance and attitude.*   Students will do well to model their grooming and dress after the executives pictured in *Business Week* and *Working Woman* and to be familiar with the business journals.

USING THE SURVEY

The survey listing is designed to be used in a job search. It enables you to take the initiative in contacting potential employers by providing information you can use to focus on companies that offer the most promising job opportunities.

In the sample from the survey listing . . . note for each employer there is a name and address of the person or department to which you should address job inquiries. The next column indicates, in brief, the nature of the employer's business.

In the third column are the specific academic credentials the employer wants in job candidates: A = accounting; B = business-marketing-economics; C = computer science; E = engineering; L = liberal arts-social sciences; M = mathematics; P = physical sciences; O = other specialties. Unless otherwise indicated, all the jobs call for a bachelor's degree.

The next column shows the kinds of jobs the employer plans to fill with new graduates. The last column notes types of candidates the company says it is having some difficulty finding.

To make best use of the listing, first select the companies and jobs for which you feel your background and interests suit you. Then do some research on each firm you've selected. Brochures and other references in your placement office library will tell you about the operations and structure of most of these firms and agencies. Also check a company's latest annual report to see how it has been performing. Consult current business periodicals to get a feeling for trends in the industries you want to work in and how they affect the companies you will apply to.

You'll score points by demonstrating this interest and knowledge when you write your job inquiry letters. For example, you might include a reference to the company's standing in its industry or comment on a bit of recent news about its product line.

Your inquiry letter should also indicate the particular job or field in which you are interested. Explain how your background suits you for it and why you're attracted to the firm.

Don't fail to ask for an interview. If you have already signed up for a campus interview with the company's recruiter, mention that fact so that the official who receives your letter can alert the recruiter to look for you. If the company hasn't scheduled a recruiting visit to your campus, suggest several dates when you could visit the company's office.

Don't waste your time, or an employer's, by writing to scores of companies you haven't bothered to learn anything about or by applying for jobs for which you clearly don't have the required credentials. The lack of focus in such an approach will be obvious, and your letters will be eliminated in the first screening.

Attach to your letter a résumé that includes your academic record, with major areas of study and your grades or grade point average. Describe your part-time and summer work experience and extracurricular activities in school, especially leadership roles you've had in campus organizations and projects. Include addresses and telephone numbers where you can be reached at school and on vacations.

Be certain your letters and résumé are neatly typed and free of spelling and grammatical errors. If you can't type, pay to have it done. If you're not sure about grammatical construction, ask someone who knows. A well-done letter and résumé will surely get the attention you seek. By the same token, badly written materials can spoil what might have otherwise been a good first impression.

"I am impressed with the caliber of students on campuses," says Elizabeth Wenzler, college relations manager for Gimbels-Midwest. "They are neat, serious and very professional. But many of the business students lack communication skills — in both writing and speaking."

Get cracking on your letter-writing campaign right away. Corporate recruiters schedule most of their hiring to coincide with June graduation dates, and there are a lot of interviews to be lined up and contacts to be nurtured between now and then.

JOB HUNTING TIPS

Changing Times asked corporate recruiters, who interview students on hundreds of college campuses each year, for tips students can use to enhance their marketability. Among those cited most often:

• Set specific, realistic career goals, and direct your job search to companies whose jobs and business fit those goals. "Too many graduates say they are interested in 'management,' or use some other vague generalization to describe their job objective," says Bill O. Miller, manager of salaried personnel for Cooper Tire & Rubber Co. Better to spend the time necessary to sharpen that objective so that you'll stand out from the crowd.

• Use the resources of your school's placement office and participate in the corporate campus interviews it coordinates.

• Take the time to learn about the companies to which you apply. Familiarity with a company's products and services, the location of its plants and offices, and the nature of its work force will impress corporate interviewers. Ignorance of such matters can create a negative impression. "We don't believe that students take advantage of the information supplied by business organizations to college and university placement offices," says Alton Wright, human resources manager for Belk Stores Services, Inc.

• Sharpen your interview skills. Sheryl Goerke, a recruiter for General Telephone Co. of the Southwest, advises a relaxed approach: "I think probably the most critical information one could give a prospective applicant is to be yourself. Often professors and other school officials give students the dos and don'ts of interviewing . . . and the students' answers end up appearing rehearsed and canned."

361

That's not to say practice can't help hone interview skills. Says Chris H. Hendrick, assistant manager of corporate recruiting for The Gap Stores, Inc., "Counselors may help students eliminate their first interview jitters by role-playing the interview process and analyzing the students' answers."

• Demonstrate that you have given serious thought to what you want to do with your life, not just for your first job but also for your long-term career and personal development.

• Be persistent in your search, and follow up all contacts with employers. Send thank-you notes to interviewers and respond promptly to all correspondence from a company.

A JOB HUNTER'S SAMPLER FROM THE SURVEY

COMPANY AND WHERE TO WRITE	PRINCIPAL PRODUCTS AND SERVICES	ACADEMIC BACKGROUND WANTED[a]	JOBS AVAILABLE	CANDIDATES IN SHORT SUPPLY
ANCHOR HOCKING CORP. Ronald A. MacKenzie Manager, Personnel Services 109 N. Broad St. Lancaster, Ohio 43130	glass tableware and packaging	A, E (mechanical, electrical, chemical, ceramic, civil) P (chemistry, physics)	finance trainee, engineers (process, R&D, supporting manufacturing)	engineers (especially mechanical)
KENDALL CO. John R. Sloan Manager of Employment and College Relations One Federal St. Boston, Mass. 02101	hospital care products	B, C, E	engineers (planning, distribution, process, project), accounting, systems marketing	industrial engineers
LAND O'LAKES, INC. College Relations Representative P.O. Box 116 Minneapolis, Minn. 55440	food marketing and processing, agricultural supply	A, B (MS), C, L, O (dairy science, dairy manufacturing, agriculture-related majors, food technology)	food sales, agriculture sales, dairy representatives, dairy management trainees, accountants, marketing assistants, business analyst programmer, food technologist	dairy science, dairy manufacturing
NEWPORT NEWS SHIPBUILDING Jay O. Dunn 4101 Washington Ave. Newport News, Va. 23607	naval and commercial ship design, construction and repair; commercial nuclear service and repair	C (programming and systems analysis), E (mechanical, electrical, civil, industrial, marine, welding), O (personnel and labor relations —master's degree)	engineers (test, design, plant, industrial, welding, planning), computer programmer analysts, labor relations supervisor	engineering, computer science

A JOB HUNTER'S SAMPLER FROM THE SURVEY (*Cont.*)

COMPANY AND WHERE TO WRITE	PRINCIPAL PRODUCTS AND SERVICES	ACADEMIC BACKGROUND WANTED[a]	JOBS AVAILABLE	CANDIDATES IN SHORT SUPPLY
SOUTH CENTRAL BELL TELEPHONE Co. College Employment Office P.O. Box 2662 3196 Highway 280 South Room 301N-C Birmingham, Ala. 35202	telecommunication service in Alabama, Kentucky, Louisiana, Mississippi, Tennessee	C (BS, MS), M (BS, MS)	programming, systems analyst, communication system representative —business systems	
3M Jennifer H. Weixel Staffing & Employee Resources 3M Ctr. Bldg. 224-1W-02 St. Paul, Minn. 55144	manufacturing— high technology	A, B, C, E, M, P	accounting, engineers (manufacturing and process), product development, EDP	chemical engineering
UNITED STATES NAVY Navy Management Programs 16101 Snow Rd. Brookpark, Ohio 44142	national defense	A, B, C, E (mechanical, electrical, civil, chemical), L, M, P, O (nursing, medicine, law)	financial analyst, navigator-pilot, intelligence analyst, physician, engineers (nuclear, aeronautical, flight), nurse, procurement officer, communications officer, ADP officer	nuclear engineers, physicians
WEYERHAEUSER Co. Dennis L. Vercillo Tacoma, Wash. 98477	forest products manufacturer	A, C (BS, MS), E (BS, MS, chemical, electrical, mechanical), O (BS, MS, pulp and paper technology)	accounting and audit trainees, engineers (process, project, plant)	

[a] *A = accounting, B = business-marketing-economics, C = computer science, E = engineering, L = liberal arts–social sciences, M = mathematics, P = physical sciences, O = other*

1. How does the 1982 job market compare with the previous year's?

   _____

2. List two qualities employers are looking for.

   a) _____

   b) _____

3. List two job hunting tips.

    a) _____

    b) _____

4. What is the purpose of the survey listing?

    _____

5. What tips does the author provide for writing letters of application?

    _____

EXERCISE 15-3

Directions: *Select a chapter from one of your textbooks, skim-read the first five pages of it, and answer the following questions.*

1. What general subject is discussed in the chapter?

    _____

2. How is the chapter organized?

    _____

3. Using your skim-reading, write a brief list of ideas or topics that are discussed in the pages you skimmed.

    _____

    _____

    _____

APPLYING WHAT YOU HAVE LEARNED

Directions: *Choose one of the reading selections at the end of the chapter. Skim-read the selection and answer the multiple choice questions that follow the selection. Do not be concerned if you are unable to answer all the questions correctly; you should expect your rate to be higher but your comprehension lower than on most other readings you have completed up to this point.*

READING SELECTION 25
CREDIT — AND HOW TO SHOP FOR IT

Richard George

Credit is nothing more than rented money. Whether it's a bank credit card, an auto loan, or an installment sales contract, you're using someone else's money, you have to pay for it. Thanks to the federal Truth-in-Lending Act, we have a simple way of measuring what this "rented money" is costing us — by the annual percentage rate (APR). Every time you borrow money, the APR must be clearly stated. To get the cheapest money, simply look for the lowest APR. Don't be confused if the merchant or lender quotes you other interest rates verbally. He may say a loan is "8 percent, simple interest." This is meaningless. Always do your comparison shopping on the basis of *annual percentage rates*.

The Truth-in-Lending law also requires lenders to be specific about finance charges. This is what the "rental fee" works out to in dollars and cents. Wherever you borrow money, the charge will be clearly stated. Look for it. When you see what the cost of the money really works out to, you may decide to postpone the purchase, or seek a better deal elsewhere.

Advertising pitches to the contrary, credit is *not* an extension of income. It's simply a convenient way of spacing out the payments for significant *durable* purchases. If your purchase is gone by the time the bill appears, maybe you shouldn't have charged it.

CREDIT AND INCOME TAXES

All interest paid on loans of all kinds is tax-deductible. Be sure to keep that in mind when working on your tax returns, especially if you make liberal use of revolving credit accounts.

You'll also do well to consider the tax implications of *any* credit transaction. The higher your income level and tax bracket, the cheaper it becomes to borrow, because of the tax deduction involved. For example, if you're in a 30 percent tax bracket (about $20,000 taxable income), and you pay $200 in interest charges on a loan in a year, the loan really costs $140 ($200 minus 30 percent).

PLASTIC MONEY

Advertising has encouraged us to think of a plastic credit card as money — and many people do. But here's an interesting point: people who charge their purchases spend more — as much as 35 percent more — than people who pay cash. So if you're having trouble balancing the family budget, one of the first steps you might take is to hide the credit cards.

Bank credit cards and department store cards are what's known as revolving credit accounts. Usually, if you pay your bill in full within 30 days, you won't have any finance charges at all. But if there's any unpaid portion of your account, you'll get socked with interest charges, which usually run about 18 percent APR — 1½ percent per month. That's not cheap.

There are two main ways of computing the interest. The best from your point of view is the "adjusted balance" method. You'll recognize this system when your statement says something like this: "A finance charge will be added on unpaid previous balances after deducting payments and credits."

This is the way it works. You pay interest on your balance only on the last day, Day 30, of your billing cycle. You could pay in full on Day 29 and get away interest-free. In fact, you can use this system for what amounts to an interest-free 59-day loan. Buy on Day 1 of your cycle. You'll get billed on Day 30, and you'll have until Day 59 to pay.

The second method of computing interest is the "average daily balance" method, and it's used by the two biggies — Master Charge and VISA (BankAmericard) — among others. It is figured by adding up the amounts owed each day of the cycle and dividing by 30. That means that if you buy something early in one cycle and pay late in the next, you're racking up a big fat average daily balance, and that's what the finance charge is levied on.

The moral of the story is this: If you're going to use a revolving credit account for a major purchase, and you know you won't be able to pay the bill in full within 30 days, try to charge at a store that uses "adjusted balance." If you *must* use the average daily balance account, try to buy late in one cycle and pay early in the next. That will minimize your average daily balance.

To organize your strategy, be sure you know the closing dates on all your accounts. You might want to write them down and keep them with your credit cards, so that when you see something you want, you can anticipate when the bill will appear, and how much time you'll have to come up with the cash. By delaying a purchase just a day or two you can often get an extra 30 days to pay.

DISCOUNTS FOR CASH

Merchants who honor bank credit cards pay for the privilege — usually 4 to 5 percent. Of course, that fee is passed on in the form of higher prices. Many merchants now give discounts if you pay with cash. Be sure to ask about it.

CREDIT BUREAUS

Credit bureaus keep track of how you pay your bills. Generally, they are huge, computerized operations that can provide a creditor — a bank, department store, loan company — with a detailed readout on your payment practices. The report includes a credit rating.

All consumers have the legal right to know what's in their credit file. If you're denied credit, the person denying it must tell you if the decision was based either entirely or partly on information in your credit file. If so, the person must give you the name and address of the credit bureau supplying the report.

If you go to that credit bureau *within thirty*

days of being denied credit, they must show you your file and explain it to you, free of charge. Otherwise they may charge you a few dollars.

If you find something in your file that's inaccurate, the credit bureau will reinvestigate it. In many cases, it finds that you're right, and corrects its records. However, if you and the bureau disagree over a certain matter, you have the legal right to have your side of the story entered into the file (in 100 words or less.)

INVESTIGATIVE REPORTS

Credit reports contain *factual, straightforward* information — and nothing else. They show what accounts you've opened, and where, how long you've taken to pay your bills, your present employment and income, how long you've worked at that job, number of dependents, and so on.

There's a different kind of report that involves *opinions* about your "character, general reputation, personal characteristics, or mode of living." This kind of information is in what's called an "investigative consumer report." If you've ever obtained a sizable insurance policy, or been considered for a big job, an investigator probably has questioned your friends, neighbors, employers, and business associates.

Unfortunately, when it comes to investigative reports, your rights are more limited. If you ask, you'll be told the "nature and substance" of the report, but not the sources of the information. If you object to the "nature and substance," you can ask for a reinvestigation, which must be done at your request. If the results of the reinvestigation are still unsatisfactory to you, you have the legal right to enter your side of the story (in 100 words or less) into your file. The problem is that since you don't know the sources of the information, it's hard to be specific in your rebuttal.

By law (the Fair Credit Reporting Act), the person who requests an investigative report must notify you within three days of the request that the report has been ordered. There's one exception. If the report is for an employment position for which you have not applied, you don't have to be notified.

Investigative reports have been the subject of a hot public debate, and numerous exposés have shown that the so-called investigators sometimes dummy up the whole report, or report that they've interviewed people they haven't. Congress has looked into the problem, but at this writing, no concrete action has been taken.

RETAIL SALES CONTRACTS

Many big ticket items — large appliances, color TVs, furniture — are sold on installment sales contracts of banks, finance companies, and some retail stores. If you buy this way, you're well-advised to read the fine print very carefully before signing.

For example, the form may not have enough lines for you to list "other accounts." The salesman may tell you it makes no difference: "Just write down 'I have no other debts,' and let it go at that." Ignore this kind of advice. Be sure to list all your debts even if you have to attach another page. If you don't, and anything goes wrong, the creditor can charge fraud.

Some such contracts include credit life insurance, so that if anything should happen to you, the loan would be paid off. You don't *have* to have credit life insurance, and if you decide you do want it, you can probably purchase it elsewhere for less. Don't sign an agreement that requires you to pay for credit life insurance you don't want.

Be sure to check the annual percentage rate and the finance charge. The APR may be quite high — over 20 percent in some cases. You can probably do better by shopping around.

Also look out for an "acceleration" clause. It sounds like this: "Any default hereunder by the Buyer, including failure to make any payment when due, may at Seller's option accelerate all remaining payments and Seller may repossess the property." In other words, if you miss one payment, the entire outstanding balance can come due at once.

Some contracts may even have a clause that says, in effect, that *nothing* can release you from the contract. That means if you buy a freezer, and it doesn't work, you're obligated to make the payments regardless.

In addition, an installment sales contract may require late-payment penalties. You may be charged $5, for example.

If the lender has to go to court to collect from you, you may be shocked to find out that, according to the contract, *you* pay for *his* lawyer's fees and court costs. Some contracts even contain "confession of judgment" clauses (now illegal in many areas) in which you agree to allow the lender to pick your lawyer, at your expense.

Signing an installment sales contract requires careful consideration because of these and other pitfalls. If you do go this route, be sure to read the fine print very carefully, and don't sign anything you don't understand.

COMPREHENSION TEST 25

Directions: *Circle the letter of the correct answer.*

1. The main purpose of the article is to
   a) discuss the advantages of buying on credit
   b) explain the various practices connected with buying on credit
   c) show how you can lose money by using credit cards
   d) explain the Truth-in-Lending law

2. The Truth-in-Lending law
   a) restricts the amount of interest a lender can charge
   b) limits the amount a lender can lend
   c) requires lenders to state the annual percentage rate of a loan
   d) details procedures for collecting unpaid loans

367

3. "Rented money" does not include
   a) auto loans
   b) bank credit cards
   c) installment sales contracts
   d) bank statements

4. Many people think of plastic credit cards as money because
   a) people would rather carry small plastic cards than the more cumbersome folding bills
   b) the government is trying to discourage paper money
   c) advertisers have encouraged us to do so
   d) banks would prefer to handle transactions with credit cards rather than currency

5. One advantage of a credit bureau is that it provides you with
   a) interest-free money
   b) a convenient method of purchasing goods
   c) a monthly statement
   d) a credit rating

6. In the phrase "any default hereunder" the word "default" means
   a) failure
   b) dispute
   c) increase
   d) error

7. If you have your choice of opening an account that charges interest on "unpaid balance" or one that charges on "average daily balance" you should choose "unpaid balance" because
   a) it allows you to use money without paying interest for up to 59 days
   b) the interest rates are usually lower

   c) it permits you to pay off your account at any rate you choose
   d) a minimum monthly payment is not required

8. If a credit bureau were to call and ask you questions about the reputation of someone you work with, you might assume that your coworker had
   a) experienced problems paying off debts
   b) recently purchased a new or used car
   c) applied for a large insurance policy
   d) applied for an oil company credit card

9. Which of the following expressions would the writer most likely agree with?
   a) You are your own worst enemy.
   b) You always get what you pay for.
   c) "Buyer beware."
   d) An old fool is a good fool.

10. This article was written primarily to
    a) engage the reader
    b) amuse the reader
    c) persuade the reader
    d) inform the reader

Selection 25:			1756 words
Finishing Time:	___ HR.	___ MIN.	___ SEC.
Starting Time:	___ HR.	___ MIN.	___ SEC.
Reading Time:		___ MIN.	___ SEC.
WPM Score:			___
Comprehension Score:			___ %
Reading Efficiency Score:			___

READING SELECTION 26
Difficulty Level: B
EIGHT WAYS TO FLUB A JOB HUNT

The old adage about learning from your mistakes is one most job hunters can verify. Valuable lessons are learned in the course of trying to find a job, though some mistakes are apparent only in retrospect.

The eight mistakes described below are culled from the experiences of people on both sides of the job search — applicants and employers, as well as agents for both. They may save you from learning the hard way.

1. Keeping your search to yourself. There are good reasons not to post a note on the bulletin board where you work. On the other hand, seeking help from no one is not the way to go either. One of the most potentially valuable elements of a job search is spreading the word among friends and business associates who might relay ideas, leads and introductions. It is possible to spread the word effectively without jeopardizing your present job. Most people will respect your request to keep your job search confidential.

2. Wasting time on blind ads. One way you can uncover leads to new jobs is in help-wanted ads in newspapers and trade journals. But preparing responses to ads that are blind — with the employer identified only by a coded box number — uses up valuable time for what is most often a fruitless effort.

Kirby W. Stanat, a former corporate recruiter, says, "The blind ad is a screen behind which a company can do all sorts of things it can't do when it identifies itself in an ad. . . . There are many reasons why companies run blind ads. They don't want their competition to know what they're up to; they don't want their employees to know; they don't want their customers to know. But perhaps the main reason is that they don't want you, the job seeker, to know what they're up to. A blind ad makes it easy for a company to discriminate against women, blacks, whites, anybody over 40,

Ivy League graduates — anybody." Some companies say that for certain jobs they have to run blind ads or they will be inundated with more replies than they can possibly handle. (Most that identify themselves will respond to every letter they receive, if for no other reason than to prevent calls or visits from applicants who don't get a response.)

The company that places a blind ad can toss out any or all of the résumés it gets without a word to anyone. It may have placed the ad for reasons other than filling a job — for example, to gauge the labor supply in a particular field or to see what kind of salaries applicants are seeking for certain types of jobs.

Says corporate executive William D. Sellers Jr., who carefully logged results from blind ads he answered during a job search some years ago, "Out of 50 letters I sent in response to blind ads, I got only two replies, a 4% return. Of 35 letters to identified employers, 27 replied — a 77% response. You are wasting stationery on a blind ad unless you can figure out who the advertiser is and contact the firm directly."

3. Botching the interview. When you get an invitation to a job interview, you are halfway toward your goal — a job offer. No matter how many encouraging responses you have gotten to job inquiry letters, with rare exceptions you will not get a job offer without an interview. So when you receive the call to come in to talk, don't squander the opportunity by failing to do your homework.

Bone up on the company and, if you can, on the person who will interview you. Have material with you that the employer might ask for — samples of your work, names and addresses of references, extra copies of your résumé. Be ready to ask pertinent questions that demonstrate your knowledge of your field.

By deciding in advance what topics you want covered in an interview, you can bring up any matters the interviewer doesn't. If you

369

haven't been through a job interview in a while, it might help you to run through some practice sessions with friends.

How do you fail an interview? There are dozens of ways, from seemingly little things like wringing your hands nervously, slouching in your chair or forgetting the basics of manners to more devastating blunders in what you say or don't say. An employment manager for a major construction company offers this advice, "If it's obvious you haven't spent any time preparing for the interview — that is, you don't know what the company does, where it does it, what kinds of jobs it has — then don't expect the company to take you very seriously."

Prior to an interview the employer has probably seen your résumé and perhaps talked with you on the phone. What employers look for in interviews is what you might call personal chemistry — how you look and act, whether you exhibit self-confidence, how you would fit in with other members of the organization.

In the brief span of the interview you want the potential employer to get to know you. If you are tense, tight-lipped, unsure of yourself and show no enthusiasm for the job or the conversation, you'll almost certainly fail this personal chemistry test.

One more thing: Don't criticize other employers. If questions come up about your reasons for leaving your present or previous jobs, take a positive approach. For example, note that you have always changed jobs to take advantage of better opportunities and that is certainly the case with the new job under discussion. Start carping about things you didn't like about other jobs or companies and you'll shift the interview to a disastrous course.

4. Talking salary too soon.   Many help-wanted ads request your "salary history" or "salary requirements." Early in a job interview the employer may ask what salary you'd be willing to accept.

If you comply with such requests at that stage of the game, you are putting yourself at a serious disadvantage. Think about the psychological situation. You want a job. You don't want to turn off a potential employer. You fear that a salary figure that is too high — even if it reflects what you honestly think you are worth or is just a little over what you are presently making — may scare off the employer. So you suggest a lower figure. Result: Even if the employer was prepared to, there is no reason to offer you more. Says executive search consultant Skott B. Burkland, "Most people negotiating for a new job don't know enough about current employment and compensation practices. They forget the employers aren't inclined to pay any more than necessary to hire employees they want."

You may be willing to forgo a salary increase or even take a cut to get into a particular field or company. But you're better off not making such a decision until you know that an employer is serious about hiring you. If you are asked about salary before you are ready to discuss it, do your best to defer the issue. Explain that because salary isn't the only factor important to you, it is open to negotiation if and when you are offered the job. If you are forced to answer at this point, give a range rather than a single figure.

5. Forgetting to compute the costs of a new job.   A new job may entail costs that your present one does not, especially if it will involve moving to a new location. Failing to take cost differences into account when you are negotiating a job offer can leave you holding the short end of the financial stick. Burkland recommends that you work up a balance sheet that compares all of the costs incidental to your present job with those of the new job and also accounts for the cost of relocating, if that is a factor.

Some work costs to compare are commuting, parking, lunch (some firms have subsidized cafeterias), sales taxes and other taxes. Relocation costs should include not only packing and moving your household goods and any difference in housing costs, but also home-hunting trips, new tags for your car, temporary housing until your family can make the move and so on. Income-tax deductions won't cover all of these under any circumstances. Burkland says you may be pleasantly surprised at how

370

willing employers are to up the ante for someone they want to hire when the facts are presented in this fashion.

6. Following only standard procedures.   You can read books about finding a job and talk to friends who have been through it recently and list things you should do in any job search — prepare a résumé . . . follow the want ads . . . mail letters to companies you want to work for. Those are all important things. But don't limit yourself to the tried-and-true steps. Thinking up the eleventh, twelfth, fifteenth way to latch onto a job lead or interview will increase your chances of success. There are lots of people vying for the same jobs, and you want to stand out from the crowd in an appealing way.

Career counselor John C. Crystal tells of one of his students, a high school teacher, who wanted to become a personal financial planner and counselor. He embarked on an ambitious exploration of the field. "He visited 55 financial planners across the country," says Crystal. "When he called for interview appointments, he told each one what he was doing — surveying those in the field to learn about the business. After his first visits he could tell successive planners that he had just talked to so-and-so, and that opened doors for him. By the time he had completed his research, he had received eight unsolicited job offers."

Be alert for opportunities to catch the attention of potential employers. It could be the chance to participate in a PTA forum, appear on a talk show, write a letter to the editor of the local paper that demonstrates your special knowledge on a particular subject. It's said that David Stockman, President Reagan's budget chief, won that job partly on the strength of his portrayal of President Carter during candidate Reagan's rehearsal sessions for the presidential election debates.

7. Dropping the ball.   Say someone who knows you are looking for a job suggests that you check with Gil Smith at the Ajax Co. Your friend doesn't know whether Smith has any jobs open or whether the Ajax Co. even employs people in

your field. But he knows Gil Smith and has given you an introduction. If you fail to follow up that lead even though it may seem tenuous, you are making a big mistake. Personal contacts are the lifeblood of a job search; even if one doesn't result in a job offer, it more often than not leads to additional contacts that might in turn lead to a job.

Also follow up on visits and correspondence with further contacts by way of a thank-you note for the interview or a letter concerning something you discussed. Nurturing the relationship may keep the person interested in aiding your search.

8. Losing hope.   Looking for a job has to be one of the hardest jobs around. It takes a lot of time, energy and organization. You have to keep up with your present job responsibilities or cope with not having a job. If it has been years since you last had to look for work, you will have to crank up the entire campaign from scratch.

In the course of your search you will face rejection repeatedly. You will spend a lot of time chasing tips down blind alleys. You will be exasperated at how slowly things seem to move. Nobody would blame you for feeling down about yourself. But that's a mistake you can't afford.

To find a job you must sell your capabilities, and tired or unenthusiastic salespeople don't make sales. You can't let the stress of the job hunt lead you to undervalue your potential or restrict your options. There is no logical reason to despair. You know the kind of work you are capable of doing. The big catch is meeting the person who needs someone like you to do a job. Logic says that will happen sooner or later.

If you've ever sold a house or a car, you know it can be a frustrating experience. Responses to your ad may come in slowly, or not at all on the first try. But you keep placing the ad and spreading the word. You know that somewhere out there is a buyer who wants what you are selling. On reflection after the sale you know you could not have anticipated just how and when the buyer would emerge. The key was maintaining confidence that all would end well. Confidence that you'll find the job you want is no less a key to a successful job hunt.

371

COMPREHENSION TEST 26

Directions: *Circle the letter of the correct answer*.

1. This article primarily discusses
   a) the motivation of employers and interviewers
   b) reasons why employers may not hear you
   c) how to make decisions about jobs
   d) mistakes to avoid in searching for a job

2. One way to discourage a potential employer during a job interview is to
   a) discuss what is wrong with your current job
   b) appear confident
   c) know too much about the company prior to the interview
   d) bring several copies of your résumé to the interview

3. When asked about salary by a job interviewer, you should
   a) always ask for a lower amount than you think the company expects you to ask for
   b) give a range of amounts
   c) ask for a higher amount than you are presently receiving
   d) say that you need time to think about it

4. One valuable element of a job search is
   a) telling friends and business associates that you are looking for a job
   b) posting a note on the bulletin board where you are presently working
   c) answering blind ads
   d) sending résumés only when requested to do so

5. Companies may run "blind ads" to
   a) discourage unqualified applicants from applying
   b) get an idea of what salaries applicants expect
   c) encourage the most qualified applicants to apply
   d) learn how much the name and prestige of a company affects the number of applicants

6. As used in the phrase, "they will be inundated" the word "inundated" means
   a) surprised
   b) flooded
   c) discouraged
   d) disappointed

7. If, during a job interview, the person conducting the interview asks you if you have any questions about the job it would be to your advantage to
   a) ask about the salary
   b) ask whether other employees like the company
   c) ask about benefits
   d) ask questions that show you know something about the company

8. To pass the "personal chemistry test" you should
   a) read about the company
   b) try to ask as many questions as you can
   c) show you are self-confident and enthusiastic
   d) openly discuss your concerns about the job

9. Suppose you applied for a job as a sales clerk, and during the interview you were asked to explain why you wanted the job. Your best answer would be to say that
   a) the job is convenient to your home
   b) you need the money
   c) your friend has told you that this is a good company to work for
   d) you can do the job well and benefit the company

10. The author compares selling a house or car to looking for a job. This comparison is made to emphasize that
    a) both situations involve luck
    b) in each situation you are trying to sell something
    c) both require a consideration of cost
    d) in each situation you are depending on another person

Selection 26:   2192 words

Finishing Time: _____ _____ _____
                  HR.   MIN.   SEC.

Starting Time: _____ _____ _____
                 HR.   MIN.   SEC.

Reading Time: _____ _____
                        MIN.   SEC.

WPM Score: _____

Comprehension Score: _____ %

Reading Efficiency Score: _____

Chapter 16:
Scanning: Rapidly Locating Information

Have you ever looked through a crowd of people searching for a particular person or sorted through a rack of clothing looking for an item of a particular size, color, style, or price? Have you ever looked across a shelf in a supermarket looking for a particular item? When you did these things, you were, in a general sense, scanning. Scanning in reading is a technique for quickly looking through reading matter to locate a particular piece of information — a fact, a date, a name, a statistic. You might be looking for the answer to a question or for a fact or detail that you need to complete an assignment. You might even be looking for a particular television program in the TV guide.

Scanning is a technique used in a variety of situations. Every time you use a telephone directory to find someone's phone number or address, you are scanning. When you check a bus schedule, look up a word in the dictionary, or locate a book on a library shelf, you are scanning. In each case, you are looking for a particular piece of information, and your *only* purpose in looking through the material is to locate that information. In fact, when you scan you are not at all interested in anything else on the page and you have no reason to notice or remember any other facts or ideas that are presented.

Although scanning is such a commonly used skill, many people have experienced problems in scanning effectively. Have you ever become frustrated when trying to locate the ad for a particular movie on the entertainment page of a newspaper or when trying to find out at which theater a particular movie is playing? Have you ever had to read a particular article completely in order to find a particular section or fact? These frustrations probably occurred because you were not scanning in the most effective, systematic manner. That is precisely the focus of this chapter — systematic scanning. Its purpose is to provide you with an organized procedure that will enable you to scan more effectively and efficiently.

HOW TO SCAN

Many people do not scan as efficiently as possible, because they randomly search through the material, hoping to stumble on the information they are seeking. Scanning in this way is time consuming, frustrating, and often forces the reader to "give up" and read the entire selection. The key to effective scanning is to approach the material in a systematic manner with your purpose clearly in mind. The following steps will enable you to systematically approach any scanning task.

Check the Organization

Before you begin to scan, check to see how the article or material is organized.

For *graphics* (maps, tables, graphs, charts, diagrams), this step is especially important. The title of the item you are scanning and other labels, keys, and legends are important to notice. They state what the graphics are intended to describe and tell you how it is presented. For example, in Figure 16-1, the title clearly announces the trend in the divorce rate that is detailed in the graph.

For *prose selections,* assessing the organization is very similar to prereading. Your purpose should be to notice the overall structure of the article so that you will be able, in one of the next steps, to predict where in the article you can expect to find the information you are looking for. Headings are especially important to notice since they clearly show how a selection is divided into subtopics.

Know Your Purpose

Fix in your mind what you are looking for. Scanning is effective only if you have a very specific purpose. Before you can begin to scan, therefore, it is useful to form very specific questions that you will attempt to answer. For example, instead of scanning for information on the topic of abortions in New York State, it would be more effective to develop questions such as:

How many abortions were performed in a certain year?
What rules and limitations restrict abortions?
Where are the majority of abortions performed?

Then, you would be scanning for specific, particular information, for scanning is really useful only for locating very specific information.

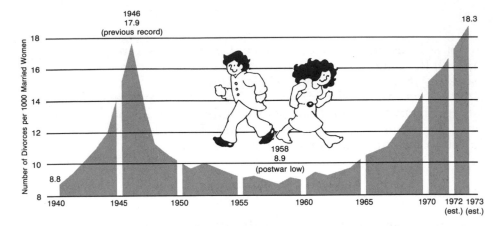

Figure 16-1. Since the mid-1960s, the divorce rate has been climbing steadily in the U.S. (Adapted from *U.S. News & World Report,* 22 April 1974, p. 43, in *Face to Face: The Individual and Social Problems,* by John Perry and Erna Perry, p. 30. Copyright © 1976 by Little, Brown and Company. Reprinted by permission.)

As a matter of fact, you could not "scan" well for information on "abortions in New York State"; you would probably end up skimming — a technique used for acquiring general information. So, the more specific your purposes and questions are, the more effectively you will be able to scan.

Anticipate Clue Words

After you have clearly established what you are looking for, you should try to anticipate clues that may help you more rapidly locate the answer. For example, if you were trying to locate the population of New York City in an article on the populations of cities, you might expect the answer to appear in digits, such as 2,304,710, or in estimate form using words such as "two million" or "three million." If you were looking for the name of the leading actress in a movie review, you should expect to find two words, both capitalized. In looking for the definition of a particular term, you might look for italics, and you might scan for the word itself or for words or phrases such as "means," "can be defined as," or "refers to." As accurately as possible, then, try to fix the image of your clue words or phrases in your mind before you begin to scan.

Identify Likely Answer Locations

Using what you have learned from checking the organization of the material, try to identify likely places where the information you are looking for might appear. You might be able to identify a column or section that could contain the needed information, you might be able to eliminate certain sections, or you might be able to predict that the information will probably appear in a certain portion of the article.

Use a Systematic Pattern

Once you know what you are looking for and can anticipate the location and form of your answer, you are ready to scan. Scanning should be organized and systematic. Do not randomly skip around, searching for clues. Instead, rhythmically sweep your eyes through the material. The pattern or approach you use will depend on the material. For material printed in narrow six- or seven-word columns, such as newspaper articles, you might move your eyes straight down the middle, catching the phrases on each half of the line. For wider lines of print, a zig-zag or Z pattern might be more effective. Using this pattern you would move your eyes back and forth, catching several lines in each movement. When you do come to the information you are looking for, it might almost seem as if the clue words stand out or "pop out" at you. This is because you have been discarding or ignoring most of the other words you processed so far and now you have fixed your attention.

Confirm Your Answer

Once you think you have located the answer you have been looking for, check to be sure you have found the correct information. That is, read the sentence or two that contains the answer, confirming that it is the information you need. Often, you can be misled by headings and key words that seem to indicate that you have found your answer when in fact you have located related information, opposite information, or information for another year, country, or similar situation.

Now let us try out this procedure. Assume that you are writing a paper on different types of school environments and you need to find out on what school program the "open classroom" setting was based. You have located a reference book on educational programs that contains the following section.

TYPES OF SCHOOL SETTINGS

There are all kinds of schools — large or small, rural or urban, public or private, rich or poor, and so forth. While it is impossible to discuss each of the numerous ways in which schools differ from each other, we can consider some of the more important dimensions and the effects they have on the development of children.

One of the dimensions that has received research attention is school size. In a well-known study, Barker and Gump focused on schools with student populations ranging between 35 and 2,200. While a wider variety of extracurricular activities was available in larger schools, there was greater participation in such activities in the smaller schools, producing stronger school identification. Perhaps as a result, dropout rates were lower in smaller schools than they were in larger ones.

Probably of greater importance is the type of curriculum or classroom structure children encounter. Until the period between 1960 and 1970 most children could be expected to be taught within a *traditional classroom* setting. This is still the most common arrangement and the one with which the majority of us are most familiar. It generally consists of children seated in rows in a rectangular classroom all listening to a teacher lecture or all working on the same task. Most of the tasks focus on developing the basic skills of reading, writing, and mathematical computation.

During the last two decades a new approach, often referred to as the *open classroom* setting, was adopted in some American schools. It was based on the British Infant School programs, but its philosophy was quite different. Greater attention was given to individuality and an emphasis on active involvement, or "learning by doing." The atmosphere in an open classroom contrasts sharply with that in a traditional setting. For example, children will be observed working individually or in groups at different tasks. Some may be in a corner reading by themselves, two or three others may be cooperating on a science project, while others may be receiving instruction from the teacher on how to operate a computer.

Is one approach better than the other? Even today there is a great deal of debate and disagreement among parents, teachers, educators, and psychologists. Groobman, Forward, and Peterson compared sixth-graders in the two types of classrooms and reported that compared to children in a traditional setting, those in an open classroom had ". . . more positive attitudes toward school and teachers and greater transfer of learning to nonschool settings." No differences were found in terms of academic expectations, self-esteem, or in actual performance. While children in the open school exhibited greater independence, their performance on standard achievement tests was not any higher.[1]

First, in assessing the organization of the material, you see that it is divided into five paragraphs, but that no additional headings are provided. Next, fixing in mind what you are looking for is an easy task since this hypothetical situation is already well defined. Then, in anticipating the form of the answer, you suspect that the name of a program would be capitalized, and that it may use words such as "school," "system," or "education." Also, since you are looking for the program on which the "open classroom" setting is based, you might also use "open classroom" and "based" as possible clue words. In choosing the likely location for the answer, you should identify the fourth paragraph because it contains the phrase "open classroom" in italics. Then, in scanning that paragraph, a Z pattern would be one effective approach and would help you locate the clue word "based" and the word "school," capitalized. Finally, suspecting that the answer to your question is the British Infant Schools, you would read the context to be sure you have identified the correct information. Although the process seems complicated when explained step-by-step, it is actually a very rapid procedure for locating particular facts and ideas.

SCANNING PARTICULAR TYPES OF MATERIALS

As is true for most of the techniques you have learned, the general procedure for scanning outlined in the previous section must be adapted to suit various types of materials. Materials to be scanned can be divided into two broad categories: columnar materials and prose material. Columnar material includes all sorts of information presented in lists, tables, columns, schedules, or charts. Examples of columnar materials include dictionaries, plane schedules, TV listings, the *Reader's Guide to Periodical Literature,* and lists of course offerings. Prose material, on the other hand, refers to any information presented in paragraph form and includes materials such as encyclopedia entries, newspapers and magazine articles, textbooks, and brochures and pamphlets. Suggestions for adapting the general scanning procedure to each of these types are offered in this section.

Scanning Columnar Materials

In scanning any information presented in list form, the most important step is to become familiar with its organization. It is essential to recognize how the writer has arranged the information. First, check to determine the overall organization and then see if it is divided in any particular way. For instance, you would note that a TV program schedule is organized by day of the week, but that it is also arranged by time. In scanning a zip code directory you would see that it is arranged alphabetically but that there is a separate alphabetical list for each state. Especially important to notice are column titles, headings, and any other clues provided about the material's organization.

Many reference books that are arranged alphabetically have guide words at the top of each page to indicate the words or entries that are included on each page. For instance, in the upper right or upper left corner of a page of a dictionary you might find the two words "cinder–circle." These guide words indicate that the first entry on the page is "cinder" and the last entry on the page is "circle." Included in various types of dictionaries and indexes, guide words are valuable shortcuts that help you locate quickly the appropriate page to scan. For lengthy alphabetical material that does not include guide words, you should check the first entry and the last entry on a page to determine if it contains the item you are looking for.

In scanning columnar material you will often be able to scan for a very specific word, phrase, name, date, or place name, and it may not be necessary to guess at the form of your answer. For example, in scanning a TV listing to find the time a particular show is on, you are looking for one very specific title. Or in checking a bank's schedule of hours, you are looking for their hours on a specific day and can scan specifically for that word.

The most effective scanning pattern for most columnar material is a straight down the column pattern, often called the arrow pattern. It is a swift, downward sweep.

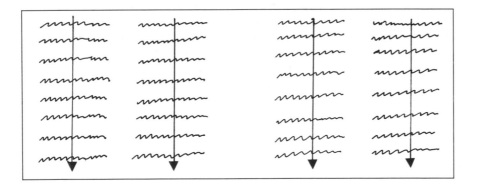

In using this pattern with material arranged alphabetically, focus on the first letter of each line until you reach the letter that begins the word you are looking for. Then focus on the first two letters until you reach the two-letter combination you are searching for. Successively widen your focus until you are looking for whole words.

For nonalphabetic materials it will be necessary, once you have selected a likely location, to scan the entire line to find the needed information.

EXERCISE 16-1

Directions: *Scan the following TV listings² to locate rapidly the following information.*

1. At what time is "The Taming of the Shrew" shown?

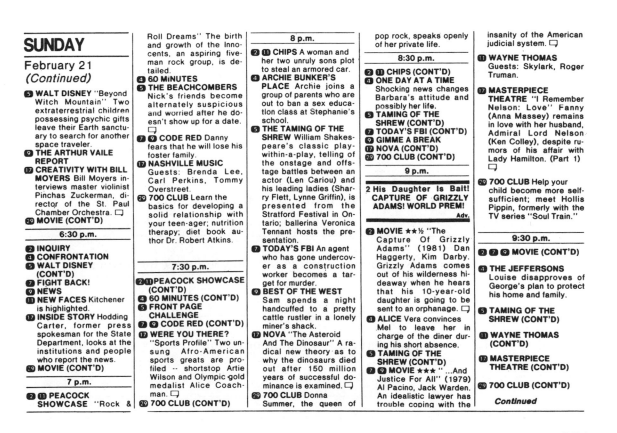

SUNDAY

February 21
(Continued)

⑤ WALT DISNEY ''Beyond Witch Mountain'' Two extraterrestrial children possessing psychic gifts leave their Earth sanctuary to search for another space traveler.

⑨ THE ARTHUR VAILE REPORT

⑰ CREATIVITY WITH BILL MOYERS Bill Moyers interviews master violinist Pinchas Zuckerman, director of the St. Paul Chamber Orchestra. ▢

㉙ MOVIE (CONT'D)

6:30 p.m.

② INQUIRY
④ CONFRONTATION
⑤ WALT DISNEY (CONT'D)
⑦ FIGHT BACK!
⑨ NEWS
⑪ NEW FACES Kitchener is highlighted.
⑰ INSIDE STORY Hodding Carter, former press spokesman for the State Department, looks at the institutions and people who report the news.
㉙ MOVIE (CONT'D)

7 p.m.

② ⑪ PEACOCK SHOWCASE ''Rock &

Roll Dreams'' The birth and growth of the Innocents, an aspiring five-man rock group, is detailed.

④ 60 MINUTES
⑤ THE BEACHCOMBERS Nick's friends become alternately suspicious and worried after he doesn't show up for a date. ▢

⑦ ⑨ CODE RED Danny fears that he will lose his foster family.

⑰ NASHVILLE MUSIC Guests: Brenda Lee, Carl Perkins, Tommy Overstreet.

㉙ 700 CLUB Learn the basics for developing a solid relationship with your teen-ager; nutrition therapy; diet book author Dr. Robert Atkins.

7:30 p.m.

②⑪PEACOCK SHOWCASE (CONT'D)
④ 60 MINUTES (CONT'D)
⑤ FRONT PAGE CHALLENGE
⑦ ⑨ CODE RED (CONT'D)
⑰ WERE YOU THERE? ''Sports Profile'' Two unsung Afro-American sports greats are profiled -- shortstop Artie Wilson and Olympic gold medalist Alice Coachman. ▢
㉙ 700 CLUB (CONT'D)

8 p.m.

② ⑪ CHIPS A woman and her two unruly sons plot to steal an armored car.

④ ARCHIE BUNKER'S PLACE Archie joins a group of parents who are out to ban a sex education class at Stephanie's school.

⑤ THE TAMING OF THE SHREW William Shakespeare's classic play-within-a-play, telling of the onstage and offstage battles between an actor (Len Cariou) and his leading ladies (Sharry Flett, Lynne Griffin), is presented from the Stratford Festival in Ontario; ballerina Veronica Tennant hosts the presentation.

⑦ TODAY'S FBI An agent who has gone undercover as a construction worker becomes a target for murder.

⑨ BEST OF THE WEST Sam spends a night handcuffed to a pretty cattle rustler in a lonely miner's shack.

⑰ NOVA ''The Asteroid And The Dinosaur'' A radical new theory as to why the dinosaurs died out after 150 million years of successful dominance is examined. ▢

㉙ 700 CLUB Donna Summer, the queen of

pop rock, speaks openly of her private life.

8:30 p.m.

② ⑪ CHIPS (CONT'D)
④ ONE DAY AT A TIME Shocking news changes Barbara's attitude and possibly her life.
⑤ TAMING OF THE SHREW (CONT'D)
⑦ TODAY'S FBI (CONT'D)
⑨ GIMME A BREAK
⑰ NOVA (CONT'D)
㉙ 700 CLUB (CONT'D)

9 p.m.

2 His Daughter Is Bait! **CAPTURE OF GRIZZLY ADAMS! WORLD PREM!**
Adv.

② MOVIE ★★½ ''The Capture Of Grizzly Adams'' (1981) Dan Haggerty, Kim Darby. Grizzly Adams comes out of his wilderness hideaway when he hears that his 10-year-old daughter is going to be sent to an orphanage. ▢

④ ALICE Vera convinces Mel to leave her in charge of the diner during his short absence.

⑤ TAMING OF THE SHREW (CONT'D)

⑦ ⑨ MOVIE ★★★ '' ...And Justice For All'' (1979) Al Pacino, Jack Warden. An idealistic lawyer has trouble coping with the

insanity of the American judicial system. ▢

⑪ WAYNE THOMAS Guests: Skylark, Roger Truman.

⑰ MASTERPIECE THEATRE ''I Remember Nelson: Love'' Fanny (Anna Massey) remains in love with her husband, Admiral Lord Nelson (Ken Colley), despite rumors of his affair with Lady Hamilton. (Part 1) ▢

㉙ 700 CLUB Help your child become more self-sufficient; meet Hollis Pippin, formerly with the TV series ''Soul Train.''

9:30 p.m.

② ⑦ ⑨ MOVIE (CONT'D)

④ THE JEFFERSONS Louise disapproves of George's plan to protect his home and family.

⑤ TAMING OF THE SHREW (CONT'D)

⑪ WAYNE THOMAS (CONT'D)

⑰ MASTERPIECE THEATRE (CONT'D)

㉙ 700 CLUB (CONT'D)

Continued

2.   What type of program is "NOVA"?

   _____

3.   What guests will appear on the Wayne Thomas show?

   _____

4.   Are there any programs on sports?

   _____

5.   How many programs are concerned with music?

   _____

EXERCISE 16-2

Directions: *Suppose you are doing a research paper on plant reproduction and you are using as a reference a book titled* Plants: Basic Concepts in Botany.[3] *Use the portion of the index that is included on page 383 to answer the following questions:*

1.   On what page(s) would you find information on reproduction of ferns?

   _____

2.   On what pages are plants' reproductive organs classified?

   _____

3.   Under what other headings should you check for further information?

   _____

4.   Does this reference contain information on how potato plants reproduce?

   _____

EXERCISE 16-3

Directions: *The table on page 385 appeared in a recent issue of* Car and Driver. *Suppose you are considering buying a new or used car and that you are interested in comparing various models. Scan the Road Test Review to find the answer to each question.*

1. What was the least expensive model tested?

    _____

2. What model is most economical in its use of fuel?

    _____

3. If you were concerned with braking ability, would it be better to buy a Volkswagen Rabbit or an Oldsmobile Cutlass?

    _____

4. Which car has the fastest acceleration: a Renault 5 Turbo, a Datsun 310-6X, or a Dodge Colt?

    _____

Scanning Prose Materials

Prose materials are more difficult to scan than columnar material. Their organization is less apparent and the information is not as concisely or obviously stated. And unless the headings are numerous and very concise, you may have to scan large amounts of material with fewer locational clues. For prose materials you must rely heavily on identifying clue words and predicting the form of your answer. It is useful to think of scanning prose materials as a floating process, in which your eyes drift quickly through a passage searching for clue words and phrases. Your eyes should move across sentences and entire paragraphs, noticing only clue words that indicate that you may be close to locating the answer.

EXERCISE 16-4

Directions: *Scan each of the prose selections on pages 386–390 to locate the answer to the question indicated. Write your answer in the space provided.*

ROAD TEST REVIEW

Quarter-mile acceleration: Elapsed time from zero through a quarter-mile distance. Car is loaded with driver, full tank of fuel, and 30 pounds of test instrumentation. With manual-transmission cars, some wheelspin is used at the starting line, but all shifts are lift-throttle. Automatic upshifts are done manually.
Top speed: Maximum average speed in two-way runs.
Braking, 70-0: Minimum obtainable stopping distance from 70 mph without sliding any tire. Since distance measurement begins with actuation of a brake-pedal-mounted contact switch, the car's brake-system-response characteristics are included in the stopping-distance results.

EPA estimated fuel economy: Each test car is driven on a chassis dynamometer, which matches both the inertia loadings (the car's weight) and the absorption loadings (aerodynamic and rolling resistance) that the engine would see on the highway. The test car follows a precise speed-versus-time trace after a cold start. The cycle runs for 7.5 miles at an average speed of 20 mph. Fuel consumption is calculated from a chemical analysis of the exhaust emissions.
Interior sound level at 70 mph: Noise level measured with a sound-level meter. The microphone is located at the driver's right ear, and results are averaged from two-way tests to cancel wind effects.

MODEL/MONTH TESTED	PRICE AS TESTED, $	1/4-MILE ACCELERATION, sec	TOP SPEED, mph	BRAKING 70-0 MPH, feet	EPA ESTIMATED FUEL ECONOMY, mpg	INTERIOR SOUND LEVEL @ 70 mph, dBA
1981 cars						
Alfa Romeo GTV6 2.5 (6/81)	17,000*	16.2	130	182	17	76
AMC Eagle SX/4 Sport (5/81)	10,616	20.0	92	210	17	81
Audi 4000 5+5 (4/81)	12,400	17.2	106	202	21	75
Blakely Bernardi (2/81)	16,150	17.6	93	227	—	—
BMW 528i (12/80)	22,380	16.3	122	214	18	72
Buick Regal Sport Coupe (6/81)	12,203	17.8	103	221	19	71
Cadillac Cimarron (8/81)	12,789	19.5	91	219	26	72
Cadillac de Ville V-8-6-4 (4/81)	17,685	18.4	101	233	15	68
Chevrolet Cavalier CL (5/81)	9000*	19.1	92	234	29	74
Chevrolet Chevette Diesel (7/81)	7591	21.8	80	232	41	75
Chevrolet Citation X-11 (12/80)	9000*	18.1	105	205	21	72
Chevrolet Malibu Classic (3/81)	9781	19.5	93	194	18	70
Chrysler Imperial (1/81)	18,311	19.4	103	235	16	68
Datsun 280-ZX Turbo (5/81)	16,500*	15.2	126	196	20	74
Datsun 310-GX (7/81)	7585	20.1	86	218	33	77
Datsun 810 Maxima (4/81)	9979	17.9	111	207	22	73
Dodge Aries K SE (9/81)	8609	18.6	93	207	25	74
Dodge Challenger (9/81)	8867	18.2	103	208	20	72
Dodge Colt (7/81)	5690	18.9	92	208	33	77
Ferrari/Amerispec 512BB (6/81)	115,000	13.6	164	203	7	82
Fiat Turbo Spider 2000 (11/81)	14,650	16.6	110	215	24	82
Ford Escort GLX (1/81)	7789	19.4	87	217	24	75
Ford EXP (3/81)	8000*	18.9	102	233	28	79
Honda Civic Four-Door (7/81)	7329	18.3	92	209	34	76
Isuzu I-Mark Diesel (5/81)	7300*	20.0	87	230	37	76
Isuzu I-Mark LS (7/81)	7095	18.8	96	202	27	74
Jaguar XJ6	27,500	18.7	111	210	15	74
Mazda GLC Custom L (7/81)	7490	19.2	92	216	35	75
Mazda RX-7 GS 5-spd (9/81)	10,220	17.0	114	218	21	73
Mazda RX-7 GSL auto (9/81)	13,010	17.7	109	201	19	74
Mazda 626 Luxury (8/81)	9685	20.5	91	227	28	75
Mercedes-Benz 300SD (4/81)	35,578	18.7	102	204	26	74
Mercedes-Benz 300TD Turbo Diesel (3/81)	32,455	19.0	102	214	26	74
Mercedes-Benz 380SEL (11/80)	45,550	17.5	107	208	18	67
Mercury Cougar GS (6/81)	10,651	19.7	—	215	19	73
Mercury Lynx RS Wagon (7/81)	8480	19.7	86	200	27	76
Oldsmobile Cutlass (11/80)	10,000*	20.6	94	246	19	67
Oldsmobile Omega ES2800 (3/81)	9531	18.2	98	205	21	72
Peugeot 505S Turbo Diesel (1/81)	15,510	19.5	94	214	28	75
Plymouth Horizon Miser (8/81)	6260	18.3	99	213	30	75
Plymouth Reliant SE (9/80)	6000*	18.3	96	227	26	75
Plymouth TC3 Turismo (6/81)	7920	18.8	105	224	25	75
Pontiac Grand Prix Diesel (7/81)	12,101	21.5	88	228	23	71
Pontiac J2000 Wagon (10/81)	10,073	20.7	87	225	25	74
Renault Le Car Five-Door (7/81)	7167	20.4	84	216	29	80
Renault 5 Turbo (8/81)	28,000	15.3	126	202	—	76
Renault 18i (12/80)	10,291	19.1	95	217	24	73
Saab 900 Turbo Automatic (4/81)	15,450	17.5	109	206	19	73
Subaru GLF (7/81)	7650	19.5	91	215	28	76
Toyota Celica Supra (6/81)	13,356	17.5	112	221	21	70
Toyota Corolla Tercel (7/81)	6238	19.6	87	204	29	78
Toyota Cressida (8/81)	12,699	17.5	106	221	19	73
Toyota Starlet (2/81)	5273	19.1	87	203	39	76
Volkswagen Rabbit LS (2/81)	8455	18.3	91	193	28	76
Volvo GLT Turbo (2/81)	13,880	17.2	106	196	18	73
1982 cars						
Bitter SC (10/81)	48,000	16.9	125	193	19	72
BMW M1 (11/81)	115,000	13.7	161	190	—	77
Chrysler LeBaron (10/81)	8000*	18.3	99	235	25	74
Continental (9/81)	20,000*	20.6	97	222	17	67
Ferrari Mondial 8 (11/81)	68,000*	16.9	138	195	10	77
Mercury Capri RS (10/81)	10,500*	15.8	127	217	18	79
Mercury Lynx GS (11/81)	7800*	18.9	92	214	26	76

*estimated

1. From what part of the pepper plant is black pepper made?

    _____

    Pepper, which has nothing whatever to do with the bell and chili pepper of the family Solanaceae, is one of the oldest and most treasured spices. It is universally incorporated in flavoring, pickling, and preserving food. New trade routes to the "Indies" were sought eagerly in the fifteenth century mostly because of the desire for pepper. Black pepper and white pepper are both obtained from *Piper nigrum*, of the family Piperaceae. The pepper plant is a high-climbing perennial vine that holds on with **adventitious roots,** which grow from leaves or stems. Black pepper is made from the dried ground fruit of the pepper plant; white pepper comes from the dried ground seeds.[4]

2. What two countries produce most of the world's supply of cloves?

    _____

    The first time that cloves were used as a spice or perfume was recorded in China in the third century B.C., and cloves are still among the most important of commercial spices because of their many uses. As a powder, they flavor sweet and savory dishes and are used in pickling and in making sauces and ketchup. Dried cloves are the desiccated, unexpanded flower buds of the evergreen tree *Eugenia aromatica* in the family Myrtaceae (myrtle), which also gives us allspice and the fruit guava. The Moluccas are the original home, but Zanzibar and Indonesia are now the world's greatest producers of cloves, growing 90 percent of the world crop.[5]

3. What object do penguins use to identify the sex of another penguin?

    _____

    At the same time as proclaiming their species, individual birds must also declare their sex to one another. Ducks do so with their head patterns for only the drakes develop them. In many species, however — among them, sea birds and birds of prey — the male and female look the same throughout the year. Their sexual identity therefore has to be conveyed by their song and behavior. The male penguin has a particularly charming way of discovering what he wants to know about his uniformly suited companions. He picks up a pebble in his bill, waddles over to a bird standing alone and solemnly lays it before it. If he gets an outraged peck and the squaring up for a fight, he knows he has made a dreadful mistake — this is another male. If his offering is met with total indifference, then he has found a female who is not yet ready to breed or is already paired. He picks up his spurned gift and moves on. But if the stranger receives the pebble with a deep bow then he has discovered his true mate. He bows back and the two stretch up their necks and trumpet a celebratory nuptial chorus.[6]

4. What organizations use group therapy to help individuals cope with their problems?

One of the most recent innovations in psychotherapy is *group therapy*. This method is based on the belief that an individual may feel freer to reveal himself when interacting with others who are also troubled. The idea is to create a community feeling in which the individual discovers that he has many experiences and feelings in common with other people. Group therapy is designed to counteract the feeling of alienation, of being "different," or totally alone. A number of techniques, including physical contact and psychodrama, are employed to facilitate interaction. Many groups like Alcoholics Anonymous, Synanon, Gamblers Anonymous, and Weight Watchers now use a modified form of group therapy with considerable success in helping individuals with specific behavioral problems. Lately family therapy also has been tried in an effort to treat the disturbed individual in the environment that possibly contributed to his disturbed behavior.[7]

5. What factors are controlled to slow the ripening of bananas?

Would you have guessed that the foremost commercial fruit is the banana? It is much more than the breakfast or dessert item that so many fruits are, since it is a staple in many countries. When eaten raw, the mature fruits are sweet and delicious, but the unripe fruits and, more commonly, the related plantain can be cooked to provide a starchy food nutritionally similar to the potato.

The banana, which has several species in the genus *Musa*, is a perennial with a short underground **rhizome** (a rootstalk) that produces both roots and shoots. All edible bananas derive from only two species in the genus *Musa*, both native to Southeast Asia, from which they have spread widely. The banana is cultivated in plantations and in gardens. A plant is started using **suckers,** shoots arising from the rootstalk. Seven to nine months later the plant will flower, but another few months are needed for the fruit to mature. The flowers grow in compact groups on a large stalk, and in many types the fruit contains no seeds. The fruit itself is white and pulpy, with a tissue of large cells filled with starch and protected by a thick skin. During the ripening much of the starch is converted to sugar.

Banana fruits for export are usually harvested before they are fully ripe and shipped at low temperatures, with carefully controlled humidity and balance between oxygen and carbon dioxide, to slow the ripening. Once at the destination, the fruits are allowed to ripen. Bananas continue to ripen even after you buy them.[8]

6.   How do birds that fly at night know where they are going?

But how do the birds manage to find their way? There seems to be no single answer: they use many methods. Some we are beginning to understand; some mystify us; and there may be some that depend on abilities we have not yet suspected. Many birds certainly follow major geographical features. Summer migrants from Africa fly along the North African coast, converging on the Strait of Gibraltar and cross there, where they can see Europe ahead of them. Then they follow valleys, flying over recognized passes through the Alps or the Pyrenees and so arrive at their summer homes. Others take an eastern route by way of the Bosphorus.

But all birds cannot use such straightforward methods. The Arctic tern, for example, has to fly at least 3000 kilometres across the Antarctic Ocean with no land to guide it. We know that some birds, flying at night, navigate by the stars for on cloudy nights they tend to get lost and if they are released in a planetarium where the constellations have been rotated so that they no longer match the position of the stars in the heavens, the birds will follow the visible and artificial ones.

Day-flying birds may use the sun. If they are to do so, they must be able to compensate for the shift of the sun across the sky each day and that means that they must have a precise sense of time. Still others appear to be able to use the earth's magnetic field as a guide. So it seems that many migrating birds must carry in their brains a clock, a compass and the memory of a map. Certainly, a human navigator would need all three if he were to match the journeys that a swallow can make within a few weeks of its hatching.[9]

7.   What is one likely cause of depression?

This form of anxiety is usually classified with the neuroses, but it is so widespread that it deserves separate coverage. The characteristic symptoms of depression are sadness, anxiety, insomnia, withdrawal from everyday life and relationships with others, a reduced ability to function and work, and generally agitated behavior. The intensity of depression varies widely: some experience only a mild sense of sadness and others are drawn into suicidal despair. In cases in which despair becomes so profound as to distort reality, the individual is said to be psychotic.

Depression is probably the most common form of mental disorder. Many people will see a physician on the pretext of a physical ailment when in reality they simply feel depressed. Not all sources of depression are clear, but one likely cause is emotional upheaval, whether as the result of losing a close friend or family member, losing one's position in the community, or losing a valued job and status. In our society, many people who are past retirement age experience depression. Presumably, their depression stems from their diminished status in society and the less-than-reverent attitude of the younger generation toward them.

The most significant danger of depression is the possibility of suicide. Suicide will be discussed later in the chapter, but it is important to note that suicide in cases of severe depression is likely to be attempted either at the beginning of the condition or when a cure seems to be successful. It is important, then, that depressed patients be kept under constant observation, even when they seem to be much better.[10]

8.   How were prostitutes thought of during Victorian times?

_____

A definition of prostitution is probably totally unnecessary. We all know that it is the exchange of sex for money or other objects of value. Curiously, prostitution has existed in almost all societies from the earliest times, although societal attitudes toward those who engaged in it have varied greatly. In some societies, and in some historical eras, prostitutes served religious functions: the act was part of ritual, or perceived as a sacrifice to the gods. At other times and in other societies they provided intellectual, as well as sexual stimulation, while wives functioned chiefly to provide heirs and keep the family alive. Often prostitutes were the only well-educated women in a time when women were generally kept in a state of vast ignorance.

For the past several centuries in the societies of Western civilization, however, prostitutes have held less exalted positions. In Victorian times, although they were widely patronized, they were despised by most people as sinful, fallen women who engaged in activities that no self-respecting woman would even think about. Today, although our norms are much more liberal with regard to marital, premarital, and extramarital sex prostitutes are still considered disreputable and promiscuous because they use sex to make a living without even the pretense of affection or feeling. We should perhaps mention in passing that prostitution is not strictly a feminine trade. There are also male homosexual prostitutes. Although they share some of the characteristics of their female counterparts, they are best discussed in the context of the homosexual subculture.[11]

APPLYING WHAT YOU HAVE LEARNED

Directions: *Choose one of the following selections, skim read it and answer the multiple choice questions that follow it. Then scan the article to locate the answers to the questions in this exercise.*

Selection 27

1.   Where is the moral looking time longer, in a bus or on the street?

   _____

2.   Name two societies in which the moral looking time is longer than in our society.

   _____

3.   Of what offense was the Spanish-speaking girl accused?

   _____

4.   How is hostility communicated through eye language?

   _____

Selection 28

1.   By how many pounds per cow has milk production risen in India?

   _____

2.   Who is Philip Handler?

   _____

3.   How much grain does the United States use to produce one pound of meat?

   _____

4.   What is the cost of clearing, transportation, and irrigation of 20 million acres of land?

   _____

READING SELECTION 27
EYE LANGUAGE

Difficulty Level: A

Julius Fast

The cocktail party was almost over when Lynn came to say goodbye. "Are you leaving alone?" I asked, surprised. Lynn is an attractive woman, and there were several good-looking men at the party.

Lynn shook her head. "See that tall blond guy near the kitchen? He'll take me home."

"You mean Jim?"

"I guess so. We haven't been introduced."

"Then how do you know he'll take you home?" I demanded.

"We've made eye contact." She grinned. "We haven't said a word, but we've been communicating for the last ten minutes."

"Across a crowded room? Honestly, Lynn. . . ."

But Lynn wasn't listening to me. She was looking at Jim, as he stood talking to another man. While I watched, she caught Jim's eye, smiled, glanced at the clock and then looked at the door of the bedroom where the coats were. A moment later, as Lynn pecked my cheek and sauntered toward the bedroom, I saw Jim smile, clap his companion cheerfully on the shoulder and turn away. He and Lynn reached the front door at virtually the same moment.

Coincidence? Not at all. As I realized later, the two of them were merely advanced practitioners in the fine art of eye contact, the single most significant element of body language. With people like Lynn and Jim, more can be communicated with one glance than with a dozen words. Mankind has used this silent skill since the first Stone-Age beauty looked back over her shoulder at a hairy, skin-clad hunter. Writers are fond of describing steely gazes and soft, tender ones, shy looks and challenging stares. Yet the eyeball itself, except for pupil size, can hardly change. It remains essentially the same through every type of glance.

What does change, then? The skin around the eye, the muscles, the lid and the eyebrow, all form a constantly mobile container for the eye itself. This expressive container, plus the tilt of the head, makes it possible for the eye to convey hundreds of different expressions and signals. The length of a look, too, is especially significant.

Look at someone, then look away. You have made a statement. Hold the glance for a second longer and you've made a different statement. Hold it for two seconds and the meaning has changed again. For every situation, there is a *moral looking time,* the amount of time that you can hold someone else's gaze without being rude, aggressive or intimate.

In an elevator, for example, the moral looking time is zero. You look up at the indicator lights, down at the floor, anywhere but into the eyes of a fellow passenger. The moral looking time is a little longer in a crowded subway or bus, and still longer out on the street. There we may catch someone's eye as we walk toward him, but we mustn't hold his glance for longer than three seconds. A glance, if it's held for less than three seconds, signals *You are another human being. I recognize you as such.* If you hold the stranger's eye for longer than three seconds, you signal: *I am interested in you.*

This interest can be a straight man-woman thing. Most men will give an attractive woman a three-seconds-plus look, and most attractive women accept it comfortably. But if one man gives another man a three-seconds-plus stare, he signals: *I know you* or *I am interested in you because you look different, strange, peculiar.* Because this glance is so ambiguous — it could imply anything from idle curiosity to sexual interest — the reaction is often hostile.

The eye game is used by men to pick up women and, more subtly, by women to pick up men. Homosexuals often identify each other on the street via extended eye contact, followed by a

392

backward glance after a few paces. If the other glances back, too, a pickup is in the offing. The eye game is also used by lonely people who would merely like to exchange a word of greeting with another human being. I've played the eye game in big cities and small towns. Holding the eye of another man a bit beyond the moral looking time in a city usually brings a frown of annoyance. In a small town it will just as readily bring a smile, a nod and a word or two of greeting.

Try it yourself, when you feel adventurous. Walk down the street playing the eye game, and see what sort of reactions you get. But be prepared for just about anything!

Just as many messages can be signaled by holding someone's gaze, others can be sent by lowering the eyes or using other means of stare. In many animal species, and in man, a prolonged gaze can be a sign of hostility. Cutting off your own gaze is a gesture of appeasement that disarms the other person's aggression.

I remember an evening I spent in a bar when I was a young soldier. I happened to catch the eye of a marine across the room. We had both had a few drinks, and the idle glance suddenly turned into a contest. Who was going to outstare the other? After a short, angry locking of eyes, I told myself: *This is silly unless I want a fight*. I broke eye contact first, the marine took it as an appeasing signal and, with a cheerful grin, came over to my table and clasped my hand. We spent a pleasant evening talking.

How do we learn the different moral looking times that enable us to function in our society? We pick them up as we do all body language, from the people around us — our parents and family first, then our friends and finally strangers. The specific rules of eye contact depend on the culture in which we live. Every group has its own regulations. Latin Americans and Arabs have longer looking times than ours; Asians and Northern Europeans have shorter ones. North African Tuaregs search each other's eyes avidly as they talk, while the Japanese pay little attention to eye contact.

Real problems can arise when the rules of different cultures get confused. For example, in America we consider a forthright glance a sign of truth, and assume that a liar avoids eye contact. But this assumption does not necessarily hold in other cultures. Take this example: In an American high school, a group of girls who had been caught smoking in the restroom were suspended by the principal, though he was troubled about one Spanish-speaking girl who had never been in trouble. "She said she wasn't involved," the principal told her teacher. "I would have believed her except that the whole time she talked to me, she didn't meet my eyes. She must have been lying."

Fortunately, the teacher, like the student, was Puerto Rican. She was able to explain to the principal that a "good" Puerto Rican girl invariably lowers her eyes as a sign of respect and obedience when she is being questioned by someone in authority. The principal promptly reinstated the girl.

COMPREHENSION TEST 27

Directions: *Circle the letter of the correct answer*.

1. Each time you look at someone you are
   a) making a statement
   b) violating the moral looking time
   c) not practicing body language
   d) trying to "pick up" that person

2. When riding in an elevator, people usually
   a) try to make conversation with other passengers
   b) stand in the middle of the elevator
   c) look at the floor
   d) make eye contact with the other passengers

3. If a gaze is prolonged beyond the moral looking time it may be taken as
   a) a sign of hostility
   b) a sign of appeasement
   c) a joke
   d) unimportant

4. Fast states that the eye game is learned first from
   a) our friends
   b) strangers
   c) parents and family
   d) teachers

5. In American culture, when a person is telling a lie, he or she will usually
   a) seek eye contact
   b) avoid eye contact
   c) use other body language cues
   d) close his eyes

6. An *ambiguous* glance is one that is
   a) very definite
   b) unclear
   c) promiscuous
   d) strange

7. If the author had not broken eye contact with the marine in the bar, probably
   a) the marine would have walked away
   b) a fight would have broken out
   c) the marine would have been appeased
   d) a conversation would have started

8. If you wanted to meet someone in your sociology class, you should
   a) make direct eye contact and hold the glance for a little longer than for a stranger
   b) sit as close as possible to him or her
   c) glance at the person and follow with a backward glance

   d) avoid eye contact and rely on body movement

9. If a Tuareg from North Africa looked into your eyes throughout a conversation with him, you could assume that he
   a) was sexually attracted to you
   b) meant nothing by this
   c) wanted to fight with you
   d) was lying to you

10. The author used the example of the cocktail party to illustrate that eye language is
    a) used only by members of the opposite sex
    b) a lost art in our society
    c) misunderstood by most people
    d) a very effective means of communicating

Selection 27:	1171 words
Finishing Time:	___ ___ ___ HR. MIN. SEC.
Starting Time:	___ ___ ___ HR. MIN. SEC.
Reading Time:	___ ___ MIN. SEC.
WPM Score:	_____
Comprehension Score:	_____ %
Reading Efficiency Score:	_____

READING SELECTION 28
ECONOMIC GROWTH AND THE FOOD CRISIS

Difficulty Level: B

Marilu McCarty

Advances in technology have helped more of the world's population live better and longer — and that's part of our problem!

Better health standards have kept larger numbers of people alive. The world's population is now almost four billion and expected to double in twenty-five years. Growing population and slowly rising living standards have increased our need for food at the rate of 30 million tons per year. As a result, the world's stockpile of food is declining by about 10 million tons per year.

THE RISE AND FALL OF THE GREEN REVOLUTION

From the early 1950s until 1972, world food production increased greatly. The Green Revolution extended scientific techniques to agriculture in the form of hybrid seed and poultry, chemical fertilizers and pesticides, and complex irrigation systems. Strains of corn, sorghum, soybeans, wheat, and rice were developed to flourish under particular climate and soil conditions.

In the United States, corn production rose to 110 bushels per acre from only 26 bushels per acre in the early 1900s. Milk production rose to 10,000 pounds per cow per year, compared with 600 in India. Chickens were bred to eat less, grow to maturity in a shorter time, and produce more eggs. As a result of such scientific advances, our twelve Midwestern states alone now feed one-fourth of the world's people.

Crop disasters in 1972 brought an apparent end to the growth in production. Much of the extra yields had come from the use of chemical fertilizers, primarily petroleum-based and now in short supply. The drop in world supplies of petroleum-based fertilizers is expected to cause a drop in crop yields of ten tons for each one-ton decline in fertilizers applied.

This presents a particular problem for underdeveloped nations that often lack the foreign exchange necessary for buying fertilizer. The problem is so severe that Philip Handler, president of the National Academy of Sciences, has predicted one million child deaths per month in these nations by the year 2025.

PROPOSALS AND PROBLEMS

What can be done? At present we are cultivating only 3.5 billion acres of arable land out of a worldwide total of 7.8 billion acres. New acreage could be brought under cultivation, although the most favorable lands are already in use. The costs in clearing, transportation, and irrigation of developing only 20 million acres of land are estimated at about $4 billion per year. Adding only 10 percent to the amount of cultivated acreage would cost at least $400 billion and could run as high as $1 trillion!

Land reform in some areas might be of help. New foods from the sea are also a possibility, but this is limited by pollution and by too intensive fishing in recent years. New varieties of seeds are still being developed, but the process is slow and costly. Fertilizer production must also be expanded, particularly in the less-developed countries.

Reduction of waste would also help relieve the food shortage. Decreased consumption in the developed nations could increase the quantities distributed to needy nations. For example, the United States uses the equivalent of seven pounds of grain in the production of one pound of meat. Reducing meat consumption would free this grain for shipment abroad. It is estimated that the average person in poor countries consumes four hundred pounds of grain per year, in contrast to the citizen of North America who consumes a ton (about one hundred pounds of which is in the form of beer or whiskey).

LIFEBOAT ETHICS?

Policy on the problem of food production must eventually deal with the problem of population growth. Some analysts are beginning to recommend what is called lifeboat ethics: In the ocean of life we are all adrift. We would like to bring all others aboard, but that would sink our boat and we would all drown. We must not exceed the carrying capacity of our system. Only those nations should be helped that are able and willing to make the tremendous effort to help themselves.

The decision to help only selected nations is similar to the principle of *triage* in battlefield casualties. Victims are divided into three groups: those who will probably survive without aid,

those who will probably survive with moderate aid, and those who will not survive without substantial aid. Limited resources are then concentrated on the second group. By implication, the third is left to perish, a morally difficult decision to make. We may not like it but, in the words of ecologist-biologist Garrett Hardin, it is like the law of gravity: "Once you know it's true, you don't sit down and cry about it. That's the way the world is."

In human terms, this may apply to the one-third of the world's population who live in the hungry nations — nations unable to feed themselves or produce goods for export which are sufficient to allow them to import food. These nations are centered in Asia and Africa below the Sahara: India, Bangladesh, Ethiopia, and others. It is estimated that one-fourth of the population of these areas live on a diet of less than 1,000 calories per day.

We continue to hope for a more acceptable alternative. Nevertheless, policy to relieve the crisis in food production will require the best efforts of scientists, sociologists, economists, and humanitarians for many years to come.

COMPREHENSION TEST 28

Directions: *Circle the letter of the correct answer.*

1. Given the present growth rate of the world population and our ability to produce food
    a) the United States will be able to feed half the world by 2025
    b) hunger will be unknown in the future
    c) the developed nations will change their eating habits
    d) we will encounter very serious problems in the near future

2. The term "Green Revolution" refers to
    a) the political situation in Ireland
    b) the increased use of scientific methods in agriculture
    c) the upheavals in underdeveloped nations
    d) the crop shortages experienced in 1972

3. Each year, the world's food reserves decline by
    a) 10 million tons
    b) 20 million tons
    c) 30 million tons
    d) 40 million tons

4. The main difficulty in increasing the world's farmlands is
    a) its high cost
    b) the scarcity of usable land
    c) rising levels of pollution
    d) the unwillingness of people to farm today

5. The system of dividing casualties into three groups and then helping just those who will be saved with minimal aid is known as
    a) lifeboat ethics
    b) musteline

c) humanitarianism

d) triage

6. When the author says "by *implication*, the third is left to perish," the word "implication" means
   a) process of elimination
   b) careful decision
   c) accident
   d) intuition

7. It is expected that crop yields will drop, especially in underdeveloped countries, mainly because of
   a) disastrous weather
   b) weak seed strains
   c) oil shortages
   d) revolutions

8. The author would likely agree with which *one* of the following statements?
   a) In the future it will most likely be possible to provide everyone with an adequate diet.
   b) If the weather could be artificially controlled, the food supply problem would no longer exist.
   c) In the future it is unlikely that every country will be able to produce or purchase enough food for survival.
   d) The principle of triage, while acceptable on the battlefield, is immoral when applied to economics.

9. By the statement that North Americans consume about a ton of grain apiece per year the writer means that
   a) we eat five times as much grain as those in poor countries
   b) we consume most of this in the form of alcoholic beverages
   c) much of this is used in the production of meat
   d) grain is the most important part of our diet

10. The concluding paragraph of this selection was written to emphasize the author's
    a) great hope for the future
    b) humorous viewpoint
    c) doubts about easy solutions
    d) distaste for the world's poor

Selection 28:			920 words
Finishing Time:	HR.	MIN.	SEC.
Starting Time:	HR.	MIN.	SEC.
Reading Time:		MIN.	SEC.
WPM Score:			
Comprehension Score:			%
Reading Efficiency Score:			

Unit Eight:
How to Increase Your Rate and Build Flexibility

Consider for a moment all the reading you have done in the past week. Most likely you have read textbook material, and you may have found time to read a newspaper article or a magazine article. Out of necessity you may have used a dictionary, checked a TV listing, read a bus schedule or various signs, labels, directions, and advertisements. Certainly an advertisement on a billboard is not as important as material contained in your textbook; nor is it as essential to remember the fabric contents of a shirt as it is to recall your lecture notes from biology. You no doubt have begun to see that what you read and how you read it depends on your purpose for reading. This section is written to enable you to increase and adjust your rate and level of comprehension to suit your purpose for reading as well as the type of material you are reading.

In Chapter 17 we will present several techniques for reading faster when the situation and material permit rapid, selective reading. Chapter 18 will contain suggestions for adjusting your rate, your level of comprehension, and your reading technique to your purpose for reading and to the type of material you are reading. Chapter 19 provides an opportunity for you to assess the progress you have made throughout your course of study and to see the improvement you have made in becoming a more efficient and flexible reader.

Chapter 17:
Techniques for Reading Faster

Up to this point in the book, we have been concerned with both the mental and physical aspects of the reading process. You have become familiar with various keys to reading efficiency and have learned techniques for understanding and retaining more of what you read. You have learned a great deal about the organization and structure of sentences, paragraphs, and passages and have developed skills for interpreting and evaluating what you read. You have also learned techniques for developing your vocabulary and have learned how to read selectively. Now you are ready to learn specific techniques that will directly improve your reading rate.

This chapter contains three techniques that will enable you to read faster. First, a technique called "pacing" is introduced that provides a structure for gradual rate increase. Next, you will learn the technique of key word reading. Key word reading involved reading *only* the essential, most important, words in a sentence. Finally, a procedure for increasing rate through rereading will be described.

PACING TECHNIQUES

An established method of improving reading rate is called *pacing*. Pacing is a useful method for forcing yourself to read slightly faster than you normally would, usually by using some mechanical or semimechanical means. It involves trying to keep up with a preestablished pace. To better understand the concept of pacing, imagine that you are in a crowd of people and suddenly everyone starts walking forward quickly. You are forced along at the pace at which the crowd is moving, regardless of how fast you want to move. Similarly, in reading you can read more rapidly if you are "forced along" by some external means.

Pacing involves pushing or forcing yourself to read faster than your normal speed while maintaining your level of comprehension. There are, of course, obvious limitations to this technique. For example, if your current leisure reading rate is 250 words per minute, it is not possible to increase your rate through pacing to 500 words per minute in one session without losing comprehension. Instead, pacing is based on small, incremental steps — 50 words per minute or less.

Pacing Methods

Because pacing is a key concept in the development of reading rate, it is often taught in reading labs and in commercial programs using specialized equipment. You may have heard about, or used, machines such as the Guided Reader or the Controlled Reader. These machines use filmstrips on which an article or story is printed. The machines expose the article, line by line, and can be set to move at a pace set by the reader. However, self-pacing techniques are almost as effective in increasing reading rate as machine-paced methods.

There are numerous ways to pace yourself for speed increase. Among the most common are these:

1. *Use an index card.* Slide a 3 × 5 card down the page as you read, moving it so that it covers up lines as they are read. This technique will force you along and keep you moving rapidly. Move the card down the page at a fixed pace, and try to keep up while reading. How fast you move the card will, of course, depend on the size of print, length of the line, etc., and will then vary for each new piece of material you read. At first you will need to experiment to find an appropriate pace. Try to move at a pace that is slightly uncomfortable and that you are not sure that you can maintain.

2. *Use your hand or index finger, or a pen or pencil.* Use your hand or index finger, pen or pencil in the same manner as the index card. Using your hand does not completely obstruct your view of the page and allows you to pick up clues from the layout of the page (to see that a paragraph is ending, that a graphic example is to follow, etc.).

3. *Use a timer or clock.* Start by measuring what portion of a page you can read in a minute. Then set a goal for yourself: determine how many pages you will attempt to read in a given period of time. Set your goal slightly above what you measured as your current rate. For example, suppose in a particular book you can read half a page in a minute. You might set as your goal to read five pages in nine minutes (forcing yourself to read a little more than a half page per minute). The next day, try to read five pages in eight or eight and a half minutes. Use an alarm clock or timer to let you know when you have used up your time.

As you begin to use one of these pacing methods, here are several suggestions to keep in mind.

1. Keep a record of your time, the amount you read, and words per minute. A quick way to estimate your speed is given in the Appendix at the end of the book.
2. Be sure that you maintain an adequate level of comprehension. To test your comprehension, try to summarize what you read. If you are unable to remember enough ideas to summarize what you read, then you have probably read too fast.
3. Push yourself gradually, across several weeks of practice.
4. Try to keep your practice material similar from day to day. That is, consistently use newspapers, or magazine articles, or the same paperback book for practice.

Why Pacing Works

Pacing is built on the principle that rate gain occurs in slow, incremental steps. Essentially, pacing provides a framework and a means to accomplish these incremental gains. Pacing is effective partly because it establishes a goal to be met, a speed to attain. It is psychologically motivating to work toward a goal, and when you attain a goal it is rewarding and encourages you to keep on working. Also, it provides a way for you to keep moving, without "getting lost in the print," so to speak. At times it is easy to become so involved with what you are reading that you become unaware of your speed and automatically shift to a slow, but comfortable speed. Pacing forces you to keep moving at a given rate unless you deliberately decide to slow down.

EXERCISE 17-1

Directions: *Select a magazine or newspaper article that you are interested in or a section of a paperback you are reading. Using one of the pacing techniques described in this section, try to increase your current reading speed by approximately 50 wpm. Record your results in the space provided.* (See the Appendix for information on how to estimate the number of words and your words-per-minute score.)

Article Used: _____

Estimated Level of Comprehension: _____

Finishing Time: _____

Starting Time: _____

Reading Time: _____

WPM: _____

KEY WORD READING

VERSION 1

KEY WORD READING NEW TECHNIQUE. FASTER THAN CAREFUL READING, DECREASE FACTUAL COMPREHENSION. WORTH LOSS, DEPENDING PURPOSE TYPE MATERIAL. (18 words)

VERSION 2

Key word reading is a new technique. Although it is faster than most of the careful reading techniques, the reader must expect a decrease in factual comprehension skill. In some situations, it is worth the loss, depending on the reader's purpose and the type of material being read. (48 words)

Were you able to understand the message conveyed in Version 1? If so, then you are already on your way to mastering the technique of key word reading. You have already read in a manner similar to key word reading. Compare the number of words in each version. Notice what is deleted in the first version that is included in the second. Did you gain much additional information about key word reading from the complete version that you had not acquired in the first?

What Is Key Word Reading?

From our example, you can see that key word reading involves skipping over nonessential words and reading only those words and phrases which carry the primary or core meaning of each sentence.

To further understand key word reading, read the following paragraph in which the key words have been underlined. Read the paragraph two ways. First, read only the underlined key words in the

404

paragraph. Can you understand the message the paragraph is conveying? Second, read the entire passage. How much additional information did you acquire?

> America's <u>only</u> <u>nonelected</u> <u>president</u>, <u>Gerald Ford</u>, became chief <u>executive</u> at a time when the <u>nation</u> desperately <u>craved</u> an <u>end</u> to <u>distrust</u> and <u>uncertainty</u>. <u>Ford</u> seemed the <u>right</u> <u>man</u> to <u>initiate</u> the <u>healing process</u>. A stolid <u>legislator</u> who had served in the <u>House</u> for <u>many years</u> <u>without</u> great <u>distinction</u>, he was an <u>open</u>, <u>decent</u>, and <u>generous</u> person, and <u>most Americans</u> seemed to <u>like him</u>.[1]

By reading only the key words, you probably were able to understand the basic message of the paragraph. Then, when you read the complete paragraph, you only learned a few additional details about Ford.

In developing skill in key word reading, it sometimes helps to think of the process as similar to that of reading a telegram, the headline in a newspaper, or a news caption which is run across the bottom of a television screen while a program is in progress.

> Telegram: ARRIVING TUESDAY 6 P.M. AMERICAN FLIGHT 321. LAGUARDIA.

> TV News Caption: AIRLINE HIJACKING LOS ANGELES. 52 HOSTAGES. FOUR HIJACKERS. IDENTITY AND PURPOSE UNKNOWN.

Both of these messages contain only the words that carry the basic meaning. Most frequently, these meaning-carrying words are nouns, action verbs, and important descriptive adjectives and adverbs. They are the words that tell the "who, what, when, and where" and frequently include names, dates, places, numbers, capitalized words, and italicized words.

EXERCISE 17-2

Directions: *To become more familiar with the idea of key words, write your response to each of the following situations using only key words. Your response should resemble a very abbreviated message such as a telegram.*

1. *Situation:* You are rushed for time but need to leave a note for your garage mechanic describing what needs repair

on your car, when you need it repaired, and that he should check with you if the cost exceeds $100.

Response: _____

_____

2. *Situation:* You are sending a cablegram to your grandmother in Florida. She is purchasing a car for you but she needs written confirmation that she has permission to register the car in your name. She also needs your address, social security number, and driver's license number.

Response: _____

_____

3. *Situation:* Your high school brother says he can't think of anything to write about for an English composition on the topic of "Deciding to Go to College." You agreed to jot down some ideas, but you forgot and now you are almost late for work. What would you write?

Response: _____

_____

When to Use Key Word Reading

You will find that key word reading is a valuable and efficient technique for some reading situations. Because key word reading involves both reading and skipping, you should expect your comprehension to be 70 percent or lower, usually in the 50–70 percent range. But, as a tradeoff for lower comprehension, you can expect an increase in rate. Actually you gain more than you lose because, although you read less than half of the material, normally you can expect to get more than 50 percent of the message. Conceivably, your rate could exceed the physical limit of 800 words per minute because you are no longer reading everything. Realistically, you might expect to achieve reading rates of between 600 and 700 words per minute when using key word reading.

Key word reading cannot be used on all types of material. There are many situations in which a comprehension level of below 80 percent is not acceptable. Especially when reading textbooks or highly technical material, your goal should be to understand everything, and key word reading is obviously not appropriate. However, there are many situations in which a level of comprehension in the 60–70 percent range is adequate. In these situations, key word reading will suit your purposes and enable you to cover the material at a high speed.

Here are a few situations in which key word reading might be an appropriate technique.

1. When you are reading magazine movie reviews to decide if you want to see the movie.
2. When you are reading encyclopedia entries to determine if this encyclopedia contains any information that you do not already have.
3. When you are reading newspaper articles to find out the key ideas and primary details in a recent local event.
4. When using reference books to gain a general idea of an author's approach and treatment of an event, idea, concept, or theory.
5. When reading professional correspondence to determine the writer's purpose and level of and nature of response required.

Aids to Key Word Reading

The ability to key word read draws on many of the comprehension skills and reading techniques you have already acquired in this book. Your knowledge of sentence structure, specifically your awareness of punctuation, and your ability to identify sentence core parts will enable you to read key words effectively. You will also be using your knowledge and familiarity with the structure of the English language, which you have acquired naturally throughout your lifetime, to help you locate key words. Though you may not be aware of them, you have learned many rules and patterns of the structure of English.

Using Sentence Structure. As you learned in Chapter 4, sentences contain core parts that tell you what the sentence is about (the subject) and what is happening in relation to that subject (the predicate). As you know, the core parts of a sentence carry the basic meaning of the sentence. To illustrate this, look at the following paragraph in which all but the core parts have been deleted. As you read through it, you will notice that you get the basic meaning of each sentence and of the paragraph as a whole.

And so, by 1968 or 1969, the country found itself caught in a giant whirlpool of anger and change. Nothing from the past, apparently, was sacred any longer. Patriotism was in bad repute: students burned their draft cards and desecrated the American flag. Chastity had become a thing of the past: college students lived in open "sin," and skirts had crawled two-thirds the way up the female thigh. Civility in public life had almost disappeared: every group was demanding "liberation" and would take to the streets, occupy public buildings, attack the police, riot, or even throw bombs to get it. Worst of all, the family was disintegrating: despite parental protest, children dressed the way they wanted, smoked "pot," and abandoned promising careers and futures to become political activists. Wives demanded that husbands share household chores so they could take jobs or go back to school.[2]

Now, read the complete paragraph. Notice that it fills you in on the details you missed by reading only key words but also notice that you did not miss any of the key ideas.

And so, by 1968 or 1969, the country found itself caught in a giant whirlpool of anger and change. Nothing from the past, apparently, was sacred any longer. Patriotism was in bad repute: students burned their draft cards and desecrated the American flag. Chastity had become a thing of the past: college students lived in open "sin," and skirts had crawled two-thirds the way up the female thigh. Civility in public life had almost disappeared: every group was demanding "liberation" and would take to the streets, occupy public buildings, attack the police, riot, or even throw bombs to get it. Worst of all, the family was disintegrating: despite parental protest, children dressed the way they wanted, smoked "pot," and abandoned promising careers and futures to become political activists. Wives demanded that husbands share household chores so they could take jobs or go back to school.

As you begin to read key words, concentrate on looking for the core parts of each sentence. Looking for sentence core parts is essentially a process of searching for the basic meaning of a sentence.

EXERCISE 17-3

Directions: *In each of the following sentences, draw a line through the words that do* not *carry the essential meaning of the sentence. Only key words should remain. After completing each sentence, check (by rereading only the words that remain) to see if the basic meaning of the sentence has been conveyed.*

Example: Work ~~should~~ ~~be~~ arranged so ~~there~~ ~~are~~ specific stopping points ~~where~~ ~~you~~ ~~can~~ feel something ~~has~~ ~~been~~ ~~accomplished~~.

1.   In some large businesses, employees are practically strangers to each other and often do not discuss problems or ideas.
2.   Criminal law as we know it today is a product of centuries of change.[3]
3.   From the standpoint of criminal law, a criminal is an individual who is legally capable of conduct that violates the law and who can be shown to have actually and intentionally engaged in that conduct.[4]
4.   By the time Congress assembled on December 4, 1865, the Republican majority — Radicals as well as most moderates — were seething with anger at the Johnson government.[5]
5.   During the 1960s the United States attained a level of material well-being beyond anything dreamed of in the past.[6]

Using Punctuation. Just as punctuation serves as an aid to comprehension, so it can be an aid in locating key words. Punctuation can help you locate the key words in a sentence by signaling what is to follow, separating nonessential parts of a sentence from the main sentence or indicating the relationships of various parts of a sentence to one another.

The use of a colon or semicolon indicates that important information is to follow. Often, you can expect to find a separate but closely related idea when a semicolon is used. When you see a colon, you may anticipate a list of items. In both cases you are alerted to look for key words ahead.

Commas, depending on their use, provide several types of clues for the location of key words. When used to separate an introductory phrase from the main sentence, the comma tells you to pay more attention to the main sentence as you look for key words.

When used to separate items in a series, the comma indicates that all items are important and should be read as key words. Commas accompanied by a conjunction are used to join two complete thoughts; you should expect to find another set of key words that function as sentence core parts. The parenthetical use of the comma tells you that the information enclosed within the commas is nonessential to the basic meaning of the sentence and may be skipped when you read key words.

Using Typographical Aids. Most printed material contains typographical features that will help you to locate key words and phrases. Typographical aids include all aspects of the words that appear in print such as boldface print, colored print, italics, capitalization, underlining, enumeration (1 . . . 2 . . . 3 . . .), or listing of information. Most typographical aids emphasize important information; others help the reader organize the information. Italics, underlining, and dark or boldface print are all used to make important information more noticeable.

Using Grammatical Structure. Your knowledge of grammar can also help you read key words effectively. You have learned that certain words modify or explain others. You know that adjectives explain or describe nouns and that adverbs give further information about verbs. Adjectives and adverbs that modify the core parts of the sentence, then, are also important in key word reading.

For example, in the following sentence you see that the adjectives and adverbs (single underlining) make the meaning of the core parts (double underlining) more complete.

The <u>psychology</u> <u><u>instructor</u></u> <u>hastily</u> <u><u>summarized</u></u> his lecture.

You also know that many words in the English language work very much like glue — they stick other, more important words together, connecting the words that carry meaning. If classified by parts of speech, these "glue words" are usually prepositions, conjunctions, or interjections (such as Oh! or Well!).

In the following sentence, all the glue words have been deleted.

. . . summary, it seems safe . . . say . . . society, . . . whole, believes . . . individuals can control their destiny.

Can you still understand the sentence? Most likely you can guess the words that were deleted. Try it. Now, compare the words you supplied with the complete sentence.

In summary, it seems safe to say that society, on the whole, believes that individuals can control their destiny.

You probably got some words exactly correct, and for others you supplied a synonym. In either case, you supplied a word that fit into the meaning of the sentence.

You will find that as you read key words, you mentally fill in the glue words that tie the sentences together. This mental ability to supply missing information is based on a psychological principle called clozure.

In key word reading, then, you are reading a stripped-down version of each sentence. You might also think of it as viewing a skeleton or forming a word outline of a paragraph or passage.

EXERCISE 17-4

Directions: *Select a magazine or newspaper article or two or three pages from a nonfiction paperback you are reading. Before beginning to read, underline the key words in the first paragraph and in five to six sentences randomly selected from the remainder of the passage. Use key word reading on the article and record your results in the space provided.* (See the Appendix for information on how to estimate number of words and your words-per-minute score.)

Source of Material: _____

Finishing Time: _____

Starting Time: _____

Reading Time: _____

Estimated Total Number of Words: _____

WPM Score: _____

APPLYING WHAT YOU HAVE LEARNED

Directions: *Select one of the reading selections at the end of this chapter and apply the technique of key word reading. Before you begin reading, underline only the key words in the first paragraph and in five or six randomly selected sentences throughout the remainder of the article. This underlining will help you to start key word reading and will remind you to continue as you read. Establish as your goal for this exercise a comprehension level of 50 to 70 percent. Push yourself to read as rapidly as possible. Answer the multiple choice questions following the selection.*

REREADING FOR SPEED INCREASE

Rereading is an effective method that you can use to build your reading rate. This technique is similar to pacing in that it involves building your rate gradually, using small increments.

To reread for speed increase use the following steps:

1. Select an article or passage and read it as you normally would for careful or leisure reading.
2. Time yourself and compute your speed in words per minute after you finish reading.
3. Take a break (five minutes or so). Then reread the same selection. Push yourself to read faster than you read the first time.
4. Time yourself and compute your speed once again. You should be able to reread the selection at a faster rate than you read it initially.
5. Read a new selection, pushing yourself to read almost as fast as you *re*read the first selection.

How fast you will be able to reread will depend on the type of selection and difficulty of its organization as well as your purpose for reading it. Of course, your rereading speed will be faster than your original speed because you are familiar with both the organization and content of the material. You know what to expect and can go back quite rapidly over ideas that are already familiar.

You are probably wondering how rereading helps you read new, unfamiliar material faster. Rereading serves as a readiness technique or as a preparation for reading the new material faster. Rereading establishes the mechanical process of more rapid eye movements and gives you preliminary practice or a "trial run" with reading at a higher reading rate. You might compare rereading to the use of training wheels when learning to ride a bicycle. The training wheels are an aid or crutch; they help the rider keep balance while learning how to steer, pedal, brake, etc. Rereading helps you learn things about reading faster while keeping your comprehension in balance. Because you already have a basic understanding of the selection from your first reading, you are free to focus and concentrate on improving your rate.

Since rereading is a readiness technique to enable you to read new material faster, it is important to include the last step of the process — the transfer of your increased speed to new, unfamiliar material. Be sure to select material that is of the same difficulty, or perhaps a little easier than the first piece of material you used. It is best to use a second selection or passage from the same book or article from which you chose the first.

As in pacing, you should not try to make dramatic rate increases in any one practice session. Increases should be gradual.

412

APPLYING WHAT YOU HAVE LEARNED

Directions: *Using one of the reading selections at the end of this chapter, follow the steps for rereading for speed increase listed in the preceding section. Answer the multiple choice questions after your first reading. Use a different reading selection from another chapter for your second reading.*

	WPM Score	Comprehension Score
First Selection	_____	_____
Rereading	_____	
Second Selection	_____	_____
Rereading	_____	

READING SELECTION 29

I'D RATHER BE BLACK THAN FEMALE

Shirley Chisholm

Being the first black woman elected to Congress has made me some kind of phenomenon. There are nine other blacks in Congress; there are ten other women. I was the first to overcome both handicaps at once. Of the two handicaps, being black is much less of a drawback than being female.

If I said that being black is a greater handicap than being a woman, probably no one would question me. Why? Because "we all know" there is prejudice against black people in America. That there is prejudice against women is an idea that still strikes nearly all men — and, I am afraid, most women — as bizarre.

Prejudice against blacks was invisible to most white Americans for many years. When blacks finally started to "mention" it, with sit-ins, boycotts, and freedom rides, Americans were incredulous. "Who, us?" they asked in injured tones. "*We're* prejudiced?" It was the start of a long, painful reeducation for white America. It will take years for whites — including those who think of themselves as liberals — to discover and eliminate the racist attitudes they all actually have.

How much harder will it be to eliminate the prejudice against women? I am sure it will be a longer struggle. Part of the problem is that women in America are much more brainwashed and content with their roles as second-class citizens than blacks ever were.

Let me explain. I have been active in politics for more than twenty years. For all but the last six, I have done the work — all the tedious details that make the difference between victory and defeat on election day — while men reaped the rewards, which is almost invariably the lot of women in politics.

It is still women — about three million volunteers — who do most of this work in the American political world. The best any of them can hope for is the honor of being district or county vice-chairman, a kind of separate-but-equal position with which a woman is rewarded for years of faithful envelope stuffing and card-party organizing. In such a job, she gets a number of free trips to state and sometimes national meetings and conventions, where her role is supposed to be to vote the way her male chairman votes.

When I tried to break out of that role in 1963 and run for the New York State Assembly seat from Brooklyn's Bedford-Stuyvesant, the resistance was bitter. From the start of that campaign, I faced undisguised hostility because of my sex.

But it was four years later, when I ran for Congress, that the question of my sex became a major issue. Among members of my own party, closed meetings were held to discuss ways of stopping me.

My opponent, the famous civil-rights leader James Farmer, tried to project a black, masculine image; he toured the neighborhood with sound trucks filled with young men wearing Afro haircuts, dashikis, and beards. While the television crews ignored me, they were not aware of a very important statistic, which both I and my campaign manager, Wesley MacD. Holder, knew. In my district there are 2.5 women for every man registered to vote. And those women are organized — in PTAs, church societies, card clubs, and other social and service groups. I went to them and asked their help. Mr. Farmer still doesn't quite know what hit him.

When a bright young woman graduate starts looking for a job, why is the first question always: "Can you type?" A history of prejudice lies behind that question. Why are women thought of as secretaries, not administrators? Librarians and teachers, but not doctors and lawyers? Because they are thought of as different and inferior. The happy homemaker

414

and the contented darky are both stereotypes produced by prejudice.

Women have not even reached the level of tokenism that blacks are reaching. No women sit on the Supreme Court. Only two have held Cabinet rank, and none do at present. Only two women hold ambassadorial rank. But women predominate in the lower-paying, menial, unrewarding, dead-end jobs, and when they do reach better positions, they are invariably paid less than a man gets for the same job.

If that is not prejudice, what would you call it?

A few years ago, I was talking with a political leader about a promising young woman as a candidate. "Why invest time and effort to build the girl up?" he asked me. "You know she'll only drop out of the game to have a couple of kids just about the time we're ready to run her for mayor."

Plenty of people have said similar things about me. Plenty of others have advised me, every time I tried to take another upward step, that I should go back to teaching, a woman's vocation, and leave politics to the men. I love teaching, and I am ready to go back to it as soon as I am convinced that this country no longer needs a woman's contribution.

When there are no children going to bed hungry in this rich nation, I may be ready to go back to teaching. When there is a good school for every child, I may be ready. When we do not spend our wealth on hardware to murder people, when we no longer tolerate prejudice against minorities, and when the laws against unfair housing and unfair employment practices are enforced instead of evaded, then there may be nothing more for me to do in politics.

But until that happens — and we all know it will not be this year or next — what we need is more women in politics, because we have a very special contribution to make. I hope that the example of my success will convince other women to get into politics — and not just to stuff envelopes, but to run for office.

It is women who can bring empathy, tolerance, insight, patience, and persistence to government — the qualities we naturally have or have had to develop because of our suppression by men. The women of a nation mold its morals, its religion, and its politics by the lives they live. At present, our country needs women's idealism and determination, perhaps more in politics than anywhere else.

COMPREHENSION TEST 29

Directions: *Circle the letter of the correct answer.*

1. Ms. Chisholm sees being female as more of a handicap than being black because
   a) sexual prejudice is more deep-seated and accepted than racial prejudice and will be harder to overcome
   b) blacks have achieved complete equality in our society
   c) women are incapable of handling higher-level jobs
   d) women are too concerned with home and family to care about politics

2. One reason Ms. Chisholm won her congressional appointment was that

a) she had a large and organized group of voting women
b) she projected a strong black, male image in her campaign
c) her opponent underestimated her intelligence
d) men refused to vote because there was a female candidate running

3. All of the following were mentioned in the essay as being typical women's occupations except
   a) secretary
   b) teacher
   c) librarian
   d) administrator

4. One stereotype produced by prejudice is that of the woman as
   a) a highly successful lawyer
   b) the "happy homemaker"
   c) an administrator
   d) a congresswoman

5. Chisholm encourages women to run for political office because
   a) women have developed the qualities of patience and tolerance that are needed in government
   b) they are ready to advance to the highly rewarding secretarial positions
   c) women in political office have a good chance to advance to important positions
   d) there are too many women in teaching positions

6. The word "tedious" as used in this passage means
   a) easy to accomplish
   b) slow and rewarding
   c) time consuming and tiring
   d) extremely interesting

7. Shirley Chisholm spent most of her years in politics
   a) serving as a congresswoman
   b) doing the background work for others
   c) serving as an ambassador
   d) working as a congressional secretary

8. Which of the following statements *best* summarizes Chisholm's view of discrimination against blacks?
   a) Discrimination against blacks has been virtually eliminated.
   b) Little progress has been made in eliminating black discrimination.
   c) Blacks have done little to eliminate discrimination.

   d) Significant progress has been made, but discrimination still exists.

9. Which of the following is the best example of the term "tokenism" as used by Chisholm?
   a) One woman is appointed to an all male board of directors of a large corporation.
   b) One woman in an office that employs eight women is promoted to the position of office supervisor.
   c) A woman is hired as an elementary music teacher, although there were male applicants.
   d) A furniture saleswoman is awarded a trip to Florida for exceeding a company-wide sales goal.

10. Chisholm proves her point in this essay by
    a) citing statistics
    b) using purely emotional arguments
    c) using humor to engage the reader
    d) giving examples from personal experience

Selection 29:			1037 words
Finishing Time:	HR.	MIN.	SEC.
Starting Time:	HR.	MIN.	SEC.
Reading Time:		MIN.	SEC.
WPM Score:			
Comprehension Score:			%
Reading Efficiency Score:			

READING SELECTION 30
HOW ADDITIVES WORK

Let's take a closer look at the different types of food additives and how they work.

Preservatives function to slow down or prevent the growth of bacteria, yeasts, or molds. These microorganisms may merely spoil the flavor and texture of the food or may actually produce an end product that is dangerous for human consumption. Some of the more common preservatives used are sodium benzoate, sorbic acid (or potassium sorbate), and sodium nitrate.

Antioxidants slow down or prevent the reaction of components of a food with the oxygen in the air. Such reaction can produce undesirable flavors, such as rancidity in fats; unpleasant colors; and loss of vitamin value.

Emulsifiers are used for smooth blending of liquids or batters. Mono- and diglycerides are commonly used emulsifiers.

Stabilizers are often added to obtain a certain texture or to preserve a food's texture or its physical condition. For example, stabilizers are used to keep a liquid thick, to slow down the melting of ice cream, to prevent the fluid in a cheese from running off like water. Algin, xanthan gum, and other gums are stabilizers.

Sequestrants combine with trace amounts of metals that may be present in a product and prevent those metals from reacting with the foods to produce undesirable flavors or physical changes (to sequester means to keep in isolation). EDTA (ethylenediaminetetraacetic acid, a synthetically produced chemical) is a sequestrant.

Acids, alkalies, and buffers regulate the acidity of a food. We all know the difference between a tart cooking apple and a less tart (but still slightly acid) eating apple. In addition to its effect on taste, however, acidity is also very important to the preservation of food. Harmful bacteria usually do not grow in foods that are acid enough. Vitamins, including the natural vitamins present in food, tend to resist destruction more in foods that are acid,

especially during the cooking process. In many foods, the preservation of the ideal flavor and color is helped by maintaining a specific acidity in the food. For these purposes, the acids make foods more acid, the alkalies make them less acid, and the buffers prevent change in acidity during storage. Citric acid is a typical acid, sodium citrate is a typical and common buffer, and sodium bicarbonate is a typical alkali.

Nutritional additives are the vitamins, minerals, and amino acids added to food either to enhance its nutritional value or to replace nutrients that might have been removed during processing. Some confusion has arisen now that vitamins are referred to by their chemical names rather than as *vitamins* in the ingredient list. It's unfortunate, but the listings of vitamins on the food label sometimes sound horrifying because their precise chemical names are given. "Vitamin B_1" is a lot more reassuring than "thiamine mononitrate."

Colors and flavors are added to make the food more appealing in appearance, smell, and taste.

Bleaching or maturing agents serve to oxidize wheat flour. While many foods must be protected against oxidation in order to preserve their quality, wheat flour used for baking must be oxidized in order to achieve the necessary quality.

Many years ago, it was possible to store flour for the necessary period of a month or longer to allow such oxidation to occur naturally with air. However, with bulk handling of flour and the massive bakeries that exist today, much flour is bleached in order to achieve artificial aging and to make the flour suitable for industrial use so that bread and cake can be produced uniformly at high speed.

Non-nutritive sweeteners sweeten without calories. Until 1978, both calcium cyclamate and saccharin were used to replace sugar in foods for those people who were supposed to restrict their intake of ordinary sweets. When

417

cyclamate was "found" to produce cancer in laboratory animals, it was prohibited under the Delaney Clause. Since 1978, saccharin alone has been used.

For years, saccharin was required to bear the statement "Contains *x* percent saccharin, an artificial sweetener to be used only by persons who must restrict their intake of ordinary sweets." Sometimes this statement was in type so small it could not be read without a magnifying glass.

Now, saccharin also has been "found" to produce cancer in laboratory animals. Under the Delaney Clause, it too would have been prohibited, but since it is the only usable artificial sweetener available, a delay in its prohibition has been granted, and even extended, to provide more time for confirmatory testing. (The granting of this delay actually required Congressional action.) In the meantime, saccharin must carry the warning:

"Use of this product may be hazardous to your health. This product contains saccharin, which has been determined to cause cancer in laboratory animals."

The history of artificial sweeteners is an example of the seriousness with which our food labeling regulations are applied, and of the problems raised by the Delaney Clause. The rationale for the delay in the prohibition of saccharin is that the danger to people that would occur through its elimination (overweight and resultant cardiac disease and stroke) is greater than the danger of cancer. In the meantime, retesting of saccharin and cyclamates, and the testing of new substances, such as aspartame, is proceeding in the hope of finding that there is no confirmable cancer-producing hazard.

Miscellaneous materials such as leavening agents and those used for other special purposes will be explained as we go through the labels further on.

COMPREHENSION TEST 30

Directions: *Circle the letter of the correct answer.*

1. The author's main purpose in writing this passage probably was to
   a) scare people into growing their own food
   b) illustrate the importance of a balanced diet
   c) encourage the government to ban unnecessary additives
   d) describe some commonly used food additives and their effects

2. Preservatives are used in food processing to
   a) retard the growth of bacteria
   b) encourage vitamin growth
   c) make food taste better
   d) give food a pleasing color

3. The reaction of metals with certain foods and the resulting bad flavors may be prevented by
   a) adding sodium nitrate
   b) the addition of a sequestrant
   c) removing the metal during processing
   d) using buffers

4. The nutritional additives include
   a) saccharin and sugar
   b) water and cyclamates
   c) vitamins and minerals
   d) sorbic acid and artificial flavoring

5. Both cyclamates and saccharin have been found to cause cancer in laboratory animals. However, saccharin is still being marketed because it
   a) is the only artificial sweetener available
   b) is not believed to cause cancer in persons who cannot eat sugar
   c) is used only in limited areas of the country
   d) is impossible to consume enough saccharin to do yourself serious harm

6. The word "rancidity" is used in the passage to mean that a food has
   a) become better tasting
   b) been fermented for other uses
   c) spoiled or become rotten
   d) had too many acids added

7. The purpose of the Delaney Clause seems to be to
   a) protect the public against potentially harmful additives
   b) control the shelf lives of packaged foods
   c) prevent delays in congressional hearings
   d) allow cyclamates to be used as additives

8. The processing of certain foods causes the natural vitamins in them to
   a) become rancid
   b) become better tasting
   c) be improved
   d) be destroyed

9. The value of most additives is that they
   a) decrease the price of the product
   b) are usually beneficial to the quality of the food

   c) do not affect the taste or texture of the food
   d) make the food organic

10. From this selection, you can conclude that the author is probably
    a) opposed to using additives in foods
    b) in favor of all food additives
    c) neither opposed to nor in favor of food additives
    d) a prominent cancer researcher

Selection 30:	899 words
Finishing Time:	_____ _____ _____ HR MIN SEC.
Starting Time:	_____ _____ _____ HR. MIN. SEC.
Reading Time:	_____ _____ MIN. SEC.
WPM Score:	_____
Comprehension Score:	_____ %
Reading Efficiency Score:	_____

419

Chapter 18:
Reading Flexibility

Throughout the book you have seen that there are many factors that control how well and how fast you read. You have also learned a wide variety of skills and techniques to apply to different types of materials and situations. The last, and perhaps the most important, step in becoming an efficient and flexible reader is to make all these factors and skills work together, combining conditions and situations with techniques that are most appropriate. This step involves a deliberate matching of material, purpose, and technique. In this chapter we will analyze the matches that efficient and flexible reading requires.

SELECTING AN APPROPRIATE COMPREHENSION AND RECALL LEVEL

A guiding principle of efficient and flexible reading is that not all materials should be read in the same way or with the same level of comprehension. It is necessary, then, to select a level of comprehension appropriate for what you are reading. The level of comprehension and recall that you choose is largely determined by your purpose for reading. For example, if your goal in reading a textbook chapter is to pass an objective exam based on that chapter, then your purpose is to learn all the important facts and ideas. For this purpose you need a very high level of comprehension and recall.

Throughout the book you have seen numerous examples and have read several discussions of how your purpose for reading shapes *how* you read. Even though you are now *aware* of the need to select a comprehension and recall level that is compatible with your purpose, it is not always easy to apply this knowledge and make deliberate decisions about how you will read material before you begin reading. Practice and frequent reminders to yourself are necessary in order to get in the habit of assessing the level of understanding and retention a particular situation and piece of reading material requires.

To select an appropriate level of comprehension and recall, you might go through the following process:

1. Clearly define why you are reading the material. Is it an assignment? Are you reading for general information, for details, for entertainment, to keep up with current events?

2. Decide what you will be required to do, if anything, after you have read the material. Will you have to pass an exam on the content? Will you be participating in a class discussion? Will you summarize the information in a short paper? Will you discuss a current event with friends? You can see that activities that follow the reading of material determine, in part, the level of comprehension that is required. For example, if you will evaluate the ideas contained in a selection, a very high level of comprehension is required. You must completely understand the ideas and their relationship to one another before you can evaluate them. On the other hand, if you are reading about a topic to prepare for a class discussion, then a moderate level of comprehension or retention is needed. Most likely, although you would need to remember all the important ideas, you would not need to recall each supporting detail.

Table 18-1 classifies in a somewhat arbitrary fashion, the levels of comprehension from which you might choose and suggests, depending on the type of followup activity required, several situations for which

Table 18-1. LEVELS OF COMPREHENSION AND RECALL

LEVELS OF COMPREHENSION	PERCENTAGE OF RECALL	TYPES OF FOLLOW-UP REQUIRED	SAMPLE SITUATIONS
Complete	100	react, evaluate, interpret	reading a poem, writing a reaction paper, analyzing a writer's theory or argument, reading a contract
High	90–100	take an objective exam, write a summary	class assignments
Moderate	70–90	discuss the ideas	class assignments
Low	50–70	be entertained, relax	reading magazines, newspapers
Selective	50 or below	recall only main ideas; get an overview, locate specific information	reading newspapers, magazines, correspondence, reference material

you might select each level. You can see that there is a complete range of comprehension or recall levels from which to choose and that your choice primarily depends on the type of followup required which is directly hinged to your purpose for reading.

EXERCISE 18-1

Directions: *For each of the following situations indicate, in the space provided, the level of comprehension that would seem appropriate. For some items there may be more than one correct answer.*

1. Reading the classified ads to find an apartment to rent.

   _____

2. Reading a friend's English paper to help him or her revise it.

   _____

3. Reading the directions for assembling some metal shelving you bought.

   _____

4. Reading a book on houseplant care to find out how often to water your new plant.

   _____

5. Reading an article in *Newsweek* on the increase in violent crime in America for a sociology class discussion.

   _____

SELECTING AN APPROPRIATE READING TECHNIQUE

Once you have established your purpose for reading and, in light of the type of followup activity required, have selected a desired level of comprehension, then you are ready to choose an approach to the material. In other words, you need to decide what techniques are best suited to accomplish your purposes. For example, if your purpose is to become generally familiar with the scope and quality of a particular film by reading a movie review and the followup you intend is a decision of whether to see the film, then a low or selective level of comprehension would be appropriate. Since you are not concerned with every fact and detail of the film, you might decide to skim the review.

On the other hand, if you were using an encyclopedia to locate information on the personality or disposition on a particular breed of dog you would first scan to locate the appropriate volume and selection and entry. Then you would skim until you found a part of the entry that deals with personality. Finally, you would read that section with a moderate to high level of comprehension. You can see, then, that in many reading situations, an efficient and flexible reader uses more than one reading technique to accomplish his or her purpose.

In choosing a technique that will suit your purposes, consider this question: What technique will enable me to accomplish my purposes most efficiently? (How can I get what I need from the material in the least amount of time?) This question will lead you to select a technique that is best suited to your purpose, to your desired level of comprehension, and to the type of material you are reading.

Let's consider the techniques that you have learned and try to identify the situations in which each would be most useful. Again, you will see in Table 18-2 that the technique you select depends on your purpose for reading.

You can see that you have a variety of techniques from which to choose. As you may have already realized while experimenting with

Table 18-2. READING TECHNIQUES FOR VARIED PURPOSES

PURPOSE/SITUATION	LEVEL OF COMPREHENSION	TECHNIQUE
reading poetry evaluating	complete	careful, word by word
textbook assignments supplemental reading library research	high, moderate	phrase reading

locate all of major ideas
  and some supporting
  details
reading newspapers,
  magazines
	low	key word reading

locate main ideas
get overview of
  organization and
  content
	selective	skimming

locate particular facts	selective	scanning

various techniques, there are occasions in which it is effective to "mix and match" techniques. That is, in reading a single piece of material, you may find that you can skim certain parts and carefully read others, or that you can read key words for some portions, skim others, and phrase read the remainder.

However, to be done effectively, mixing and matching of techniques requires accurate assessment of the structure of the material and of the relative importance of various portions of the article. You must be familiar with the overall structure of an article in order to know where to use which technique, and you must have an overview of the content to be able to identify parts that are important and deserve thorough reading and those which are less important and can be read with lower comprehension.

ADJUSTING YOUR RATE ACCORDING TO PURPOSE

As mentioned earlier in the book, many adult readers read everything at the same rate. They read newspapers at the same speed as they read a technical report and a poem at the same speed as a magazine ad. This habit may be at the root of inefficient, inflexible reading, causing a reader to waste valuable time on material that is unimportant and to spend too little time concentrating on what is important. To overcome this habit it is necessary at first to adjust consciously to suit your purpose. Just as you selected an appropriate comprehension or recall level and an appropriate technique to suit your purpose, you should also adjust your reading rate. That is, depending on your purpose for reading a particular piece of material, you need to decide at what rate you can handle the material effectively. Rate, as you may have already realized, is not independent of such factors as comprehension and technique. The rate you choose must be low enough to provide adequate comprehension. Similarly, the technique you choose in part determines the rate at which you read. Skimming, by its nature, involves a very high reading rate; thorough word-by-word reading is necessarily slow.

As a general rule, the less specific your purpose is for reading, and the less comprehension you require, the faster you can afford to read. You can think of rate and comprehension as tradeoffs: as you increase one, you decrease the other. To read effectively, you have to maintain a balanced rate and comprehension. If you feel you are losing comprehension, then you should slow down. When it seems very easy to follow the author's train of thought, then speed up.

Unfortunately, there are no rules for how fast is "too fast," or what rate is considered slow. In this case you must rely on your judgment and the "feeling" you receive as you read. If you feel you are missing something, slow down. As a check, you might even go back and reread that section to see if you really did miss any information. Often, when trying to read faster, you become uncomfortable and afraid that you are missing ideas. Often this insecurity is unfounded and only the result of trying a new approach.

ADJUSTING YOUR RATE TO THE MATERIAL

Just as you adjust your reading rate to suit your purpose, you should also adapt it to suit the material you are reading. From your own experience as well as from the variety of reading selections you encountered in the book, you have realized that some materials are well organized and easy to read, whereas others use fewer organizational aids, difficult vocabulary, and complicated sentences and paragraphs, and are difficult to read.

Throughout the book, you have learned numerous skills that will help you read even difficult material more effectively. You have learned how to use various organizational aids, how to approach difficult vocabulary, how to untangle difficult sentences, how to recognize the structure of paragraphs, and so forth. Although these techniques will enable you to comprehend accurately and read a little faster, they cannot fully compensate for vast differences among types of materials. It is still necessary to read difficult material at a slower rate than more easy material.

The easiest way to assess the difficulty of a selection is to preread it. Prereading will reveal how well organized the material is and will give you a "taste" of the difficulty of language and content. Then, once you have made a quick estimate of a material's level of difficulty, you can adapt your rate accordingly.

As was true for adjusting your rate to suit your purpose, there is no rule of thumb to use in deciding how much to slow down or speed up to compensate for differing degrees of difficulty. Again, you are left to use your judgment and rely on a feeling for whether you are being as efficient as possible.

APPLYING WHAT YOU HAVE LEARNED

Directions: *Choose one of the selections at the end of the chapter. Define your purpose for reading and your desired level of comprehension and record them below. Then choose an appropriate reading technique and read the selection. After reading the selection, answer the multiple choice questions.*

Selection: _____

Purpose: _____

Expected Level of Comprehension: _____

READING SELECTION 31
A VERY SHORT HISTORY OF SOME AMERICAN DRUGS FAMILIAR TO EVERYBODY

Difficulty Level: A

Adam Smith

Our attitude toward the word "drug" depends on whether we are talking about penicillin or heroin or something in-between. The unabridged three-volume Webster's says a drug is "a chemical substance administered to prevent or cure disease or enhance physical and mental welfare" or "a substance affecting the structure or function of the body." Webster's should have added "mind," but they probably thought that was part of the body. Some substances that aren't drugs, like placebos, affect "the structure or function of the body," but they work because we *think* they're drugs.

We are a drug-using society. We take, for example, twenty thousand tons of aspirin a day, almost one aspirin per person in the whole country. Aspirin is a familiar drug from a family called salicylates, specifically, acetylsalicylic acid. It lowers body temperature, alleviates some types of pain, and stimulates respiration.

Nicotine is a familiar and widely recognized drug, a stimulant to the central nervous system. It is addictive. The toxic effects of nicotine have been detailed at great length by the Surgeon General. Americans smoke 600 billion cigarettes a year.

Alcohol is also a widely recognized drug. In the United States 70 million users spend $10 billion a year. Five million of the 70 million alcohol users are said to be addicts, that is, they have a physical dependence on the drug. Alcohol is unique, says the pharmacology textbook, because it is "the only potent pharmacological agent with which self-induced intoxication is socially acceptable." Alcohol is so much a part of everyday life we do not think of it, on the rocks or straight up, as a drug or a potent pharmacological agent.

Then there is the family of drugs called the xanthines. Americans take xanthines at the rate of 100 *billion* doses per year. Xanthines are alkaloids which stimulate portions of the cerebral cortex. They give you "a more rapid and clearer flow of thought, allay drowsiness. . . . motor activity is increased. There is a keener appreciation of sensory stimuli, and reaction time to them is diminished." This description, again from the pharmacology textbook, is similar to descriptions of cocaine and amphetamine. Of course, the xanthine addict pays a price. He is, says Sir Clifford Allbutt, Regius Professor of Medicine at Cambridge, "subject to fits of agitation and depression; he loses color and has a haggard appearance. The appetite falls off; the heart suffers; it palpitates, or it intermits. As with other such agents, a renewed dose of the poison gives temporary relief, but at the cost of the misery."

Xanthines are generally taken orally through "aqueous extracts" of the plants that produce these alkaloids, either in seeds or leaves. In the United States the three most common methylated xanthines taken are called caffeine, theophylline and theobromine. The seeds of *Coffea arabica* contain caffeine, the leaves of *Thea sinensis* contain caffeine and theophylline, and the seeds of *Theobroma cacao* contain caffeine and theobromine. In America the three are known as "coffee," "tea" and "cocoa," and they are consumed daily, at the rate of billions of pounds a year. They are generally drunk as hot drinks, but Americans also drink cold drinks containing caffeine from the nuts of the tree *Cola acuminata*. The original drinks ended in the word "cola," but now there are many "colas" which do not bear that name in the title. The early ads for Coca-Cola said it gave you a lift.

Coffee, tea, cocoa and cola drinks are all drugs. Caffeine is a central nervous system stimulant, theophylline less so, and theobromine hardly at all. All xanthines increase the production of urine. Xanthines act on smooth muscles — relaxing, for example, especially in the case of theophylline, bronchi that may have been constricted. Like the salicylates — aspirin — xanthines can cause stomach irritation. Caffeine can cause sleeplessness, and researchers have found that it causes chromosome breaks.

Maxwell House, meet the Regius Professor of Medicine. Is the stuff good to the last drop, or another dose of the poison? Is it a food, to be sold in supermarkets, or a stimulant to the central nervous system like the amphetamines? "The popularity of the xanthine beverages depends on their stimulant action, although most people are unaware of any stimulation," says the giant pharmacology text.

It is surprising to find substances we think of so cheerfully, perkin' in the pot, listed as drugs. That's the point. In our society, there are some drugs we think of as okay drugs, and other drugs make us gasp. A coffee drinker who drinks coffee all day and cannot function without it is just a heavy coffee drinker, but someone using a non-okay drug is a "drug user" or an "addict."

Consumer Reports asked: how did drugs with such potential hazard spread without arousing the legal repression and social condemnation aroused by other drugs? They were domesticated, it said. There was no illegal black market, the dosages were relatively small, and some people buffered the drug effect with cream and sugar.

The worst of what our society thinks of as "hard drugs" comes from the unripe capsule of the opium poppy. In the nineteenth-century United States, you could buy opiates at grocery stores and drugstores, and by mail. Godfrey's Cordial — a molasses, sassafras and opium combination — was especially popular. Genteel Southern ladies in lace and ruffles, smelling of verbena and other sweet things, sounding like

Scarlett O'Hara, were slugging down daily a combination of opium and alcohol called laudanum. The first surveys of narcotics showed that women outnumbered men three to one, because "the husbands drank alcohol at the saloon, and the wives took opium at home."

The point of this capsule history is not to warn people from the perilous xanthines. (I drink them all, *Coffea arabica* and *Thea sinensis*, sweetened, no cream, please, and *Theobroma cacao* on cold winter days, and *Cola acuminata* on warm summer ones, and I have to be paying attention to be aware of the stimulant action.)

Nor is it to diminish the danger of illegal narcotics. (Legal narcotics are part of legitimate medicine.) There is no comparison between legal, domesticated, mild, buffered drugs and illegal and undomesticated ones, but it is society that has produced the legalities and the domestication. Illegal narcotics, producing huge profits and employing the worst criminal elements, are merchandised to the least stable elements of society, producing tremendous social problems.

A Coke at snack time, a drink before dinner, a cup of coffee after dinner, a cigarette with the coffee — very relaxing. Four shots of drugs. Domesticated ones. It would be rather comic to have addicts sneaking down dark alleys for a shot of coffee, but nicotine is so strong that when currencies fail — Germany right after World War II, for example — cigarettes become currency.

In some Muslim countries, you can sit and smoke hashish all day at a café, but possession of alcohol will land you in jail; in the United States you can sit in a saloon ingesting alcohol all day, but possession of hashish will land you in jail.

The drug taken by the astronauts of inner space was, at that time, legal. It was also nonnarcotic and nonaddictive. It crops up in the story not only because it was used in the exploration of the mind, but because so many explorers in meditation, biofeedback and other disciplines went through a stage with it.

Lysergic acid diethylamide was invented by the Swiss. Curious to think of the Swiss, the symbol of sobriety and industry, watchmaking and cuckoo clocks, as having invented LSD, Librium and Valium, psychedelics and tranquilizers, the turn-ons and the turn-offs, but then the Swiss have been in the drug business since Paracelsus of Basle, roughly a contemporary of Columbus.

COMPREHENSION TEST 31

Directions: *Circle the letter of the correct answer.*

1. The major conclusion you can draw from this passage is that
   a) the effects of certain narcotic drugs are dependent on where they were manufactured
   b) Americans consume many types of drugs routinely, but are often unaware of their effects
   c) xanthines are popular solely because they may be taken by mouth
   d) alcohol addiction is America's most serious drug problem

2. Two of the most widely used drugs in the United States are
   a) ethyl and dioxin
   b) alcohol and aspirin
   c) cyanide and glycerine
   d) codeine and analgesics

3. It is hard for many Americans to think of which of the following as a drug?
   a) "pep pills"
   b) hashish
   c) cocaine
   d) alcohol

4. Cola drinks, tea, and coffee are examples of the group of drugs known as
   a) salicylates
   b) norepinephrines
   c) xanthines
   d) saccharides

5. The author admitted to regularly consuming coffee, tea, cocoa, and cola drinks and that the stimulant effect of these drugs was
   a) hallucinogenic
   b) not noticed at all
   c) noted only if he specifically looked for it
   d) strong enough to make him dizzy

6. The word "placebo" was used in this passage to mean a (n)
   a) narcotic
   b) inactive substance
   c) addictive drug
   d) opium derivative

7. The writer suggests that you might be arrested for smoking hashish in the United States, but not for drinking alcohol because alcohol
   a) is not as harmful to your body
   b) is not addictive but hashish is
   c) is produced in this country, whereas hashish is not
   d) consumption is socially accepted but smoking hashish is not

8. The effects of drinking a Pepsi, though not nearly as extreme, would be similar to taking
   a) amphetamines
   b) DES
   c) penicillin
   d) LSD

9. If a person drinks coffee steadily all day while at work, his coworkers are most likely to think of him as
   a) an addict of depressant drugs
   b) a heavy user of placebos
   c) not susceptible to caffeine effects
   d) the user of an "okay" drug

10. When the author says "Maxwell House, meet the Regius Professor of Medicine," he intends to
    a) actually introduce them to each other
    b) emphasize the commonplace nature of drugs
    c) refer the coffee company to medical research
    d) frighten us into switching from coffee to tea

Selection 31:   1269 words

Finishing Time: _____ _____ _____
                  HR.   MIN.   SEC.

Starting Time: _____ _____ _____
                 HR.   MIN.   SEC.

Reading Time: _____ _____
                          MIN.   SEC.

WPM Score: _____

Comprehension Score: _____ %

Reading Efficiency Score: _____

READING SELECTION 32
SCRAMBLE ON THE POLAR ICE

It appears frozen in time, an icy world surrounded by frigid seas where winds of 100 m.p.h. are not uncommon. No human is known to have set foot upon it until the 19th century, and even today it exposes unwary travelers to the greatest dangers. Temperatures regularly plunge to −100° F or below. Giant crevasses can open in the ice, swallowing men and machines. Sudden storms often blend ground and sky into one snowy blur that hopelessly disorients the most skilled aviators.

During his doomed dash to the South Pole in 1912, British Explorer Robert Falcon Scott was right enough when he called it this "awful place." But Antarctica, half again as large as the continental U.S., is also a world of spectacular beauty. Beyond its great central plateau, where the ice is more than two miles thick, are towering mountains, volcanoes, and glaciers as big as Rhode Island that creep inexorably toward the sea at rates of up to two miles a year. There are even curious, snow-free "dry valleys" where the winds have sculpted the rocks into a phantasmagoria of surreal shapes.

Though Antarctica gets less precipitation than the Sahara (less than 2 in. a year), nearly two-thirds of the world's fresh water is locked up in the polar icecap. Even bacteria are barely able to cling to life in the interior, but the coastal regions abound with seals and penguins, to say nothing of the whales that come from round the world to winter in Antarctica's icy, protein-rich waters.

This forbidding continent has lately become more than the testing ground for explorers in mukluks and wooden sledges. It is being eyed acutely for mineral wealth, once deemed far too difficult and expensive to mine. Geologists have already confirmed that it holds great quantities of iron and coal, including perhaps the world's largest coal field, running more than 1,500 miles along the Transantarctic Mountains. There are strong indications of other treasures as well. More than 200 million years ago, before the world's continents began their slow drift apart, Antarctica was attached to South America, Africa, India and Australia as part of a great landmass that scientists call Pangaea (Greek for whole earth). In strata similar to those of its long-separated continental cousins, Antarctica, like the tip of South America and southeastern Australia, may possess uranium.

During the six-month austral, or southern, summer, when the South Pole is bathed in sunlight 24 hours a day, geologists from the U.S., Australia and New Zealand explored the rocky mountains of Northern Victoria Land. They found signs of such valuable metals as tantalum and lithium, used for making high-strength alloys. The Dufek Massif in the Pensacola Mountains, similar to South Africa's Bushveld, may have platinum and chromium, both strategic metals.

The greatest prize may be oil. In the 1972–73 season, the deep-sea drill ship *Glomar Challenger* found the hydrocarbons ethane, methane and ethylene in shallow sediments at the bottom of the Ross Sea. All three are regarded as indicators of oil. Since then one Gulf Oil executive has estimated that there may be 50 billion bbl. of oil under the ice-covered Weddell and Ross seas, comparable to Alaska's estimated reserves. At present, extracting it would be prohibitively expensive, but geologists are convinced that drilling may soon become technologically practical in Antarctica as well.

Ecologists wonder what an oil spill or blowout in the Antarctic might do to the fragile environment. But there are still larger questions: Who owns these resources and how could any rush to exploitation be regulated? Earlier in the century, seven nations laid claims to wedge-shaped slices of the Antarctic pie. Three of these claims, those of Chile, Argentina and Britain, overlap. Neither the U.S. nor the Soviet Union has staked out any territory, nor does either country recognize anyone else's claim. For the time being at least, all territorial squabbling has been put in a sort of legal cold storage by a 1961 international pact called the Antarctic Treaty. Under its terms, the signatories — there are 14, including the U.S. and U.S.S.R. — pledged themselves to three key things: keeping Antarctica free of nuclear weapons, forbidding military activity, freely exchanging scientific information about the continent. Also implicit in the treaty is an agreement that no country will act unilaterally on its own claim.

But the treaty is subject to review. And as geologists find new evidence of the extent of Antarctic wealth, some countries are becoming increasingly vocal about asserting rights to any resources found within their territories or off their shores. These waters teem with krill — small, shrimplike protein-rich crustaceans that are being exploited not only by wintering whales, but by fleets of Soviet, Japanese, West German and Polish fishing boats.

Until now, the American interest has been primarily scientific. The U.S. maintains four stations, the largest a sprawling collection of huts and machines on Ross Island, overlooking McMurdo Sound, at the edge of the Ross Ice Shelf. Equipped with everything from bars to laundromats, it serves as the central depot for U.S. operations in Antarctica. During the southern summer, the McMurdo base has a population of more than 800 people. Most are support personnel, provided by the U.S. Navy and a private contractor, for the teams of scientists who descend upon Antarctica each year.

The scientific investigations range from learning more about the continent's effects on the world's climate to unraveling the physiological mystery of how animals like large-eyed Weddell seals survive so harsh a climate. But the scientists acknowledge that the allure of Antarctica is itself a powerful magnet. Says Geologist Edmund Stump of Arizona State University: "Walking over a ridge that no man has set foot on before produces a spell that eventually captures us all."

The most intriguing American outpost is at the pole itself. Located under a giant geodesic dome, the station serves as an invaluable high-altitude (9,200 ft.) geophysical observatory. Because of the pristine quality of the air and the funnel-like shape of the earth's magnetic field at the antipodes, scientists are able to measure the amount of carbon dioxide and pollutants in the atmosphere and register the influx of cosmic rays from space (a hint of solar activity) with much greater ease than at any other place on the earth's surface. The station also acts as a laboratory for the study of human behavior in isolation. Last week the season's final flight took off from the pole. Left behind until November, when flights resume, were 17 people, including one visiting Soviet scientist, an atmospheric physicist. During the long polar night, radio will be their only contact with the outside world.

Though information gathered at the polar station is scientifically valuable and could even help doctors select and prepare the best possible crews for long space journeys, the reason for the American presence at the pole is as much geopolitical as geophysical. It gives the U.S. a unique toehold in all the Antarctic claims except the Norwegian, which stops short of the pole proper. Says Bernhard Lettau, polar oceanography manager for the National Science Foundation, which runs the U.S.'s $67.4 million-a-year Antarctic scientific effort: "The pole is highly symbolic. By being here we maintain our status as first among equals of the treaty nations and prevent the Soviets from grabbing our base."

That does not seem likely for the moment. But like other government agencies, NSF has been struck by the budget ax; for fiscal 1982, the Antarctic program has been effectively cut by 10%, curtailing scientific activity and delaying needed repairs at McMurdo. Meanwhile, the Soviet Union continues to expand its operations on the ice, with a total of seven research bases strategically scattered over nearly all of the claimed pie slices.

This disturbs U.S. officials. Says NSF Chief Polar Scientist Frank Williamson: "You can't tell me that a continent that occupies the whole bottom of the world isn't valuable. But our current investment here consists of six airplanes, seven helicopters and just over 1,000 people. It's minuscule compared to what we might be able to gain." From all the hints the

Antarctic is giving, the list of possible gains is likely to keep growing.

COMPREHENSION TEST 32

Directions: *Circle the letter of the correct answer.*

1. This article describes
   a) the battle between the United States and Russia to acquire new territories
   b) a desolate region that is of questionable research value
   c) a potentially rich, valuable, but unexploited region of the world
   d) the conflict between United States and Russian scientists

2. Although scientists have found evidence of oil under Antarctica's seas, they have not begun drilling operations because
   a) weather conditions are unpredictable
   b) specific regions containing oil have not been identified
   c) drilling is too expensive
   d) drilling rights have not been established

3. All of the following are conditions included in the Antarctica Treaty except
   a) forbidding any military action
   b) prohibiting nuclear weapons placement in Antarctica
   c) freely exchanging scientific information about Antarctica
   d) the United States and Soviet Union would divide Antarctica's territory between themselves

4. Because of Antarctica's unique position at the South Pole, scientists can *best* measure
   a) fluctuations in temperature
   b) amounts of pollutants in the atmosphere
   c) thickness of glaciers
   d) magnitudes of stars

5. Chief Polar Scientist Frank Williamson feels the American investment in Antarctica at the present time is

   a) extravagant
   b) minimal, considering the area's potential
   c) too narrowly research oriented
   d) too expensive

6. When referring to the *allure* of Antarctica, the author is referring to its
   a) threatening characteristics
   b) dependencies
   c) obvious disadvantages
   d) attractiveness

7. If a severe energy crisis should develop in the world you could expect
   a) all interest in exploration of the Antarctic to come to an abrupt halt
   b) a sudden surge of interest in the Antarctic
   c) a shift of manpower
   d) a dramatic decline in the amount of funds devoted to Antarctic research

8. If you owned a section of land in the Antarctic, the most valuable natural resource you might find is
   a) lithium
   b) coal
   c) uranium
   d) oil

9. The author is most likely to agree with which of the following statements on Antarctic exploration?
   a) It is a losing investment.
   b) Human life should never be risked unless national security is at stake.
   c) The possible gains justify the expense.
   d) Cost effectiveness does not allow us to allocate additional funds.

433

10. The author presents his case by
    a) threatening a Soviet takeover of Antarctica
    b) quoting from political and scientific reports
    c) giving examples of valuable discoveries in other regions
    d) presenting facts and statistics about the region

Selection 32:	1370 words

Finishing Time: ___ ___ ___
HR.   MIN.   SEC.

Starting Time: ___ ___ ___
HR.   MIN.   SEC.

Reading Time: ___ ___
MIN.   SEC.

WPM Score: ___

Comprehension Score: ___ %

Reading Efficiency Score: ___

434

Chapter 19:
How Much Have You Improved?
Posttests

Now that you have completed the text, no doubt you have acquired many new skills and have polished many existing skills. Through your day-to-day reading of textbooks, reference material, magazines, and newspapers, most likely you have noticed that you can approach various types of material with a new level of efficiency and flexibility. Also, most likely you have demonstrated increasing levels of efficiency and flexibility in your week-to-week progress with the end-of-chapter reading selections.

Now it is time for you to measure your overall improvement. You may recall that in Chapter 2 you completed pretests that assessed your skill level at the beginning of the course. This chapter contains similarly structured, equally difficult posttests. By comparing your performance on the pretests with that of the posttests, you will see how much you have improved.

MEASURING YOUR READING EFFICIENCY

To assess your present level of reading efficiency, complete the following posttest. Be sure to time yourself accurately and to read the passage as directed.

Reading Efficiency Posttest

1. Assume that the following article on computers appeared in the magazine you are reading. You realize that computers influence our daily lives so you decide to find out as much as you can about computers from reading the article. Read the article with the purpose of learning as much as you can about computers.
2. Before you begin reading, record the time in minutes and seconds in the space on page 439 marked Starting Time. Then begin reading the selection. Read it only once. When you finish, record the time in the space marked Finishing Time.

3. Complete the comprehension questions that follow the selection. Do not look up the answers. Refer to the selection only when answering a question that refers to a particular term, sentence, or paragraph.

4. Score your answers using the Answer Key. Record your score (number correct multiplied by 10) in the space marked Comprehension Score.

5. Use the words-per-minute conversion chart on pages 456–457 to find the average number of words that you read per minute and record it in the space marked WPM Score.

6. Compute your Reading Efficiency Score and record it on the Posttest Summary on page 452.

READING EFFICIENCY POSTTEST
MAY THE SOURCE BE WITH YOU

For most families, household utilities usually mean electricity, the heating system and a supply of fresh water. But when middle-income New Yorkers next month begin moving into a newly completed 52-unit condominium at 260 West Broadway in Manhattan's Tribeca district, they will find not just sinks, tubs and electrical outlets, but builder-installed computer terminals. The inconspicuous machines, which look like small television sets with a keyboard, are hooked up to a McLean, Va., firm that styles itself an "information utility." Its daunting name: the Source.

The Source and its 12,000 nationwide customers are part of the still small, but explosively growing, new business of consumer data banks. For fees that can amount to as little as a few cents a month, the data banks are using computer technology and telephone lines to provide household subscribers with the opportunity to summon up-to-the-minute information on everything from the action on Wall Street to the best shopping bargains available from brand-name discount houses around the country.

For years major corporations have earned extra income by marketing the sort of research and scientific information that routinely get produced and then filed away in the normal course of business. Data banks buy the information, put it in their own computers and then resell it either to other corporations or perhaps to large research institutes.

One such bank, DIALOG Information Services Inc. of Palo Alto, Calif., buys reports, statistics and doctoral dissertations from some 140 different corporations, universities and even the government. When using the service, a subscriber dials a toll-free 800 number and connects his telephone receiver to a coupler device that links his office computer to the DIALOG computer. He can then transmit queries and receive the answers within seconds. Cost for such services can run as high as $300 an hour, a sum that businesses can afford much more readily than the average individual can.

But the mushrooming popularity of personal computers has now begun to
spur the development of data banks specially tailored for individual consumers.
The Source, which is a subsidiary of *Reader's Digest*, offers subscribers everything
from financial planning to word processing. Source subscribers can monitor the
schedule of current legislative activities in the Congress, check the latest changes
in airline schedules and send "electronic mail" to other subscribers by using
Source computers as a kind of space-age postal system. Gerald Reinen, a
Massachusetts business consultant, reports that not only does he use the Source
for business applications at the office but his children use it at home when they
want to look up movie reviews.

Another consumer data bank, CompuServe Inc., of Columbus, offers
electronic copies of stories in ten major national newspapers, including the
Washington *Post* and the New York *Times* on the same day that the newspapers
hit the stands. Also available is current news from the Associated Press wire
service. Through its Microquote data base, CompuServe provides constantly
updated information on any of more than 40,000 different stocks, bonds and
commodities.

Prices are not cheap. The Source charges customers a one-time sign-up fee of
$100, plus a monthly fee of $10, whether the system is used or not. Additional "on-
line" fees can be anywhere from $4.25 to $30 an hour, depending upon the time of
day and the nature of the information requested. CompuServe requires an initial
sign-up fee of $19.95, but fees for on-line usage during business hours are higher
than the Source's.

Before he can communicate with a data bank, a subscriber needs either a
personal computer, which can cost anywhere from $1,500 to $8,000, or one of the
much less expensive electronic keyboards that retail in hobby shops for under
$400. There is a serious drawback to the keyboards, though. While cheaper to buy,
they often wind up being more expensive to use. Reason: keyboards lack computer
memory power, and thus can communicate with data banks only at the pace of the
human typing information into the machine, which is fairly slow by computer
standards.

In contrast, personal computers can be preprogrammed to ask questions
before they are ever connected to data banks. Moreover, once connected, via a toll-
free call over a household telephone line, the personal computers can transmit
requests for data at superfast speeds. This can cut a subscriber's on-line usage
from hours to minutes, or even seconds, at a time, resulting in huge savings in
monthly bills. Says Marshall Graham, president of the Source: "Our equipment is
constantly in operation, but the average bill to our customers is no more than about
$25 per month."

Though total subscribers to both the Source and CompuServe now number
fewer than 27,000, the Source alone expects to have 20 times that many on-line
customers within three years. Meanwhile, a number of other companies, including
CBS, Warner Amex, Cox Broadcasting and Time Inc., are working to bring similar
services into the home via so-called interactive cable-television systems. Such
systems would use a television cable instead of a telephone line to transmit the
data, and permit viewers to extract information by means of specially modified
television sets equipped with keyboards. Tests are now under way with cable
subscribers in San Diego, Columbus, Dallas and elsewhere. Whatever the actual
transmission technology, it seems that people are becoming increasingly hungry

437

for the information wizardry that computers are bringing about, especially now that the magic can be brought right into the home.

COMPREHENSION TEST

Directions: *Circle the letter of the correct answer.*

1. This article was written to describe
   a) the increasing popularity of electronics
   b) the trend toward home computers
   c) the problems of national data banks
   d) the costs of computer time

2. To use a data system such as the Source, a customer must do all of the following except
   a) pay a sign-up fee
   b) write a simple conversion program
   c) purchase a home computer or keyboard
   d) pay an "on-line" hourly usage fee

3. The cost of subscribing to the Source involves a
   a) $10 sign-up fee
   b) $30 wiring/installation fee
   c) $100 sign-up fee
   d) $60 wiring/installation fee

4. Personal computers may be connected with the data bank through
   a) basic electronic wiring systems
   b) interactive video
   c) cable hookups
   d) ordinary telephone lines

5. According to the article, the minimum cost of a personal computer is about
   a) $400
   b) $800
   c) $1,500
   d) $2,500

6. The term "spur" means
   a) defer
   b) restrict
   c) direct
   d) encourage

7. It may be cheaper in the long run to use a personal computer rather than a keyboard to communicate with a data system because
   a) keyboards use up more data system computer time
   b) keyboards do not provide a printed record of the information
   c) keyboards require a fast accurate typist
   d) keyboards have more difficulty reprogramming and correcting errors

8. The article suggests that
   a) businesses can afford data bank links more than private individuals

b) data bank links will soon be used by everyone
c) electronic computing is becoming the most popular hobby in the country
d) cable subscribers are a particular breed of mechanical geniuses

9. Which one of the following groups of people is most likely to subscribe to the Source?
a) small business men and women interested in reaching clients in their local community
b) a national advertising firm that wants to advertise a product to potential consumers
c) lawyers interested in locating information on their clients
d) a wine importer who is attempting to increase the popularity of "light," low-calorie wines

10. The writer's attitude toward computer data banks is one of
a) suspicion and distrust
b) shock
c) excitement and amazement
d) envy

Efficiency Posttest:		903 words
Finishing Time:		
	HR. MIN.	SEC.
Starting Time:		
	HR. MIN.	SEC.
Reading Time:		
	MIN.	SEC.
WPM Score:		
Comprehension Score:		%
Reading Efficiency Score:		

MEASURING YOUR READING FLEXIBILITY

The following posttests are designed to measure your current level of reading flexibility. It consists of three reading selections with very specific directions for completing each. As you work through this post-test, be sure to read and follow the directions carefully.

Reading Flexibility Posttest 1

1. Assume that the following selection was assigned by your psychology instructor. You are expected to read the material carefully so that you can take an exam based on its content. Read this selection in order to be able to recall most of what you read.

2. Before you begin reading, record the time in minutes and seconds in the space on page 444 marked Starting Time. Then begin reading the selection. Read it only once. When you finish, record the time in the space marked Finishing Time.

3. Complete the comprehension questions that follow the selection. Do not look back at the selection to answer the questions unless a question refers to a particular word, sentence, or paragraph.

4. Score your answers using the Answer Key. Record your score (number correct multiplied by 10) in the space marked Comprehension Score.

5. Use the word-per-minute conversion chart on pages 456–457 to find the average number of words that you read per minute and record it in the space marked WPM.

6. Compute your reading efficiency score and fill in the Posttest Summary on page 452.

FLEXIBILITY POSTTEST 1
LEARNED HELPLESSNESS

James Geiwitz

The basic task of motivation psychologists is to explain why we approach certain objects and events and avoid others. We approach situations that we perceive are likely to result in pleasant emotions, and we avoid those likely to lead to unpleasant emotions. If we are put unavoidably in a situation eliciting an unpleasant emotion, like anger or fear (or hunger), we will try to reduce the emotion by appropriate behaviors such as fighting or fleeing (or eating).

But what if the individual who is unavoidably experiencing an unpleasant emotion thinks that there is nothing he can do to alter his unfortunate state of affairs? What if he's frustrated and angry, but perceives "the government" or "the system" at fault; how does one punch out the system? What if he's afraid of his boss? How does one flee from one's boss, without losing one's job? What if an individual, frustrated and fearful, feels helpless to improve his state?

The research literature on psychosomatic illness provides part of the answer, for people who cannot extricate themselves from negative emotions eventually get sick. The person is depressed and frightened, sees no answer to his problems; the body seems no longer willing to fight back, and the bacteria, viruses, and cancerous cells gain ground. In extreme cases, such as voodoo curses, the individual feels he is helpless to avoid death; he gives up, and the body quits.

What is the nature of this feeling of helplessness? How do angry or fearful people come to feel that there is nothing they can do? These questions have been the subject of considerable research lately, with some interesting results. The research began with some rather traditional "avoidance learning" tasks involving dogs.

HELPLESS DOGS

Dogs are good leapers. Laboratory investigations of dog behavior, for this reason, often utilize a device known as a shuttlebox. The shuttlebox has two compartments separated by a barrier wall that can be hurdled by a dog trying, for example, to escape electric shocks. A typical study of escape and avoidance learning begins with a warning signal (for example, the lights dim); ten seconds later a shock is delivered to the feet through an electrified floor. Most dogs quickly learn to leap over the barrier to the safe side of the box as soon as the shock comes on; eventually they learn to leap when the lights dim, avoiding shock altogether.

Most dogs do this, but not dogs who have learned to feel helpless. Helpless dogs were trained in the following way: Twenty-four hours before their shuttlebox test, they were placed in hammock-like harnesses and subjected to several painful but not injurious shocks. There was nothing the dogs could do to prevent the shocks or to escape from them once they began.

These dogs reacted quite differently in the shuttlebox. On the first trial with shock, they ran around and howled, then settled down to constant whining, with few motions that could be interpreted as attempts at escape. After 50 or 60 seconds, the shock was stopped automatically, and soon the second trial began. After a few trials, the dogs would do virtually nothing but whine; they appeared to have given up. These dogs had learned helplessness. It was as if they had become fatalists, believing shocks were simply part of life.

The psychologists who discovered learned helplessness viewed the phenomenon as an active, not a ⟨passive⟩ learning. The dogs who were shocked for no reason were not passive in their harnesses; they struggled, they barked, and they bit the air, but everything they tried had one thing in common: It didn't work. They learned that nothing helps.

HELPLESS HUMANS

Although most of the research on learned helplessness has used dogs as subjects, the same basic experiment has been successfully repeated with college students. The students were exposed to an offensively loud noise; nothing they did had any effect on the noise. Later these students were tested in a kind of "finger shuttlebox," in which they could escape from the noise by moving a finger to the other side of the box. In contrast to control subjects who had no prior exposure to the noise and who learned the shuttle easily, the helpless humans passively endured the loud sound.

Psychologist Martin Seligman, who has done much of the research on helplessness, thinks the shuttlebox situation has analogies in real life. He describes one young boy named Archie, age 15. Archie is waiting for his chance to quit school. School has been an unending series of shocks and failures for him: questions with no answers because he doesn't know some of the words in the questions, interactions without joy because the other kids think he's stupid. Nothing he does seems to have any effect on these "shocks." Archie is ready to enter the shuttlebox of life, and he has learned how to be helpless. He is likely to endure passively any shocks he encounters outside of school, just as he does in school. His changes of success, obviously, are not good.

In extreme states of helplessness, humans begin a zombie-like existence. Nazi

441

concentration camps were full of what Bettelheim called "walking corpses." Some mental patients could also be so labeled, not because of their original mental disorders but because they develop an intense feeling of hopelessness. One group, were they not led from a hospital fire, would have burned, motionless and emotionless.

NEW HOPE FOR THE HOPELESS

Learned helplessness involves a situation in which the subjects learn that an aversive event is not affected by anything they do. Nothing helps. Once they have learned this, is there anything we can do to help them "unlearn" helplessness? Can we return to them a confidence in their ability to affect their environment? If you were the experimenter, what would you do to help the helpless dogs? Obviously they must learn that eliminating the painful shock is now within their control. But how? How do you teach a helpless dog to move off an electrified grid?

The psychologists tried a number of tricks. They dropped meat on the safe side. They took down the partition between the compartment and called the dog: "Here, boy." Boy stayed there, however, and finally the researchers were forced to take extreme measures; they dragged the dog on a leash to safety. They continued dragging the dog until it responded without force. It took many, many trials before each dog caught on that it could affect the shock and pain by moving, but eventually all the dogs were cured.

The helplessness of the dogs given uncontrollable shocks was overcome with great difficulty. The helplessness of humans may present even more difficulties. What is the human equivalent of dragging an animal into a more pleasant state? I don't know. If that question has an answer, can it be done without violating moral or legal codes? How much better it would be if we could *prevent* the development of hopelessness!

Another study of learned helplessness provides relevant data. Dogs that had had experience with shock they *could* control were not affected by later experience with inescapable shock; they learned the shuttlebox trick as well as dogs with no prior experience of any kind. In other words, it is enough for dogs to learn that their behavior is effective *sometimes*. They are then relatively immune to the effects of a situation in which they are helpless, and they don't carry over the hopelessness to new situations. The implication for the parents and teachers of human learners is that they should do all in their power to present at least some situations in which a child can see that his or her ability counts for something, makes a difference.

COMPREHENSION TEST

Directions: *Circle the letter of the correct answer.*

1. Learned helplessness refers to a(n)
   a) feeling of being unable to control one's circumstances
   b) response that humans make to fear
   c) reaction to unpleasant experiences
   d) attempt to control emotional reactions

2. Dogs who trained in situations where they could not avoid shocks
   a) tried to escape the shock in the shuttlebox
   b) did not try to avoid the shock in the shuttlebox
   c) eventually learned to avoid shock in the shuttlebox
   d) occasionally leaped to avoid the shock

3. Helplessness can be unlearned
   a) easily if directly taught
   b) if the unlearning occurs soon after the original learning
   c) when the individual is aware of the learning
   d) only with great difficulty

4. A group of college students was exposed to an uncontrollable loud noise. Then they were placed in a situation where they could control the noise and they
   a) did not try to control the noise
   b) could not figure out how to control the noise
   c) controlled the noise immediately
   d) controlled the noise only after repeated trials

5. Research on the causes of illness suggests that
   a) illness is purely a matter of exposure to bacteria
   b) emotions are related to illness
   c) illness can be caused by other people
   d) some people think they are sick when they really are not ill

6. "Passive" learning is
   a) inactive
   b) indirect
   c) active
   d) direct

7. The term "shuttlebox of life" means that
   a) life is as confining and restricting as a box
   b) life has its share of shocks and failures
   c) people are physically moved back and forth in life
   d) scientists have developed a shuttlebox for humans

8. Of the following groups of people you would most expect a sense of helplessness in
   a) priests
   b) accountants
   c) abused children
   d) divorced women

9. Based on the information contained in the passage, if Archie, the young boy waiting to quit school, found himself in a job situation which he disliked and found difficult and unrewarding, you would expect him to
   a) discuss his situation with his supervisor
   b) do nothing to correct the problem
   c) complain to friends
   d) quit and look for another job

10. The author describes learned helplessness mainly by
    a) giving arguments and proof
    b) offering statistical evidence
    c) explaining principles of psychology
    d) presenting personal experiences

Flexibility Posttest 1:   1269 words

Finishing Time: _____ _____ _____
                     HR.   MIN.   SEC.

Starting Time: _____ _____ _____
                     HR.   MIN.   SEC.

Reading Time: _____ _____
                          MIN.   SEC.

WPM Score: _____

Comprehension Score: _____ %

Reading Efficiency Score: _____

Reading Flexibility Posttest 2

1. Assume that you have found the following article in a magazine that you are paging through. The title suggests that the article is about *television programs through satellites.* You enjoy watching TV, but are dissatisfied with what shows are currently being shown, so you decide to read the article *only* for the purpose of finding out what new offerings may become available. You are not interested, at this time, in details about satellites and are reading to locate only most important ideas. Read the selection then locate *only* these ideas.

2. Before you begin reading, record the time in minutes and seconds on page 448 in the space marked Starting Time. Then begin reading the selection. Read it only once. When you finish, record the time in the space marked Finishing Time.

3. Complete the comprehension questions that follow the selection. *Do not look back at the selection to answer the questions.*

4. Score your answers using the Answer Key. Record your score (number correct multiplied by 20) in the space marked Comprehension Score.

5. Use the words-per-minute conversion chart on pages 456–457 to find the average number of words that you read per minute and record it in the space marked WPM.

6. Compute your Reading Efficiency Score and record it on the Post-test Summary on page 452.

FLEXIBILITY POSTTEST 2
TUNING YOUR TV
TO THE SATELLITES

Picture this scene: Friends drop in and you ask the assembled group, "Would you like to see a program live from Moscow?" You fiddle with the controls on the TV set, a small motor hums as it automatically adjusts reception, and everybody settles back to watch the Bolshoi. Thanks to a new-fangled antenna, the screen brightens up with brilliant ballet, unedited and uninterrupted.

Too good to be true? Not long ago it would have sounded like pie in the sky. But right now in places blessed with unencumbered access to the sky, viewers with the proper equipment can get a whole raft of programming that's not available on regular channels, and some people can even bring in that ballet from Moscow.

The new brand of TV entertainment is beamed from an overhead satellite directly to your own special antenna, a space-age contraption ten feet or so in diameter that looks like a huge sand dollar propped on edge in your yard. Besides pulling down programs from several pay-TV broadcasts, it can eavesdrop on original transmissions from network correspondents before the evening news is edited and packaged, pluck from the air cartoons broadcast in French from Canada and bring from the heavens numerous religious programs. On any day a flick of the dial snares 50 to 60 different programs.

Satellite transmission is growing by leaps and bounds. There are now 12 commercial U.S. satellites, and soon there will be 13 (each with several channels) orbiting the earth.

In places where cable TV is unavailable and conventional reception is poor, dish owners can still enjoy a smorgasbord of entertainment.

HOW THE DISH WORKS

The large dish antenna, along with its related equipment, is called an earth station, a high-tech name that may make the buyer feel better about its price. Your own earth station can easily run a hefty $7,500. And one of these days, some broadcasters may be billing earth-station owners each month for the privilege of tuning in their satellite programs.

Satellite reception can work only when there are no buildings, trees or other obstacles in a direct line between the antenna and the satellite in the sky. The dish, usually set in concrete on the ground, latches onto signals beamed from satellites orbiting the earth 22,300 miles above the equator. With an orbit speed synchronized to the earth's rotation, these satellites, in effect, stand still in the sky,

445

meaning they remain in the same position relative to the dish. Broadcasters send TV signals to the satellite, which converts them to another frequency and transmits them to earth.

Special electronic equipment amplifies the signals reaching your antenna, but the oversized dish itself is the crucial part. The dish must face the particular satellite whose programming you want to tune in. You can turn the dish manually or — for a few hundred dollars more — buy equipment that allows you to rotate it automatically from inside the house.

WHAT YOU GET

Currently, there are an estimated 5,000 earth-station owners, many of them hobbyists or people with a knack for television electronics. Because a single satellite, SATCOM I, provides the bulk of U.S. satellite TV programs, many earth-station owners keep their antenna aimed at SATCOM I. Among its offerings are first-run movies, live coverage of the U.S. House of Representatives, religious programs and Cable News Network. SATCOM I is the satellite closest to the horizon and therefore is easily blocked by a tree or building. If you cannot get SATCOM I, there are still plenty of viewing options from other commercial satellites.

KEEPING IT LEGAL

You can install an earth station without a license, but assembling groups of people and charging a fee for viewing is very likely to be challenged as illegal. Owners of apartment houses, hotels or condominiums might also get in a jam by picking up satellite programs gratis and passing them on to tenants. Running a cable across the street or other public property to share programs with a neighbor would invite legal questions.

The Communications Act isn't crystal clear about whether you need permission from satellite broadcasters to pick up their signals. In any case, some services, such as religious broadcasters, welcome all viewers. Some others are likely to be charging a fee to viewers within a few years. They can do this by scrambling broadcasts so that special decoding equipment is needed to receive their shows, then charging a rental fee for the use of the decoder. Still other broadcasters say they don't intend to bother with charges until earth stations become prolific enough to make the collection effort financially worthwhile.

There may be no choice in the matter if Congress passes a law forbidding earth-station owners to intercept satellite programs without permission from broadcasters.

SHOULD YOU WAIT TO BUY?

If the high price of earth-station equipment isn't enough to put you off, there is another important consideration. By the middle to late 1980s there will probably be several new satellites whose broadcasts can be received with equipment that will be not only much less expensive but also much smaller. In the works are dish antennas as small as two and a half feet across, less than a third the size of today's giants, designed to fit on the rooftops of private homes. They will tune in to a new type of satellite, more powerful than today's but with fewer channels. You may be able to receive programs from several such direct broadcast satellites (DBS) without having to change the position of the rooftop antenna.

Applications from nine companies interested in DBS programming have been accepted for processing by the FCC. More than likely, not all of these will yield new services, but within the next several years there may be as many as 25 or 30 DBS channels in each time zone.

For example, the government has accepted the application of the Satellite Television Corp., a subsidiary of COMSAT, to build the first satellites for its DBS plan. Beginning with service for the eastern time zone, STC intends to offer three channels of commercial-free television in each of the four continental U.S. time zones for a subscription fee of less than $20 a month, plus the cost of the receiving equipment. Subscribers may be able to purchase equipment outright for about $100 and rent the indoor and outdoor electronic gear for $10 or less per month.

Good as it sounds, the quality and versatility of DBS programs will depend partly on whether cable TV beats it to the punch in filling the void left by the regular networks. The case for DBS is not helped by opposition from the major networks and their affiliates, which contend that DBS broadcasts would displace local programs. Nevertheless, CBS has applied for permission to operate a DBS broadcasting system.

Whether you become an earth-station owner now or later or whether you simply opt for the conventional offerings depends on your own interests and priorities. But one thing is certain: Because of satellites, your choices are becoming more numerous and complicated. You may have to put a little more effort into understanding and selecting your entertainment alternatives.

COMPREHENSION TEST

1. What equipment would you need to purchase to tune in on satellite broadcasts?

   _____

2. What factors determine how well you will be able to receive satellite broadcasts?

   _____

3. What legal restrictions currently limit satellite reception in your own home for personal use?

   _____

4. About how much do satellite TV receivers cost? (State a general price range.)

   _____

5. Should you wait to buy earth-station equipment? If so, why?

_____

Flexibility Posttest 2:	1196 words
Finishing Time: ___ HR. ___ MIN. ___ SEC.	
Starting Time: ___ HR. ___ MIN. ___ SEC.	
Reading Time: ___ MIN. ___ SEC.	
WPM Score: _____	
Comprehension Score: _____ %	
Reading Efficiency Score: _____	

Reading Flexibility Posttest 3

1. The following selection is taken from a reference book on plant biology. Assume you are completing a writing project on this topic and need to find the answer to a particular question. Read the following selection only for the purpose of finding the answer to this question:

   To what three families do most root-crop plants belong?

2. Before you begin reading, record the time in minutes and seconds in the space on page 450 marked Starting Time. Then begin reading the selection. Read it only once. When you finish, record the time in the space marked Finishing Time.

3. Answer the question that followed the selection. *Do not look back at the selection to find the answer.*

4. Score your answer using the Answer Key. Record your score in the space marked Comprehension Score. Your score will be 100 if you answer correctly, zero if you cannot answer or if you answer incorrectly.

5. Use the words-per-minute conversion chart on pages 456–457 to find the average number of words that you read per minute and record it in the space marked WPM.

6. Compute your Reading Efficiency Score and record it on the Post-test Summary on page 452.

FLEXIBILITY POSTTEST 3
THE EARLIEST AGRICULTURE

Watson M. Laetsch

From the work of many scholars, archaeologists, botanists, and other scientists, we can reconstruct with fair accuracy how the plant revolution, at least the one in the Middle East, most probably got under way.

The Fertile Crescent of the Middle East is a land of varied habitats and was an early abode of human beings along the Tigris and Euphrates rivers. To the east lie the rugged Zagros Mountains, unsuitable for permanent settlement but offering good hunting and a cool summer for nomadic bands. West of its foothills, dry and windswept steppes dip gradually to the rich flood plains along the rivers. It seems likely that the base camps of wandering tribes lay in the foothills, but the men and women who lived there went far afield. They dwelt in the fertile bottomlands during the cooler seasons, and in the burning summers they migrated east to the mountains. Whenever they traveled they subsisted on game and the edible plants they found. Their food grew wild, each crop maturing in its season, and it was varied and plentiful because of the varied habitats that lay between rivers and hills.

The opportunity, an invitation almost, to bring the sources of food to where they wanted them, rather than always migrating to where the food was, must have gradually become obvious to the nomads as they watched how plants reproduced themselves and grew. Undoubtedly, as the women gathered the wild grain, they brought it back to the encampment, spilling some seeds, throwing some onto a garbage heap after a meal, or otherwise accidentally scattering them near the camp. Some of these seeds, variants hardier than the parent plants, in time would hold and grow. The women, seeing this, may well have reasoned that these plants came from the grain they had brought home, and they might experimentally scratch or dig a few holes in the ground and plant more. Seeing plants thrive when supplied ample water, they would bring water to them, at first in gourds, then in ditches or canals as their planted fields spread. And so, slowly, generations may have come to realize that they could stay in one place and grow the plants they needed by their homes.

The earliest evidence for agriculture is from the Zagros Mountains, but perhaps this is because the climate is dry, preserving remains better than elsewhere, and because many scientists look there for evidence of early farming. But half a world away, in the Tehuacán Valley south of where Mexico City stands today, other people were trying similar experiments with other plants. In Mexico maize (corn) was probably among the first seeds planted.

Another birthplace for agriculture was around the middle reaches of the Yellow River in northern China, the center for the domestication of the cereal grains we call millet. These are annual grasses that are grown in semiarid regions, now a staple food for millions in Asia and Africa.

Scientists also have evidence that *root-crop agriculture* in the humid tropics is very ancient. In this type of agriculture, the starchy underground stems and roots are the food. Root-crop plants are mostly species in three families — taro, cassava, and yams (not our yam, which is a sweet potato). These are easy to raise, have high yields, and are the staple and sometimes only food of people in many parts of the tropics.

Fossil remains are less likely to turn up in the tropics, however, so our record of early agriculture is somewhat biased. Decay is rapid there, and the difficulty of finding sites suitable for exploration in places like the jungles of Southeast Asia has made them less attractive to archaeologists than places like the arid Mideast, where signs of ancient settlements litter the landscape. Thus most of our evidence about early agriculture comes from temperate regions.

The first *economic plants*, as useful plants are called today, were hardy plants to begin with; they flourished in the new and favorable environment created for them by human care. Competing vegetation was cleaned out so that the planted crops could grow better. As time went by a domesticated crop was regularly grown in cultivated fields, and other plants were added — figs, dates, olives, grapes. Just how these and other plants first cultivated were transformed into their domesticated versions we will never know. Some of the change probably was natural and accidental, some probably was deliberate as cultivators learned more about what they were doing. Either way, our debt to these primitive first farmers is huge. They domesticated most of the food plants we eat today, laying the basis for agriculture as it developed right up to modern times.

COMPREHENSION TEST

1. To what three families do most root-crop plants belong?

_____

Flexibility Posttest 3:		816 words	
Finishing Time:	___HR.___	___MIN.___	___SEC.___
Starting Time:	___HR.___	___MIN.___	___SEC.___
Reading Time:		___MIN.___	___SEC.___
WPM Score:	_____		
Comprehension Score:	_____		%
Reading Efficiency Score:	_____		

EVALUATING YOUR PROGRESS

Now that you have completed all of the posttests, you are ready to evaluate your improvement. First, fill in the necessary information on the Evaluation Chart (page 453). To locate your pretest reading efficiency scores, turn back to page 33 (Pretest Summary). Copy in your posttest reading efficiency scores from the Posttest Summary on page 452. Now subtract each pretest score from the corresponding posttest score. The answer will reflect your gain — the amount you improved.

Reading Efficiency

You increased your reading efficiency if your score increased between the pretest and posttest. Because the amount of improvement that students make depends on their incoming level of skill as well as how hard they worked throughout the course, it is not fair to quote an "average" amount of gain to which you compare yourself. In fact, the score is not intended to compare you to some group standard. Instead, it is designed to provide measurable evidence of your improvement.

Reading Flexibility

You can evaluate your reading flexibility in two ways. First you can compute your gain on each test and assess your improvement by how much you increased your Reading Efficiency Score in each of the three posttests. Second, and more important, you can evaluate the amount of difference between each of the three posttest Reading Efficiency Scores as compared to your pretest scores. If you have become a more flexible reader (and no doubt you have) then you will see greater differences among the posttest scores than among the pretest scores.

POSTTEST SUMMARY

1. Reading Efficiency Score: _____

2. Reading Flexibility

   Posttest 1

       Comprehension Score: _____

       WPM Score: _____

       Reading Efficiency Score: _____

   Posttest 2

       Comprehension Score: _____

       WPM Score: _____

       Reading Efficiency Score: _____

   Posttest 3

       Comprehension Score: _____

       WPM Score: _____

       Reading Efficiency Score: _____

EVALUATION CHART

1. Reading Efficiency

   Posttest RES: _____

   Pretest RES: − _____

   Gain: _____

2. Reading Flexibility

   Test 1 (Careful Reading)

   Posttest RES: _____

   Pretest RES: − _____

   Gain: _____

   Test 2 (Skimming)

   Posttest RES: _____

   Pretest RES: − _____

   Gain: _____

   Test 3 (Scanning)

   Posttest RES: _____

   Pretest RES: − _____

   Gain: _____

Appendix:
How to Estimate
Your Reading Rate

When you are reading material for more than a minute or two, it is useful for you to have a quick method for estimating the amount of words read. Counting every word you read is time-consuming; so, instead, estimate the amount you read as follows:

1. After you have chosen a passage in a book or article, count the total number of words in any three lines. Divide the total by three (3). Round off to the nearest whole number. This will give the average number of words per line.
2. Count the number of lines in the article or book (or on one page if it is longer than one page). Multiply the number of words per line by the total number of lines. This will give you a fairly accurate estimate of the total number of words.
3. As you read, time yourself. Record both minutes and seconds of your starting time (for example, 4:20:18). Start reading when the second hand of the clock reaches twelve. Record your finishing time. Subtract your starting time from your finishing time.
4. Divide the total reading time into the total number of words. To do this, round off the number of seconds to the nearest quarter of a minute and then divide. For example, if your total reading time was 3 minutes and 12 seconds, round it off to 3¼ or 3.25 minutes and then divide. Your answer will be your words-per-minute score.

    Example:

    Total number of words on 3 lines: 23
    Divide by 3 and round off: 23 ÷ 3 = 7⅔ = 8
    Number of lines in article: 120
    Multiply number of words per line by number of lines:
        8 × 120 = 960 (total words)
    Subtract starting time from finishing time: 1:13:28
                                                  − 1:05
                                                    ‾‾‾‾‾‾
                                                    8:28
    Round off to nearest quarter minute: 8.5 minutes
    Divide time into total number of words:
        960 ÷ 8.5 = 112 + a fraction (your reading rate)

Words-per-Minute

Reading time	Pretests				Reading Selection													
	Effic.	Flex. 1	Flex. 2	Flex. 3	1	2	3	4	5	6	7	8	9	10	11	12	13	14
1:00	839	1083	1430	746	1055	1020	1678	986	924	757	1095	1329	1123	1625	864	858	1345	1407
1:15	671	866	1144	597	844	816	1342	789	739	606	876	1063	898	1300	691	686	1076	1126
1:30	559	722	953	497	703	680	1119	657	616	505	730	886	749	1083	576	572	897	938
1:45	479	619	817	426	603	583	959	563	528	431	626	759	642	1121	494	490	769	804
2:00	420	542	715	373	528	510	839	493	462	379	548	665	561	813	432	429	673	704
2:15	373	481	636	332	469	453	746	438	411	336	487	591	499	722	384	381	598	625
2:30	336	433	572	298	422	408	671	394	370	303	438	532	449	650	346	343	538	563
2:45	305	394	520	271	384	371	610	359	336	275	398	483	408	591	314	312	489	512
3:00	280	361	477	249	352	340	559	329	308	252	365	443	374	542	288	286	448	469
3:15	258	333	440	230	325	314	516	303	284	232	337	409	346	500	266	264	420	433
3:30	240	309	409	213	301	291	479	282	264	216	313	380	321	464	247	245	384	402
3:45	223	289	381	199	281	272	447	263	246	201	292	354	299	433	230	229	359	372
4:00	210	271	358	187	264	255	420	247	231	189	274	332	281	406	216	215	336	352
4:15	197	255	336	176	248	240	395	232	217	178	258	313	264	382	203	202	316	331
4:30	186	241	318	166	234	227	373	219	205	168	243	295	250	361	192	191	299	313
4:45	177	228	301	157	222	215	353	208	195	159	231	280	236	342	182	181	283	296
5:00	168	217	286	149	211	204	336	197	185	151	219	266	225	325	173	172	269	281
5:15	160	206	272	142	201	194	320	188	176	144	209	253	214	309	165	163	256	268
5:30	153	197	260	136	192	185	305	179	168	137	199	242	204	295	157	156	245	256
5:45	146	188	249	130	183	177	292	171	161	132	190	231	195	283	150	149	234	245
6:00	140	181	238	124	176	170	280	164	154	126	183	222	187	271	144	143	224	235
6:15	134	173	229	119	169	163	268	158	148	121	175	213	180	260	138	137	215	225
6:30	129	167	220	115	162	157	258	152	142	116	168	204	173	250	133	132	207	216
6:45	124	160	212	111	156	151	249	146	137	112	162	197	166	241	128	127	199	208
7:00	120	155	204	107	151	146	240	141	132	108	156	190	160	232	123	123	192	201
7:15	116	149	197	103	146	141	231	136	127	104	151	183	155	224	119	118	186	194
7:30	112	144	191	—	141	136	224	131	123	101	146	177	150	217	115	115	179	188
7:45	108	140	186	—	136	132	217	127	119	98	141	171	145	210	111	111	174	182
8:00	105	135	179	—	132	128	210	123	116	95	137	166	140	203	108	107	168	176
8:15	102	131	173	—	128	124	203	120	112	91	133	161	136	197	105	104	163	171
8:30	—	127	168	—	124	120	197	116	109	—	129	156	132	191	102	101	158	165
8:45	—	124	163	—	121	117	192	113	106	—	125	152	128	186	—	—	154	161
9:00	—	120	159	—	117	113	186	110	103	—	122	148	125	181	—	—	149	156
9:15	—	117	155	—	114	110	181	107	100	—	118	144	121	176	—	—	145	152
9:30	—	114	151	—	111	107	177	104	—	—	115	140	118	171	—	—	142	148
9:45	—	111	147	—	108	105	172	101	—	—	112	136	115	167	—	—	138	144
10:00	—	106	143	—	106	102	168	—	—	—	110	133	112	163	—	—	135	141

456

Conversion Chart

					Reading Selection													Posttests			
15	16	17	18	19	20	21	22	23	24	25	26	27	28	29	30	31	32	Effic.	Flex. 1	Flex. 2	Flex. 3
853	794	829	1368	647	742	1200	2528	723	1313	1756	2192	1171	920	1037	899	1269	1370	903	1269	1196	816
682	635	663	1094	517	594	960	2022	578	1050	1405	1754	937	736	830	719	1015	1096	722	1015	957	653
569	529	553	912	431	495	800	1685	482	875	1171	1461	781	613	691	599	846	913	602	846	797	544
487	454	474	782	370	424	686	1445	413	750	949	1253	669	526	593	514	725	783	516	725	683	466
427	397	415	684	324	371	600	1264	362	657	878	1096	586	460	519	450	635	685	452	635	598	408
379	353	368	608	288	330	533	1124	321	583	780	974	520	409	461	400	564	609	401	564	532	363
341	318	332	547	259	297	480	1011	289	525	702	877	468	368	415	360	508	548	361	508	478	326
310	289	301	497	240	270	436	919	263	477	639	797	426	335	377	330	461	498	328	461	435	297
284	265	276	456	216	247	400	843	241	438	585	731	390	306	346	300	423	457	301	423	399	272
262	244	255	421	199	228	369	778	222	404	540	674	360	283	319	277	390	422	279	390	368	251
244	227	237	391	185	212	343	722	207	375	502	626	335	263	296	257	363	391	258	363	342	233
227	212	221	365	172	198	320	674	195	350	468	585	312	245	276	240	338	365	241	338	319	218
213	199	207	342	162	186	300	632	181	328	439	548	293	230	259	225	317	343	226	317	299	204
201	187	195	322	152	175	289	595	170	309	413	516	276	216	244	211	299	322	212	298	281	192
190	176	184	304	144	165	267	562	160	292	390	487	260	204	230	200	282	304	201	282	266	181
180	167	175	288	136	156	253	532	152	276	370	461	247	194	218	191	267	288	190	267	252	172
171	159	166	274	129	148	240	506	145	263	351	438	234	184	207	180	254	274	181	254	240	163
162	151	158	261	123	141	229	482	138	250	334	418	223	175	198	171	242	261	172	242	228	155
155	144	151	249	118	135	218	460	131	239	319	399	213	167	189	163	231	249	164	231	217	148
148	138	144	238	113	129	209	440	126	228	308	381	204	160	180	156	221	238	157	221	208	142
142	132	138	228	109	124	200	421	121	219	293	365	195	153	173	150	212	228	151	212	199	136
136	127	133	219	104	119	192	404	116	210	281	351	187	147	166	144	203	219	144	203	191	131
131	122	128	210	—	114	185	389	111	202	270	337	180	142	160	138	195	211	138	195	184	126
126	118	124	203	—	110	178	374	107	195	260	325	173	136	154	133	188	203	134	188	177	121
122	113	118	195	—	106	171	361	103	188	251	313	167	131	148	128	181	196	129	181	171	117
118	110	114	189	—	102	166	349	—	181	242	302	162	127	143	124	175	189	125	175	165	113
114	106	110	182	—	—	160	337	—	175	234	292	156	123	138	120	169	183	120	169	159	109
110	102	107	177	—	—	155	326	—	169	227	283	151	119	134	116	164	177	117	164	154	105
107	—	104	171	—	—	150	316	—	164	220	274	146	115	130	112	159	171	113	159	150	102
103	—	100	166	—	—	145	306	—	159	213	266	142	112	126	109	154	166	109	154	145	—
100	—	—	161	—	—	141	297	—	154	207	258	138	108	122	106	149	161	106	149	141	—
—	—	—	156	—	—	137	289	—	150	201	251	134	105	119	103	145	157	104	145	137	—
—	—	—	152	—	—	133	281	—	146	195	244	130	102	115	100	141	152	100	141	133	—
—	—	—	148	—	—	130	273	—	142	190	237	127	—	112	—	137	148	—	137	129	—
—	—	—	144	—	—	126	266	—	138	185	230	123	—	109	—	133	144	—	134	126	—
—	—	—	140	—	—	123	259	—	135	180	225	120	—	106	—	130	141	—	130	123	—
—	—	—	137	—	—	120	253	—	131	176	219	117	—	104	—	127	137	—	127	120	—

Reading Progress Graph

Directions: For each reading selection you complete, record the date and selection number. Then place a dot at the words-per-minute score, and the comprehension score you achieved, in the appropriate column. Connect the consecutive dots to form a line graph. Record your Reading Efficiency Scores in the boxes provided.

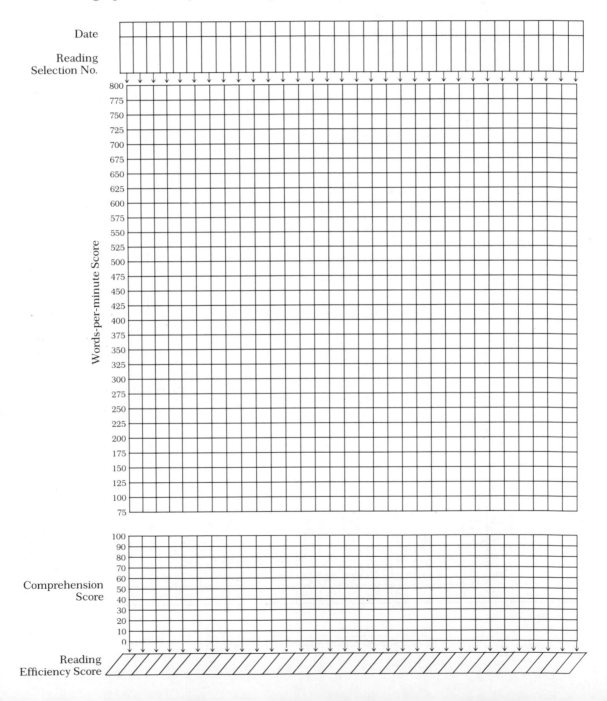

Answer Key

Answers are not included in this key for those exercises that require long subjective responses or underlining of passages. The comprehension tests for reading selections and pretests and posttests are structured so that item 1 tests your understanding of the main idea of the selection, items 2–5 test your retention of details, item 6 is related to vocabulary, and items 7–10 are concerned with your ability to interpret and evaluate what you have read.

CHAPTER 2

Reading Efficiency Pretest

1. a		6. a	
2. b		7. a	
3. c		8. b	
4. d		9. d	
5. d		10. b	

Reading Flexibility Pretest 1

1. b		6. a	
2. b		7. c	
3. d		8. a	
4. c		9. d	
5. a		10. b	

Reading Flexibility Pretest 2

1. mini TV; projection TV
2. any two of the following: automatic picture control, electronic tuning, remote control, built-in cable capacity, beefed-up sound, auxiliary jacks
3. between $2,000 and $4,000; between $200 and $600
4. front projection (one- or two-piece); rear projection
5. the picture you get

Reading Flexibility Pretest 3

1. Robert Hooke

CHAPTER 3

Exercise 3-1

1. What are the wrong questions?

    or

    What are the right questions?

2. What is the hospital patient's plight?
3. What effects did college have on the author?
4. How do the thinking of men and machines compare?
5. How are Ghana and Rhodesia different?
6. What are magnetic fields and lines of force?
7. How do x rays and visible light compare?

Reading Selection 1

1. d	6. b
2. a	7. d
3. c	8. a
4. c	9. a
5. d	10. b

Reading Selection 2

1. b	6. b
2. b	7. b
3. c	8. d
4. c	9. b
5. d	10. b

CHAPTER 4

Quiz on Hypnosis

1. T	6. T
2. T	7. F
3. F	8. T
4. T	9. T
5. F	10. T

Reading Selection 3

1. c	6. a
2. d	7. a
3. a	8. c
4. c	9. c
5. b	10. d

Reading Selection 4

1. b	6. d
2. b	7. a
3. a	8. d
4. a	9. a
5. b	10. c

CHAPTER 5

Exercise 5-1

1. stress is defined
2. political scientists are interested
3. government may employ, allow, or prevent
4. power and authority are central
5. majority have no cause

Exercise 5-2

1. professor summarized; he gave
2. you can relieve; people don't know
3. mind and body are not separate, independent; change is accompanied
4. communication skill involves; listening skills involve

Exercise 5-3

1. second
2. second
3. second
4. second
5. first

Exercise 5-4

1. you don't realize; you realize
2. urbanization and rise have removed
3. we have little understanding
4. it is apparent
5. applicability was recognized

Reading Selection 5

1. b	6. c
2. c	7. d
3. d	8. c
4. c	9. a
5. a	10. c

Reading Selection 6

1. c	6. d
2. a	7. d
3. c	8. d
4. a	9. c
5. c	10. d

CHAPTER 6

Exercise 6-1

1. coffee beans, or the processing of coffee beans
2. buying motives
3. swaddling
4. communication with other worlds
5. space exploration

Exercise 6-2

1. Parents often influence the children's choice of dating partners by offering or withholding resources.
2. We must study planets other than earth to learn about the processes that created earth and the other planets.
3. Self-concepts change constantly, as shown by the example of the college student.
4. Bundling was a courtship custom in which a couple slept in the same bed but sexual contact was forbidden.
5. Teachers treat boys and girls differently, rewarding different types of behaviors for each.

Exercise 6-3

1. first sentence
2. third sentence
3. first sentence
4. last
5. first

Exercise 6-4
1. Physical anthropologists specialize in particular areas of study and work with other scientists in performing their tasks.
2. Although the food service industry is an expanding market, it is difficult to develop restaurants as successful businesses.
3. Overweight people, regardless of their age, suffer rejection by their peers.
4. Color has many uses and serves important functions in a variety of situations.
5. A speaker's purpose can vary widely depending on the audience and situation.

Exercise 6-5
1. three categories of instruments with the names or descriptions of the instruments that are included in each
2. a definition of storage and retrieval and a listing of implications
3. a description of the scientific objections followed by a description of the religious objections
4. a listing of various narcotics and a description of their relative strength and aftereffects
5. a discussion of the unmeasurable factors

Exercise 6-7
1. illustration-example
2. illustration-example
3. description
4. facts and statistics
5. reasons

Exercise 6-8
1. first, second, finally; markers for important information
2. for example; continuation
3. for this reason, therefore, moreover; continuation
4. and, additionally; continuation
5. on the contrary; change in thought

Reading Selection 7

1. a
2. d
3. c
4. b
5. d
6. b
7. a
8. c
9. a
10. b

Reading Selection 8

1. b
2. b
3. d
4. a
5. a
6. c
7. b
8. d
9. c
10. a

CHAPTER 7

Exercise 7-1
1. cause-effect
2. comparison-contrast

3. chronology
4. listing of information
5. statement-support

Reading Selection 9

1. b	6. c
2. a	7. b
3. d	8. b
4. b	9. c
5. b	10. a

Reading Selection 10

1. c	6. b
2. b	7. a
3. d	8. d
4. b	9. b
5. d	10. c

CHAPTER 8

Exercise 8-1

1. computers; their use in the home
2. businesses; employee alcohol consumption and programs to curb it
3. vitamins; whether they are worth while
4. movie ratings; their effectiveness
5. vegetarianism; its effects on health

Reading Selection 11

1. a	6. a
2. c	7. c
3. c	8. c
4. d	9. b
5. d	10. b

Reading Selection 12

1. b	6. d
2. c	7. a
3. a	8. c
4. c	9. c
5. b	10. d

CHAPTER 9

Exercise 9-3

1. categorization
2. mnemonic devices
3. visualization or sensory modes (drawing the skull)
4. visualization
5. categorization

Reading Selection 13

1. d	6. d
2. b	7. d
3. d	8. c
4. b	9. b
5. b	10. d

Reading Selection 14

1. d	6. a
2. a	7. c
3. c	8. b
4. b	9. c
5. c	10. c

CHAPTER 10

Reading Selection 15

1. b		6. a	
2. b		7. a	
3. c		8. b	
4. b		9. c	
5. d		10. a	

Reading Selection 16

1. c		6. b	
2. a		7. b	
3. c		8. d	
4. a		9. a	
5. c		10. a	

CHAPTER 11

Word Awareness Quiz

1. The *Random House College Dictionary* lists 135 meanings.
2. poverty that results from changes such as the decline or disappearance of an industry from a particular area
3. c
4. a chemical compound that is an ingredient in chlorine bleach
5. c
6. no
7. hoax

Exercise 11-2

1. gobble
2. chat, gossip, confer
3. just, impartial, objective
4. notorious, distinguished, illustrious
5. gang, pack, assembly
6. snatch, withdraw, grab, seize
7. talent, aptitude, knack, gift
8. mutt, curr, mongrel
9. hasty, speedy, quick
10. stumble, trip

Exercise 11-3

	Positive	*Negative*
1.	polish	decontaminate
2.	display	expose
3.	gaze	stare
4.	become acquainted	encounter
5.	toss	hurl
6.	request	demand
7.	relinquish	abandon
8.	entrust	relegate
9.	overlook	neglect
10.	joke	ridicule

Reading Selection 17

1.	a	6.	d
2.	b	7.	b
3.	d	8.	c
4.	a	9.	a
5.	c	10.	b

Reading Selection 18

1.	b	6.	b
2.	b	7.	c
3.	b	8.	a
4.	d	9.	b
5.	b	10.	a

CHAPTER 12

Tests A and B

1.	a	6.	e
2.	e	7.	a
3.	b	8.	d
4.	a	9.	c
5.	b	10.	b

Exercise 12-1
1. the tendency . . . reactions
2. the process . . . environment
3. drawing a . . . principles
4. questioning
5. disfigured

Exercise 12-2
1. characteristics of metal
2. thinking or knowing
3. weaknesses
4. irrational fear of a particular object or situation
5. ways to contend or deal with situations

Exercise 12-3
1. silent, uncommunicative
2. out of date
3. far away
4. gave in
5. having two or more wives or husbands at the same time

Exercise 12-4
1. weak, feeble
2. unprincipled, not concerned with right and wrong
3. to bring back into favor
4. mysterious, dreadful, frightening
5. absurd, ridiculous

Exercise 12-5
1. lack of agreement or uniformity
2. freed from guilt
3. persistent, stubborn

4. change or flow
5. gloomy, horrible

Exercise 12-6

1. not correctly told
2. to phrase again in a different way
3. between offices
4. to trace a line around, encircle
5. not reversible
6. below standard
7. above the natural
8. communication over a distance by radio or telephone
9. not qualified
10. to divide further
11. to go beyond the limits
12. overly critical
13. one who pretends to be an intellectual
14. prevention of (against) conception
15. equal in quantity, value, or force

Exercise 12-7

1. arrangement of events in order of time
2. method of using light to compose matter for printing
3. looking into one's own mind
4. science that deals with the study of life (plants and animals)
5. beneath the earth's surface.
6. to catch (take) one's attention
7. change (turn) from one form to another
8. device that unrolls speech or script to speaker or actor, unseen by audience
9. belief in one God
10. movement of goods from one country to another

Exercise 12-8

1. for example
2. del' ə tir' e əs
3. Greek, French, and Italian
4. 5,280 feet
5. a conclusion or inference that does not follow from the information at hand
6. addenda
7. a short diagonal line used between two words to show that either may apply
8. violet, tired, rind
9. peoples who speak a semitic language (Hebrews, Arabs, etc.)
10. yes; as a verb

Exercise 12-9

1. make a pretense, feign, or pretend
2. a vehicle that can travel on water or land
3. hard-surfaced area in front of an airplane hangar
4. prevented or avoided
5. drawn into conflict

Reading Selection 19

1. c	6. b
2. b	7. d
3. a	8. a
4. a	9. b
5. c	10. b

Reading Selection 20

1. c	6. b
2. b	7. a
3. c	8. a
4. a	9. c
5. a	10. c

CHAPTER 13

Exercise 13-1

1. The woman is interested in meeting the man.
2. The teenager is a stranger; the dog is unfriendly.
3. Your brother ate the missing cookies.
4. An accident or crime has occurred.
5. She changed her mind or she confused the days.

Reading Selection 21

1. b	6. d
2. b	7. c
3. a	8. d
4. b	9. b
5. a	10. c

Reading Selection 22

1. b	6. c
2. a	7. d
3. c	8. a
4. b	9. b
5. a	10. c

CHAPTER 14

Reading Selection 23

1. d	6. b
2. c	7. a
3. c	8. a
4. b	9. c
5. b	10. a

Reading Selection 24

1. d	6. a
2. b	7. c
3. d	8. a
4. a	9. c
5. b	10. c

CHAPTER 15

Exercise 15-1

1. Massachusetts Society for the Prevention of Cruelty to Animals
2. to show how farm animals can be raised efficiently and with loving care
3. They are kept clean and provided with ample living quarters.
4. yes; tours, exhibits, computer games

Exercise 15-2

1. at least as strong as the previous year
2. good attitude toward work; communication skills, self-confidence; businesslike appearance and attitude

3. any two items listed under the heading "Job Hunting Tips"
4. to enable readers to contact potential employers
5. show knowledge of the company; be specific; request an interview; type neatly and correctly

Reading Selection 25

1. b	6. a
2. c	7. a
3. d	8. c
4. a	9. c
5. d	10. d

Reading Selection 26

1. d	6. b
2. a	7. d
3. b	8. c
4. a	9. d
5. d	10. b

CHAPTER 16

Exercise 16-1
1. 8 P.M.
2. informational program or documentary
3. Skylark, Roger Truman
4. yes — "Were You There?"
5. 4

Exercise 16-2
1. 107, 108, 126
2. 70, 77, 94
3. check under specific topics
4. yes

Exercise 16-3
1. Toyota Starlet
2. Chevrolet Chevette Diesel
3. Volkswagen Rabbit
4. Renault 5 Turbo

Exercise 16-4
1. fruit
2. Zanzibar and Indonesia
3. pebble
4. Alcoholics Anonymous, Synanon, Gamblers Anonymous, Weight Watchers
5. temperature, humidity, balance of oxygen and carbon dioxide
6. They navigate by the stars.
7. emotional upheaval
8. despised as sinful, fallen women

Applying What You Have Learned
Selection 27
1. street
2. Latin Americans, Arabs
3. smoking
4. prolonged gaze

Selection 28
1. 600
2. president of the National Academy of Sciences
3. seven
4. four billion

Reading Selection 27
1. a	6. b
2. c	7. b
3. a	8. a
4. c	9. b
5. b	10. d

Reading Selection 28
1. d	6. a
2. b	7. c
3. a	8. c
4. a	9. c
5. d	10. c

CHAPTER 17

Reading Selection 29
1. a	6. c
2. a	7. b
3. d	8. d
4. b	9. a
5. a	10. d

Reading Selection 30
1. d	6. c
2. a	7. a
3. b	8. d
4. c	9. b
5. a	10. b

CHAPTER 18

Exercise 18-1
1. selective
2. complete
3. high
4. selective
5. moderate

Reading Selection 31
1. b	6. b
2. b	7. d
3. d	8. a
4. c	9. d
5. c	10. b

Reading Selection 32
1. c	6. d
2. c	7. b
3. d	8. d
4. b	9. c
5. c	10. d

CHAPTER 19

Reading Efficiency Posttest

1.	b	6.	d
2.	b	7.	a
3.	c	8.	a
4.	d	9.	b
5.	c	10.	c

Reading Flexibility Posttest 1

1.	a	6.	a
2.	b	7.	b
3.	d	8.	c
4.	a	9.	b
5.	b	10.	c

Reading Flexibility Posttest 2

1. large dish antenna
2. presence of obstacles between antenna and the satellite
3. none
4. $7,500
5. Yes; equipment will be less expensive and much smaller.

Reading Flexibility Posttest 3

1. taro, cassava, and yams

References

CHAPTER 3

1. Gerald Leinwand. *The Pageant of World History.* Boston: Allyn and Bacon, 1971, p. 394.
2. Kenneth J. Neubeck. *Social Problems: A Critical Approach.* Glenview, Ill.: Scott, Foresman, 1979, p. vii.
3. Marilu McCarty. *Dollars and Sense,* 2nd ed. Glenview, Ill.: Scott, Foresman, 1979, p. 209.
4. Martin J. Gannon. *Management: An Organizational Perspective.* Boston: Little, Brown, 1977, p. 107.
5. Irwin Unger. *These United States,* Vol. II, 2nd ed. Boston: Little, Brown, 1982, p. 814.
6. Richard George. *The New Consumer Survival Kit.* Boston: Little, Brown, 1978, p. 69.
7. George, p. 97.
8. George, p. 103.
9. Morris K. Holland and Gerald Tarlow. *Using Psychology,* 2nd ed. Boston: Little, Brown, 1980, pp. 8–9.
10. George, p. 219.
11. George, p. 214.
12. George, p. 213.
13. George, p. 138.

CHAPTER 4

1. Holland and Tarlow, p. 60.
2. Holland and Tarlow, p. 157.
3. Holland and Tarlow, pp. 152–153.

CHAPTER 5

1. Holland and Tarlow, p. 80.
2. James C. Coleman. *Contemporary Psychology and Effective Behavior,* 4th ed. Glenview, Ill.: Scott, Foresman, 1979, p. 281.
3. Coleman, p. 266.
4. Coleman, p. 256.
5. Clayton Reeser and Marvin Loper. *Management: The Key to Organizational Effectiveness.* Glenview, Ill.: Scott, Foresman, 1978, p. 34.

CHAPTER 6

1. S. Joseph DeBrum et al. *General Business.* Cincinnati: South-Western Publishing Co., 1971, p. 353.
2. Paul G. Hewitt. *Conceptual Physics,* 4th ed. Boston: Little, Brown, 1981, p. 440.
3. Roger Chisholm and Marilu McCarty. *Principles of Economics.* Glenview, Ill.: Scott, Foresman, 1978, pp. 91–92.
4. Watson M. Laetsch. *Plants: Basic Concepts in Botany.* Boston: Little, Brown, 1979, p. 146.
5. Richard Buskirk. *Principles of Marketing,* 3rd ed. New York: Holt, Rinehart and Winston, 1970, p. 135.
6. Mary J. Gander and Harry W. Gardiner. *Child and Adolescent Development.* Boston: Little, Brown, 1981, pp. 7–8.
7. Louis Berman and J. C. Evans. *Exploring the Cosmos,* 2nd ed. Boston: Little, Brown, 1980, p. 427.
8. Berman and Evans, p. 362.
9. DeBrum, p. 565.
10. Geiwitz, pp. 482–483.
11. Edward J. Fox and Edward W. Wheatley. *Modern Marketing.* Glenview, Ill.: Scott, Foresman, 1978, p. 83.
12. David Knox. *Exploring Marriage and the Family.* Glenview, Ill.: Scott, Foresman, 1979, p. 180.
13. Berman and Evans, p. 438.
14. Buskirk, p. 138.
15. Knox, pp. 13–14.
16. Knox, p. 37.
17. S. L. Washburn and Ruth Moore. *Ape into Human,* 2nd ed. Boston: Little, Brown, 1980, pp. 169–170.
18. Hewitt, p. 524.
19. Chisholm and McCarty, p. 123.
20. Bernard Campbell. *Humankind Emerging,* 3rd ed. Boston: Little, Brown, 1979, p. 93.
21. Laetsch, p. 151.
22. Fox and Wheatley, pp. 287–288.

23. Geiwitz, pp. 363–364.
24. Joseph B. Aceves and H. Gill King. *Introduction to Anthropology*. Glenview, Ill.: Scott, Foresman, 1979, p. 61.
25. Washburn and Moore, p. 171.
26. Gander and Gardiner, p. 48.
27. John Perry and Erna Perry. *Face to Face*. Boston: Little, Brown, 1976, p. 128.
28. Aceves and King, pp. 18–19.
29. Fox and Wheatley, p. 26.
30. Henrietta Fleck. *Introduction to Nutrition,* 2nd ed. New York: Macmillan, 1971, p. 418.
31. Frans Gerritsen. *Theory and Practice of Color*. New York: Van Nostrand, 1975, p. 9.
32. Alan H. Monroe and Douglas Ehninger. *Principles and Types of Speech*, 6th ed. Glenview, Ill.: Scott, Foresman, 1967, p. 115.
33. Geiwitz, pp. 543–544.
34. Perry and Perry, pp. 130–131.
35. Gary Wasserman. *The Basics of American Politics*, 3rd ed. Boston: Little, Brown, 1982, p. 10.
36. Wasserman, p. 57.
37. James E. Crouch and J. Robert McClintic. *Human Anatomy and Physiology*, 2nd ed. New York: Wiley, 1976, p. 120.
38. Gordon B. David. *An Introduction to Electronic Computers*. New York: McGraw-Hill, 1965, p. 2.
39. Chester R. Longwell and Richard F. Flint. *Introduction to Physical Geology*, 2nd ed. New York, Wiley, 1962, p. 402.
40. Brian M. Fagan. *World Prehistory*. Boston: Little, Brown, 1979, p. 14.
41. Leonard Broom and Philip Selznick. *Sociology*, 3rd ed. New York: Harper and Row, 1963, p. 574.
42. Broom and Selznick, p. 455.
43. Stephen Crane. "Bride Comes to Yellow Sky," in James B. Hall and Elizabeth C. Hall, *The Realm of Fiction*. New York: McGraw-Hill, 1977, p. 192.
44. Chisholm and McCarty, p. 253.
45. Buskirk, p. 141.
46. Ernest Hemingway. "In Another Country," in Hall and Hall, p. 418.
47. Burton Wright and John Weiss. *Social Problems*. Boston: Little, Brown, 1980, pp. 137–138.
48. Wright and Weiss, p. 243.
49. Geiwitz, p. 97.
50. Philip G. Zimbardo. *Psychology and Life,* 10th ed. Glenview, Ill.: Scott, Foresman, 1979, p. 157.
51. Geiwitz, p. 265.
52. Buskirk, p. 140.
53. Zimbardo, p. 169.
54. Wasserman, p. 10.
55. Monroe and Ehninger, pp. 305–306.
56. Holland and Tarlow, pp. 92–93.

57. Robert R. Arnold et al. *Introduction to Data Processing*. New York: Wiley, 1966, p. 1.

CHAPTER 7
1. Laetsch, p. 146.
2. Laetsch, p. 55.
3. Howard Gardner. *Developmental Psychology*, 2nd ed. Boston: Little, Brown, 1981, p. 28.
4. Geiwitz, p. 60.
5. Zimbardo, p. 227.
6. DeBrum, p. 433.
7. Berman and Evans, p. 115.
8. Laetsch, p. 152.
9. Laetsch, p. 11.
10. Wasserman, p. 197.
11. Wasserman, p. 198.
12. Wright and Weiss, p. 31.
13. Wright and Weiss, p. 64.

CHAPTER 8
1. Broom and Selznick, pp. 65–66.
2. Philip Smith. "Breathe Your Troubles Away." Reader's Digest (April 1981), p. 85.
3. Roger Penske. "Fifty-five Is Fast Enough." Reader's Digest (April 1981), p. 13.
4. David Roberts. "Is It Worth the Risk?" Reader's Digest (April 1981), pp. 170–171.
5. Fred Warshofsky. "Strategic Minerals: The Invisible War." Reader's Digest (February 1981), p. 81.
6. Neubeck, pp. 246–247.
7. Zimbardo, p. 305.

CHAPTER 10
1. John Dorfman et al. *Well-Being: An Introduction to Health*. Glenview, Ill.: Scott, Foresman, 1980, pp. 172–173.
2. Dorfman et al., p. 278.
3. Fox and Wheatley, p. 49.
4. Dorfman et al., pp. 208–209.

CHAPTER 13
1. Katherine Anne Porter. "Portrait: Old South," in Tibbetts and Tibbetts, *Strategies: A Rhetoric and Reader*. Glenview, Ill.: Scott, Foresman, 1979, p. 88.
2. John Updike. "Eclipse," in Joyce Steward, *Contemporary College Review*. Glenview, Ill.: Scott, Foresman, 1978, p. 69.

CHAPTER 14
1. John J. Palen. *City Scenes,* 2nd ed. Boston: Little, Brown, 1981, p. 14.
2. Fox and Wheatley, pp. 443–444.

References

CHAPTER 16
1. Gander and Gardiner, pp. 361–362.
2. *Buffalo Courier Express*, 27 February 1982, p. 11.
3. Laetsch, p. 507.
4. Laetsch, p. 152.
5. Laetsch, p. 153.
6. David Attenborough. *Life on Earth*. Boston: Little, Brown, 1979, p. 188.
7. Perry and Perry, p. 427.
8. Laetsch, pp. 143–144.
9. Attenborough, pp. 184–185.
10. Perry and Perry, p. 408.
11. Perry and Perry, p. 456.

CHAPTER 17
1. Under, 1982, p. 871.
2. Unger, 1978, p. 897.
3. Hugh D. Barlow. *Introduction to Criminology*, 2nd ed. Boston: Little, Brown, 1981, p. 12.
4. Barlow, p. 16.
5. Under, 1982, p. 421.
6. Unger, 1982, p. 848.

Index

TO THE STUDENT:

As educational publishers, it is our job to continually improve our texts and make them more useful to instructors and students. One way to improve a book is to revise it, taking into account the experience of people who have used it. We need to know what you learned and what you found confusing, as well as what you enjoyed and what you disliked. Your instructor may be asked to comment on this text later, but right now we want to hear from you, the person who paid for this book and read it.

Please help us by completing the questionnaire and returning it to College English Developmental Group, Little, Brown and Company, 34 Beacon Street, Boston, Massachusetts 02106.

School: _____

Instructor's Name: _____

Title of Course: _____

1. Which of chapters 1 to 19 did you read for class? _____

   _____

   Which chapter did you find the most interesting? _____

   Why? _____

   Which chapter did you find the least interesting? _____

   Why? _____

2. What useful skills have you learned from this text? _____

   _____

3. Please give us your reactions to the selections: Keep   Delete

   PRETESTS
      Cross-County Inns Are In   _____   _____
      Nonverbal Communication   _____   _____
      The New TVs: Getting Bigger, Getting Smaller   _____   _____
      Second Revolution: Plant Migrations and Agricultural
        Improvements   _____   _____

   READING SELECTIONS
     1. Musical Sounds   _____   _____
     2. Electronic Data Processing   _____   _____
     3. Weddings, Old and New   _____   _____
     4. What Causes Cancer?   _____   _____
     5. The Non-Runner   _____   _____

	Keep	Delete
6. Child Abuse	———	———
7. Who's Afraid of Math, and Why?	———	———
8. Chuck Berry: Folk Poet of the Fifties	———	———
9. Surgical Search for Youth	———	———
10. Auto Insurance	———	———
11. An Ugly New Footprint in the Sand	———	———
12. Cloning: A Generation Made to Order	———	———
13. The Biosphere	———	———
14. The Creative Side of Advertising	———	———
15. The Appreciation of Humor	———	———
16. Archaeological Sites	———	———
17. Wine Labels	———	———
18. Touching—and Being Touched	———	———
19. The Singing Whales	———	———
20. Time in the Cinema	———	———
21. The Nightmare of Life Without Fuel	———	———
22. Flirtation — the Signals of Attraction — Deciphered	———	———
23. The "Flickering Blue Parent"	———	———
24. Violence in Sports	———	———
25. Credit — and How to Shop For It	———	———
26. Eight Ways to Flub a Job Hunt	———	———
27. Eye Language	———	———
28. Economic Growth and the Food Crisis	———	———
29. I'd Rather Be Black Than Female	———	———
30. How Additives Work	———	———
31. A Very Short History of Some American Drugs	———	———
32. Scramble on the Polar Ice	———	———

POSTTESTS

	Keep	Delete
May the Source Be With You	———	———
Learned Helplessness	———	———
Tuning Your TV to the Satellites	———	———
The Earliest Agriculture	———	———

4. Do you intend to keep this book for your personal library?   ——— Yes   ——— No

5. If you have any additional comments, questions, or concerns about EFFICIENT AND FLEXIBLE READING, please tell us about them.

Signature (optional): _____ Date:_____

Address (optional): _____